Criminal Law

Essays in Honour of J C Smith

Professor J. C. Smith

Criminal Law

Essays in Honour of J C Smith

EDITED BY

Peter Smith LLB

Senior Lecturer in Law, University of Nottingham

WITH A FOREWORD BY

The Rt Hon Lord Edmund-Davies

A Lord of Appeal in Ordinary

London
Butterworths
1987

United Kingdom	Butterworth & Co (Publishers) Ltd, 88 Kingsway, LONDON WC2B 6AB and 61A North Castle Street, EDINBURGH EH2 3LJ
Australia	Butterworths Pty Ltd, SYDNEY, MELBOURNE, BRISBANE, ADELAIDE, PERTH, CANBERRA and HOBART
Canada	Butterworths. A division of Reed Inc., TORONTO and VANCOUVER
New Zealand	Butterworths of New Zealand Ltd, WELLINGTON and AUCKLAND
Singapore	Butterworth & Co (Asia) Pte Ltd, SINGAPORE
South Africa	Butterworth Publishers (Pty) Ltd, DURBAN and PRETORIA
USA	Butterworths Legal Publishers, ST PAUL, Minnesota, SEATTLE, Washington, BOSTON, Massachusetts, AUSTIN, Texas and D & S Publishers, CLEARWATER, Florida

British Library Cataloguing in Publication Data

Criminal law : essays in honour of J. C. Smith.
1. Criminal law —— England
I. Smith, Peter II. Smith, J. C.
(John Cyril)
344.205 KD7869

ISBN 0 406 50110 6

Typeset by
The Castlefield Press, Wellingborough.

Foreword

Academic lawyers have acquired during this century an ascendancy and influence over the development of our law far greater than I believe they had ever earlier possessed. And this is particularly true of our criminal law.

In that field I have had the great advantage of working with a trio of academic giants, each of them a member of the Criminal Law Revision Committee during my Chairmanship. By their teaching, their widely circulated textbooks and writings, and in other ways, they have made a contribution to legal education and law reform the significance of which is, as yet, only partially appreciated.

Professor John Smith, one of that giantesque trio, is the recipient of this Festschrift. I would readily expatiate upon his just entitlement to this high honour were that necessary. But the first essay in this volume will fill any lacunae in the reader's knowledge of the achievements of this scholar of the highest quality.

The essays are directed to considering many branches of the criminal law. Their reader will find much wisdom, deep learning, sharp criticism, valuable instruction, and bold and challenging submissions. Not surprisingly, therefore, I must not be regarded as necessarily agreeing with all the conclusions of all the essayists.

I am nevertheless glad to be associated with this timely collective tribute to an academic lawyer whose outstanding qualities of character and learning have enabled him to render great public service. And I hope that the volume will meet with the appreciative reception I believe it merits.

Edmund-Davies
December 1986

Preface

This volume of essays in honour of John Smith is published in the session in which he retires from the Chair of Common Law at the University of Nottingham after a long and distinguished career in law teaching and legal scholarship. It is a mark of the high regard in which John is held that the first tentative suggestion of such a volume was immediately welcomed by colleagues, publishers and potential contributors alike and their co-operation in its production was readily forthcoming.

It seemed appropriate to devote the volume to criminal law, as the subject in which John has published the bulk of his work and with which he is most commonly associated, although this inevitably meant that invitations to contribute would be restricted to those with an interest in the field. In the event, amongst the contributors (whose essays have been written simultaneously and specifically for inclusion in this volume) are former students, current and former colleagues, and those who have collaborated with John in the development and exposition of the criminal law. Lord Edmund-Davies, by accepting an invitation to write the foreword, has indicated the special reputation which John has achieved amongst practitioners, and in his appreciation, Alan Prichard relates aspects of John's work and character not always apparent to those who only encounter him professionally. The contributors represent all those whose contact with John, in whatever capacity, has resulted in the esteem and goodwill out of which this book was conceived and in which it is presented.

The combined efforts of authors and publishers normally produce profit for both parties, but in this case, through the generosity of the contributors and the publishers, all profits accruing from the volume will be devoted to a purpose to be determined by John. It is, of course, impossible to predict precisely what purpose John will select, but there can be little doubt that it will, in some way, encourage and develop the teaching and study of law — a task to which John has dedicated himself for the best part of forty years.

My work as editor has been minimal. This reflects both the diligence of the contributors and the expertise of the publishers. I am grateful to them and to the two secretaries in the Nottingham law department whose collaboration in the production of the final manuscript was hampered by the attempt to keep the volume secret from John!

The essays were all submitted by the end of September 1986 and only later amendments of the most pressing kind were permitted at the page proof stage.

Peter Smith
Nottingham
January 1987

Contents

Table of legislation

References in this Table to *Statutes* are to Halsbury's Statutes of England (Fourth Edition) showing the volume and page at which the annotated text of the Act will be found.

UNITED STATES OF AMERICA

Table of cases

John Smith: an appreciation

A M Prichard

John Smith was born and brought up in County Durham. To one southerner at least the image of that county is one of honesty of endeavour and minimum of flamboyance. If that image is accurate then John Smith is a true son of that county. Indeed, only in one particular could he ever have been regarded as a renegade: as a boy he was a passionate enthusiast not for Sunderland, or Middlesbrough or even Newcastle United, but for the all-conquering Arsenal of the thirties. Otherwise he can fairly look upon himself as an untainted northerner, greatly blessed in being able to regard Yorkshiremen as southerners.

Coincidences do happen. Not one of those who taught John at St Mary's Darlington could have envisaged that a decade later the school roll would contain the name of Brian Hogan and that the two names would become linked in legal scholarship in the way that they have. To eavesdrop on the two as they compare remembrances of their old school is almost as intriguing as when they dispute on the criminal law. Suffice it to say that John has the happiest recollections of his school days.

On leaving school John had no particular career yet in mind, but then the War was on — the 1939–45 one, not 'the Kaiser's' as John, venerable in appearance from a very early age, had occasion once to correct a wrongly-guessing judge. John joined the Royal Artillery and saw arduous service in India and Burma. At the end of the war he succumbed to the pressing invitation of the government to extend his service an extra year. As a result a grateful country was in due course to reward him by denying him — by three short months — the right to count his service for pension purposes: a meanness accorded to too many of his generation.

In the turmoil of the war one happy meeting was to have a most profound effect on John's career and on the course of English law. John attended a lecture on the law given as part of the army's educational programme. The lecturer was Freddie Odgers, one of the most outstanding and remarkable law teachers of our time: a man utterly incapable of making even the most dry-as-dust principles appear to his pupils other than exciting and exhilarating. From that occasion stemmed not only John's deep friendship and admiration for Freddie, but also John's own lifetime enthusiasm for the law.

From the Army John duly went to read law at Downing College Cambridge under the strikingly disparate tuition of Whalley Tooker and Clive Parry. For ex-servicemen the first degree was compressed into a two year tripos. After gaining a First in that John stayed on to get another First in the LL B (as it was then characterised). While sitting for those exams in 1950 he received an invitation to attend for interview at Nottingham University: a timely intervention in characteristic terminology from Clive Parry happily induced Roger Crane to arrange for postponement of the interview till the exams were finished. The result was another — and the greatest — of the inspired selections that Roger made in his unique achievement of founding two university law schools — first Nottingham from 1946 and twenty years later Queen Mary College.

When John arrived, the young department had already given the start to a teaching career for Tony Honoré and Lee Sheridan, as well as to Hamish Gray and Tony Thomas, who both still remained; it was not only highly regarded, but was already a lively, companionable, fun-loving department where the happiness of the students was as important as their intellectual development. Throughout the years since that character has been maintained, not always without effort, but frequently assisted by the policy of regularly appointing young people to the staff on estimates of potential. That policy was begun by Roger Crane and continued by Harry Street in his four short but vitally effective years as head before he returned to Manchester: it has always been sustained by John. It has often meant that all too quickly some of those appointed have been lured away as soon as their talent has become evident, and this in turn has often meant that severe strains from freezing of posts or, at the least, the need for radical realignment of teaching duties have had to be faced. However, throughout there has been a heartening spontaneity of response to fill gaps and to undertake new ventures. That response, one suspects, has always derived from the quality of leadership and the example that originally Roger and Harry, and then for over thirty years, John, have given.

In his early years at Nottingham he not only quickly learnt his trade of teaching and began to write in a manner that always commands notice and respect, but also fitted in two most important experiences. The first was a pupillage: not, it may surprise, at the common law Bar, but in the heart of Chancery in Sir John Pennycuick's chambers with the famous and formidable J H Stamp as pupil-master. At that time John would readily have developed into an Equity lawyer, but in the early 1950s Trusts was the most fiercely coveted teaching subject at Nottingham, as at other law schools, and not without regret John concentrated on the more common law side of English law. In those years too John was prominent in the teaching of mercantile law, and from that exposure as well as to Equity has come not only his own command of the wide contexts of both contract and criminal law, but also his insistence that those who seek to reform those laws as well as merely to teach or to practice them must have a deep awareness of those same contexts.

The other formative experience of those years was the year he spent in the United States on a Commonwealth Scholarship (as Harkness awards were then known) at Harvard. That year, 1952–53, incidentally saw another young lecturer, Peter Stein, begin his teaching career at Nottingham before going off to Aberdeen to join David Daube: so Nottingham can proudly boast of having given a start to both the country's Regis Professors as well as to a most impressive roll-call of other academic lawyers.

John's experience at Harvard was to have a profound effect on English academic legal training. He quickly appreciated the value of casebook teaching as a supplement, but not a total substitute for the time-honoured English law teaching techniques. (He also extracted wry humour from attending a class given by the arch-priest of realist jurisprudence, Jerome Frank, to find that it was an unwaveringly traditional and far from exciting exposition of black-letter law.) Harvard, indeed all the great law schools of the Eastern seaboard of the States, were in one of their liveliest and most stimulating eras of academic activity, and John has always been deeply aware of his debt to that experience. Nor was it a purely academic exercise — the summer of 1953 saw him driving with friends made at Harvard right across America and gave him an enduring love of that country.

On his return in 1953 he found in the collaboration with Tony Thomas and in the enthusiastic and shrewd encouragement and guidance of Harry Street the means to introduce the case-method of teaching to an English law school and to adapt it to the special circumstances of such schools, in particular the greater youth of the English undergraduate law student and the much smaller potential market for the sale of any casebook. When this writer arrived at Nottingham in 1954 (as a replacement for Tony Thomas as it happened), the venture was under way. Stencilled prototypes were being used to mount a comprehensive case-method for the first time this side of the Atlantic. Within a year or two the first edition of *Smith and Thomas* was published. This was a casebook that differed radically from the so-called casebooks such as Winfield on Tort or Cheshire and Fifoot on *Contract*: they merely sought to provide the user of their companion textbooks with abstracted materials to employ when out of reach of a law library. Even the more sophisticated works such as *Cockle on Evidence* and Nathan's *Equity through the Cases*, which included much useful pedagogic material, formed a totally different genus from *Smith and Thomas*, where the cases were carefully selected and passages from judgments specially picked for their *teaching* potential, rather than their actual enshrinement of doctrine. As it happens, of course, contract is so lively a subject that many of the principal cases do form excellent teaching vehicles, so that *Smith and Thomas* has a dual value — a basis for case-teaching and a supplement to any chosen textbook where teaching is by traditional lectures.

One of the most remarkable features of *Smith and Thomas* is its compactness for its purpose. North American casebooks have a market that enables them to be two or three times the length of the English ones. With such generous space they can quite easily provide sufficiently diverse material for different teachers to develop personal choices of approach and selection of items. Within the confines of a few hundred pages only, *Smith and Thomas* has had to be a much more precise production: intended to be used and capable of being used by a wide assortment of teachers. Given the constraints, probably no such work could be less idiosyncratic. It has held its special position and the respect of its users for over thirty years now. It has also enabled generations of law students at Nottingham, where contract has always been taught in the first year, to achieve a basic case technique right from the start. To this end a special teaching flair has been the vital extra element.

Contract has probably remained John's favourite subject despite his gradual development of a paramountcy in criminal law and related disciplines such as evidence and sentencing. His conviction that the criminal law should be codified to achieve a necessary measure of certainty and predictability where 'moving with the times' should be left to parliamentary action has not been matched by the least enthusiasm for the same process for contract. In the latter area judge-made law can, in his view, better achieve the adaptability needed by businessmen without sacrificing too much of predictability. That judgment once again reflects the shrewd insight of a man who can achieve perspective whilst still attaining mastery of detail.

In 1955 the law department for the first time began the session with the same staff as a year before, but in the following spring it looked distinctly possible that all five members would be leaving that year. John in particular was emerging as a strong candidate for an Oxbridge fellowship or a provincial chair. As it happened only Harry Street departed in 1956, although Hamish Gray left a year later to put the law school at the University of Canterbury at Christchurch, New Zealand, on the international map: he had been at Nottingham ten years and had played a major role in establishing the school and the University. He is remembered still with great warmth and gratitude by graduates of those years.

The University made a bold and inspired decision, backing their own appreciation of academic potential on the evidence of John's six years as law teacher and writer. He succeeded Harry as head of department with a Readership in Law and at the end of 1957 he was promoted to the Chair in Law (the title of which was changed to the Chair of Common Law when Jack Garner was appointed Professor of Public Law in 1964 and the department for the first time had two chairs). In the same year of 1956 Brian Hogan joined the staff, with Ian Brownlie replacing Hamish a year later and David Williams being appointed to a new lectureship a year later still. This was the start of a period of consolidation badly needed for the department. Dick Webb was to give fifteen years of lively and invaluable service from 1953 until he departed to a chair in Auckland; Brian to remain ten vital years, and Ian and David till 1963; while John and the present writer opted to stay in Nottingham. These early years of John's headship were richly formative of the department, of its staff and of John himself.

1957 had been an expensive one for the law students. With characteristic generosity they provided not only a leaving present for Hamish but also wedding presents for the other four staff. Ian Brownlie also married that year, so that over a long vac a wholly bachelor department was transmogrified into a totally married one. Like a good captain John attended all his colleagues' weddings before being married himself. His bride, Shirley, had begun a secretarial career in the department before moving out to work in a solicitors' office. Those who know them will be aware how much John's success has depended on Shirley and the security of his family life. Her loyalty and enthusiasm for the department have always been characterised by a total refraining from interference.

In those days the intake of the department was some twenty or so students and included several outstanding overseas students, especially from Ghana and Malaysia, who have been distinguished ever since not only by the brilliance of their careers but also by their generous loyalty to the department. Entry standards were in no way so high as they were to become in the '70s and '80s, but most students were very able and some brilliant. The memory is of a group that worked well, but who were also happy and fun-loving, giving the law school an esprit de corps which has happily been preserved even into a period when the intake is four or five times as great. That continuity has been matched by the evolution of John's style of leadership: always judicious and humane, preferring the looser rein so long as it created no illusion that liberties might be taken; a reluctance to interfere in the academic processes of his colleagues, yet an always open door and readiness to give unconfined time, encouragement and judgment to staff and student alike. A very special talent John has always enjoyed and made the most of is the ability to interrupt sustained work to deal with any query or matter that crops up, long or short, and then quickly to reimmerse himself in the work. How much effort and discipline are needed to achieve this remarkable gift is impossible to gauge, so calm and unflurried is the aspect he shows to the interrupter.

Within five years of becoming head of department, John's talents as administrator were clearly recognised and he was elected Dean. Despite the efforts of Harry and then John and strong support from several quarters including ex-students, Nottingham had opted against the traditional structure of a faculty of law. Instead, law was and remains part of a Faculty of Law and Social Sciences. Whatever the pros and cons (and there are several on each side of the argument), leading a young, very disparate faculty called for patience, firmness, fairness, good humour, judgment and imagination. All those John displayed most impressively, along with a chairmanship that achieved expedition without the least hint of railroading. Those three years as Dean confirmed the already existing conviction in the University that in John it had a professor always worth listening to and never sensibly to be disregarded. A decade or so later John was to be an outstanding Pro-Vice-Chancellor, acting for most of his four year term as deputy to the VC. During those four years, years of strain and tension in the university world and in the departments that made it up, John relinquished the headship of the department to Jack Garner. If Jack's style was markedly — and endearingly — different, his paramount aims were always to preserve and to promote the character of the department that John had built up; and that aim was fully and loyally achieved. Otherwise for thirty years till 1986, with the one year's absence for the session 1981–82 which John and Shirley spent at Osgoode Hall in Canada and a few shorter breaks (in particular the summer term and vacation of 1985 when John had a sabbatical to work on 'the Code'), John has held the headship and could fairly be said to have 'made' the department.

Outside the University among legal academics John's reputation rose quickly in the 1950s, and has been rising ever since; and not just among academics — judges, practitioners, police, laymen, have all come to admire and to approach him for help, which is never refused. In 1955 Harry Lawson showed his usual perspicacity by choosing John to be book review editor of the SPTL Journal and a year or two later John commenced operating as the Case and Comment Editor of the Criminal Law Review. For nearly three decades his commentaries have been a vital vehicle for the development — and, when it is needed, correction — of the criminal law. They have been one of the main reasons for the great success of that journal and the great width of its circulation. Always concise, pointed, frank and honestly written, they have not always endeared him to the higher judiciary, but while John will never barb or acidify his criticisms, he consistently draws the line between due deference and hypocrisy. Moreover, the criticisms are firmly founded on the best of bases — sensible self-criticism and a generous openness to argument. An endearing incident exemplifies this. In May 1985 John took a case-method class on a recent decision of the House of Lords and used as the basis for it his own freshly written commentary for the Review. In the class his arguments were spiritedly challenged by a bright student backed by others. John came out at the end delighted, saying that that was what a case class should be like. He then went upstairs, tore up his commentary and rewrote it, taking into account the challenges his students had made.

It was only a matter of time before John's mastery of the criminal law would win him a key role in governmental reform of that law. In the 1960s he served on the sub-committee of the Criminal Law Revision Committee that prepared the Theft Act 1968. Thereafter he has been on the full Committee, and later on the Policy Advisory Committee of the Home Office. These contributions had already won for him the award of the CBE. Then most recently has come the huge effort that John, Edward Griew and Ian Dennis have put in on the draft Criminal Code for the Law Commission, to be followed by a wide range of talks on the codification issue.

Other distinctions that have given him quiet pleasure whilst signalling the regard in which he is held have been appointment as Queen's Counsel, election to the Bench of Lincoln's Inn, election as Fellow of the British Academy and the awards of LL D by his old University of Cambridge and by the University of Sheffield. It was at Cambridge too that he chaired the SPTL annual conference during his year of office as President.

All in all, it is doubtful whether any academic, at least in modern times, has achieved as much in any other branch of law. Yet, as John has always maintained, there is one figure whose brilliance and inspiration must take pride of place — Glanville Williams. Before Glanville started teaching the criminal law, with the emergence in due course of the classic of all legal works, *The General Part*, the topic had been a Cinderella subject, never really popular with students and over-intricate in details with confusion and anomaly where there should have been principle. It is a great testimony to Glanville — and to John following his lead — that criminal law is now such a lively subject and has attracted so many of the best legal academic brains to its study and development, as this volume will clearly demonstrate. Of all the distinctions which John has achieved one suspects that the admiration and friendship Glanville has accorded him are the greatest and dearest to him.

The present writer has had the privilege of being John's colleague for over thirty-two years now. Nearness notoriously affects judgment. Even so, certain insights can be relied upon with safety. Three examples of John's qualities will suffice perhaps to show his special value. The first example is his public lectures. Right from his inaugural lecture on mens rea back in 1958, those events — and they are 'events' however low the key — have always brought enlightenment and enjoyment to all the audience from expert through to absolute layman: the clarity of mind is such that every sentence containing information or argument is utterly lucid to all, while the gentle asides are always pitched right and never overdone.

The second example, one specially cherished by the present writer, demonstrates his quiet sense of fun and ready enjoyment of a joke against himself. It was with great glee that John, always plagued by allusions to his age, recounted how his elder son, Mark, coming home from his first history lesson at prep school, had asked him, 'Daddy, were you in the Crusades?'

The third example is the way the busiest of men unostentatiously found time to visit frequently and regularly throughout a long vacation a student hospitalised far from home.

His mind is of course special, but so also are his humour, kindness, loyalty, modesty, integrity and total reliability. They all combine to make him not just an outstanding academic, but even more a much loved friend, colleague and teacher.

Defining criminal offences without harm

Andrew Ashworth

In its discussion of the nature of an actus reus, *Smith and Hogan* states that the most frequent form of criminal offences is to require 'proof of an act or an omission (conduct)', and that 'usually it must be proved that the conduct had a particular result'.[1] In an article published in 1971,[2] Professor J C Smith deplored the element of chance which this way of defining offences allows into the determination of criminal liability. And, despite the passing of the Criminal Attempts Act 1981, which reduces the effect of chance by penalising most impossible attempts, many of the examples given in that 1971 article are still with us: chance plays a considerable role in accomplice liability and in liability for manslaughter and for causing death by reckless driving. Nevertheless, towards the end of the article Professor Smith came down in favour of result-oriented definitions as the normal mode of definition, arguing that wider adoption of a mode of definition which did not incorporate the results of conduct would have the demerit of extending the criminal law without yielding any significant benefit in terms of general deterrence. Later, in an article published in 1978, he added a further reason for this general approach: 'The fact is that we all react quite differently when an act causes harm from when the same act does not.'[3] Result-oriented offences, supported by the law of attempts in cases where the intended harm does not result, usually cover the ground satisfactorily.[4]

These arguments and counter-arguments reveal a tension within systems of criminal law — a tension between conduct and results, between intentions and outcome, between what D is trying to do or believes he is doing and what the position actually turns out to be. The aim of this essay is not to debate the deep theoretical issues which underlie and contribute to this tension,[5] but rather to examine the texture of English criminal law, as it is presented by *Smith and Hogan*,[6] in order to shed light on other, perhaps more practical questions. Why is one mode of definition chosen rather than another? Do the different modes of definition affect individual rights and police powers? How does the inchoate mode of definition relate to the law of attempts? Is there, generally speaking, any difference in the reach of the criminal law between a result-oriented crime under-pinned by the law of attempts and a substantive offence defined in the inchoate mode? It is hoped that reflection on these issues will have implications for both the reform and the codification of English criminal law.

In order to lay a foundation for answers to the questions posed, it will be necessary to consider the anatomy of a wide range of criminal offences. First, however, an analytical framework must be sketched so that the different styles of definition can be recognised and evaluated.

1 Modes of definition

Two principal modes of definition will be distinguished, the inchoate and the result-oriented.[7] The inchoate mode is characterised by a style of defining criminal offences which proscribes the doing of certain acts in order to produce a certain outcome. It is the outcome which the law wishes to prevent, but the offence is so defined as to penalise D for trying to produce it, whether or not the outcome resulted. A clear example would be the offence of unlawfully administering to another a poison or noxious thing with intent to aggrieve or annoy, contrary to s 24 of the Offences against the Person Act 1861. Variations on this mode abound: for some crimes it is sufficient that the specified outcome was 'likely to be caused', and in perjury there is no reference to any outcome at all. The second mode of definition is the result-oriented mode, which requires proof that D's act, done with the required culpability, actually caused the proscribed result. The crimes of murder and rape provide clear examples. It is not suggested that all crimes fall neatly into one or the other of these categories.

2 Results: ends and means

In brief and general terms, it may be said that the criminal law has two aims. The first is to protect those interests which are most central to life in society (leaving less important interests to be protected by government regulation or civil actions, and others still by informal social pressures). The protection operates by way of prevention based on general deterrence, the assumption being that the declaration and enforcement of the criminal law causes fewer violations of the protected interests to take place. This does not imply that the criminal law is the sole or even the principal means of social protection of the interests. The second aim of the criminal law is to establish an authoritative framework for the official response to lawbreaking. It is to provide and delineate the authority of the state to deal with offenders, by prescribing the conditions for criminal liability and by granting to the courts circumscribed powers to sentence convicted offenders, to order them to pay compensation to their victims, and to make various other orders. This framework is not limited to situations in which a protected interest has actually been violated: the general protective aim leads to the creation of many preventive offences, including (for example) crimes of possession as well as the inchoate offences of attempt, conspiracy and incitement.

There is room for much debate about which interests do and which interests do not justify the protection of the criminal law. In order to focus upon the subject-matter of this essay, it will be assumed that there is agreement that the criminal law should protect at least the safety of the person, sexual integrity, and property. However, it cannot be adequate to refer generally to the protection of sexual integrity when that is something an adult is largely free to yield as he or she wishes, nor to the protection of property when it too may be yielded voluntarily. It is in this context that another proposition — that citizens should be protected from force, fear and fraud — comes into its own. Freedom from force corresponds with the protection of physical safety: violence of a certain degree is criminalised almost unconditionally.[8] For all property offences and most sexual offences, the distinction between the consensual and the non-consensual is crucial, and for this reason the elements of fear and fraud become important.[9] With these general remarks in mind, it is now time to consider some patterns of liability in English criminal law.

3 Fear and threats

The various offences of making threats or causing fear have different structures. The first group takes the inchoate form and penalises the making of a threat to invade a protected interest. It includes threatening to kill,[10] threatening to damage or destroy property belonging to another,[11] making an unwarranted demand with menaces,[12] and threatening violence for the purpose of securing unlawful entry to occupied premises.[13] There are no parallel offences of threatening another's sexual integrity. The hallmark of this first group is that the making of the threat constitutes the crime. There is no requirement that the threat should actually have caused fear in the intended victim or another, so long as it is established that it was intended to have this effect.[14] Indeed, there may be no requirement that the threat was even communicated to the intended victim; thus in *R v Solanke*[15] D's threat to kill his wife was contained in a letter sent to his probation officer, but the offence of making a threat to kill was nonetheless committed. In terms of the tension described at the beginning of this essay these offences tend to minimise the role of chance in criminal liability by concentrating on the doing of an act with intention rather than on the achievement of the intended consequence, on intentions rather than outcomes.

Threats offences in the second group require not only the actual causing of fear but also proof of actual harm caused to one of the traditional interests. Examples are robbery, insofar as it consists of stealing by using a threat of violence;[16] rape, insofar as it consists of having unlawful sexual intercourse with a woman in circumstances where her apparent 'consent' is vitiated by the threats made to her by D;[17] procuring a woman by threats or intimidation to have unlawful sexual intercourse;[18] and, possibly, assault.[19] This result-oriented mode of definition places emphasis on the violation of the traditional interests of sexual inegrity, personal safety or property and relegates the use of fear to a description (albeit essential) of the method used. In this connection it may be observed that serious offences against the person, including manslaughter and causing grievous bodily harm, may be committed in circumstances where D threatens or frightens V into a course of conduct which causes death or injury, as the case may be.[20] All these result-oriented offences are underpinned by the law of attempts, of course, but such conduct as making a threat to steal by force or to violate a woman sexually may not always amount to an attempt to commit one of these crimes.

There is a further group of offences which penalise conduct which was likely to produce fear in bystanders. Each of the three new offences against public order — riot, violent disorder and affray — requires a use or threat of violence '. . . such as would cause a person of reasonable firmness present at the scene to fear for his personal safety.' Not only does that form of definition require no proof that any person of reasonable firmness did fear for his safety, but for each offence the Act stipulates that '. . . no person of reasonable firmness need actually be, or be likely to be, present at the scene.'[21] Other new crimes introduced by the Public Order Act follow a similar pattern.[22]

Why have the different approaches to definition been adopted? The first group of offences seems to have a similar rationale to the modern English law of attempts: a person who has gone so far as to utter a serious threat has crossed the threshold of criminal culpability, irrespective of the result of his action. The making of the threat is sufficient, without proof that it caused fear in, or was even communicated to, the intended victim.[23] Indeed, both the first and third groups could be regarded as species of inchoate offences, enabling the police to step in before any harm has actually been done. The criminal law has general doctrines of attempts, conspiracy and incitement but not threats. A threat will usually fall short of an attempt, but a firm (non-frivolous) threat may be as unambiguous in its portents as a conspiracy and no less likely to foreshadow the infliction of harm than an incitement of another.

Whilst the first and third groups of offences resolve the fundamental tension in favour of intentions and against outcomes, the second group shows that the tension is not always resolved in the same way. It would be possible to define these offences differently, and to avoid passing through the subtleties of the concept of consent by devising an offence of making an unwarranted sexual demand with menaces,[24] or an offence of making a threat in order to obtain unlawful sexual intercourse, in place of the result-oriented crimes of rape and of '. . . procuring a woman by threats or intimidation to have unlawful sexual intercourse.' However, these offences are designed for cases in which the threat has been carried out, where the primary consideration appears to be that '. . . we all react quite differently when an act causes harm from when the same act does not.'[25] It does seem strange that a person who threatens to rape or to rob another may incur no criminal liability because he has not yet done an act 'more than merely preparatory' to rape or robbery, but the explanation is probably that the criminal law has not in practice been found wanting in this respect.

4 Deception and falsehoods

The various deception offences fall structurally into two groups. The first group follows the inchoate mode of definition, penalising the use of a deception for certain purposes without requiring that those purposes have been attained. The main offences in the Forgery and Counterfeiting Act 1981 are the most obvious examples. The making, the use and the possession of a false instrument[26] are all offences which depend on the intention with which the conduct takes place: no actual deceiving, let alone obtaining, is required. If it is established that D intended to induce another to accept the instrument as genuine, and by reason of so accepting it to do or not to do some act to his own or any other person's prejudice, the offences are complete. The whole purpose of penalising forgery is preventive. The offences of false accounting[27] and false statements by a company director[28] take a similar form, since they are complete without proof of any deception or obtaining thereby.[29]

Offences in the second group are characterised by the result-oriented mode of definition, and typically require that the deception should have operated on another so as to cause D to obtain something thereby. Thus the basic offence of obtaining property by deception[30] and the more recent offences of obtaining services[31] and evasion of liability[32] all require proof of both the means and the end. Child-stealing also falls within this category, since it may be committed where D by fraud leads or entices away or detains a child under the age of 14 unlawfully.[33] Among the sexual offences, rape may be committed where D practises a deception on V so as to induce her to consent to unlawful sexual intercourse, if the deception is a sufficiently fundamental one (as to the nature of the act or as to D's identity as V's husband).[34] Where the deception is not so fundamental, there is the lesser offence under s 3 of the Sexual Offences Act 1956 of procuring a woman by false pretences or false representations to have unlawful sexual intercourse.[35]

There is a wide gap between the requirements of the two groups of deception offences. To what extent is their reach assimilated by the application of the law of attempts to the result-oriented crimes? Acts such as publishing a statement about a company which is known to be misleading or concealing a will or furnishing misleading information for the purpose of an account or record may in themselves constitute the actus reus of offences defined in the inchoate mode.[36] If in all cases D was pursuing a plan to obtain property from V, would the acts done amount to an attempt to obtain property by deception? The test introduced by the Criminal Attempts Act 1981 is whether the act was 'more than merely preparatory' to the commission of the substantive offence. In two cases decided under the pre-1981 law, it was held that for an insured person to inform the insurance company falsely that his property had been stolen and to enquire whether and how a claim might be made was insufficient to amount to an attempt to obtain by deception.[37] The Law Commission hoped that the new test would broaden the ambit of attempts,[38] but the very imprecision of that test rendered any such change uncertain. It had been argued that the matter should have been put beyond doubt by the inclusion in the 1981 Act of a non-exhaustive list of forms of conduct which would as a matter of law amount to 'more than merely preparatory' steps, thereby ensuring a change in the law whilst leaving the courts with flexibility to apply the test to other situations.[39] One of the categories suggested for inclusion in the list, following the example of the Model Penal Code, was 'preparing, stating or acting a falsehood for the purpose of an offence of fraud or deception.'[40] Had this excellent suggestion been adopted, one consequence would have been the virtual assimilation of attempts to commit result-oriented deception offences with those deception offences defined in the inchoate mode. Instead, the Criminal Attempts Act leaves the interpretation of the new test largely to the jury or magistrates in each case.[41] Not only has an opportunity for certainty without inflexibility been lost, but there may remain a significant difference in the reach of the criminal law according to the mode of definition used.

Are there any reasons why offences in the second group could not be defined satisfactorily in the inchoate mode, or offences in the first group defined as result-oriented crimes? Presumably the basic offence of obtaining property by deception could be drafted so as to penalise a person who makes a false representation in order to cause V to transfer property to D. This would dispense with the necessity to prove that there was a deception by D which caused the obtaining: the focus would instead be upon the definition of 'false representation' (or whatever term was used)[42] and upon the representor's intention. Correspondingly the forgery offence of using a false instrument with intent, etc, could be defined in the result-oriented mode: it would penalise a person who induces another to do or not to do some act to his own or any other person's detriment, by using a false instrument which D intends V to accept and V does accept as genuine. What would be the practical difference between the two modes? At the trial stage, the crucial issue for offences in the inchoate mode is the intention or purpose of the person using the false instrument or making the false representation. For result-oriented offences it is necessary to prove that V was deceived and that this caused the obtaining, etc, by D, and there has been a succession of reported cases in which these elements have presented problems for the courts.[43] These difficulties might be circumvented by using the law of attempts, but in cases where D has achieved what he set out to achieve this would (for those who prefer result-oriented definitions) be a strange approach, suggesting a weakness in concentrating on results.

The practical difference between the two modes of definition at the stage of law enforcement lies in the degree of certainty. If the offence is defined in the inchoate mode, the police or others know that they can intervene when the false instrument is tendered or the false representation made. There is far less uncertainty than under the imprecise 'more than merely preparatory' test of the law of attempts. The greater certainty of the inchoate mode of definition brings a keener preventive edge to the law, but there remains the question whether this is bought at too high a price. The Forgery and Counterfeiting Act spreads its net very wide, covering the making and possession, as well as the use, of a false instrument. Whether there was either a practical need or theoretical justification for using the inchoate mode to extend the criminal sanction this far has been doubted.[44] It must therefore be borne in mind that the inchoate mode of definition, whilst it may reduce the role of chance, reduce problems of proof and increase the preventive effectiveness of the law, also has a potential for extending the reach of the criminal law.

5 Surveying the field

This discussion of two areas of criminal liability, for threats and deception, should have conveyed an impression of the variations of approach in English criminal law. But two swallows do not make a summer, and, without testing the general proposition that result-oriented crimes are more usual, it is proposed to consider a broad range of crimes which are defined in the inchoate mode. It should perhaps be borne in mind that the law of attempts, which operates to extend the reach of result-oriented crimes, seems generally to apply no less to crimes defined in the inchoate mode and therefore extends their reach too.

Starting with chapter 11 of *Smith and Hogan*, we find that s 58 of the Offences against the Person Act 1861 penalises the unlawful administration of any poison or other noxious thing or the use of an instrument or other means with intent to procure a miscarriage. The essence of this offence is an attempt to procure a miscarriage, and it takes the inchoate mode to what was then an unusual extreme by providing that it can be committed even if the woman is not in fact pregnant.[45] One reason for creating this specific offence was probably that the ambit of the law of attempts was unsettled in the early nineteenth century. The Criminal Attempts Act 1981 now establishes a test for the actus reus of attempt, and therefore the draft Criminal Code includes a result-oriented offence of abortion which is to be supported by the general law of attempts.[46]

In chapter 12 of *Smith and Hogan*, following several offences against the person which adopt the result-oriented mode, we come to the offences of administering poison.[47] Section 23 of the Offences against the Person Act 1861 is result-oriented, penalising the unlawful administration of any poison or noxious thing which endangers the life or inflicts grievous bodily harm upon another. Section 24 takes a more inchoate form, penalising the unlawful administration of poison, etc, with intent to injure, annoy or aggrieve the victim. If it is true that the law of attempts was not fully settled by 1861, this might explain the need for this additional offence. When the Criminal Law Revision Committee reported on these offences, it discarded s 23 as a model because it contains no requirement of mens rea as to the result it proscribes (endangerment of life or serious bodily harm). Its recommendation was for a new offence along the lines of s 24, supporting this on the ground that the general offences of causing injury and attempting to cause injury would not necessarily cover all 'poison' cases.[48] Clause 80 of the draft Criminal Code seeks to implement this. Yet the logic used to support this rare departure from the result-oriented mode in offences against the person seems at best incomplete. If s 23 is unacceptable because of the absence of a fault requirement, why not insert one? Would there be any objection to an offence of causing substantial interference with another's bodily functions by the administration of a substance, etc, intending or being reckless as to such a result? Attempts to commit such an offence would cover further ground, but some consequences of adopting the inchoate mode are (a) that an attempt to administer a substance constitutes an offence whereas if the causing of substantial interference with bodily functions were required as the actus reus, an act more than merely preparatory to the administration would not necessarily amount to an attempt; and (b) that administering a substance reckless as to whether it would cause substantial interference is an offence, whereas it would otherwise be non-punishable as a merely reckless attempt.

It is convenient to deal here with a group of six offences relating to transport which survive in the 1861 statutes.[49] The Criminal Law Revision Committee noted that conduct endangering the safety of rail users would not be covered entirely by their proposed offences of causing serious injury or injury and attempts to commit such crimes, because some of the acts done might not amount to conduct 'more than merely preparatory' to the causing of injury, and some of them could not be proved to have been done with intent to cause injury.[50] The gist of the Committee's recommendation, as now embodied in clause 81 of the draft Criminal Code, is to create an endangerment offence which in effect imposes liability for reckless and negligent 'attempts'. This development taps into a sphere of conduct where chance (in terms of actual results, outcomes and facts) has traditionally been a determinant of criminal liability. In brief, a person who does certain acts reckless as to whether he will cause injury or damage may be liable for a serious offence if such a consequence happens to result, yet free from any criminal liability if no such consequence happens. English law's general reluctance to embrace the concept of a 'reckless attempt'[51] may be supported on the basis that the amount of criminal law should be kept to a minimum,[52] but an exception here is surely justified by reference to the risks to the safety of large numbers of people and to the element of manifest wrong doing in placing obstructions on or otherwise interfering with the railways.

Chapter 12 of *Smith and Hogan* deals with two other cognate offences. Under the Night Poaching Act 1828 it is an offence unlawfully to enter or to be on land at night, armed, for the purpose of taking or destroying game. No poaching, injuring or threatening need take place: the offence is constituted by the act of trespass with the required purpose and weapon.[53] The two forms of bomb hoax offences under s 51 of the Criminal Law Act 1977 are similarly inchoate.[54] An offence is committed if an article is placed or dispatched with the intention of inducing a belief that it is likely to explode: no proof that anyone did entertain such a belief is necessary. An offence is also committed if information known or believed to be false is communicated to another with the intention of inducing a belief that there is a bomb likely to explode: again, no proof that D succeeded in inducing such a belief is required.

Turning to chapter 13, several sexual offences involving threats and deception have already been discussed, but the abduction offence in s 19 of the Sexual Offences Act 1956 is worth mentioning here. It penalises the taking of an unmarried girl under the age of 18 against the will of her parent or guardian with intent that she should have unlawful sexual intercourse.[55] No proof that intercourse has taken place is necessary, even though this is evidently the mischief against which this offence (as distinct from that in s 20) is directed. The difficulty of proving that there has been intercourse is presumably the reason for adopting the inchoate mode. The Criminal Law Revision Committee, in following this approach, gave no reason for doing so,[56] but perhaps it was thought too obvious to be worth spelling out.

Chapter 15 of *Smith and Hogan* brings us to theft and related offences, where examples of the inchoate mode abound. Theft itself is ambiguous in this respect. According to the interpretation of 'appropriates' in *R v Morris*,[57] the actus reus is complete as soon as D assumes the rights of an owner of the property — indeed, as soon as D assumes '*any* of the rights of an owner'.[58] So long as D does this dishonestly and with the intention of depriving the owner permanently of the property, the crime has been committed. Whether it follows that theft is an offence defined in the inchoate mode depends on one's view of the real mischief against which the offence is directed.[59] If it is any temporary interference with an owner's rights by someone bent on permanent deprivation, theft may be regarded as a result-oriented crime. If the real mischief is the loss of property or at least a substantial interference with the owner's rights, the crime of theft is defined in the inchoate mode inasmuch as it penalises an extremely preliminary and possibly innocent act (any assumption of the rights of an owner) accompanied by an ulterior intent (permanently to deprive) which goes much further than could ever be insisted upon in a result-oriented definition — since to require proof of permanent deprivation would mean that no prosecution for theft could succeed unless the owner had died without recovering his property! The Theft Acts contain other examples of the inchoate mode, such as burglary contrary to s 9(1)(a) of the 1968 Act, which criminalises entry into a building as a trespasser with one of the specified intents.[60] However, the sister offence of burglary in s 9(1)(b) is one of several examples of the result-oriented mode of definition, which has already been seen to characterise the many Theft Act offences of obtaining by deception.[61]

Examples of the inchoate mode are not hard to find among offences relating to the administration of justice. Chapter 19 of *Smith and Hogan* contains perhaps the clearest example of all — the Perjury Act 1911. It might be thought that the offence of perjury is designed to protect courts from being misled by lying witnesses. What it penalises is a witness who makes a statement which he knows to be false or does not believe to be true. No matter that the court is not misled. No matter, even, that the statement is in fact true.[62] Perjury is based on the beliefs and acts of the defendant with no mention of outcomes or even possible effects, in this respect anticipating s 1 of the Criminal Attempts Act by seventy years. All the offences concerned with perverting the course of justice take the inchoate form, although none of them is statutory.[63] The basic offence is doing an act which has a tendency and is intended to pervert the course of justice, which depends partly on the objective likelihood that the course of justice would be perverted, and there are also offences of attempt, conspiracy and incitement. *Smith and Hogan* states that ' . . . the charge always seems to have taken the form of an inchoate offence — incitement, conspiracy or attempt — even though justice has been manifestly defeated in fact.'[64] The obsolescent offence of embracery consists of an attempt to influence a juror unfairly,[65] and the modern offence of contempt of court may be committed by any act which either has a tendency or is intended to obstruct or prejudice the course of justice in present or future proceedings.[66] Both these formulations show that the offence of contempt is complete irrespective of whether the course of justice is actually obstructed or prejudiced. Only if it were argued that the mischief is not interference with justice but the mere doing of an act likely or intended to produce this consequence, which is contemptuous towards the court, could contempt be described as a result-oriented offence. Last, in this field of law, is the offence under s 4 of the Criminal Law Act 1967, which consists of doing any act with intent to impede the apprehension or prosecution of an arrestable offender. Again, no proof of any actual impeding is required by the definition of the offence.[67]

Chapter 21 of *Smith and Hogan*, on offences against the security of the state, contains one of the most far-reaching offences in the inchoate mode known to English law — doing any act preparatory to the commission of an offence against the Official Secrets Act.[68] This appears to be a deliberate widening of the ambit of the criminal sanction so as to criminalise the very early stages of a spying operation and thus to allow the security services or police to intervene before any damage is done.[69]

6 Some issues of principle

Nothing in this essay has cast doubt on the claim that the result-oriented mode of definition is more common than the inchoate mode among English criminal offences. It has, however, shown that in many branches of the criminal law there are important offences defined in the inchoate mode. Some of them, such as forgery, counterfeiting and perjury, are defined in a purely inchoate manner and depend entirely on the intention with which D does certain preliminary acts. Some offences relating to public order and the administration of justice adopt the inchoate mode with an objective requirement: 'doing a preliminary act likely to . . . '. Others are phrased in an alternative subjective-objective form, such as the 'breach of the peace' offence — conduct of a certain kind intended or likely to cause a breach of the peace. It need hardly be observed that there are significant differences between these formulations, but the question which they raise as a whole is whether the harm-plus-culpability model should be regarded as the natural approach to defining criminal offences. Is the inchoate mode more acceptable, equally acceptable, or suitable only where some special justifications are present? Let us consider some of the issues of principle raised by the different types of definition.

(a) The public interest in preventing harm It needs little argument to

establish that there is a public interest in minimising the frequency with which interests protected by the criminal law are violated. The law itself is not the only and may not be the primary social mechanism for this, but it is recognised that one function of law enforcement agents is to prevent crimes (or, alternatively put, to prevent invasions of protected interests). To this end the law contains a range of preventive crimes, including the inchoate offences of attempt, conspiracy and incitement. It does not, however, contain a general inchoate offence of threatening to commit a crime. It was argued above that there is a strong affinity between threatening and inciting, conspiring and attempting.[70] The offence of assault applies generally to threats of bodily harm which cause fear, but its maximum penalty of one year's imprisonment may be insufficient for the more serious threats.[71] The inchoate offences themselves, on the other hand, take their elements and maximum penalty from the crime threatened. Serious consideration should surely be given to the merits of an additional form of general inchoate offence, instead of the piecemeal and patchy approach of existing English law to threats. It must be added, however, that the ambit of the law of attempts may not be thought sufficient for the proper prevention of crime. The 'more than merely preparatory' test introduced by the Criminal Attempts Act 1981 is not only imprecise in the guidance it gives to law enforcement officers and susceptible to different interpretations in the courts, but it may also fail to cover some forms of preparation for offending which ought to be covered. Of course it is for debate what forms of preparation should and should not be criminalised. But the absence from the 1981 Act of a non-exhaustive list of acts amounting to an attempt has left considerable doubt in the area of fraud and deception which does not afflict forgery, false accounting and false statements by company directors, since those offences are defined in the inchoate mode, and which could be avoided if the other deception offences in the Theft Act were similarly re-defined. The formulation of the law of attempts, and its relationship with other offences, are therefore matters for discussion in the context of the proper extent of crime prevention.

(b) The inchoate mode and individual rights The inchoate mode of defining offences may have the advantage of increased certainty, but, as was noted when discussing the provisions of the Forgery and Counterfeiting Act,[72] that advantage may be bought at too high a price. There are recognised dangers in defining offences without requiring actual harm, and these have been debated most vigourously in the context of the law of attempts. One danger is that of premature condemnation: if D is held guilty of a crime before he has done all (or almost all) the acts necessary to violate the protected interest, he is being deprived of an opportunity to repent or give up for some other reason. The danger is greater when the system of criminal law pushes the actus reus of attempt further back from the completed offence, especially if there is no provision for a defence of abandonment. The danger is equally present in the various threats offences, possession offences and wherever the inchoate mode of definition renders D liable to conviction even though a further act would have to be done to violate the protected interest. Another danger lies in excesses of state power: offences which require proof of results or of acts harmful in themselves depend on open and objective facts, whereas the law of attempts may leave room for charges to be brought on the basis of alleged confessions, admissions or previous misconduct of a similar kind, unsup-

ported by objectively incriminating facts.[73] The point is relevant to offences defined in the inchoate mode, even though many of them require proof of what might be termed a 'non-innocent' act. These offences do not typically take the wide form of penalising 'any act done with intent to . . . ' although there are a couple of examples of this in s 4 of the Criminal Law Act 1967[74] and s 7 of the Official Secrets Act 1920,[75] and some would place theft in this category.[76] But the usual form is to penalise a preliminary act such as entering premises as a trespasser, administering a substance, placing an obstruction on a railway line, or words or behaviour which are threatening, abusive or insulting. These acts are all 'non-innocent' in the sense that they are sufficiently wrongful in themselves to call for an explanation, and in the absence of a convincing explanation might warrant an inference of the intent which constitutes the other principal ingredient of the offence.[77]

Insofar as offences defined in the inchoate mode require some form of non-innocent act, then, some of the dangers of the law of attempts are reduced. But those dangers are still present to a greater extent than in result-oriented offences, and this should prompt deep consideration before the inchoate mode is adopted in a certain sphere of conduct. The outer boundaries of the criminal law must be set with due respect for individual rights as well as crime prevention.

(c) Ease of proof One reason for adopting an inchoate mode of definition is that it reduces problems of proof. In what circumstances, if any, is this a sufficient justification? One example of this reasoning is provided by the offence of taking an unmarried girl under 18, etc, with intent that she should have unlawful sexual intercourse;[78] another example is the definition of the bomb hoax offences.[79] But the 'ease of proof' explanation emerges most clearly in the public disorder and public nuisance offences, where it is thought likely that members of the public would be reluctant to come forward and give evidence that they were either put in fear or annoyed by D's behaviour. Even though it might be thought that the creation of fear in bystanders is part of the essence of the major crimes of riot, violent disorder and affray, the Public Order Act 1986 goes so far as to include an express dispensation from proof that any member of the public was even at the scene, let alone put in fear — a dispensation which virtually undermines the rationale of the offence.[80] These dispensations undoubtedly smooth the path of the prosecutor and make it correspondingly more difficult for defendants to obtain an acquittal, but do they unfairly favour the prosecutor? Do they infringe a defendant's rights? The questions reach far into a realm of disputation about individual rights and the interests of the state which cannot be fully considered here, but some issues can be raised. Does it seem right to convict a person of a serious public order offence without the need to hear evidence from any member of the public? Should police evidence and court inferences suffice for conviction? It would certainly be unjust if a meritorious prosecution were to fail because no member of the public wished to 'get involved' to the extent of coming to court and giving evidence; but is it not unjust in another way if a meritorious defence were to fail because witnesses who do come to court to say that they were not put in fear or to dispute the prosecution's interpretation of the acts done are ruled, because of the definition of the offence, not to be speaking to the main issue? There is little doubt that the public order and the public nuisance[81] offences have been defined so as to favour the convenience of prosecutors. That

does not *necessarily* infringe a defendant's rights because he surely cannot be said to have a right to an unmeritorious acquittal. It does, however, indicate that these questions of definition ought to be approached with a keen eye to the balance of interests and rights, and with a sound basis in systematic evidence (rather than forensic lore) about the difficulties of prosecuting and defending these cases.

(d) Criminalising reckless and negligent 'attempts' One consequence of defining an offence in the inchoate mode may be that it provides for the conviction of reckless (and sometimes of negligent) actors who, if the offence were defined in the result-oriented mode, would not be liable to conviction because English law requires proof of intention in order to constitute the crime of attempt. For example, if the breach of the peace offence were defined along the lines of 'causing a breach of the peace by using threatening, abusive or insulting words or behaviour', then an attempt would require proof of an intention to cause a breach of the peace. The effect of the present inchoate mode of definition is, however, that D is liable to conviction if he does one of the specified acts in circumstances in which it is 'likely' to lead to a breach of the peace — a form of liability for negligence which, if it is accepted that the real mischief is actual public disorder, amounts to what might be called a negligent attempt. More frequently the effect of the inchoate mode is to render liable the reckless attempter, and English law has set itself against this as a general feature of the law of attempts.[82] The usual arguments are that the criminalisation of reckless attempts would extend the criminal sanction widely and unnecessarily (since there has been no call for such a general extension), and that it would go against the popular understanding of the concept of an attempt (since 'the very idea of an attempt is one of trying or striving to achieve a result').[83] The counter-argument is essentially the same as that in favour of penalising factually impossible attempts: when D knowingly takes the risk that a prohibited result will occur or that a particular circumstance exists, his liability or non-liability should not be dependent on chance, since his culpability is the same. Moreover, if recklessness is sufficient for the completed offence, is it not illogical that it should be insufficient for the attempt? In Scots law and many other European systems, recklessness is generally sufficient for an attempt.[84] Although English law rejects the general doctrine, we have noticed several offences defined in the inchoate mode which have this effect, most notably the many 'endangerment' offences which penalise acts likely to disrupt means of transport.[85] Those offences tend to have two features which might be thought sufficient to justify liability even if the general argument for criminalising reckless attempts is rejected: firstly, they specify acts which are non-innocent, such as placing an obstruction on a railway line; secondly, they are aimed at situations in which the consequences could be particularly serious, such as injury or death to one or many citizens. The first feature is important from the point of view of individual rights (see (*b*) above), whilst the second suggests the general principle that, the more remote from the protected interest the definition of a crime is taken, the more serious must be the potential harm to that interest in the circumstances defined. In broad terms, and without concluding the specific arguments, it is more justifiable to criminalise a negligent attempt if the potential danger is to life and limb, possibly of many people, whereas there may be little or no social justification for penalising reckless attempts to violate less central interests.

(e) Legal definitions and popular beliefs No lawyer, let alone one who has any interest in the reform of the criminal law, can afford to ignore popular feeling. The administration of criminal justice is itself dependent on laymen, as magistrates and as jurors, and it would be unsatisfactory if the form and scope of the law were to become out of step with popular beliefs. In this context the many offences defined in the inchoate mode discussed in this essay might be thought to be incompatible with '. . . the fact . . . that we all react differently when an act causes harm from when the same act does not.'[86] What should we make of this apparent conflict? One possibility is that few members of the public do have an opinion on such matters, so that the apparent conflict is unimportant in this sphere. Another possibility is that popular reactions are rather more complex than a simple concentration on results. This might explain a popular tendency to focus on results in relation to offences against the person, whilst raising little objection to the inchoate mode in which theft and forgery (for instance) are defined,[87] and viewing with equanimity a sentence of ten years' imprisonment for 'doing an act preparatory to' a breach of the Official Secrets Act.[88] If there is an inconsistency between the inchoate mode of definition and popular beliefs, it may be a selective one and may in any event be less important than some of the arguments of principle raised earlier.

(f) Keeping the criminal law to a minimum The welter of inchoate offences, crimes of possession and other offences defined in the inchoate mode prompts deeper reflection on another of the principles mentioned at the beginning of the essay, that of keeping the amount of criminal law to a minimum. Even if we welcome it as a sound utilitarian principle, exactly how and where it should bite remains to be debated. It would certainly be wrong to use the principle simply as a ground for opposing any and every new offence, for then it would operate purely to preserve the status quo — to defend the existing boundaries of the criminal law. Rather, it should be capable of use as a critical principle throughout the criminal law, restricting the criminal sanction to major invasions of and threats to the central interests and relegating minor invasions of non-central interests to other less stigmatic and less costly procedures. In order to use the principle in this way, criminal lawyers need a ranking of interests which goes beyond the simple physical/sexual/property interests assumed above and which also ranks public, social and environmental interests.[89] Without at least a general impression of what our priorities should be and where the threshold of criminal liability should be set, the principle of keeping the criminal law to a minimum cannot function properly as a critical standard. Criminal lawyers have perhaps tended to concentrate unduly on the issues raised by mens rea, defences and the other personal conditions of liability, and to give insufficient attention to the social reach of the criminal sanction and the substantive principles of criminalisation.[90] It is not that these issues of priority have been entirely ignored, for there are examples in English law's restriction of the law of attempts to indictable offences and in its refusal to penalise reckless and negligent 'attempts' save in certain situations of potential gravity. But we should also be asking whether it is justifiable to criminalise as theft any mere assumption of an owner's rights with intent, etc, whilst refusing to penalise a reckless attempt at rape as such,[91] whether it is right to criminalise threats to cause criminal damage but not threats to cause non-serious injury,[92] and so on. There is also the point that when an offence is defined in the inchoate mode, the

law of attempts usually applies to extend the reach of the criminal sanction even further. In some cases of trying to do a non-innocent act such as entering as a trespasser in burglary, this extension might be acceptable. In other crimes such as theft and making a false instrument, the extension may be less justifiable. What seems to be missing is an overall consideration of the priorities — in terms of the interests to be protected, the importance of prevention and the protection of rights — at these outer edges of the criminal sanction.[93] The definitions of many of the offences considered above go a considerable distance back from the actual violation of interests worthy of the criminal law's high protection, and we must be satisfied that this is the product of careful and principled choice rather than tradition and happenstance.

7 Conclusions

The form in which criminal offences are defined surely deserves closer and wider-ranging attention than it has hitherto received. Criminal lawyers have become accustomed to debating whether a definition should be framed objectively or subjectively in a particular respect. But another choice — that between the inchoate and result-oriented modes of definition — must not be overlooked. This choice not only lays bare the tension between outcomes and intentions as the foundation of criminal liability — a tension which, as the many offences defined in the inchoate mode suggest, can be resolved in favour of intentions without jeopardising public confidence in the law — but also raises issues about the interests which deserve the protection of the criminal law, about priorities among those interests, about the proper scope of the inchoate offences themselves, about the earliest stage at which the law ought to intervene and criminalise, about the punishment of recklessness and negligence, and about the value of certainty in the criminal law. Underlying what may appear to be technical issues of definition there are deep questions of principle and practice about individual liberty and social policy. Those of us who accept both the proposition that intentions should be more important than outcomes in determining criminal liability and the proposition that the reach of the criminal law should be kept to a minimum have a great deal more thinking to do.

NOTES

1 JC Smith and B Hogan *Criminal Law* (5th edn, 1983) p 31; hereinafter, references to this work will be abbreviated to *S&H*.

2 'The Element of Chance in Criminal Liability' [1971] Crim LR 63. An earlier version of that paper is referred to by PR Glazebrook, 'Should we have a Law of Attempted Crimes?' (1969) 85 LQR 27, in discussing some of the points examined below.

3 'Some Problems of the Reform of the Law of Offences against the Person' (1978) 31 CLP at p 15.

4 See R Cross *The English Sentencing System* (3rd edn, 1981) pp 151–157.

5 I have tried to do this elsewhere: 'Belief, Intent and Criminal Liability' in JS Bell and JM Eekelaar (eds), *Oxford Essays in Jurisprudence: Third Series* (forthcoming). Cf GP Fletcher

Rethinking Criminal Law (1978) for a different theoretical and historical approach.

6 This essay is limited to those crimes discussed in detail by Smith and Hogan (see note 1, above), and does not survey the 7,000-odd crimes known to English law.

7 For other distinctions of this kind, see GH Gordon *Criminal Law of Scotland* (2nd end, 1978) p 61; GP Fletcher, *op cit* pp 115–122 and 388–390.

8 Except where the limited doctrine of consent operates: see *S&H* pp 357–361.

9 This is not to suggest that fear and fraud are the only matters relevant to consent: see *S&H* p 408.

10 Offences against the Person Act 1861, s 16, as amended by Criminal Law Act 1977, Sch 12; *S&H* p 333; draft Criminal Code, cl 68.

11 Criminal Damage Act 1971, s 2; *S&H* p 650; draft Criminal Code, cl 83.

12 Theft Act 1968, s 21; *S&H* p 550.

13 Criminal Law Act 1977, s 6; *S&H* p 753.

14 Another example is the offence of using threats to suppress evidence, recommended in Law Com no 96 *Offences relating to Interference with the Course of Justice*, draft Bill, cl 9.

15 [1969] 3 All ER 1383, CA.

16 Theft Act 1968, s 7; *S&H* p 503.

17 Sexual Offences (Amendment) Act 1976, s 1; *S&H* pp 408–409.

18 Sexual Offences Act 1956, s 2; *S&H* p 413.

19 *S&H* p 351; draft Criminal Code, cl 77. Technically the offence of assault lies between the first group (which does not require the actual causing of fear) and the second (which requires that and more).

20 See *S&H* pp 289–290 and pp 373–375.

21 Public Order Act 1986, ss 1(4), 2(3) and 3(4).

22 Eg the two variants of the breach of the peace offence in ss 4 and 5 of the 1986 Act, which are inchoate in slightly different ways.

23 The offences of threatening to kill or to cause damage require that the threat be communicated to another, 'intending that that other would fear it would be carried out', but this usage of the word 'fear' might be no more than a contextual synonym for 'believe'. Otherwise it might no longer be possible to convict D on the facts of *R v Solanke* (above, n 15), where D's threat to kill his wife was communicated only to his probation officer, who probably had no 'fear' personally. See also *R v Syme* (1911) 6 Cr App Rep 257, CCA.

24 The gain/loss requirement in Theft Act 1968, s 21, would be eliminated: a model for this approach is provided by cl 15 of the draft Bill appended to Law Com no 96.

25 Above, n 3 and text thereat.

26 See s 1, 3 and 5 of the 1981 Act; *S&H* pp 614–620.

27 Theft Act 1968, s 17; *S&H* p 538.

28 Theft Act 1968, s 19; *S&H* p 538.

29 Further examples of the same approach may be found in cl 23, 24 and 26 of the draft Bill appended to Law Com no 96.

30 Theft Act 1968, s 15; *S&H* p 519.

31 Theft Act 1978, s 1; *S&H* p 522.

32 Theft Act 1978, s 2; *S&H* p 525.

33 Offences against the Person Act 1861, s 2; *S&H* p 389.

34 *S&H* pp 408–411.

35 Sexual Offences Act 1956, s 3; *S&H* p 413.

36 Theft Act 1968, ss 17 and 19.

37 *Comer v Bloomfield* (1970) 55 Cr App Rep 305; *R v Ilyas* (1984) 78 Cr App Rep 17.

38 Law Com no 102 *Attempts, and Impossibility in relation to Attempt, Conspiracy and Incitement*, paras 2.38 and 2.52.

39 See Law Commission Working Paper no 50, paras 78 et seq, and the article by Ian Dennis 'The Elements of Attempt' [1980] Crim LR at pp 766–772; for a possible model, see cl 11 (3) of the draft Bill appended to Law Com no 96.

40 See LCWP no 50, para 86, and [1980] Crim LR 772.

41 S 4(3), followed by cl 53(4) of the draft Criminal Code.

42 See ATH Smith 'The Idea of Criminal Deception' [1982] Crim LR 721 at p 724.

43 See *S&H* pp 512–518, for a critical appraisal.

44 See the comments on the Law Commission's Working Paper on forgery by E Griew [1970] Crim LR 548 and PR Glazebrook [1970] Crim LR 554.

45 S 58 provides, however, that the woman herself cannot be convicted of the attempt if she is not in fact pregnant, and this exception to the impossibility principle is preserved in cl 72(2) of the draft Criminal Code.

46 By cl 70 and 71(1); cl 72 preserves an extended inchoate offence of supplying articles for

abortion. Reference should also be made to the offence of concealment of birth (*S&H* p 334), which uses the inchoate terminology of 'endeavouring to conceal' the birth.
47 *S&H* pp 379–381.
48 Criminal Law Revision Committee, 14th Report *Offences against the Person* (Cmnd 7844 of 1980), pp 84–87.
49 For the offences of placing wood on rail lines with intent to obstruct a locomotive, exhibiting false signals with intent to endanger any ship and concealing or removing buoys provided for the guidance of shipping, see *S&H* p 653. S 32, 33 and 34 of the Offences against the Person Act 1861 create further railway offences.
50 14th Report (n 48, above), para 193.
51 *S&H* pp 256–258; Law Com no 102, pp 8–13.
52 See ns 1 and 2 above, and text thereat.
53 *S&H* p 402.
54 *S&H* p 403.
55 *S&H* p 426.
56 15th Report *Sexual Offences* (Cmnd 9213 of 1984), pp 90–92; the Committee recommended reducing the age-limit to 16 and extending the offence to sexual offences with boys.
57 [1984] AC 320, HL.
58 See Lord Roskill in *R v Morris*, above, and JC Smith *Law of Theft* (5th edn, 1984) p 18.
59 See the discussion of the historical development by GP Fletcher, *op cit*.
60 *S&H* p 566. It could be said that a s 9(1)(a) burglary is not inchoate since it requires entry of a building as a trespasser. However, since there is no general crime of trespass on premises, this could hardly be described as the mischief at which the offence is aimed.
61 See pp 10–11 above, and also the offences in s 2 of the Theft Act 1978.
62 *S&H* pp 695–696. Under the Law Commission's proposed Bill, cl 3(1)(a), the offence would require the making of a false statement: Law Com no 96.
63 *S&H* pp 700–704.
64 *S&H* p 700; the Law Commission's proposed offence takes a similar form (Law Com no 96, cl 8).
65 *S&H* p 705.
66 *S&H* p 717, and Contempt of Court Act 1981, ss 1 and 2.
67 *S&H* pp 707–708. There is no crime of attempting to commit this offence: Criminal Attempts Act 1981, s 1(4)(c).
68 Official Secrets Act 1920, s 7; *S&H* p 791.
69 Cf also the offence of seditious libel, discussed by *S&H* pp 783–786, which is defined in an inchoate mode.
70 See p 10, above.
71 See n 19, above.
72 See n 44 above, and text thereat.
73 See the discussion of this point by GP Fletcher in (1975) 23 UCLA Law Rev 293 at p 298, replying to P Robinson at (1975) 23 UCLA Law Rev 266.
74 See n 67 above, and text thereat.
75 See n 68 above, and text thereat.
76 Cf Glanville Williams *op cit*, ch 32.
77 On innocent and non-innocent acts, see GP Fletcher *Rethinking Criminal Law*, p 232.
78 See n 56 above, and text thereat.
79 See n 54 above, and text thereat.
80 Cf ATH Smith 'The Metamorphosis of Affray' (1986) 136 NLJ 521, and Smith & Hogan *Criminal Law: Cases and Materials* (3rd edn, 1986), pp 390–391.
81 Eg the offence in Sexual Offences Act 1985, s 1(1), and the proposed offence of committing sexual acts where they are likely to be seen by members of the public: CLRC 15th Report (above, n 56), Part X.
82 Law Com no 102, pp 10–13.
83 *S&H* p 256. For the development of Professor JC Smith's views on this, see (1957) 70 Harv LR 422 at pp 434–435; [1962] Crim LR 135; and [1971] Crim LR at pp 72–73.
84 Eg GH Gordon *Criminal Law of Scotland* (2nd edn 1978), pp 264–267; GP Fletcher *Rethinking Criminal Law* (1978), pp 445–449.
85 See p 13 above, and KJM Smith 'Liability for Endangerment: English Ad Hoc Pragmatism and American Innovation', [1983] Crim LR 127.
86 Above, n 3 and text thereat.
87 See n 44 above, and text thereat.
88 The *Schulze* Case (1986) Times, 11 July.
89 A start has had to be made on this difficult task in relation to sentencing: see, for example,

J Floud and W Young *Dangerousness and Criminal Justice* (1981), chs 1 and 4, and A von Hirsch *Past and Future Crimes* (1986), ch 6.

90 A rare example of relevant discussions is what has come to be known as the Hart-Devlin debate on the relationship between law and morality.

91 If this is indeed the position on attempted rape: cf *R v Pigg* [1982] 2 All ER 591, CA with *S&H* p 257, Glanville Williams at [1983] Crim LR 365 and Richard Buxton at [1984] Crim LR 25.

92 The CLRC's argument against criminalising threats to cause non-serious injury was that this would bring too many venial matters into the criminal law (14th Report, para 218). Yet this kind of objection has been met by referring to prosecutorial discretion in, for example, the 15th Report, para 5.21.

93 There is a short discussion of some of the issues in Law Com no 102, paras 2.123 to 2.126, but compare Criminal Attempts Act 1981, s 1(4), with such questions as the need for offences of attempting to threaten, to administer a substance, to communicate false information, to make a false instrument, to steal, etc.

Hearsay-logic and hearsay-fiddles: Blastland *revisited*

D J Birch

Students frequently complain that the hearsay rule is illogical. My favourite answer is that most of the time it is not, but it has a logic all of its own, to grasp which it may first be necessary to compromise one's common sense. Those who are well-versed in this 'highly technical'[1] branch of the law of evidence have frequently to apologise for reaching conclusions which 'are such as would seem to a layman to be completely out of this world',[2] and the common sense approach of the man who assumes that he can admit that he has a packet of Players in his pocket because that is what it says on the label[3] will simply not do as hearsay-logic.

Fundamental to hearsay-logic are two basic propositions which the student must master. Firstly, the hearsay rule operates upon everything from the 'most worthless gossip' to the 'weightiest opinion'.[4] All evidence which fits the definition of hearsay is liable to exclusion, no matter how reliable, because the benefits of excluding hearsay evidence as a class are assumed to outweigh the claim a particular item of evidence may have to be accorded very great weight.[5] Secondly, the job of admitting reliable hearsay is left to hearsay exceptions, but it is not true to say either that what is admitted under the exceptions is invariably reliable, or that what is left out is of no worth. Of course the exceptions exist to perform the function of separating the wheat from the chaff, but we all know that the motley varieties of threshing implements, being of different vintages and designed with no overall purpose in mind, are apt to leave much nourishing grain on the threshing-room floor, while occasionally offering up for consumption the sort of fibrous husky residue which sticks in the throat.[6] With hearsay exceptions as with the rule itself, the dominant consideration is classification, rather than individual credit worthiness:

> 'The whole development of the exceptions to the hearsay rule is based on the determination of certain classes of evidence as admissible or inadmissible and not on the apparent credibility of particular evidence. No matter how cogent particular evidence may seem to be, unless it comes within a class which is admissible, it is excluded.'[7]

These two fundamental principles of hearsay-logic combine to ensure that occasional injustice is inevitable. If this were all, most students could be induced to go along with hearsay-logic, but it is not all. There exists, side by side with hearsay-logic, the hearsay-fiddle. This occurs, for example, when a court brazenly announces, aided and abetted by the absence of any full and binding judicial definition of hearsay, that evidence bearing all the characteristics of hearsay is nothing of the sort. This is generally done in order to admit reliable evidence which does not fit within a hearsay exception.[8] Thus, for example, where it was necessary to prove that the repossession of goods had not been undertaken by a firm's head office, a local branch manager was permitted to testify that he had telephoned head office and been told that there was no record of any such repossession.[9] This evidence was clearly tendered for the hearsay purpose of persuading the court that what the manager had been told was true, and it is generally accepted by academic commentators that to label the evidence non-hearsay was a fiddle perpetrated in order to admit reliable information which, labelled as hearsay, would have been inadmissible.[10] The hearsay-fiddle may also be employed in order to pass off as hearsay, evidence which is not really guilty of that charge, but this is a less common phenomenon, partly because there is more than one way of disposing of evidence which it is considered undesirable to admit.[11]

The overall picture of the hearsay rule in criminal cases is one of hidden tension between the apparently inexorable hearsay-logic and the judicially unacknowledged but ever-present hearsay-fiddle. The ability to work a hearsay-fiddle depends, as has already been observed, on the absence of any comprehensive judicial definition of hearsay. If the House of Lords could be provoked into properly defining hearsay, the game would be up. It might be supposed that if ever there was a case in which such intervention was called for, it would be one in which the Court of Appeal succeeded in applying hearsay-logic side by side with what could be accused of being a hearsay-fiddle. Such a case was *R v Blastland*,[12] but the result was not as anticipated. If anything, we are further away from a definition of hearsay since the House of Lords pronounced upon the case, the difficulty being almost entirely side-stepped. Nevertheless the decision sheds an interesting light both upon the use of hearsay-logic and the circumstances in which, in future, the tension produced in the fabric of the rule by the hearsay-fiddle might prove too strong to be ignored. It shows hearsay-logic at its worst, disabling a man from defending himself, and the absence of any sure dividing line between hearsay and non-hearsay as the defect it is. It is proposed to examine the decision with a view to exposing these weaknesses, and to consider what might be done about them.

R v Blastland

B was charged with the buggery and murder of a 12-year old boy, F. The circumstantial evidence against him was strong. Forensic examination established a sexual connection between them which B sought to explain away by testifying that he had given the boy money, and had then attempted to bugger him with his consent, but had failed to do so. He admitted acts of masturbation and oral sex in order to account for the presence of semen in the child's stomach. At this point in events, however, a third person came on the scene: he was, according to B, 'a very tall man with dark wavy hair [who] had a donkey jacket on.' It was B's contention that he panicked and fled at the sight of this figure, leaving the boy behind.[13] The inference was that as B had not buggered and murdered the child, this other man must have done so. There seems little doubt that this 'other person' was a person subsequently traced and interviewed by the police who, because he was not charged, was referred to only as Mark. Some information about him was placed before the jury at B's trial in the form of formal admissions by the prosecution, including his involvement in consensual buggery with a sixteen-year-old boy on two occasions, and his propensity to frequent public lavatories for the purpose of sexual activity with men. Further evidence about M was available but was not made the subject of admissions, and it was this which B sought to introduce. It consisted of:

(a) confessions made by M in the course of police interrogation;
(b) statements made by M on the night of the murder and the following day in which his state of mind was revealed, in particular his knowledge about the murder at a time when it was not generally known.

At B's trial, all of the evidence was rejected as hearsay. The Court of Appeal dismissed his appeal for the same reason.[14] Leave to appeal to the House of Lords was sought with regard to both classes of statement, but granted only in respect of (b).[15] That appeal was dismissed, chiefly on the ground that such evidence was irrelevant. It is not clear whether the House of Lords was also of the opinion (i) that the evidence was hearsay; or (ii) that it was inadmissible by analogy with the hearsay rule. What is clear is that, in the outcome, the jury were rightly kept in ignorance throughout the trial of all of the statements made by M. M was not called as a witness, an application by the defence to call him and treat him as hostile having been refused by the trial judge.

Hearsay-logic and the third-party confession

If the confession made by M had not been excluded, it would have been impossible to deny the relevance of the other statements, particularly as the ability of the maker of a confession accurately to describe the details of the offence is regarded as the best indication of the reliability of what he says.[16] This function of the inter-relationship of the confession and the other statements can only be exploited, however, if the confession is admissible, and the obstacle to its admissibility is that it is hearsay, being tendered in order to establish the truth of what is asserted. Applying hearsay-logic, this obstacle can only be surmounted if the confession can be received under an exception to the hearsay rule. Now, our system is well-geared to the reception of confession evidence, but only when the confession emanates from the accused. A confession by B would be admissible against him at his trial under what is now s 76 of the Police and Criminal Evidence Act 1984, provided that the prosecution could establish that it was free from the taints of unreliability or oppression. The confession of M, however, stands on an entirely different footing, although it must be as relevant as the confession of B, if it is accepted that the crime must have been the work of either M or B. However, s 76 does not apply unless the confession is that of 'an accused person',[17] so that this avenue to admissibility is closed to M's confession, and it cannot be tendered in evidence unless some other hearsay exception is applicable.

According to recent case law, no such exception exists. In *R v Turner*,[18] B was charged with robbery. His defence was that the offence had been committed by S, but that a prosecution 'supergrass' witness had decided to 'frame' B and protect S by substituting B's name for S's in his account of the robbery. In support of this defence B sought to introduce out-of-court statements by S in which he admitted his part in the robbery. The refusal of the trial judge to allow him to do so was upheld on appeal, Milmo J commenting:

> 'It would have been hearsay evidence which did not come within any of the well settled exceptions to the general rule that hearsay evidence is not admissible. That the categories of these exceptions are now closed and cannot be added to without legislation was made clear by Lord Reid in *Myers v DPP*.'[19]

The Court of Appeal in *R v Blastland* was happy to be bound by *R v Turner*, dismissing B's appeal on the confession point with a short 'We need say no more about that.'[20] Commenting on the refusal of leave on the point when dismissing B's appeal to the House of Lords, Lord Bridge referred to the general rule that such a refusal does not necessarily constitute approval of the law as stated by the court below, but added:

> 'However, the decision of the Court of Appeal (Criminal Division) in *Turner* . . . was itself based on the majority decision of your Lordships' House in *Myers v DPP* . . . which established the principle, never since challenged, that it is for the legislature, not the judiciary, to create new exceptions to the hearsay rule. To admit in criminal trials statements confessing to the crime for which the defendant is being tried made by third parties not called as witnesses would be to create a very significant and, many might think, a dangerous new exception.'[21]

In both *R v Turner* and *R v Blastland* it was assumed that to admit the evidence would be to create a new exception to the hearsay rule. Hearsay-logic since *Myers v DPP*[22] has dictated, as Lord Bridge and Milmo J correctly observe, that it would be a usurpation of the role of Parliament for courts to create further exceptions to the hearsay rule. This abdication of what was regarded by the minority in *Myers* as an important judicial function[23] may have led directly to the modern-day preference for the hearsay-fiddle of declaring evidence not to be hearsay for spurious reasons as a means of admitting evidence for which a new exception would otherwise have been created.[24]

Be that as it may, if either Lord Bridge or Milmo J intended to state, as it seems they did, that to admit a third party confession would violate the *Myers* principle, it is submitted that this need not be the case. It is clear that *Myers* prevents the creation of any new exception. It is equally clear that it does not exclude the possibility of tinkering with existing exceptions. The Privy Council's decision in the later case of *Ratten v R*[25] is regarded as representing English law, and to have effectively expanded and re-explained the res gestae exception under which spontaneous statements are received. It is surely not arguable that, because of *Myers*, only the legislature should have been regarded as competent to lay to rest the inconvenient nineteenth-century precedents which were held by the Privy Council to be inconsistent with the rationale of that exception:[26] indeed it could hardly be supposed that Parliament should be considered the appropriate body for such a purpose.[27] It has even been held since *Myers* that the courts may go beyond the reversal of erroneous precedent when dealing with an existing exception, and in effect remove a restriction on admissibility which has been rendered obsolete by modern business practice.[28] Of course the line will have to be drawn somewhere, or else the result would eventually be to create what would in effect constitute new exceptions. Tinkering is one thing, major surgery another.[29]

Insofar as tinkering with an existing exception does not appear to have been canvassed in *R v Turner* or *R v Blastland*, let us embark on an exercise in hearsay-logic and consider what, if anything, it could have achieved. The common law exception most suitable to be doctored would have been the declaration against interest. This is encumbered with two inconvenient limitations: the declaration must be against the pecuniary or proprietary interest of the declarant, and the declarant must have died before the trial.

The first limitation may be amenable to re-interpretation: it has certainly been much criticised. It was imposed in 1844 by the House of Lords in the *Sussex Peerage Case*.[30] A clergyman, since deceased, admitted to his son that he had officiated at a marriage, the celebration of which might have exposed him to criminal proceedings under the Royal Marriage Act of 1772. It was held that a declaration which exposed the speaker to criminal proceedings was not admissible as a declaration against interest. However the House was also clearly of the opinion that, even if such a declaration had been admissible, the facts of the case would not have satisfied the relevant conditions:[31] there was no proof that the declarant knew that the statement was against his penal interest at the time, and in any event it was part of the case of the party seeking to rely on the declaration that no criminal proceedings could have been taken against the clergyman.

The reason given for rejecting the evidence was not directly related to the potential unreliability of the particular statement. Declarations against penal interest were declared inadmissible because it was realised that to acknowledge such an exception as of general application would result in the confession of a third party being admissible *against* a defendant in a criminal trial. It was this proposition which was characterised, in Lord Brougham's famous phrase, as:

> '. . . one of the most monstrous and untenable propositions that can be advanced.'[32]

Certainly the principle that third party confessions could not be tendered against an accused was well established in 1844,[33] and to apply the exception for statements against interest so widely that statements of deceased persons implicating a defendant were admissible would have produced a conflict. It does not necessarily follow, however, that the hearsay exception must be confined to interests other than penal interest in order to avoid this result.[34] In Canada, a series of cases in which such statements were tendered by the *defence* resulted in the partial rejection of the *Sussex Peerage Case*, and acceptance that statements against penal interest could, in theory, be proved.[35] However in *Lucier v R*[36] the Supreme Court flatly rejected the contention that, mutatis mutandis, such statements could be tendered for the prosecution; the differences between the two cases being said to be 'a very real one.'[37] Here then, is one possibility; it would be possible, consistently with the *Sussex Peerage Case*, to acknowledge a one-sided hearsay exception. To English ears, however, the suggestion has an odd ring: it is almost a boast with us that the hearsay rule cuts both ways.[38] Furthermore it has been stated in Australia as a ground for refusing to allow declarations against penal interest on behalf of the defence that this step would necessarily involve permitting the introduction of such statements by the prosecution.[39] Nevertheless the argument is worth advancing, as it is the intrinsic one-sidedness of the confession exception[40] which has brought about the difficulty in the first place.

In any event, the removal of the *Sussex Peerage Case* from the scene would not have helped in *Turner* or *Blastland*, as the second limitation, requiring death of the declarant, would have come into play and resulted in the evidence being rejected. This limitation has been with the exception almost from the start,[41] and to remove it judicially goes beyond what could be justified under *Myers v DPP* as it was just such a limitation on the reception of records made by persons acting under a duty which the House in *Myers* felt unable to lift. The restriction is admittedly illogical, as there may be many other reasons for being unable to call a witness; a fact of life which modern statutory exceptions readily admit.[42] In cases such as *Blastland* it might be argued that a witness who, if called, could refuse to answer questions on the grounds of self-incrimination is in real terms as unavailable to the defence as if he had died.[43] That, however, is not the point, applying hearsay-logic. Confessions of deceased persons *might* be admissible if their reception could be squared with *Myers* and the *Sussex Peerage Case*. Confessions of live but potentially hostile witnesses might be analogous, but that alone is no warrant for admitting them and if, as seems likely, *Myers* is authority against the removal of the limitation of the exception to declarations by persons since deceased, the harsh but inevitable conclusion is that the exception is saddled with an illogical limitation and nothing can be done about it.

Thus hearsay-logic puts paid to the defence tendering a third party's acknowledgment of guilt as either a confession or (at least if he is still alive) as a declaration against interest. These two exceptions were canvassed first because, if the evidence in *Blastland* and *Turner* had a meritorious claim to be admitted at all, it was on the strength of the rationale underlying both of these two exceptions, that what a man says against himself may fairly be presumed to be true. But it is legitimate when applying hearsay-logic to look beyond exceptions of this kind: evidence can be received under *any* exception, the conditions of which it satisfies, and if the satisfaction of these conditions is purely coincidental and not related to those features of the evidence which it is claimed make it reliable, then that is the luck of the game. So it is worthy of note that there is at least one other possibility[44] for admission of the evidence in a case of the *Blastland*[45] type. Note that it can be achieved without doctoring the facts in any way so as to make the evidence more creditworthy. Under s 68 of the Police and Criminal Evidence Act 1984,[46] a statement in a documentary record, compiled by a person acting under a duty from information supplied by a person who may reasonably be supposed to have personal knowledge of the matters dealt with, is admissible provided the supplier of the information is unavailable for one of a number of reasons listed in the section. Hostility to the party calling the evidence is not one of them, but it is good enough if the supplier is dead, ill, abroad, or cannot be found.[47] The record of a police interview with a suspect who confesses but who is not subsequently charged seems to qualify as a documentary record, so that if the interviewee was unavailable to testify for one of the stated reasons his confession would be admissible on behalf of the person eventually charged with the offence, notwithstanding that the third party would have been an unwilling witness or that the defence is greatly relieved not to have to call him. The fact that the third party is dead or ill does not, of course, make his statement any more reliable, nor does his being abroad (unless perhaps he has fled there). In a recent case which attracted the attention of the Press, a 'have-a-go-nun' foiled a bank raid by tripping up the robber. She was, however, reluctant to come forward to testify for various reasons, though a police spokesman said that she would have been a useful witness. But if she had gone abroad as a missionary, or become ill, or died, anything she had said to the police and which had been recorded could have been given in evidence under s 68,[48] notwithstanding that she would have been reluctant to give the evidence in person, and her reluctance would in all probability have been respected.

Common sense and the third party confession

One of the upsetting things about hearsay-logic is that it encourages one to play games of the sort outlined above and discourages direct consideration of what should be more important issues. Is the evidence reliable? Even if it is not, ought not D to have the right to claim that it should be evaluated by the jury?[49] If the prosecutor decided to proceed against D rather than the third party, it must have been clear to him that the third party's confession was worthless; perhaps he appeared to be the sort of person who confessed to things he has not done because he could not stand the pressure of interrogation,[50] or perhaps it seemed that he was protecting D. Whatever the reason, it could be placed before the jury along with the other evidence. Such a course might occasionally lead to the acquittal of a guilty defendant, but in terms of fairness it has more to offer than the hearsay-logic solution which, though ostensibly geared to reliability, may exclude much which is reliable and vice versa.

As an interesting footnote, the Criminal Justice Bill before Parliament at the time of writing proposes the radical step of rendering admissible all first-hand documentary hearsay statements.[51] A third party confession would thus be admissible if written, but not if oral. However, the Bill further provides that the court may in its discretion exclude the documentary hearsay if to admit it would not be in the interests of justice.[52] It is submitted that it would be better to abrogate the hearsay rule altogether than to tempt courts to decide that admitting a third party confession is not in the interests of justice.

Hearsay-fiddles and the evidence of M's 'state of mind'

The remainder of the evidence which was excluded in *Blastland* was described as evidence of M's 'state of mind.' Had this been admitted together with the confession, a significant amount of confirmatory evidence would have emerged, quite probably sufficient to raise a reasonable doubt in the minds of most juries.[53] M knew within a very short while after the killing that murder had been done; he knew who the victim was, where he lived,[54] and he knew something of the boy's movements on the night in question. When M arrived home that night, he was 'shaking like a leaf', according to J, his common-law wife. The following day he was still giving out details of the murder before the body had been found, and in a manner which suggests a state of considerable excitement on his part: when a visitor to his home asked, 'How are you, Mark?' he responded, 'Do you know there's been a murder?'

This was the evidence rejected by the Court of Appeal as hearsay: a proposition not actively dissented from by the House of Lords,[55] although the ratio of their decision seems to have been that the statements were irrelevant. Is the evidence hearsay?

This is the point at which the uncertainty created by the absence of any full definition of hearsay comes into play. However it will be argued that the evidence is not, properly understood, hearsay, and that the Court of Appeal may have been resorting to a hearsay-fiddle in order to avoid the otherwise amusing but inconvenient paradox that direct, confession evidence of M's guilt was inadmissible hearsay while indirect evidence of his 'state of mind' was not.

In order to advance the argument, my own hearsay colours must be nailed to the mast. Firstly, in what material respect is it contended that the hearsay rule is unclear? It is submitted that in this context the relevant question to which no defiinitive answer has been given is:

> 'is [the hearsay rule] confined to statements (ie representations of fact by words or conduct) which were intended to be assertive when they were made, or does it extend to words or conduct which, though not intended to be assertive by the speaker or agent, are nonetheless treated by the party tendering them in evidence as equivalent to an express assertion of fact?'[56]

In other words, does the hearsay rule only apply when the speaker is trying to convey that what he says is true (he claims 'X speaks French') or is it enough that an inference that he must have believed in the truth of the proposition in question can be drawn from what he says or does, even though he is not trying to communicate that fact? (He speaks and writes to X using the French language.)

There is much to be said for treating both types of statement as hearsay, as both depend on the credit to be given to the speaker. Both involve reliance on the reasoning 'the speaker believed such-and-such, therefore it is true',[57] although in one case the belief is asserted by the speaker and in the other it is deduced by the listener. Both are subject to the 'hearsay dangers' of ambiguity, insincerity, defective memory and lack of perception, though not necessarily to the same degree.[58]

However, judicial support for treating non-assertive statements and conduct as hearsay is rare in English law. There is, of course, the case of *Wright v Doe d Tatham*,[59] in which letters written to one M whose sanity was in issue were tendered to show that, as they were not the sort of letters one might write to a lunatic, therefore the writers must have believed M to be sane. The evidence was rejected as hearsay; the lack of oath and cross-examination being regarded as every bit as fatal to evidence tendered as the equivalent of an assertion of sanity as to an assertion itself.[60] Furthermore it was held that the mere fact that the writers had acted on their beliefs by sending the letters was of no consequence. Even if they, and numerous others, had elected M to Parliament it would have amounted to no more than the equivalent of the assertion 'I vote for [M] because I believe him to be competent,' and thus rejected as hearsay.[61] Were the rules otherwise, it was said, 'it would lead to indiscriminate admission of hearsay evidence on all manner of facts.'[62]

Despite the apparent logic of this approach, it is seldom applied, although it is left to academic writers to explain what is wrong with it. It is not simplifying their counter-argument too far to state it as the converse of the proposition just put: if the rule is stated so widely as to cover non-assertive words and conduct, 'there would be no end to the situtations in which the rule would apply.'[63] 'Every human action can be presented as an implied assertion of the actor's belief in the satisfaction of the conditions under which he would be prepared to perform it.'[64] The limitation is not necessarily put forward as a logical one, and its proponents do not always concur as to its application,[65] but it is regarded as desirable in practice.

Whereas the courts have refrained from any express rejection of *Wright v Doe d Tatham* in favour of the 'assertion' theory, it is not difficult to find cases the results of which square with the more restrictive view of hearsay. Thus in *Mawaz Khan and Amanat Khan v R*[66] it was held that the unsworn statements of co-defendants in which they each told lies in a manner suggestive of a conspiracy to fabricate a joint story were admissible as prosecution evidence. The statements were adduced:

> 'Not for the purpose of establishing the truth of the assertions contained therein, but for the purpose of asking the jury to hold the assertions false and to draw inferences from their falsity.'[67]

The inference to be drawn was that 'the recourse to falsehood leads naturally to an inference of guilt',[68] in other words 'D lied, therefore he believed himself to be guilty, therefore he was guilty'. Because the inference of guilt comes about indirectly through a deduction as to belief, rather than directly through an assertion of guilt such as a confession, it is not a hearsay statement.

Now it may well be that the turning of a judicial blind eye to the *Wright v Doe d Tatham* concept of hearsay is the biggest hearsay-fiddle of the lot, but the present purpose of the writer is not to suggest that that is so, but rather that the preponderance of authority favours confining the rule to assertions. This being so, it would be inappropriate, and a hearsay-fiddle, to revert to the broader, *Wright v Doe d Tatham* concept simply as an expedient to exclude non-assertive words or conduct which it is considered desirable to exclude.[69] Now let us return to the conclusion of the Court of Appeal in *Blastland* and ask again: was the evidence hearsay?

The evidence which was rejected was said to be evidence of M's 'state of mind'. This expression is susceptible of three meanings. Firstly, there is the 'state of emotion' of a person who has just committed a murder. Secondly, there is the 'state of belief in his own guilt' which a killer may manifest and which is aptly described as an implied admission. Thirdly, there is the 'state of knowledge' of information of which a murderer might be expected to be in possession.[70]

There is no hearsay problem involved in using M's statements to support an inference that he was in an emotional state of mind. This could be deduced from the way the statements were made, and from the fact that they were made at all, without reference to the truth of anything imparted by M. Consistently with this view, the Court of Appeal regarded the use of the evidence in this way as inappropriate not on the grounds of hearsay, but on the grounds of relevance. M's state of emotion *after* the killing was not relevant, although it would have been permissible to prove:

> 'His state of mind at or before the moment that the appellant saw him there . . . if it was him . . . and evidence might have been admitted as to this.'

This is an unnecessary and inappropriate restriction on the use of evidence of emotion. Just as the state of emotion of a murderer before a killing might be expected to be something out of the ordinary (anger, perhaps, or depression) so the state of his feelings afterward can be anticipated to be unusual. One might expect him to be shocked, tearful or unable to sleep. Failing to show any emotion after committing murder is so unusual that it might provide an indication of mental abnormality:

> 'That he appeared detached and unconcerned did not strike the doctor at the time as remarkable, owing to his acquaintance with the phlegmatic disposition of the labouring class in East Anglia, but he agreed that it was remarkable for even an East Anglian to sleep soundly after committing murder.'[71]

Thus if the question is which of two mentally normal men committed a murder, evidence that one was upset afterwards ought to be relevant. Thus the evidence should not have been rejected either for the reason given by the Court of Appeal, or because it was hearsay.

Having rejected the possibility that the evidence might serve to show M's emotion at a relevant time, the Court of Appeal reasoned that the statements must have been tendered for some other purpose, and it was this which was characterised as hearsay. At trial the hearsay label was attached on the basis that the statements were implied admissions. As was indicated above, this is the sort of analysis which one might apply to statements in which M's belief in his guilt was revealed. The Court of Appeal, however, does not seem to have proceeded via this sort of analysis. It seems to have reasoned (a) M's statements were assertions of knowledge; (b) this evidence was tendered only in order to show that M might have been present and might have been the murderer; (c) thus there was reliance on the truth of M's assertions.

> 'The defence sought in reality to admit the evidence of Mark's state of knowledge in order to ask the jury to infer that he may have been present and the murderer. That is outside the state of mind line of cases and over the border into the province of fact and truth.'[72]

The reference to the 'state of mind line of cases' is to those authorities in which a person's relevant state of emotion was proved, either as non-hearsay or (if in the form of an assertion) by way of exception to the hearsay rule.[73] But it does not follow that because those authorities were inapplicable, and because the purpose of tendering the statements was to lead to an inference of guilt, the statements were hearsay. First, let us distinguish between the statements as assertions of knowledge and as indications of belief. Insofar as M asserted knowledge, his statements were potentially hearsay. This is not because it was necesssary to rely on M's statements to prove the truth of the facts related, because this could easily be proved by other evidence. A hearsay problem would arise if reliance were placed on the statement to prove that M *knew* what he claimed to know. As a general rule, it is not possible to prove the fact of knowledge by an assertion of it without breaking the hearsay rule, and rightly so.[74] Even if what the speaker claims to know can be verified, it may be that he was guessing, or using the verb 'to know' in an unusual sense, eg to connote belief, as in 'I know that my Redeemer liveth'. However the hearsay rule applies only where reliance is placed on the assertion rather than on the fact that it has been made. In exceptional cases a claim of knowledge may establish knowledge without reliance on the credit to be given to the speaker (ie independently of its assertive quality) because the fact that the statement is *made* demonstrates knowledge, as where the speaker correctly asserts the combination of a safe, or a telephone number. The argument is not 'Why would he say such a thing, unless he believed it to be true? (therefore it is true)' but 'how *could* he have said such a thing, unless he knew it?'[75] M's statements surely fell into this category.

There remains the possibility of using M's statements as an implied admission of guilt. Here, no hearsay problem arises because there is no assertion by M, express or implied, to this effect. M's belief in his guilt had to be inferred by the listener, as where an accused person tells lies, or runs away. However, if such statements are not hearsay, we have the odd result vis-à-vis the third party who confesses *and* makes such statements, that his confessions are inadmissible, but not the statements from which his belief in his own guilt can be deduced. Lord Bridge seems to have had this paradox in mind when he said:

> '. . . if it is right, the argument does appear to lead to the very odd result that the inference that Mark may have himself committed the murder may be supported indirectly by what Mark said, though if he had directly acknowledged his guilt this would have been excluded.'[76]

This is the context in which he came close to applying the hearsay rule by analogy, holding that to admit such evidence was:

> '. . . in the light of the principles on which the exclusion of hearsay depends, to be open to still graver objection than allowing evidence that he had directly committed the crime.'[77]

It is, of course, extremely unlikely that in *Blastland* reliance was being placed on M's statements as implied admissions at all. A more suitable case for the investigation of the paradox identified above is if it is assumed that the third party (a) confesses and (b) lies about the offence, or runs away. In *R v Steel*[78] D sought to adduce evidence of a third party's statements with a view to proving them to be lies. The Court of Appeal held that the evidence was 'in all probability' hearsay, but was in any event, 'an irrelevance'.[79] Without seeking to bandy words on the question of relevance, why was the evidence 'in all probability' hearsay? D's statements are not hearsay if proved only in order to show that they are false.[80] How can it be otherwise with the statements of another? One thing is clear: we cannot have a different concept of hearsay according to whose statements are in issue; or at least, not without very good reason.

The real reason why there has been some dithering over the question whether a third party's lies constitute hearsay is that D's lies will be admitted in any event, either as original evidence or, if hearsay, as admissions. The third party's lies throw the hearsay problem into sharp focus: admit them as original evidence, and it renders almost ridiculous the exclusion of the third party's confession.

So far it has proved possible to avoid apparently ridiculous consequences by rejecting evidence such as the esoteric knowledge in *Blastland*, or the lies in *Steel*, as being, if not hearsay, insufficiently relevant. This will not be an escape route which is open in all cases; indeed it is doubtful whether the evidence about M in *Blastland* was properly rejected. According to the House of Lords:

> 'What was relevant was not the fact of Mark's knowledge but how he had come by that knowledge . . . [His statements] provided no rational basis whatever on which the jury could be invited to draw an inference as to the source of that knowledge.'[81]

Lord Bridge referred with approval to *R v Roberts*[82] in which R sought to defend himself by proving that E, the brother of his co-defendant, had detailed knowledge of the offence. This was rejected as insufficiently relevant because, on the facts, the offence could have been committed by all three men: even if the evidence showed E was involved, it did not show that R was not.

In *Blastland*, of course, the case is different. Either B committed the crime, or M did. If only two people could have committed an offence, the fact that one of them possessed detailed knowledge about it would normally be highly relevant. However, Lord Bridge seemed to reason that because M could have acquired his knowledge as a witness, evidence about it was irrelevant. The short answer to this is surely that to make such an assumption is to usurp the function of the jury.

If this criticism is valid, the hearsay issue in *Blastland* should not have been avoided by the House of Lords and, if confronted, it is submitted that the answer provided at trial and by the Court of Appeal would not have held water: it was a hearsay-fiddle to dismiss M's statements as within the rule of exclusion.

What would the neighbours say?

To sum up, it is hard to avoid the conclusion that the courts fiddle the concepts of hearsay and relevance to admit only evidence which it is considered desirable to admit. The concept of hearsay as applied to lies, for example, may vary according to whether the lies are told by D or another, as may the concept of relevance. Legal relevance may have to vary in this way for a variety of reasons, including the risk of raising too many side-issues. It is, however, indefensible that the concept of hearsay should vary at all, and the sooner the rule is fully defined the better.

It is rather a long shot, but the initiative may come from Europe, as Mr Blastland has taken his case to Strasbourg under the European Convention on Human Rights. However, his chances of success are not great. The Convention guarantees, inter alia, a general right to a fair trial (Art 6(1)) and a collection of minimum rights best regarded as aspects of a fair trial (Art 6(3)). These include the right to examine prosecution witnesses and 'to obtain the attendance and examination of witnesses on his behalf under the same conditions as witnesses against him' (Art 6(3)(d)). There is no corresponding specific guarantee of the right to adduce relevant evidence in non-testimonial form. If such a right exists it must be deduced from the general guarantee of a 'fair trial', which is not defined but which has been interpreted as importing more than the sum total of guaranteed 'minimum rights', so that a trial may be unfair notwithstanding that those rights have not been violated. Thus in theory it is possible to argue that the inflexibility of a rule requiring the exclusion of reliable out-of-court statements might deprive D of a fair trial.

In practice, however, Art 6 is unlikely to be used as a mechanism for the review of domestic courts' rules of evidence:

> '[Article 6] implies that a party . . . should have a reasonable opportunity to put his case under conditions which do not place him at a substantial disadvantage vis à vis his opponent . . . It does not, however, lay down rules as to the evidence as such, and in particular to its admissibility and probative value, these questions being essentially dependent on domestic legislation.'[83]

Thus the European Commission has in the past refused to uphold complaints based on the reception of hearsay evidence against an applicant,[84] and on the refusal to allow hearsay evidence to be given for him.[85] Where a rule of evidence, such as our own hearsay rule, operates (in theory anyway) equally for both prosecutor and defence, the purpose of the Convention may be said to be fulfilled insofar as it is designed to ensure 'equality of arms' for the individual against the State. So the prospects of the United Kingdom receiving a dressing down from Europe over our hearsay rule does not appear all that great. Far better to put our own house in order, and the sooner the better.

NOTES

1 *Myers v DPP* [1965] AC 1001 at 1019, per Lord Reid.
2 Cross 'The Periphery of Hearsay' (1969) 7 MULR 1 at 3.
3 A Commentary by [JCS] on *Bird v Adams* [1972] Crim LR 174 at 175 questions this particular operation of the hearsay rule.
4 *Wright v Doe d Tatham* (1838) 7 LJ Ex 340 at 367 per Williams J.
5 'It is said that an injustice has been done. I think that the ordinary rules of evidence do sometimes do an injustice. The rules are made to meet the general run of cases, and it cannot be helped if in particular cases they work an injustice.' *R v Cargill* (1913) 8 Cr App Rep 224 at 229, CCA per Channell J.
6 There is also the colourful analogy of the 'crazy quilt made of patches cut from a group of paintings by cubists, futurists and surrealists' (Morgan and Maguire, 'Looking Backward and Forward at Evidence' (1937) 50 Harv LR 909), of which Lord Reid's observation that 'A policy of make do and mend is no longer adequate' is particularly pertinent: *Myers v DPP* [1965] AC 1001 at 1022.) I prefer the threshing room, however, in which some ancient flails are left propped up against the walls, their usefulness all but over, and shiny new machinery can be seen which has so many working parts that the major interest is to see which breaks down first.
7 *Myers v DPP* [1965] AC 1001 at 1024, per Lord Reid.
8 See Ashworth and Pattenden 'Reliability, Hearsay Evidence and the English Criminal Trial' (1986) 102 LQR 292.
9 *R v Muir* (1983) 79 Cr App Rep 153.
10 Ashworth and Pattenden, *op cit* at 311, *Cross on Evidence* (6th edn), p 559.
11 For example, on grounds of insufficient relevance. See, eg *R v Steel* (1981) 73 Cr App Rep 173, discussed below.
12 [1986] AC 41, [1985] 2 All ER 1095, [1985] 3 WLR 345.
13 B's account in court differed significantly from his signed statement to the police.
14 (1985) Times, 22 January (transcript from Lexis).
15 It is clear that (a) was regarded as inadmissible hearsay.
16 *Re Van Beelen* (1974) 9 SASR 163 at 216–7.
17 It is argued in *Cross on Evidence* (6th edn), p 545 that D may prove the confession of a co-accused under the section. The safeguards would be inapplicable.
18 (1975) 61 Cr App Rep 67.
19 Ibid at 87.

20 (1985) Times, 22 January (transcript from Lexis).
21 [1986] AC 41 at 52–3.
22 [1965] AC 1001.
23 'That the court should be slow to introduce or further adapt exceptions is reasonable. That the court should debar itself forever from introducing further exceptions or adapting them under any circumstances, however unforeseen or unforeseeable, would be unreasonable.' [1965] AC 1001 at 1038, per Lord Pearce.
24 Ashworth and Pattenden, op cit (n 8 above), p 297.
25 [1972] AC 378.
26 Particularly *R v Bedingfield* (1879) 14 Cox CC 341, which had won the approval of the House of Lords in *R v Christie* [1914] AC 545 and of the Privy Council in *Teper v R* [1952] AC 480, PC.
27 It would be rather fun to see the proposition '*Bedingfield* is more useful as a focus for discussion, than for the decision of the facts' reduced into statutory form. (*Ratten v R* [1972] AC 378 at 390, PC).
28 *R v Halpin* (1975) 61 Cr App Rep 97, CA (public documents).
29 'Since . . . 1886, there appears to be no case in which any new exception, or any considerable extension of an existing exception has been approved.' *Myers v DPP* [1965] AC 1001 at 1021 per Lord Reid. According to Lord Morris in the same case, 'firmly established conditions' may not be removed (at 1028). According to O'Sullivan JA (dissenting) in *Lucier v R* (1980) 50 CCC (2d) 535 at 552 'the discussion of the Law Lords [in *Myers*] is useful as a caution against wholesale reformulation of longstanding rules.'
30 (1844) 11 CL & Fin 85. Until 1844 there seems to have been no restriction: *Middleton v Melton* (1829) 10 B & C 317 at 323, per Bayley J; *Gleadow v Atkin* (1833) 1 Cr & M 410 at 425, per Vaughan B.
31 (1844) 11 CL & Fin 85 at 110, per Lord Lyndhurst LC, (with whom Lords Brougham, Denman and Cottenham concurred), and at 114 per Lord Campbell.
32 Ibid at 112.
33 So well established that it formed a corner-stone of Starkie's arguments seven years earlier against the admissibility of the famous letters in *Wright v Doe d Tatham*: 'these letters are *res inter alios*, and can no more bind parties to the cause than the admission of a stranger, or in a criminal case, the confession of another accused person.' (1837) Ad & E 313 at 353.
34 A restriction which is open to criticism because it results in the 'arbitrary and tenuous distinction' that what a man says affecting his pocket is of more weight than what he says affecting his liberty. *O'Brien v R* (1977) 76 DLR (3d) 513.
35 *O'Brien v R* (1977) 76 DLR (3d) 513; *Demeter v R* (1977) 34 CCC (3d) 137. See also *R v Pelletier* (1978) 38 CCC (2d) 515. The Canadian courts are not bound by *Myers v DPP* : *Ares v Venner* (1970) 14 DLR (3d) 4.
36 (1982) 132 DLR (3d) 244, reversing the Manitoba CA, which was split 2–1 against making such a distinction (O'Sullivan JA dissenting).
37 The Supreme Court has been criticised for failing to explain the distinction (Gold, Case Comment on *Lucier v R* (1983) 21 Osgoode Hall LJ 142, and see Paciocco, 'The Constitutional Right to Present Defence Evidence in Criminal Cases' 1985 Can Bar Rev 519). See instead the judgment of O'Sullivan JA in the court below (1980) 50 CCC (2d) 535 at 549.
38 See eg *Sparks v R* [1964] AC 964, PC, and the comments of Milmo J in *R v Turner* (1975) 61 Cr App Rep 67 at 88, CA.
39 *Re Van Beelen* (1974) 9 SASR 163 at 206.
40 Not in the same sense that it can only be used against the defendant, but in the sense that only confessions by accused persons can be tendered.
41 Not quite from the start: *Walker v Broadstock* (1795) 1 Esp 458; *Doe d Hindly v Rickarby* (1803) 5 Esp 4, discussed by Baker 'The Hearsay Rule' (1950) at 65.
42 See, eg Police and Criminal Evidence Act 1984, s 68, discussed below. The common law of Scotland seems not to suffer the same exclusive morbid preoccupation with death: see Scottish Law Commission Memorandum No 46 (1980) p 136; Wilkinson 'The Rule Against Hearsay in Scotland' (1982) JR 213.
43 Seemingly not acceptable in Canada: *Demeter v R* (1977) 75 DLR (3d) 251 at 251 (and see *R v Agawa and Mallett* (1975) 28 CCC (2d) 379), indicating that 'unavailability' will probably be restricted to death, ill-health and absence from the jurisdiction. Contrast *Hines v Commonwealth* (1923) 117 SE 84: 'If he were alive and present and claimed his privilege, he would not be available as a witness, and the exception would apply with as much reason as if he

were dead or absent.' For the problems which arise if D calls the confessing party as his own witness, see *Chambers v Mississippi* 410 US 284 (1973), holding that the cumulative effect of the rules that D could not impeach his own witness and could not introduce evidence of out of court confessions made by the witness was to deprive D of a fair trial.

44 Another possibility if a confession emerges with sufficient promptness might be the res gestae.

45 The proposal would not work for *R v Turner* (1975) 61 Cr App Rep 67 unless the statement was made in the same form as in *Blastland*.

46 Not in force when Blastland was tried.

47 S 68(2). Or he cannot be expected to remember what he said, or cannot be identified, neither of which is likely to be relevant to a third party confession.

48 Sch 3, para 2 prevents the giving in evidence without the leave of the court of a 'document setting out the evidence which a person could be expected to give as a witness . . . prepared for the purpose of any pending or contemplated proceedings,' which might apply to a formal statement made by the nun, but would not be in any sense an apt description of a third party confession which, at the time it is prepared, is intended for use if necessary against the maker.

49 Admittedly this was not thought to be the case in *R v Williams* (1985) 50 OR (2d) 321, decided under the Canadian Charter of Rights and Freedoms which guarantees inter alia the right to a fair trial (s 11(d)).

50 As in *Re Van Beelen* (1974) 9 SASR the third party admitted the untruth of his statement with the words, 'I am a nut. I had to tell you something.'

51 Criminal Justice Bill 1986, clause 14.

52 Ibid, clause 16. The court must have regard to whether it is likely to be possible to controvert the statement if the maker does not testify, and to how far the statement supplies evidence not otherwise readily available.

53 See the argument of counsel to the effect that this was the view taken by the Court of Appeal: [1986] AC 41 at 44.

54 Which was a long way both from M's home and the scene of the murder.

55 Lord Bridge applauded the manner in which the view that the evidence was hearsay had been put by Bush J, but appeared to find it unnecessary to comment on the reasoning behind it. [1986] AC 41 at 53.

56 Cross 'The Periphery of Hearsay' (1969) 7 MULR 1 at 11.

57 What Professor Tribe describes as a 'trip' into the head of the person making the statement or doing the act relied on: Tribe 'Triangulating Hearsay' (1974) 87 Harv LR 956 at 958.

58 See, eg Morgan 'Hearsay Dangers and the Application of the Hearsay Concept' (1948) 62 Harv LR 177; McCormick 'The Borderland of Hearsay' (1930) 39 Yale LJ 489; Weinburg 'Implied Assertions and the Scope of the Hearsay Rule' (1973) 9 MULR 268.

59 (1837) 7 Ad & El 313; on appeal (1838) 7 LJ Ex 363 at 382 HL.

60 Ibid, per Coleridge J at 363; Williams J at 366; Patterson J at 370; Aldeson B at 372; Bosanquet J at 373; Parke B at 376; Vaughan J at 377; Littledale J at 379; Tindal CJ at 382.

61 Ibid at 364, per Coleridge J.

62 (1837) 7 Ad & El 313 at 354, per Parke B.

63 Cross 'The Periphery of Hearsay' (1969) 7 MULR 1 at 13.

64 *Cross on Evidence* (6th edn), p 473.

65 The statement 'Hello X' tendered to prove recognition by the speaker may be regarded as hearsay (Cross 'The Periphery of Hearsay' (1969) 7 MULR 1 at 12), or original evidence (*Cross on Evidence* (6th edn), p 471).

66 [1967] 1 AC 454.

67 Ibid at 462.

68 Ibid at 463.

69 It may be, of course, that the 'true' hearsay rule lies between the two extremes canvassed of assertion and belief, and the stark choice presented is insufficiently subtle. It does not much matter what the rule is, as long as it remains constant.

70 This last meaning is unusual. In the Court of Appeal O'Connor LJ concluded 'knowledge is not a state of mind' which leaves much to the imagination.

71 *R v Rivett* (1950) 34 Cr App Rep 87 at 90.

72 Transcript from Lexis.

73 There is an (extremely unhelpful) school of thought, supported by some authority, that such declarations are receivable as original evidence. See *Phipson on Evidence* (13th edn), para 7–34; *Lloyd v Powell Duffryn Steam Coal Co* [1914] AC 733. *Cross on Evidence* (6th edn), p 590 deals with them as exceptions to the hearsay rule, which they surely must be.

74 *R v Gunnell* (1886) 16 Cox CC 154.

75 See *R v Cowell* (1940) 27 Cr App Rep 191; *State v Scott* (1925) 235 Pac 380.
76 [1986] AC 41 at 53.
77 Ibid at 54.
78 (1981) 73 Cr App Rep 173
79 Ibid at 186.
80 *Mawaz Khan and Amanat Khan v R* [1967] AC 454.
81 [1986] AC 41 at 54.
82 (1984) 80 Cr App Rep 89.
83 Application 7450/76 9 D & R 108 (1977) at 110.
84 *X v Austria* (1972) 15 YB ECHR 264.
85 *Huber v Austria* (1972) 17 YB ECHR 314.

The mental element for accessories

I H Dennis

Introduction

In an earlier *Festschrift* John Smith published a seminal essay on the law of complicity.[1] His authoritative analysis of the terms used to describe secondary participation in crime was the first major re-examination of this subject since the second edition of *The General Part*[2] and it marked the beginning of a revival of interest in a somewhat technical but fascinating area. Since 1978 the literature has burgeoned. George Fletcher's influential *Rethinking Criminal Law*[3] contained a substantial section on the theory of accessorial liability. Several important articles have subsequently appeared in journals in England,[4] Australia[5] and the United States,[6] fuelled partly by a steady flow of case law and partly by a growing realisation of the extent to which this central topic in criminal law had been neglected in academic writing.

This revival of scholarly interest in complicity has coincided in England with the preparation and publication of the Law Commission's Draft Criminal Code.[7] It is betraying no secret to say that the code team[8] found one of the hardest parts of their work the drafting of the provisions dealing with parties to crime. In particular the mental element for accessories proved an exceptionally complex matter. The law on this topic is almost entirely judge-made, but the cases to be taken account of are frequently characterised by looseness of terminology, by incomplete exposition of the law and by judicial uncertainty about underlying theory. The task of the codifier in achieving the goals of clarity, completeness and coherence in a legislative draft is thus rendered formidable. Since the code team's work was published, a series of further cases has appeared dealing with the question of accessorial mens rea. These cases raise fundamental issues about the nature of the mental element required for liability as an accessory, and prompt the thought that a re-appraisal of this important topic is overdue. Accordingly it is the purpose of this essay to explore the implications of the recent case law in the light of the Draft Code and against the background of renewed academic analysis and speculation on the topic of complicity.

1 The construction of accessorial liability

It is helpful to recapitulate briefly the way in which accessorial liability is constructed. Definitions of offences are descriptive generally only of the conduct of the perpetrator of the offence, the 'principal in the first degree' in the old language of felonies. This is the person whose acts are the most direct cause of the relevant prohibited harm or state of affairs:[9] the person who kills or steals or who is in possession of a controlled drug or who omits to report an accident. Such a person will be liable for the offence as a principal offender if he does the acts specified for the offence with the mental state or other fault element required for the offence.[10] In the case of secondary parties, whom the Draft Code refers to as accessories, the sources of liability are general doctrines of common law rather than offence definitions. These doctrines of complicity are generally applicable to all offences, whether statutory or common law; and thus whenever a particular offence is enacted or declared to exist, its scope must be taken to extend beyond its definition to include common law forms of secondary liability.[11]

It follows of course that the conduct sufficient for accessorial liability need not be and generally is not the same as that specified by the offence definition. This explains how it is, for example, that a woman can be liable for rape as an accessory and that an unmarried man can 'commit' bigamy despite the inability of both to comply with the offence descriptions of liability as a principal. A woman cannot have penile intercourse with another woman but she can procure or encourage a man to do so without consent.[12] A bachelor cannot himself marry a second time but he can certainly assist his married friend to go through a second ceremony of marriage in the lifetime of the first spouse.[13] Equally, since the source of culpability as an accessory is not the offence definition, there is no logical imperative that the mental element for an accessory should be the same as that required for a principal. It would be perfectly possible to say as a normative proposition that no one could be convicted as an accessory to an offence *unless* he had the mens rea required by the definition of the offence, but there is no logical inconsistency in refusing to take this position. And we find, for example, that in *DPP for Northern Ireland v Maxwell*[14] the House of Lords seems to have indicated that it is sufficient for an accessory to know the perpetrator's intent or possible intent without sharing that intent himself. This point will be returned to later. For the moment it is worth noting in passing that if a separate offence of complicity or facilitation[15] existed with lesser penalties than those for relevant substantive offences it would be much less controversial for a lesser mental element to suffice for a secondary party.

But this point must remain controversial for as long as the accessory is made liable for the offence committed by the principal. The convicted accessory is liable to the same stigma and penalties as the principal despite the fact that he is not the direct cause of the occurrence of the offence. *If* the justifying theory for this position is that there is an equivalence of culpability between principal and accessory,[16] and *if* the function of a mens rea requirement is to ensure that stigma and punishment are applied only to those who deserve them, then it would appear that an accessory should have at least an equivalent blameworthy state of mind to the principal before he can be convicted. Indeed it is arguable that his mental state should be more blameworthy. His causal connection with the offence is less direct and may well appear immaterial.[17] Thus it may not be possible to say with confidence that he has brought about or contributed to a prohibited harm in the same way as a principal. Reduced culpability in this respect would then suggest greater culpability in respect of the mental element before the claim for equivalent treatment can be convincingly made out.

This analysis leads to the issue of potential tensions in the construction of accessorial liability. If the mental element is framed by reference simply to the conduct required for an accessory, reflecting the separate source of liability, there is a danger of overlooking the significance of the offence itself and mens rea safeguards against unfair conviction of the principal. The natural tendency is to think in terms of whether the accessory's conduct was intentional in the sense that his act of assistance or encouragement was voluntary and was done with knowledge of the relevant circumstances. This indeed is the language of many of the judgments in cases of strict liability in the principal.[18] But such simple ideas of voluntariness and knowledge need expansion when more complex crimes are involved. If an offence requires a specific intent to cause a harmful result, it seems incoherent to hold an accessory liable for the offence when he did not have such an intent either in relation to the result or in relation to furthering the principal's act.[19] On the other hand to incorporate the full mens rea of the offence as part of the mental element which must be proved against the accessory may produce a complex and extensive requirement with considerable evidential difficulties for the prosecution. Further tensions arise in cases where the accessory acts with a 'good' motive or in the course of some lawful trade or occupation. For example, does a doctor who prescribes contraceptives to a girl under sixteen become an accessory to unlawful sexual intercourse?[20] Does a retailer of a commonplace article become liable for an offence committed with it if he knows of the buyer's criminal intention at the time of sale?[21] It is debatable the extent to which voluntariness of the act and knowledge of the circumstances are a satisfactory basis for deciding such cases. But if a purpose to promote the commission of the offence is required, does that make accessorial mens rea too narrow and fail to secure the conviction of those who ought to be convicted? Such tensions are a large part of the explanation of the complexity of this subject.

It is proposed to consider the mental element for accessories under two main headings of the intention to aid and abet and the mens rea of the offence committed by the principal. The first is a convenient encapsulation of the general requirement applicable to all cases of complicity, and the question is what state or states of mind are comprised within this notion. The second is specific to the particular offence concerned, and the question is the extent to which the mens rea required for a principal must be proved against an accessory. This ordering of the issues reflects the approach of the Draft Code. Clause 31(4) provides:

> 'A person has the fault [required for liability as an accessory] if he
>
> (a) intends that what he does shall, or is aware that it will or may, cause, assist or encourage the principal to do an act of the kind he does and in the circumstances specified for the offence; and
>
> (b) where a result is an element of the offence, is, in respect of that element, at fault in the way required for liability as a principal.'

A final introductory point concerns the heads of secondary liability. An orthodox statement of the law is that a person may be convicted in respect of an offence perpetrated by another if he has procured, assisted or encouraged the perpetrator to commit the offence.[22] This principle is normally assumed to describe the totality of secondary liability, an assumption reinforced by the statutory procedural provisions that persons who aid, abet, counsel or procure the commission of offences are liable to be tried and punished as principal offenders.[23] Occasionally, however, reference is made to a further principle of secondary liability based on conspiracy. In *Chan Wing-Siu v R*[24] the Judicial Committee of the Privy Council considered the liability of three appellants for offences of murder and wounding with intent alleged by the Crown to have been committed in the course of an attempted robbery. Sir Robin Cooke, delivering the judgment of the Board, said:[25]

> '. . . it should first be recalled that a person acting in concert with the primary offender may become a party to the crime, whether or not present at the time of its commission, by activities variously described as aiding, abetting, counselling, inciting or procuring it. In the typical case in that class, the same or the same type of offence is actually intended by all the parties acting in concert. In view of the terms of the directions to the jury here, the Crown does not seek to support the present convictions on that ground. The case must depend rather on the wider principle whereby a secondary party is criminally liable for acts by the primary offender of a type which the former foresees but does not necessarily intend.
>
> That there is such a principle is not in doubt. It turns on contemplation or, putting the same idea in other words, authorisation, which may be express but is more usually implied. It meets the case of a crime foreseen as a possible incident of the common unlawful enterprise. The criminal culpability lies in participating in the venture with that foresight.'

The suggestion that 'common purpose' is an alternative form of secondary liability to aiding and abetting is doubtful. The origins of this principle are traceable to the institutional writers, notably Foster, who declared that a person would be liable as an accessory in respect of felonies committed by one whom he had solicited to act if such crimes were probable incidents of the carrying out of the felony solicited.[26] Such liability would exist irrespective of whether the accessory contemplated the commission of those crimes or not. Foster's principle proved influential in the United States where it gave rise to the so-called *Pinkerton*[27] doctrine of accessorial liability of conspirators for all crimes done in furtherance of the conspiracy or which are reasonably foreseeable as natural consequences of carrying it out. But it is submitted that the principle in this form does not now form part of English law. Its distinctive feature, as stated by Foster, is the element of objective liability in the sense that the putative accessory need not have contemplated the commission of the offence in question if it was a probable consequence of the conspiracy. Although early English cases dispensed with a requirement of subjective contemplation in such situations,[28] the modern authorities make it clear that conspirators cannot be convicted of an incidental offence committed in the course of carrying out the common purpose in the absence of knowledge on their part that it might occur.[29] This is a significant move. Once the element of subjectivity is firmly established in the proposition about conspiracy, it is difficult to see how the liability differs from liability for aiding and abetting. The better view is that conspiracy is simply *evidence* from which aiding and abetting may be inferred so that, for example, a spectator at an illegal event may be held to be encouraging the offence despite his apparent inactivity if his presence is pursuant to a prior agreement to commit the offence.[30] Gillies has commented in terms that the doctrine of common purpose 'does not represent a substantive addition to, or a supplanting of the general principles of complicity.'[31] Its continued attraction for the courts may however be explained in terms of its utility as a convenient expression of how the general principles of complicity apply in a frequently recurring fact situation, namely the commission of an 'incidental' offence by one of a group pursuing a common criminal purpose (the 'foundational' offence).[32] Murder committed in the course of a robbery is a paradigm case. It may well be easier to explain to a jury the operation of the aiding and abetting principle by reference to a common purpose of robbery and what the robbers have impliedly agreed may happen in the course of carrying it out, than by using the actual language of aiding and abetting which might suggest that the jury had to look for acts of positive assistance or encouragement at the time of the murder. This seems to be the best explanation of the reference in *Chan Wing-Siu v R* to the Crown not seeking to support the convictions on the ground of the intended aiding and abetting of the offences. It is suggested, however, that it was not a 'wider principle' on which the Crown did rely. Rather it was the same general principle which applies to tacit acts of assistance and encouragement via a conspiracy as well as express forms of aiding and abetting.[33] The court may however have been misled into believing that more than one general principle is involved by the existence of more than one theory of accessorial liability (see later).

2 The intention to aid and abet

This is a convenient phrase to describe the general requirement of mens rea which is applicable to all cases of complicity, but its apparent simplicity is misleading. On analysis it comprises a number of distinct mental elements consisting of three matters of knowledge concerning the offence with which the accessory is charged. To these must be added the issue of the accessory's mental attitude towards the commission of that offence. The matters of which knowledge is generally required for accessorial liability are:

(a) the principal's intention to do the acts constituting the offence;
(b) any relevant circumstances specified by the definition of the offence;
(c) that the accessory's act will amount to participation in the commission of the offence.

Each of these will be examined, and then the question of whether the accessory must have an intention to promote the commission of the offence will be considered.

(a) KNOWLEDGE OF THE PRINCIPAL'S INTENTION TO DO THE ACTS CONSTITUTING THE OFFENCE

A preliminary statement of the law might be that a person cannot be convicted of an offence as an accessory unless at the time of performing the conduct alleged to amount to participation he knew that the principal was committing or intended to commit the acts constituting the offence. For example, in *Johnson v Youden*[34] two partners in a firm of solicitors acting for a builder who was selling a house at a price above a permitted maximum were acquitted of aiding and abetting the builder's offence on the ground that they had not been dealing with the transaction and thus had no knowledge of the builder's actions. Lord Goddard CJ declared:[35] 'Before a person can be convicted of aiding and abetting the commission of an offence, he must at least know the essential matters which constitute that offence.' That statement of principle was approved by the House of Lords in *Churchill v Walton*,[36] and in *DPP for Northern Ireland v Maxwell*[37] Viscount Dilhorne said: 'In my opinion it is clear that a person cannot properly be convicted of aiding and abetting in the commission of acts which he does not know may be or are intended.' This fundamental point need not be laboured. Aiding and abetting always requires mens rea in this respect; doctrines of strict[38] and vicarious[39] liability have no application.

However, a number of points do need to be made by way of expansion of the general principle. Firstly, given that the accessory knows that the principal is intending to commit an offence, how specific does this knowledge have to be? Is it material that the accessory may not know the particulars of the offence to be committed, that is, such matters as date, time, place, identity of property to be entered or stolen, and so on? In the leading case of *R v Bainbridge*[40] the Court of Criminal Appeal upheld a direction to a jury that it was sufficient if the defendant knew that the type of offence which was in fact committed was intended. An argument founded, inter alia, on *R v Lomas*,[41] that the accessory must know the details of the particular crime which was in fact committed was expressly rejected. This decision created some ambiguity by its use of the words 'type of offence',[42] and in *DPP for Northern Ireland v Maxwell*[43] the House of Lords restated the test. In that case the defendant, a member of an illegal organisation which had been engaged in terrorist activities involving murders and bombings, drove his own car to guide a group of men in a second car to a remote public house at night. A bomb was thrown by one of the men into the public house but did not in the event cause injury or damage. The defendant was charged with offences of doing an act with intent to cause an explosion by a bomb[44] and possession of a bomb with intent to endanger life or cause serious injury to property.[45] His story was that he knew he was 'on a job' for the organisation, but had no knowledge of what the men in the second car were carrying or what they intended to do on reaching the public house. The trial judge[46] found that the defendant did know that he was taking part in an attack on the public house involving the use of violence by means of bomb, bullet or incendiary device in which people would be endangered or premises seriously damaged. Upholding his conviction on both counts the House of Lords held that the test is one of the accessory's contemplation. It was not necessary that he should have actual knowledge of the particular offence intended by the principal offender. It was necessary, and sufficient, that he should have contemplated the commission of one or more of a number of crimes by the principal and intentionally lent his assistance in the commission of such an offence. Provided therefore, that the crime in fact committed is one which the accessory knew or contemplated was on the principal's 'shopping list', it is immaterial after *Maxwell* and *Bainbridge* that the accessory does not know which particular crime is intended, or the precise details of any of them. So if A supplies B with explosives, thinking that B is intending (a) to kill or injure by means of a bomb; or (b) to cause damage to property by means of a bomb with intent to endanger life; or (c) to cause an explosion likely to endanger life, A will be guilty if B does any of those acts anywhere at any time using the explosives supplied by A. On the other hand, if B uses the explosives to frighten security guards into handing over money A will not be liable for robbery since this is not an offence whose commission by B he has contemplated.

pave

Secondly *Maxwell* demonstrates that the principal need not have expressly informed the accessory of his intentions. In many cases involving a conspiracy he will have done so. But the accessory does not have to 'know' what is in the mind of another in the sense of having received direct evidence of it from the other. It will be enough if the accessory has inferred the existence of the other's intentions from all the circumstances, including of course the other's actions and words.[47] For example, A and B are charged with the murder of P, and it is proved that A stabbed P in the course of a robbery by A and B of P's shop. Once B admits that he saw A pocket a knife before setting out on the burglary, it may readily be concluded that B must have contemplated on the basis of this circumstantial evidence of A's state of mind that A was intending to use it to kill or cause serious injury if the need arose. Indeed many of the 'common purpose' cases turn on the question whether the accessory knew that the principal was in possession of a murderous weapon when they embarked on their unlawful enterprise.[48] If he did not know this, he cannot be an accessory to its use, at least if there was no other evidence to suggest that the principal was intending to commit murder.[49]

Thirdly, however, the circumstances may be ambiguous as to the principal's intention. The potential accessory may, for example, supply goods or information on request to a person whose intentions are unclear. The supplier knows that there is a possibility that the recipient of the information is intending to commit an offence with its help, but equally he contemplates that the information may be sought for other lawful purposes. Is awareness of a possible intention on the part of the principal sufficient to inculpate the accessory if the offence which the principal may be intending is in fact committed? This point arose recently in connection with the statutory offence of aiding and abetting suicide.[50] The executive committee of the Voluntary Euthanasia Society (formerly 'Exit') published a booklet entitled 'A guide to self-deliverance' for distribution to members of the society who wished to obtain copies. In *A-G v Able*[51] the Attorney-General sought declarations against five members of the executive committee that the supply of the booklet was unlawful as constituting an offence under s 2 of the Suicide Act 1961 or an attempt to commit that offence depending on whether the recipient of the booklet did or did not commit suicide following the advice contained in the booklet. The Attorney's argument in essence was that the defendants knew, on the basis of the restricted distribution of the booklet to members of the society, that it would be supplied to a class of persons actually intending to commit suicide or who were likely to be contemplating suicide. If, with this knowledge, the defendants supplied the booklet on request, intending it to assist or encourage suicide or knowing that it would be likely to do so, they would necessarily be guilty of the full offence or of an attempt. Woolf J took the view that the defendants' liability fell to be determined by the common law principles of accessoryship, although he noted that the liability under s 2(1) of the Suicide Act 1961 is in form that of a principal offender.[52] Applying those principles, he held that before an offence could be established to have been committed, three matters would need to be proved. First, that the supplier of the booklet had the necessary intent, that is, he intended the booklet to be used by someone contemplating suicide and intended the booklet to assist or otherwise encourage him. Second, that with that intention he supplied the booklet to such a person who read it. Third, except in the case of an attempt, that such a person was assisted or encouraged by reading it to take or attempt to take his own life. However, it would be for the jury to say in each case whether these matters had been proved. It could not be inferred that they would necessarily be proved in all cases. For example, the booklet might have nothing to do with the suicide or attempted suicide of a particular recipient, as where a long period of time elapsed between the distribution and the attempt at suicide.[53] Accordingly it could not be said in advance that any particular supply would amount to an offence, and thus it would not be appropriate to grant the declarations sought.

Stripped to its essentials, this judgment really amounts to a refusal to usurp the function of the jury in relation to inferences as to intention to be drawn from the evidence in each case. The prosecution will have to adduce evidence of the defendant's intention in respect of each particular supply of the booklet. Where the recipient has informed the supplier of his intention to commit suicide, there will be little difficulty in inferring the defendant's intention to assist or encourage suicide by sending the booklet.[54] But such an intention to assist or encourage will not apparently exist simply by virtue of the supplier's knowledge that the booklet is likely to assist or encourage those who have decided or do decide after reading it to take their own lives. The judgment seems to envisage, for example, that the supplier may say that he thought a particular recipient had requested the booklet for purposes of information or research, and therefore that the supply was not intended to facilitate an attempt at suicide.[55] More will be said later about this conception of intention.

The main interest of the judgment for present purposes lies in the statement by Woolf J that '. . . as long as there is the necessary intent to assist those who are contemplating suicide to commit suicide if they decide to do so, *it does not matter that the supplier does not know the state of mind of the actual recipient*.'[56] (Emphasis supplied.) Read in the context of the preceding two paragraphs this seems to be saying that it is sufficient that the supplier knows that 'there is a real likelihood that the booklet is required by one of the substantial number of members of the society who will be contemplating suicide.'[57] It need not be proved therefore that the supplier knew that the particular recipient was actually contemplating suicide, much less that the recipient had already taken a decision to do so. It will be enough that the supplier realises from the circumstances the likelihood that the recipient has the intention to commit suicide or is contemplating doing so.

It may be assumed that this decision is not intended to be confined to the statutory offence in question. Given that it purports at this point to state a general principle of complicity, is it correct? One writer[58] has argued that in cases of assistance other authorities indicate that the principal must have taken a decision to commit the offence before assistance is provided and that the accessory must be aware of this before he acts. Woolf J's judgment would be inconsistent with such a requirement. However, it may be doubted whether the law is settled as narrowly as suggested. Taking the cases relied on, the point at issue was not considered in *Johnson v Youden*[59] where the two acquitted partners had no knowledge at all of the circumstances disclosing the builder's intention; he was outside their contemplation altogether. Lord Simon's observation in *DPP for Northern Ireland v Lynch*,[60] that '. . . it must be foreseen [by the accomplice] that the instrument or other object or service supplied will probably (or possibly and desiredly) be used for the commission of a crime', seems to be directed to what I have identified above as the third element of the intention to aid and abet rather than this first issue of the accessory's knowledge of the principal's state of mind. Lord Parker's statement in *R v Bainbridge*[61] that '. . . there must be not merely suspicion but knowledge that a crime of the type in question was intended' was concerned to establish that the accessory had to know the species of crime in fact committed, and that knowledge of a general criminal intent on the part of the principal was not sufficient. There was no discussion of whether it was necessary in all cases for the principal to have a settled intention and for this to be known to the accessory.

In the absence of clear authority to the contrary Woolf J's decision must be taken to state the law, and it indicates that the first element of the intention to aid and abet has a wide scope.[62] However, the scope should not be overstated. In *Able* there was only one relevant act which the 'principal' could have had in mind, and it was quite clear that the defendant knew that the booklet was likely to assist or encourage the act if he decided to do it. But where a person provides goods or services suspecting they may be intended or contemplated for use in *some* criminal purpose, but having no evidence what that purpose might be, the principle of *Bainbridge* and *Maxwell* indicates that he cannot be guilty of aiding and abetting. Accordingly it is submitted in the light of the decision in *Able* that the principle may be restated as follows.

It is sufficient for this element of the intention to aid and abet that at the time of rendering assistance or encouragement to the principal, the putative accessory either:

(i) knows (because he has been so informed) that the principal is intending or contemplating the commission of the acts constituting the offence in fact committed; or

(ii) is aware (because he has inferred it from the circumstantial evidence) that the principal may be intending or contemplating the commission of the acts constituting the offence in fact committed.

In both situations the accessory must have contemplated the species of offence in fact committed, but it is immaterial that he was not aware of the precise details.[63] It is also immaterial that he did not regard the commission of the offence by the principal as probable or likely provided that he realised it was a reasonable possibility.[64]

(b) KNOWLEDGE OF THE CIRCUMSTANCES SPECIFIED BY THE DEFINITION OF THE OFFENCE

It is helpful to distinguish this aspect of the accessory's knowledge from his knowledge of the principal's intended acts, although it must be admitted that the distinction is not pure. Circumstantial elements of the offence can often be incorporated into a description of the principal's act, as when we say that a person 'drove an overloaded lorry on the highway'.[65] However, in analysing the elements of criminal liability, it may be material to subtract from that description the circumstances that the lorry was 'overloaded', and that it was driven 'on a highway'. These circumstances are specified by the definition of the offence as ones whose existence makes the otherwise lawful act of driving a lorry into an offence. The distinction between acts and the specified circumstances in which they take place is important for accessorial liability in relation to offences of strict liability. Frequently a principal offender can be criminally liable in respect of an act done in certain specified circumstances despite his ignorance of those circumstances. It is no defence, for example, for a butcher charged with exposing unsound meat for sale to say that he did not know the meat was unsound.[66] In most cases of this type even absence of negligence is no answer. What then is the position of a person charged with aiding and abetting the commission of an offence of strict liability?

The stock answer is that aiding and abetting is a common law notion and therefore requires mens rea.[67] Accordingly, strict liability has no application to accessories. It is not, however, entirely clear what it is necessary or sufficient for the prosecution to prove by way of mens rea. In *Callow v Tillstone*[68] proof of negligence on the part of a veterinary surgeon in his examination of the carcase of a heifer was held insufficient to sustain a charge against him of aiding and abetting the exposure by a butcher of unsound meat for sale. The Divisional Court did not state in terms that proof of knowledge was required, although it appears that the court may have accepted a distinction drawn by counsel between negligence and knowingly counselling the doing of the act.[69] Since 1950[70] the statement of principle by Lord Goddard CJ in *Johnson v Youden* has been frequently cited in support of a claim that the accessory must be proved to have had knowledge of the essential matters which constitute the offence. Such a requirement is consistent with what has been described here as the first element of the intention to aid and abet. It would certainly be odd if a distinction of substance could be found between these two aspects of accessorial knowledge, given the facility with which the second may be absorbed in a description of the first. However, care must be taken when running the two together not to suggest that the accessory must know or believe that the principal has mens rea himself in respect of each circumstance of the offence. For example, a statement that the accessory 'must know that the principal is intending to expose unsound meat for sale' is misleading in that it suggests a need for knowledge on the accessory's part that the principal knows the meat to be unsound. A better and more accurate statement is to say that the accessory must know (or contemplate) that the principal is intending to expose certain meat for sale which the accessory knows to be unsound.

It may be asked therefore to what extent the authorities support a concept of 'knowledge' in relation to circumstantial elements similar to the 'knowledge' discussed in relation to the principal's acts. Actual knowledge will of course be sufficient, as where the defendant observes the specified circumstances with his own senses. Equally, 'wilful blindness', where the defendant contemplates or suspects the possible existence of the specified circumstances as a matter of inference from other circumstances of which he is aware but where he deliberately refrains from seeking to acquire actual knowledge, will be regarded as equivalent to such knowledge.[71] 'Connivance' is a useful term to describe this state of mind.[72] There is, however, some difficulty whether in this context knowledge includes recklessness. In *Carter v Richardson*[73] the supervisor (D) of a learner-driver (E) was charged with aiding and abetting E to drive with excess blood alcohol. D did not of course know the precise level of alcohol in E's blood, but the justices found that he did know that E had consumed 'excessive' alcohol. (The offence took place on Christmas Day, and D and E had been together for some time.) The justices then convicted D, apparently on the basis that he had been reckless whether E was over the limit and that recklessness was sufficient mens rea for aiding and abetting. This characterisation of D's state of mind was almost certainly unnecessary. Given the circumstances of the case and D's knowledge that E had consumed excessive alcohol, it was virtually an irresistible inference that D must have contemplated that E was over the limit.[74] On that basis the case was a perfectly straightforward example of connivance. On appeal the Divisional Court had no difficulty in rejecting the argument that D had to be proved to have actual knowledge of the level of alcohol in E's blood. Such a requirement would make the law of accessories unworkable in breathalyser cases. Lord Widgery CJ, in an unreserved judgment, held that the justices' findings of fact were sufficient to sustain the conviction. This would have been enough to dispose of the appeal and the justices' comments about recklessness could then have been quietly forgotten. However, Lord Widgery added that the justices' statement was correct that recklessness was sufficient for aiding and abetting.

It is submitted that this should be regarded as a dictum only, given that it was unnecessary for the decision. No authority was cited to support the proposition—indeed no authorities of any kind were cited in the case. There is moreover a difficulty in knowing exactly what is meant by recklessness in this context. If it refers to a realisation by D that E may be over the limit and the deliberate taking of that risk by supervising E's driving, then it adds nothing to the idea of wilful blindness or connivance.[75] If, on the other hand, it refers to the idea that D gave no thought at all to whether E was over the limit because he did not care whether he was,[76] then the matter is problematic. Recklessness in that sense would seem to call into question a number of cases which assume a requirement of awareness under the first and third elements of the intention to aid and abet,[77] and would considerably enlarge the ambit of accessorial liability. If Lord Widgery had intended to develop the law in this way it is very surprising that there was no further discussion of the matter. The better view must surely be that he was doing no more than restating a familiar principle in different terminology to deal with a common factual situation. On that basis the case is not authority for any new proposition.

In conclusion it is suggested that knowledge in the second element of the intention to aid and abet bears the same meaning as in the first element. It is sufficient that the accessory knew that the specified circumstances existed when he performed his act of complicity, or that he contemplated that they would or might exist. The state of awareness may be described indifferently as 'wilful blindness', 'shutting of eyes' or 'connivance'.

(c) KNOWLEDGE THAT THE ACCESSORY'S ACT WILL AMOUNT TO PARTICIPATION IN THE COMMISSION OF THE OFFENCE

It is not enough that the accessory, knowing of the principal's criminal intention, does an act which objectively assists or encourages the execution of that intention.[78] In *R v Clarkson*[79] a group of soldiers stood by and watched some of their fellows carry out a series of rapes. The Courts-Martial Appeal Court held that on a charge of aiding and abetting rape it was necessary to prove both encouragement in fact (which might be inferred from their non-accidental presence in the room) and an intention to encourage. If the defendants did not realise that they were giving encouragement, '. . . it would not be a case in which, to use the words of Hawkins J, the accused person "wilfully encouraged".'[80] In *DPP for Northern Ireland v Lynch*[81] Lord Simon, discussing assistance as a form of aiding and abetting, said '. . . it must be foreseen that the instrument or other object or service supplied will probably (or possibly and desiredly) be used for the commission of a crime.' The reference to probability and the parenthesis in this proposition seem to be directed to the requirement of an 'intention' to aid and abet (discussed below). What is significant for present purposes is the requirement of foresight that the accessory's act will or may aid in the commission of the offence.

One interesting feature of *Clarkson* has implications for the mental element of accessories generally. The defendants in that case had apparently all been drinking for some time before the rapes occurred. It is assumed in the judgment of the court that they could rely on evidence of intoxication in denying that they had had an intention to encourage the commission of rape. This certainly suggests that the mental element of accessoryship involves proof of a specific intent for the purposes of the law on intoxication.[82] Were the mental element to involve basic intent, and thus to be satisfied by recklessness,[83] the defendants would be presumed to have realised the likely consequences of their presence at the scene, namely that they would encourage the rapists or discourage the victim. If *Clarkson* is right on this point, it provides further ammunition against an extended interpetation of *Carter v Richardson*. However, Lord Simon in *Lynch* said that aiding and abetting did not involve proof of a specific intent,[84] which seems to contradict the argument just put. But Lord Simon was not concerned at any point in his speech with intoxication and he did not refer to *Clarkson*. He was using the term 'specific intent' as part of an argument denying that the accessory had to be proved to have had a specific intent to 'further the aim of the principal offender.' In other words 'specific intent' was being equated with motive as part of an affirmation that a motive to assist or encourage did not have to be proved. On this basis the significance of *Clarkson* is unaffected.

To summarise the argument so far: although the authorities are not entirely clear or consistent, the better view is that the mental element required for an accessory involves proof of three matters of knowledge. Such knowledge is required to exist at the time of the alleged act of participation. It is not restricted to actual knowledge, but includes awareness of possibilities, such awareness being variously described in terms of contemplation, foresight, wilful blindness and connivance. There appears to be no distinction in substance between these terms in this context. The question which must now be considered is whether such knowledge amounts by itself to the intention to aid and abet, or whether something more is needed.

(d) COGNITION, INTENTION AND PURPOSE

The three matters of knowledge are issues concerning the *cognition* of the accessory. They do not by themselves presuppose or involve any further enquiry into the accessory's mental *attitude* towards the commission of the offence by the principal. It is sometimes asserted that such an enquiry need not be made. The intention to aid and abet, it is said, will be satisfied by proof of a voluntary act of participation done with the requisite knowledge.[85] In particular there is no requirement of a motive to further the commission of the offence. It will be immaterial on this view that the accessory had no desire for the offence to occur. His indifference, even his wish that it should not occur, will be no defence.

This account of the law needs careful examination, because there are at least four authorities which suggest the need for some qualification. The first is the old case of *R v Fretwell*.[86] D supplied corrosive sublimate to a woman (P) who was pregnant by him. He supplied it at her request and as a result of her threat to kill herself if he did not do so. He knew she intended to take it to procure abortion. She took the substance in his absence and subsequently died. He was charged with murder, the substance of the allegation being that he was an accessory before the fact to P's self-murder. On a case reserved, the court of five judges held that he could not be convicted. Erle CJ, giving the main judgment, held that D could not be an accessory because he was unwilling that P should take the poison:

> 'He procured it for her at her instigation, and under a threat by her of self-destruction. He did not administer it to her, or cause her to take it, and the facts of the case are quite consistent with the supposition that he hoped and expected that she would change her mind and would not resort to it.'[87]

Such reasoning suggests that clear evidence of disapproval of or non-consent to the principal's act may negative the mental element required for an accessory.[88] In *A-G v Able* Woolf J said that *Fretwell* was inconsistent with *NCB v Gamble* and was confined to its own facts.[89] This, with respect, is difficult to accept. There was no evidence in *Gamble* of any threats by the driver of the lorry to coerce the weighbridge operator into handing over the ticket which enabled the driver to leave the defendant's colliery. The operator was at best indifferent whether the driver took the overloaded lorry on the highway; he probably thought it was none of his business. *Gamble* and *Fretwell* are thus distinguishable on the facts. In *Gamble* it can fairly be said that the operator handed over the ticket *in order to* enable the driver to drive his lorry out of the colliery on to the highway.[90] In that sense he had intended to help the principal to commit the offence, and it was immaterial that he had no interest in or emotional satisfaction from the commission of the offence. *Fretwell* did not supply the poison *in order that* the woman should take it; his reason for acting was to avoid the otherwise tragic outcome of the woman's suicide. It is noticeable that *Fretwell* was cited by Devlin J in *Gamble* without disapproval as authority for the proposition that 'proof that the article was knowingly supplied is not conclusive evidence of intent to aid.'[91]

This analysis suggests that the 'intention' to aid and abet incorporates an element of purpose. This is not purpose in the sense of giving assistance 'with the motive of endorsing the commission of the offence' or as an express indication of approval of the principal's intended act. As Devlin J said, '... an indifference to the result of the crime does not of itself negative abetting.'[92] Rather it is purpose in the sense of the defendant's reason for acting; the outcome or state of affairs that he had decided to achieve by his act. If it can fairly be said that the outcome the defendant had decided to achieve was assistance or encouragement of the principal's intended act, then the intention to aid and abet is established. Proof only of a voluntary act of assistance or encouragement with the requisite knowledge is *evidence* of such a purpose, but does not constitute its equivalent. In many cases it will be fair to infer the intention/purpose from the doing of the act with the requisite knowledge, particularly where the defendant gives no evidence of his real intention/purpose. But where he does do so, it will be a question for the court or jury what his intention was.

A number of recent authorities afford clear support for this view. In *R v Clarke*[93] the defence to a charge of aiding and abetting burglary was that D had taken part in the burglary with the intention of assisting the police by passing on information about the identity of his co-accused and of enabling the stolen goods to be recovered. The trial judge had directed the jury to convict D on the basis of his admission of voluntary participation with knowledge of the circumstances. On appeal it was held that the defence should have been left to the jury. It seems clear that the Court of Appeal thought that the defendant's intention 'not to further but to frustrate the ultimate result of the crime'[94] could negative the mental element required for accessoryship. A distinction was drawn between this case, and the case where a person acts in order to help the principal carry out his plan even though he is antipathetic to the crime or indifferent to it.[95] In *R v Anderson*[96] a similar view was taken of the liability of an informer or undercover agent for conspiracy. Lord Bridge, in a speech with which the other members of the House of Lords agreed, said that a person who joins a conspiracy in order to betray it will not be guilty of conspiracy himself. He does not join the agreement intending to play some part in the agreed course of conduct in furtherance of the criminal purpose, and hence he lacks the necessary mens rea.[97] Normally such intention will be inferred from the act of joining the agreement, but as before this inference may be displaced by evidence from the defendant himself of his 'real' intention. Given that conspiracy is one form of aiding and abetting, this tends to confirm the decision in *Clarke*.

In *Gillick v West Norfolk and Wisbech Area Health Authority*[98] the question of the meaning of intention to aid and abet arose in a particularly acute and sensitive form. The plaintiff sought a declaration that certain advice in a circular issued to doctors by the Department of Health and Social Security was unlawful. The advice indicated that in exceptional cases doctors might give contraceptive advice and treatment to girls under 16 to protect them from the harmful effects of sexual intercourse. One ground of alleged unlawfulness[99] was that a doctor treating a girl in this way would become an accessory to an offence of unlawful sexual intercourse with the girl. On a pure 'knowledge' approach to accessorial mens rea, the argument for liability is unanswerable. The doctor knows that the offence is very likely to be committed,[100] and he knows that the provision of contraceptive advice or treatment is likely to assist or encourage its commission. In the House of Lords Lord Brandon founded his dissenting opinion entirely on this criminal law point, assuming without argument that the requisite mens rea would necessarily be present if a doctor chose to prescribe contraception. The majority of the Lords, however, disagreed. Lords Fraser, Scarman and Bridge all took the view that liability depended on the doctor's intention.[101] It had been conceded in argument that if a doctor prescribed contraceptives with the intention of encouraging intercourse he would clearly be liable as an accessory. But, according to Lord Fraser, a doctor who honestly intended to act in the best interests of the girl would be unlikely to commit an offence.[102] Such a case would occur where contraception was prescribed in order to prevent the girl suffering an unwanted pregnancy, or to protect her from the risk of sexually transmitted disease.[103] Lord Scarman concluded that the bona fide exercise by a doctor of his clinical judgment in this respect 'must be a complete negation of the guilty mind which is an essential ingredient of the criminal offence of aiding and abetting the commission of unlawful sexual intercourse.'[104]

Both Lord Scarman and Lord Bridge agreed with the analysis of the mental element made by Woolf J at first instance.[105] Woolf J was the only judge out of the nine who heard the case to deal in detail with this aspect of it. He distinguished the case of the doctor intending to encourage sexual intercourse from the case of the doctor who is 'firmly against' it and who prescribes contraceptives only because he feels he has to in the best interests of the girl.[106] The latter is not liable for aiding and abetting. In terms of the preceding analysis, this amounts to a straightforward application of the concept of intention as purpose. The 'innocent' doctor does not prescribe contraceptives in order that intercourse shall take place, but in order that health shall be preserved and unwanted outcomes avoided. A similar approach can now be seen to have been employed by Woolf J in *A-G v Able*.[107] The distributor of the booklet is liable for aiding and abetting suicide only if he supplies it in order to assist or encourage a person intending or contemplating suicide. If the supply is for other purposes, such as information or research, no offence will be committed. In *Gillick* Woolf J felt constrained to distinguish propositions he took to be established by *NCB v Gamble*[108] and *DPP for Northern Ireland v Lynch*.[109] These were that the mental element for aiding and abetting is satisfied by proof of a voluntary act done with knowledge of the circumstances, and that nothing more is needed. However, the attempted distinctions are unconvincing,[110] and the better view is that it was not necessary to make them. Devlin J never said in terms in *Gamble* that knowledge alone was all that was required. He commented at one point that it was not conclusive evidence of intent to aid,[111] and added later that it was always open to the defendant to give evidence of his real intention.[112] Lord Simon's comments in *Lynch* were, as stated above, directed to rejecting any necessity for a motive or desire on the part of the accessory to promote the commission of the offence. There is nothing inconsistent in accepting this while maintaining that the accessory must still act with the intention/purpose of facilitating the acts the principal intends to do. A person may deliberately sell a gun for use in a robbery without having the slightest interest in whether the robbery is successful. He has no motive or desire to rob, but there is no difficulty in saying that he acted in order to assist the buyer in carrying out the robbery and thus intended to aid and abet.

The significance of *Gillick* is that it does for intention in relation to accessories what *R v Moloney*[113] and *R v Hancock*[114] appear to have done for intention in relation to principal offenders. These latter decisions have aroused a good deal of controversy. The narrowing they have made in the law of murder is referred to below. It seems reasonably clear, however, that the concept of intention involved in those cases is the same as that discussed here. According to the judgments, intention in relation to the results of acts is something to be inferred from a person's words and deeds and the circumstances of the case.[115] His admission that he foresaw certain results as probable, highly probable or even virtually certain is evidence of the intention with which he acted, but no more than that.[116] Foresight is neither a species of intention itself nor equivalent to intention. Given then that what is being inferred is not motive or desire, and the judgments are insistent upon this,[117] the inferences can only be as to the defendant's reasons for acting. The question to be asked must be what was the defendant's purpose, in the sense of the result that he acted in order to bring about.[118] Purpose in this sense may be distinguished from desire or motive; a person may have no desire or motive to go to the dentist, in the sense that he hopes and expects to be enriched or pleased by doing so, but it may certainly be his purpose to make a visit.[119] The jury will frequently infer that a person acted in order to bring about those results of his acts which were likely to occur, particularly when that person gives no evidence of his reasons for acting. Where such evidence is given, as in *R v Steane*,[120] it will generally then be a jury question what the person's 'real' intentions were. It is no coincidence that *Steane* is cited as a leading authority on the exculpatory effect of a defendant's testimony about his intentions in both *NCB v Gamble* and *Moloney*.

This analysis of the 'intention' to aid and abet has important implications for the Draft Code. Clause 31, dealing with accessories, has no provision encompassing the general requirement which has been identified as a purpose to assist or encourage the principal's act. Further consideration of this point, however, needs to be postponed until the other main aspect of accessorial mens rea has been discussed.

3 The mens rea of the offence

(a) THE ACCESSORY'S KNOWLEDGE OF THE PRINCIPAL'S MENS REA

The first element of the intention to aid and abet, discussed above, is knowledge on the part of the accessory of the acts intended by the principal. 'Acts' is a flexible term in criminal law discourse. In this context it is helpful to distinguish physical acts from the specified circumstances in which they are done for the reason already given. We may take it, however, for the purposes of further discussion, that 'acts' includes the consequences of an act as well as the physical act itself. Now it was implicit in the earlier discussion of the principal's 'intended acts' that the accessory should be aware of any necessary mental element on the part of the principal in relation to his acts.[121] Logically it is difficult to see how an accessory could know that he is participating in another's crime if he does not know of the other's guilty mind. So in *R v Quick, R v Paddison*[122] an accessory's conviction for assault was quashed as unsafe when the Court of Appeal held that the principal's defence of automatism ought to have been left to the jury. As Lawton LJ said '. . . if Quick acted without conscious volition, it is most unlikely that Paddison would have known what he intended to do.'[123] In relation to results, a number of the 'common purpose' cases indicate that in the event of a joint attack on P by D (the accessory) and E (the principal who causes P's death), D's liability depends on what he intended or contemplated E might do. If he did not foresee that E might strike P with intent to kill or cause serious injury D cannot be liable for murder.[124] Similarly, if the accessory is unaware of a necessary ulterior intention on the part of the principal, he cannot be liable for aiding and abetting the commission of the offence requiring such an intention.[125]

(b) SUFFICIENCY OF KNOWLEDGE—HOW FAR MUST THE MENS REA OF THE OFFENCE BE SHARED?

According to Glanville Williams, 'Knowledge of the perpetrator's intent or possible intent is sufficient, without having the intent yourself.'[126] So in *DPP for Northern Ireland v Maxwell*[127] the defendant was liable because he guided the principals to their destination in order that they could carry out their attack. It was immaterial that it was not his own purpose to cause an explosion or to endanger life or to cause serious damage to property by means of a bomb. Similarly, the person who supplies a gun for use in a robbery may have no specific intention himself to deprive the victim permanently of his property. Nonetheless he will still be liable for robbery because he intentionally aided and abetted the principal to commit the offence. If the accessory and principal are acting in concert to rob or to cause an explosion then of course the intention will be shared, but these examples indicate that conspiracy is not a necessary condition of accessorial liability.[128] Maxwell was a minor figure in the organisation which carried out the attack and seems to have had no access to the decision-making process. Similarly, the supplier of the gun or the car for use in a robbery may be a peripheral figure, not part of the group who planned the robbery. The rationale for liability in such cases seems to be that there is an intentional contribution to the commission of the offence. Where assistance is knowingly given, albeit without a conspiracy, it may be inferred that the accessory had consented to the principal's act and did something in order to facilitate it.[129] Such conduct and such a state of mind are then regarded as sufficiently equivalent to the principal's culpability to justify liability to equivalent punishment. The interests of crime prevention can also be invoked to discourage any stricter requirement of accessorial intention.[130] There is a clear social need to deter those who are minded to facilitate the commission of offences, and requiring shared purpose with the principal offenders would make the achievement of that policy considerably more difficult. This argument has considerable force when used in relation to the suppliers of articles which can only be used, or which are commonly used, for criminal purposes. It has dangers, however, when applied to persons pursuing particular trades or occupations whose goods and services are not generally used for criminal purposes. This point will be returned to in the concluding section of this essay.

What is the position with regard to result-crimes? If the principal is required to have a particular mental element in respect of a result of his act, is it sufficient again that the accessory has knowledge of this element without sharing it? For example, can an accessory be convicted of murder even if he himself cannot be proved to have had an intention to kill or cause serious injury? In *Chan Wing-Siu v R*[131] the Judicial Committee of the Privy Council indicated on one interpretation that the answer is 'Yes'. The court rejected a defence argument that, in the absence of an agreement to kill, an accessory could not be liable for murder unless he foresaw that the principal would probably kill or cause serious injury. This argument was consistent with the law of murder as it then stood in relation to principal offenders. Before *R v Moloney*[132] the law appeared to be that a person was guilty of murder if he did an act foreseeing that it would probably cause death or serious injury and the act did in fact kill.[133] A direct equivalence for an accessory would be doing an act of assistance or encouragement knowing that the principal would probably act with the intent to kill or cause serious injury.[134] The Privy Council effectively rejected any need for direct equivalence, holding that the accessory need only have contemplated that the principal might *possibly* act with that intent. This approach is then justified in terms of a theory of authorisation, discussed below. Two points may be noted about the decision now. Firstly, it is consistent with the law just considered in relation to those specific intents spelt out in the definition of conduct-crimes for the principal. Secondly, there are several references in the judgment to the idea of an accessory *taking the risk* that a co-adventurer may act with the intent for murder. For example, a person may think that the risk of a co-adventurer acting in that way is altogether negligible. Then, according to Sir Robin Cooke:

> 'If [the jury] think there is a reasonable possibility that the case is in that class, taking the risk should not make that accused a party to such a crime of intention as murder or wounding with intent to cause grievous bodily harm.'[135]

Risk-taking is the language of recklessness, and it is one of the reasons why *Chan Wing-Siu* may be a doubtful authority. In *Moloney* Lord Bridge emphatically rejected any form of recklessness as sufficient mens rea for murder.[136] He stressed that murder is a crime of specific intent, and denied that foresight or contemplation of death or serious injury as probable consequences was a species of intention or equivalent to intention. His remarks were directed to principal offenders, but the restrictive approach contrasts curiously with the expansive liability for accessories apparently adopted by the Privy Council. There is however an alternative interpretation for the decision which avoids inconsistency with *Moloney*. This makes use of the concept of conditional intention. *Chan Wing-Siu* was presented by the Crown as a 'common purpose' case in which the three defendants armed themselves with knives to carry out a robbery. The murder and wounding were offences committed in the course of the attempted robbery. If each defendant had contemplated murder and wounding as offences which his co-adventurers might find it necessary to commit to carry out the robbery, then it could fairly be inferred that each had agreed to these incidental, and conditional, additions to the common purpose. Therefore each accessory would have had an implied intention to kill or cause serious injury. Understood in this way the decision would not in fact detract from the principle that murder is a crime of specific intent for all parties.

If this last point is right, it follows that result-crimes differ from conduct-crimes in an important respect. Conduct-crimes, such as those involved in *Maxwell*, require only that the accessory know of the principal's mens rea. He need not share it in those cases where he gives assistance without being part of a conspiracy to commit the crime. Result-crimes, however, require that the accessory have the mens rea in relation to the prohibited result which is prescribed for the principal. There are several examples where this has been spelt out in the cases. In *R v Smith*[137] Thesiger J directed the jury in a case of concerted assault causing death in terms described by the Court of Criminal Appeal as legally unassailable. He said at one point:[138]

> 'Several persons . . . present at the death of a man may be guilty of different degrees of crime — one of murder, others of unlawful killing, which is called manslaughter. Only he who intended that unlawful and grievous bodily harm should be done is guilty of murder. He who intended only that the victim should be unlawfully hit and hurt will be guilty of manslaughter if death results.'

In *R v Reid*[139] Lawton LJ distinguished between liability for murder and manslaughter in similar terms.

> 'When two or more men go out together in joint possession of offensive weapons such as revolvers and knives and the circumstances are such as to justify an

inference that the very least they intend to do with them is to use them to cause fear in another, there is, in our judgment, always a likelihood that, in the excitement and tensions of the occasion, one of them will use his weapon in some way which will cause death or serious injury. If such injury was not intended by the others, they must be acquitted of murder; but having started out on an enterprise which envisaged some degree of violence, albeit nothing more than causing fright, they will be guilty of manslaughter.'[140]

These citations make it clear that if the accessory does not contemplate his co-adventurer having the intention to kill or cause serious injury, he (the accessory can only be liable for murder if he himself had such an intention at the time of the assault. Where he does have such contemplation, it can usually be inferred that killing or the causing of serious injury has been tacitly agreed as part of the common purpose. The intention in the latter case may be conditional, but this does not affect the substance of the requirement. Thus where it is unclear which of two attackers inflicted the fatal blow, and it is also unclear whether they were acting in concert, each must be independently proved to have had the intention to kill or cause serious injury before he can be convicted of murder, either as principal or as accessory.[141]

Finally, if the mens rea specified for a particular result is less than intention, for example, recklessness, there is clear authority that intention to aid and abet the principal's act and recklessness as to the result must be proved against the accessory.[142]

It is submitted in the light of the above that cl 31(4)(b) of the Draft Code accurately states the present law. This is subject to the acceptance of the 'conditional intention' analysis of *Chan Wing-Siu*. If, however, there is a wider principle that the accessory's foresight of the principal's specific intention is sufficient by itself for result-crimes, the clause will need reconsideration. The objection to such a principle is its inconsistency, both with *Moloney* and with a number of other authorities on liability for aiding and abetting result-crimes. The rationale of the distinction between conduct-crimes and result-crimes falls to be considered in connection with the theory of accessorial liability.

4 The mental element and the theory of accessorial liability

The analysis of the mental element for accessories demonstrates that the law is complex and difficult to state with confidence. One obvious cause of complexity is the nature of accessorial liability itself. It is derivative in the sense that it is founded on the wrongful act of another and comprises doctrines which stipulate the conditions under which liability arising out of that wrongful act may be attributed to persons who have not directly caused the harm involved.[143] Thus the mental element has two points of reference rather than one — the wrongful act of the accessory as well as the wrongful act of the principal — and a detailed working out of their relationship in terms of concepts of knowledge and intentionality seems inescapable. In addition there appears to be more than one justifying theory of accessorial liability underpinning the mental element. This may help to explain why the law is imprecise as well as complex.

American writers have commented on the relative dearth of studies of complicity theory.[144] Compared to other central topics the literature is certainly underdeveloped. This is not the place to embark on a detailed appraisal of the recent American approaches, partly because space does not permit and partly because those writers tend to build on American case law, which differs in some respects from English law.[145] Nonetheless they do offer important insights, and the articles by Kadish and Dressler,[146] in particular, are helpful in understanding the principles underlying the English law.

A convenient starting point is to suggest that complicity theory has developed two principles of attribution for determining when an accessory incurs liability arising out of an offence apparently perpetrated by another. The first is a principle of agency. The central notion is that one person authorises another to act on his behalf in the achievement of some criminal purpose. Where the person authorised has no mens rea for the offence or has a defence, it is common to speak of the situation as one of 'innocent' agency.[147] In such a case the person doing the authorising will usually have instigated the other to act and can be identified as the prime mover in the offence. Accordingly he is then characterised as the principal offender and the mens rea for the offence will have to be proved against him. But the principle is not restricted to cases of innocent agency. It serves also to accommodate cases where the accessory has instigated, solicited or conspired with the principal offender to commit an offence. In these cases the criminal purpose is held in common rather than by the accessory alone. Reflecting traditional conspiracy doctrine, the act of one is treated as the act of all,[148] unless the act done was not authorised, expressly or impliedly, by the other parties.[149] The implication of this theory for the mental element is that each party to the common purpose will usually have the mens rea for the offence. He will generally either intend to commit the offence himself, or intend that one or more of his co-adventurers should do so. It is, however, now possible to be a party to a conspiracy without necessarily having the intention that the foundational offence should be committed. In *R v Anderson*[150] the House of Lords held that it was sufficient for conspiracy that a person intended to play some part in the agreed course of conduct in furtherance of the criminal purpose which the agreed course of conduct was intended to achieve. Thus the defendant was liable for conspiracy to effect an escape from prison where he agreed for reward to supply diamond wire to be smuggled into the prison by his co-conspirators. It was immaterial that it was not his purpose that the escape should take place. In terms of liability if the offence is in fact committed this case shows that conspiracy doctrine now straddles the two theories of accessoryship discussed here. In those cases where the criminal purpose is held in common, it can plausibly be said that each party is the agent of all the others for its achievement. But where the criminal purpose is not held in common, the position of the person who intends to play only a limited role cannot convincingly be said to approximate to that of a 'principal' for whom all the other conspirators are agents. In such cases the theoretical basis of his liability as an accessory is a principle which does not treat the act of another as 'his' act.

Such a principle already exists to ground liability for alleged accessories who were never parties to an agreement for the commission of the offence. The agency principle cannot deal happily with the independent supplier of goods and services who knowingly assists or encourages the criminal schemes of others, but who is not part of such schemes. It would not be accurate to say of Bainbridge or Maxwell or Haslam (the weighbridge operator in *NCB v Gamble*) that he had 'authorised' the acts of the principal offenders in those cases. The agency principle presupposes that the accessory is in some position of authority or influence over the perpetrator, or is at least in a position to negotiate with him on equal terms. This is not generally true of the peripheral supplier of goods and services. In these cases the law seems to have espoused a theory of what might be called substantial participation in the offence. On this approach culpability is based on the causal contribution which the accessory has made to the commission of the offence. The causation can be of the 'but for' type, as in the *A-G's Reference (No 1 of 1975)*[151] (defendant procured the principal to commit a driving offence of strict liability by secretly lacing his drinks). 'But for' causation is not necessary, however; it will be sufficient if the accessory's acts are a concurrent cause of the crime. He may, for example, provide the means or the opportunity for the principal to commit the offence.[152] It will be immaterial that the principal would have committed the offence in any event. The harm is attributable to the accessory because he has caused (in an extended sense) its occurrence. In some cases the contribution may appear to be relatively slight, as where it consists simply of encouragement of the principal without the elements of overt assistance or prior agreement.[153] However, causation theory generally requires only that contributions be substantial in the sense of more than merely trivial or minimal,[154] and in this sense there is nothing unusual about its application to accessories.

The principle of substantial participation constitutes an acknowledgment that there will be cases where accessories, for example, suppliers of goods and services, do not share the principal's criminal purpose. In these cases, as suggested above, it is enough that the accessory has knowledge of what that purpose is or may be, plus the intentional supplying of aid in order that the principal's intended act may be committed. To require a full sharing of the criminal purpose, especially in crimes requiring an ulterior intention, would be unduly restrictive. It would inhibit the conviction and punishment of those who knowingly facilitate the commission of offences, and this in turn would be offensive to notions of retributive justice. It would not be acceptable, for example, for the supplier of lethal weapons for use in a robbery to escape liability on the ground that he had no wish for the robbery to be successful and therefore lacked mens rea for robbery. There is a sufficient equivalence of culpability in the idea of an informed consent to the robbery.[155] Utilitarian considerations of crime prevention also argue strongly for liability to be based primarily on knowledge in such cases. If more knowing facilitators are deterred, perhaps fewer offences will be committed.

These two principles, agency and substantial participation, have not been articulated in terms in the cases. Nonetheless, together they offer the most convincing account of the forms of aiding and abetting identified in John Smith's earlier essay.[156] Is either fully adequate on its own? Agency will not do as a way of rationalising the liability of non-conspirators, and substantial participation may work unsatisfactorily when complicity in 'incidental' offences is being determined. However, the existence of two theoretical principles has caused difficulty for the mental element for accessories. This is because they tend to pull in different directions. The agency principle, to be coherent, entails that the accessory shares the mens rea for the offence with the principal.[157] Substantial participation, on the other hand, entails that the accessory knows of the principal's mens rea without necessarily sharing it (although of course he may do). If we then return to the distinction already noted between conduct-crimes and result-crimes, one explanation for it becomes apparent. The leading authorities in respect of accessorial mens rea for conduct-crimes are all substantial participation cases,[158] whereas for result-crimes the leading authorities are agency cases.[159] *Chan Wing-Siu v R*[160] is thus particularly significant. If it is *not* regarded as a case of conditional intention, it represents a move towards the substantial participation theory in a clear agency case; the accessory's foresight of the principal's possible murderous intention is sufficient by itself to make the accessory liable. At the same time, other recent cases such as *R v Clarke*[161] and *Gillick*,[162] which are clearly examples of substantial participation rather than agency, strongly suggest that the intention to aid and abet the principal's *acts* is itself a specific intent in the sense of purpose. It may be therefore that the two theories are tending to converge in terms of their impact on the mental element.

If this is so, the way forward for the Criminal Code becomes clearer. With hindsight, cl 31 (4) of the Draft Code looks unsatisfactory because it reflected, but did not resolve, the theoretical uncertainty exposed by the recent cases. The problem must now be tackled more convincingly. Assuming for this purpose that hiving off cases of facilitation to a separate offence is not an available option, the best solution would appear to be to tie accessorial liability more clearly to a theory of substantial participation in the commission of the offence. The implications of doing so will of course require careful detailed consideration. The mental element would consist of knowledge of the principal's intended or contemplated act (including knowledge of any specified fault on the part of the principal in relation to results of the act or in the form of an ulterior intention) plus the specific intention to participate in such acts. Such a requirement would not be without its own problems. 'Common purpose' cases might need somewhat different handling, and interpreting 'intention' in the way suggested raises issues going beyond the scope of this essay. Nevertheless these must be confronted if satisfactory codification of this topic is to be achieved.

NOTES

1 'Aid, Abet, Counsel and Procure' in *Reshaping the Criminal Law* (essays presented to Glanville Williams, ed PR Glazebrook, 1978) pp 120 ff.

2 Glanville Williams *Criminal Law The General Part* (2nd edn 1961) (hereafter referred to as Williams *CLGP*).

3 (1978), pp 634 ff.

4 See in particular D Lanham 'Accomplices and Transferred Malice' (1980) 96 LQR 110 and 'Accomplices and Withdrawal' (1981) 97 LQR 575; KJM Smith 'Assisting in Suicide — The Attorney-General and the Voluntary Euthanasia Society' [1983] Crim LR 579; RD Taylor 'Complicity and Excuses' [1983] Crim LR 656; AJ Ashworth 'The Draft Code, Complicity and the Inchoate Offences' [1986] Crim LR 303.

5 See in particular D Lanham 'Accomplices, Principals and Causation' (1980) 12 Melbourne ULR 490; 'Complicity, Concert and Conspiracy' (1980) 4 Crim LJ 276 and 'Limitations on Accomplice Liability' (1982) 6 Crim LJ 306. Reference should also be made to the monograph by P Gillies *The Law of Criminal Complicity* (Sydney, 1980) to which I am indebted.

6 See in particular L Westerfield 'The Mens Rea Requirement of Accomplice Liability in American Criminal Law — Knowledge or Intent' (1980) 51 Miss LJ 155; P Robinson 'Element Analysis' (1983) 35 Stanford LR 681 and 'Imputed Criminal Liability' (1984) 93 Yale LJ 609; SH Kadish 'Complicity, Cause and Blame: A Study in the Interpretation of Doctrine' (1985) 73 Cal LR 323; J Dressler 'Reassessing the Theoretical Underpinnings of Accomplice Liability: New Solutions to an Old Problem' (1985) 37 Hastings LJ 91. Earlier American articles still of considerable value are FB Sayre 'Criminal Responsibility for the Acts of Another' (1930) 43 Harv LR 689 and RM Perkins 'Parties to Crime' (1941) U Pa LR 581.

7 Codification of the Criminal Law: A Report to the Law Commission (Law Com No 143, 1985), and the Draft Criminal Code Bill contained therein.
8 Professor JC Smith, Professor EJ Griew and Mr IH Dennis. Mr PR Glazebrook was originally a member of the team, but withdrew in January 1984.
9 Hale, 1 PC 437. See Glanville Williams *Textbook of Criminal Law* (2nd edn 1983) p 329.
10 Draft Code, cl 30(1)(a).
11 Complicity is one of a number of doctrines which extend criminal liability beyond the paradigm set out in an offence definition. Others include voluntary intoxication and vicarious liability. See generally Robinson 'Imputed Criminal Liability' (1984) 93 Yale LJ 609 who adds transferred intent to the list, *sed qu*.
12 *R v Ram and Ram* (1893) 17 Cox CC 609.
13 Cp *R v Brawn* (1843) 1 Car & Kir 144.
14 [1978] 3 All ER 1140, HL.
15 It is not my purpose in this essay to join the debate whether such an offence should be introduced into English law. It exists in a number of American codes (New York Penal Law Art 115; Proposed Federal Criminal Code s 1002) and has received some support in England. See in particular R Buxton 'Complicity in the Criminal Code' (1969) 85 LQR 252; 'Complicity and the Law Commission' [1973] Crim LR 223 and 'The Working Paper on Inchoate Offences: (1) Incitement and Attempt' [1973] Crim LR 656 and JR Spencer, 'Trying to help another person commit a crime', later in this volume. For an argument in favour of a system of lower maximum penalties for accessories, see C Clarkson and H Keating, *Criminal Law Text and Materials* (1984), pp 442–447.
16 The theoretical basis of accessorial liability is considered later.
17 It is not necessary to prove that encouragement by the accessory had any causal potency: *R v Calhaem* [1985] 2 All ER 266, although on the facts this case was one of criminal agency. See also JC Smith and B Hogan *Criminal Law* (5th edn 1983), p 122.
18 Most notably *Johnson v Youden* [1950] 1 KB 544 (Lord Goddard CJ); *National Coal Board v Gamble* [1959] 1 QB 11 (Devlin J). See also Lord Simon in *DPP for Northern Ireland v Lynch* [1975] AC 653 at 698–9, HL.
19 This matter is considered in detail below in connection particularly with the decisions of the House of Lords in *R v Moloney* [1985] AC 905, HL and of the Privy Council in *Chan Wing-Siu v R* [1985] AC 168.
20 *Gillick v West Norfolk and Wisbech Area Health Authority* [1986] AC 112.
21 Cf *Cook v Stockwell* (1915) 84 LJKB 2187; *Cafferata v Wilson* [1936] 3 All ER 149; Williams *CLGP* pp 366–380.
22 Halsbury's *Laws of England* 4th edn, Vol 11 (1976) para 42; Draft Code cl 31(1)(a).
23 Accessories and Abettors Act 1861, s 8; Magistrates' Courts Act 1980, s 44; *Gould & Co Ltd v Houghton* [1921] 1 KB 509. Assist and encourage are frequently used as modern synonyms for the older language of aid, abet and counsel.
24 [1985] AC 168.
25 At 175.
26 *Crown Law* (1762) 370. Foster's account is a very clear statement of the early common law as recorded by Plowden (note to *R v Saunders and Archer* (1573) 2 Plowd 473), Coke (3 Inst 51), Hale (1 PC 617), Hawkins (2 PC 446) and Blackstone (4 Comm 37), and see generally Sayre *op cit*, n 6 at pp 696–700.
27 *Pinkerton v United States* 328US 640 (1946), well discussed in W LaFave and A Scott *Criminal Law* (1972) 513 ff. See also D Lanham 'Complicity, Concert and Conspiracy' (1980) 4 Crim LJ 276, 284 ff.
28 *Mansell and Herbert's Case* (1556) 2 Dyer 128b; *Lord Mohun's Case* (1692) Holt KB 479; *Ashton's Case* (1698) 12 Mod Rep 256. Gillies (*op cit* (n 5) p 93) argues that the earliest authorities were not consistent on this point, but the cases he cites in the supporting footnotes do not really bear him out. At best they recognise the principle that if the perpetrator *deliberately* departs from the criminal purpose to commit a crime outside the scope of its execution the accessory is not liable, the classic illustration being the contemporary case of *Saunders and Archer* (n 26 above). The principle is now embodied in the Draft Code c 31(6).
29 *Davies v DPP* [1954] AC 378, HL; *R v Anderson* [1966] 2 QB 110; *R v Lovesey* and *R v Peterson* [1970] 1 QB 352; *R v Penfold* (1979) 71 Cr App Rep 4, CA; *Borg v R* (1970) WAR 194 (citing *Russell on Crime* (12th edn, 1964) Vol 1, 162); *Johns v R* (1980) 143 CLR 108; *Miller v R* (1980) 55 ALJR 23. The move to subjective contemplation began in the nineteenth century (*Duffey and Hunt's Case* (1830) 1 Lew CC 194; *Macklin and Murphy's Case* (1838) 2 Lew 225; *R v Price* (1858) 8 Cox CC 96; *R v Skeet* (1866) 4 F & F 931; *R v Caton* (1874) 12 Cox CC 624), but the judges were not consistent (*R v Bernard* (1858) 1 F & F 240; *R v Betts and*

Ridley (1930) 22 Cr App Rep 148) until relatively recently. Stephen accepted Foster's view and incorporated it in the *Digest* (Art 20). His draft Code of 1879, ss 71 and 72 made the accessory liable in effect for negligence in respect of probable consequences. See further Glanville Williams *CLGP* p 402.

30 *R v Coney* (1882) 8 QBD 534 at 558 (Hawkins J). Cf Glanville Williams *CLGP*, p 353.

31 *Op cit* (n 5), p 91.

32 This convenient terminology is employed by Gillies, p 90, cited in *McLean* (1981) 5 A Crim R 36.

33 The point is well illustrated by the direction to the jury by Byles J in *R v Price* (1858) 8 Cox CC 96 and in the judgment of the High Court of Australia in *Miller v R* (1981) 55 ALJR 23. For discussion of whether there is a wider principle only in relation to the mental element, see below.

34 [1950] 1 KB 544.

35 At 546.

36 [1967] 2 AC 224 at 236–7, HL.

37 [1978] 3 All ER 1140 at 1144, HL.

38 *Bowker v Premier Drug Co Ltd* [1928] 1 KB 217; *Johnson v Youden*, n 34 above; *Thomas v Lindop* [1950] 1 All ER 966.

39 *Ferguson v Weaving* [1951] 1 KB 814; *John Henshall (Quarries) Ltd v Harvey* [1965] 2 QB 233.

40 [1960] 1 QB 129.

41 (1913) 9 Cr App Rep 220. See the explanation of this case by Devlin J in *R v Bullock* [1955] 1 WLR 1.

42 It was unclear whether Lord Parker CJ, who delivered the judgment of the court, meant that the accessory had to foresee the particular species of offence in fact committed (*eg* office-breaking, as opposed to any other offence), or whether it would be sufficient if the accessory foresaw the commission of a particular genus of offences (*eg* breaking and entering generally).

43 [1978] 3 All ER 1140. For discussion see Glanville Williams *Textbook of Criminal Law* (2nd edn, 1983), pp 351 ff.

44 Explosive Substances Act 1883, s 3(a).

45 Ibid, s 3(b).

46 MacDermott J, sitting without a jury under the Emergency Provisions (Northern Ireland) Act 1973.

47 In this context such phrases as 'wilful blindness' and 'shutting of eyes' should be taken to convey the idea that if the accessory is aware of the circumstances disclosing the principal's intentions, it will be no answer for him to say that he deliberately refrained from making enquiry whether his suspicions about those intentions were correct. As Devlin J put it in *Roper v Taylor's Central Garages Ltd* [1951] 2 TLR 284 at 288: 'The case of shutting eyes is actual knowledge in the eyes of the law.' See further Glanville Williams, *CLGP*, pp 157–159; EJ Griew 'Consistency, Communication and Codification: Reflections on Two Mens Rea Words' in *Reshaping the Criminal Law* (n 1 above), particularly at pp 69–75.

48 See eg *Duffey and Hunt's Case* (1830) 1 Lew CC 194; *R v Price* (1858) 8 Cox CC 96; *Davies v DPP* [1954] AC 378; *R v Smith* [1963] 3 All ER 597; *R v Anderson* [1966] 2 QB 110.

49 If there was an agreement to kill or cause serious injury to P by one means, and the principal killed P by some other means, the accessory would still be liable for murder. The principal would not have varied the substance of his authority: Hawkins 2 PC 316; Blackstone 4 Comm 37.

50 Suicide Act 1961, s 2(1).

51 [1984] QB 795.

52 Which means that it is possible to attempt this offence: *R v McShane* (1977) 66 Cr App Rep 97.

53 [1984] QB 795 at 812. The example is unconvincing, because if the booklet is supplied with the intention that it should assist or encourage a person contemplating suicide, this would seem necessarily to amount to an act 'more than merely preparatory' to the commission of the offence and thus to be an attempt contrary to s 1(1) of the Criminal Attempts Act 1981. It is the last act which the supplier of the booklet intends to do, and it would be immaterial that the booklet has no effect on the recipient. Cf *R v Hensler* (1870) 11 Cox CC 570. See also the case-note on *Able* by JC Smith in [1984] Crim LR 35.

54 But apparently the booklet would not be supplied in such circumstances in view of the written undertaking required of the member of the society that he has '. . . no present intention of taking my life and that I am not contemplating self deliverance in the foreseeable future.' See KJM Smith 'Assisting in Suicide — The Attorney-General and the Voluntary Euthanasia Society' [1983] Crim LR 579, 585 n 30, who argues, rightly, that the legal efficacy of this kind of disclaimer must be very doubtful.

55 [1984] QB 795 at 800.

56 Ibid at 811.

57 Ibid at 810. The qualifications of 'real' likelihood and 'substantial' numbers are inserted presumably to indicate that the accessory must know that there is more than a remote or merely negligible risk that the recipient is contemplating suicide.
58 KJM Smith *op cit* (n 54).
59 [1950] 1 KB 544.
60 [1975] AC 653 at 698.
61 [1960] 1 QB 129, CCA.
62 This is assuming that the decision in *Able* is not restricted to its context of complicity in suicide. But there is nothing in the judgment to support such an interpretation, and Woolf J's reliance on leading authorities on complicity suggests that he thought he was stating principles of general application.
63 For discussion of the implications of this position see AJ Ashworth 'The Elasticity of Mens Rea' in *Crime, Proof and Punishment* (ed CFH Tapper, 1981), pp 45, 49, 64–68.
64 *Chan Wing-Siu v R* [1985] AC 168, approving *Johns v R* (1980) 143 CLR 108; *Miller v R* (1980) 55 ALJR 23; *R v Gush* [1980] 2 NZLR 92. If the accessory thought, for example, that the possibility of murder being done in the course of an unlawful enterprise of robbery was so remote as not to be a real risk at all, he would be liable only for manslaughter and not murder if death occurred: *R v Tomkins* [1985] 2 NZLR 253. Cf *R v Jubb, R v Rigby* [1984] Crim LR 616, CA; Lexis: 'probably' is the appropriate word.
65 *NCB v Gamble* [1959] 1 QB 11.
66 *Hobbs v Winchester Corpn* [1910] 2 KB 471, CA.
67 Smith and Hogan *op cit* p 130.
68 (1900) 83 LT 411. See also *Bowker v Premier Drug Co Ltd* [1928] 1 KB 217.
69 Ibid at 412.
70 The authorities up to this time were not consistent. *Callow v Tillstone* and *Bowker v Premier Drug Co Ltd* should be compared with *Provincial Motor Cab Co Ltd v Dunning* [1909] 2 KB 599 and with *Carter v Mace* [1949] 2 All ER 714, both of which in substance applied vicarious liability principles to charges of aiding and abetting offences under road traffic legislation. In *Davies, Turner & Co Ltd v Brodie* [1954] 3 All ER 283, *Carter v Mace* was held to have been decided on its own facts and to lay down no general principle. However, vicarious liability survives for accessories in South Australia: *Lenzi v Miller* [1965] SASR 1; *Kurucz v Mayne* [1966] SASR 82. *Cf R v Glennan* [1970] 2 NSWR 421, rejecting strict liability and negligence for accessories. For discussion, see Gillies *op cit*, pp 74–82.
71 *Roper v Taylor's Central Garages Ltd* [1951] 2 TLR 284; *Poultry World v Conder* [1957] Crim LR 803; *D Stanton & Sons Ltd v Webber* [1972] Crim LR 544.
72 Smith and Hogan *op cit*, p 110; Glanville Williams *CLGP*, p 867; JLL Edwards '*Mens Rea in Statutory Offences*' (1955) pp 194 ff.
73 [1974] RTR 314.
74 In *Crampton v Fish* (1969) 113 Sol Jo 1003 another Divisional Court had had no difficulty in finding knowledge proved against the accessory on similar facts.
75 See the authorities cited in n 72 above. The Law Commission Working Paper no 43 (1972) on Parties took the view that even subjective recklessness was insufficient and that actual knowledge of the external elements of the offence should be required (see ibid, p 49). No authorities were cited or discussed. This highly restrictive approach was justified by the need not to bring within the criminal law persons acting in the ordinary course of business dealings. The better view is that such persons should be dealt with according to the requirement of an 'intention' to aid and abet the principal's act, discussed below.
76 An example of *Metropolitan Police Comr v Caldwell* recklessness [1982] AC 341, anticipated in this context by *Glennan* [1970] 2 NSWR 421. On one view *Davies, Turner & Co Ltd v Brodie* [1954] 3 All ER 283 supports the view that a failure to entertain suspicions which a reasonable man would have had on the basis of facts known to the defendant and about which enquiry should have been made will be sufficient for aiding and abetting, but it is very difficult to distinguish this from negligence, which is clearly not sufficient. Cf Glanville Williams *CLGP*, p 159; Gillies *op cit* pp 77–79.
77 *Bainbridge* (n 40 above); *Maxwell* (n 43 above); *R v Clarkson* [1971] 3 All ER 344; *Lynch* (n 18 above).
78 *R v Allan* [1965] 1 QB 130, CCA; *R v Jones and Mirrless* (1977) 65 Cr App Rep 250, CA.
79 [1971] 3 All ER 344.
80 *R v Coney* (1882) 8 QBD 534 at 558.
81 [1975] AC 653 at 698.
82 Smith and Hogan *op cit*, p 194.
83 *DPP v Majewski* [1977] AC 443.

84 [1975] AC 653 at 698.

85 The clearest expression of this view is by Lord Simon in *DPP for Northern Ireland v Lynch* [1975] AC 653 at 698–9, basing himself on the judgment of Devlin J in *NCB v Gamble* [1959] 1 QB 11. See also Gillies *op cit*, p 59; Cross and Jones *Introduction to Criminal Law* (10th edn, 1984), p 455; Smith and Hogan *op cit*, p 126.

86 (1862) Le & Ca 161.

87 (1862) Le & Ca 161 at 164.

88 *Russell on Crime* (12th edn, 1964) Vol 1, pp 151–2 explains *Fretwell* as reflecting a requirement laid down by the institutional writers of approval of the principal's act as well as knowledge; Hale 1 PC 616; Hawkins 2 PC 445. In modern law the requirement of approval seems to have been absorbed into the 'intention' to aid and abet: see, for example, *A-G v Able* [1984] QB 795 at 809–811.

89 [1984] QB at 811, citing the 4th edition (1978) of Smith and Hogan *op cit*, pp 120–121. Glanville Williams also considered the decision indulgent: *CLGP*, p 368.

90 Devlin J rejected the NCB's argument that the weighbridge operator (Haslam) had no option but to deliver the ticket after the weighing. Once it is decided that there was a choice, the inference is inevitable, in the absence of evidence from Haslam, that he delivered the ticket in order to enable the driver to carry away the load. See [1959] 1 QB 11, 22.

91 Ibid, 22–23, also citing *R v Steane* [1947] KB 997 to the same effect. The cases are analogous since Fretwell was reacting to a kind of duress in the same way as Steane, reluctantly doing the act required in order to avert the act threatened.

92 Ibid at 23. Cf Model Penal Code, art 2.06(3)(a).

93 (1984) 80 Cr App Rep 344.

94 Ibid at 348.

95 Ibid at 347, instancing *DPP for Northern Ireland v Lynch* [1975] AC 653 (antipathy) and *NCB v Gamble* [1959] 1 QB 11 (indifference). The case of duress presents a problem for the meaning of intention discussed in this essay. It is plausible for anyone, such as Lynch, charged with aiding and abetting an offence, to say that he acted only in order to avoid a threat and not in order to help the principal commit his intended act. Such a plea, if unrestricted, would make all the policy-influenced restrictions on the general defence of duress irrelevant as far as accessories were concerned. As long as the intention to aid and abet includes foresight of the probable consequences of doing certain acts of assistance the problem does not arise, as the decision in *Lynch* impliedly recognised. If the narrow view of intention prevails, claims of no mens rea based on duress will have to be treated in the same way as pleas of intoxication, ie as cases involving general policy implications to be governed by special rules.

96 [1986] AC 27.

97 Ibid at 39.

98 [1986] AC 112, HL.

99 There were a number of others not material for the purposes of this essay.

100 This is in fact one of the five conditions which must be satisfied before contraceptive advice and treatment can be given without parental consent: see ibid (n 98), per Lord Fraser at 174, with whom Lords Scarman and Bridge agreed.

101 Ibid at 175, 190, 194.

102 Ibid at 175. Lord Fraser said that the doctor intending to act in the best interests of the girl would be unlikely to commit an offence under s 28 of the Sexual Offences Act 1956. This seems clearly to be an error. The offence aided and abetted would be the commission of unlawful sexual intercourse under s 5 or 6 of the Act. An argument that doctors prescribing contraception would be criminally liable under s 28 was rejected by Woolf J at first instance and not renewed on appeal.

103 These examples may be deduced from the speeches of Lord Fraser (at 174–5), Lord Scarman (at 190–1) and Lord Bridge (at 194).

104 Ibid at 190. This explicit statement that the ground of non-liability is the absence of mens rea for aiding and abetting makes it difficult to sustain the argument that the decision recognises and applies a general defence of necessity: see JC Smith in [1986] Crim LR 114. None of the relevant authorities on necessity were cited to the House of Lords and the word does not appear in any of the speeches. If a general defence was being utilised it is remarkable that its parameters were not explored in more detail. For a a view of the criminal law point which accords with that discussed here see Glanville Williams 'The Gillick Saga' (1985) 135 New LJ 1156, 1181.

105 [1984] 1 All ER 365.

106 Ibid at 371.

107 [1984] QB 795.

108 [1959] 1 QB 11.
109 [1975] AC 653, HL.
110 They were that the doctor may have insufficient knowledge of the circumstances of the offence and that he does not supply anything essential for the commission of the offence. The first is answered by *R v Bainbridge* [1960] 1 QB 129, CCA (not cited to Woolf J), and the second by saying that it is true but immaterial, since it is enough for aiding if the doctor facilitates intercourse by removing inhibitions against it (as Lord Brandon recognised: [1986] AC 197).
111 [1959] 1 QB 11 at 22.
112 Ibid at 23.
113 [1985] AC 905.
114 [1986] AC 455. A further addition to authorities supporting a 'purpose' construction of intention in relation to aiding and abetting may be *Thambiah v R* [1966] AC 37, in view of the way in which the Privy Council analysed the evidence in the case.
115 [1985] AC 913 at 928–9, [1986] AC 469 at 472.
116 Any doubt that remained after *Moloney* whether foresight of virtual certainty amounted to intention per se or was still only evidence of intention seems to have been resolved in favour of the latter by *R v Hancock* [1986] AC 455 at 471–2 and by *R v Nedrick* [1986] 1 WLR 1025.
117 See Lord Bridge at [1985] AC 926; Lord Lane CJ at [1986] 1 WLR 1027.
118 For a similar view see J Stannard 'Mens Rea in the Melting-Pot' (1986) 37 NILQ 61.
119 I am indebted to Stannard, ibid at 69, for this helpful illustration. Equally, if I am attacked by a madman with an axe I may purposely cause his death as the necessary means of saving myself, but in the ordinary usage of language I have no desire or motive to kill him. See further RA Duff 'Codifying Criminal Fault: Conceptual Problems and Presuppositions' in *Criminal Law and Justice* (ed IH Dennis, forthcoming).
120 [1947] KB 997, CCA.
121 Cf Law Commission Working Paper no 43, Proposition 7(1); Gillies *op cit*, pp 61 ff. If D (the putative accessory) believes that E (the putative principal) lacks mens rea for the offence which D knows is being committed by E, the case will be one of innocent agency.
122 [1973] QB 910.
123 Ibid at 923.
124 *Davies v DPP* [1954] AC 378; *R v Smith* [1963] 1 WLR 1200; *R v Betty* (1963) 48 Cr App Rep 6; *R v Anderson, Morris* [1966] 2 QB 110; *R v Penfold* (1979) 71 Cr App Rep 4.
125 *DPP for Northern Ireland v Maxwell* [1978] 3 All ER 1140, HL.
126 *Textbook of Criminal Law* (2nd edn, 1983), p 352. See also *CLGP*, p 394. Other texts suggest however that the accessory must have the mens rea of the offence: Halsbury, *Laws* (n 22 above), para 42, but cf para 45; Gillies *op cit*, pp 56–7.
127 [1978] 3 All ER 1140.
128 *R v Kupferberg* (1918) 34 TLR 587, CCA. See further S Carpenter 'Should the Court Aid and Abet the Unintending Accomplice: The Status of Complicity in California' (1984) 24 Santa Clara LR 343, discussing *People v Beeman* 199 Cal Rptr 60 (1984), 674 P 2d 1318.
129 The element of consent forms a link with the underlying theory of the common purpose cases, as Lowry LCJ recognised in his judgment in the Court of Criminal Appeal for Northern Ireland in *Maxwell*: [1978] 3 All ER 1140 at 1162. See further Kadish, *op cit* (n 6 above) at 354–5.
130 For discussion see Westerfield *op cit* (n 6 above), pp 175 ff.
131 [1985] AC 168.
132 [1985] AC 905.
133 *Hyam v DPP* [1975] AC 55, HL; *R v Cunningham* [1982] AC 566, HL; *Leung Kam-Kwok v R* (1984) 81 Cr App Rep 83.
134 In *R v Jubb, R v Rigby* [1984] Crim LR 616, CA; Lexis: the Court of Appeal approved a direction substantially to this effect.
135 [1985] AC 168 at 179.
136 [1985] AC 905 at 920.
137 [1963] 1 WLR 1200.
138 Ibid at 1206.
139 (1976) 62 Cr App Rep 109, CA.
140 Ibid at 112. See also *R v Betty* (1963) 48 Cr App Rep 6; *R v Lovesey, R v Peterson* [1970] 1 QB 352, CA; *R v Penfold* (1979) 71 Cr App Rep 4; Archbold, *Criminal Pleading, Evidence and Practice* (42nd edn 1985) para 29–8.
141 *Mohan v R* [1967] 2 AC 187, PC.
142 *R v Swindall and Osborne* (1846) 2 Car & Kir 230 (manslaughter by furious and dangerous

driving); *R v Salmon* (1880) 6 QBD 79 (manslaughter by gross negligence); *R v Baldessare* (1930) 144 LT 185 (manslaughter by reckless driving); *R v Creamer* [1966] 1 QB 72, CCA (constructive manslaughter); *R v Robert Millar (Contractors) Ltd* [1970] 2 QB 54, CA (causing death by dangerous driving); Gillies *op cit* 71–74.

143 Fletcher *op cit* (n 3 above), p 636.

144 Fletcher *op cit*, p 637, n 4; Dressler *op cit* (n 6 above), pp 91–2.

145 For example, Federal courts require proof of purpose in the accessory to promote the commission of the offence: *US v Peoni* 100 F 2d 401 (1938), and see Westerfield *op cit*, pp 158 ff. On the other hand adherence to a conspiracy may entail accessorial liability for all offences reasonably foreseeable as consequences of carrying out the conspiracy: *Pinkerton v US* 328 US 640 (1946), (n 27 above). Neither rule applies in England.

146 See n 6 above.

147 *R v Michael* (1840) 9 C & P 356; *R v Manley* (1844) 1 Cox CC 104; *R v Cogan, R v Leak* [1976] QB 217.

148 *DPP v Doot* [1973] AC 807 at 827 (per Lord Pearson).

149 *R v Anderson* [1966] 2 QB 110 is the leading modern authority for a principle going back to the sixteenth century: *R v Saunders and Archer* (1573) 2 Plowd 473.

150 [1986] AC 27.

151 [1975] QB 773, CA.

152 All cases of assistance clearly fall within the scope of substantial participation; see Hart and Honore *Causation in the Law* (2nd edn 1985), pp 51–61; cf Kadish *op cit*, pp 357–361.

153 Where the accessory has instigated the principal the case may be regarded indifferently as either agency or substantial participation, since it may be supposed that the accessory has the mens rea for the offence in any event. Encouragement of a principal who has independently decided to commit the offence shows the causal link at its most attenuated; it appears sufficient that the encouragement *might* have made a difference to whether the principal committed the offence: Kadish *op cit*, pp 361–2. A case such as *Clarkson* [1971] 3 All ER 344 is on the borderline of causal contribution, and is doubted by Glanville Williams *Textbook of Criminal Law* (2nd edn 1983), pp 346–7.

154 Smith and Hogan *op cit*, p 279; Draft Criminal Code cl 21.

155 Kadish *op cit*, pp 354–5; cf Dressler *op cit*, pp 109–111.

156 See n 1 above.

157 As exemplified in the tendency found in some authorities to treat all conspirators as principals in the offence committed pursuant to the agreement: see Lanham 'Complicity, Concert and Conspiracy' (1980) 4 Crim LJ 283 ff; Fletcher *op cit*, p 660. Innocent agency cases provide further examples.

158 *NCB v Gamble; Bainbridge; DPP for Northern Ireland v Maxwell.*

159 See the cases cited in n 137, 139, 140 and 142 above.

160 [1985] AC 168.

161 (1984) 80 Cr App Rep 344.

162 [1986] AC 112, HL.

States of mind, presumptions and inferences

Edward Griew

Law students agree in finding criminal law a difficult subject. It is also strangely difficult to teach. In the first weeks of the academic year, when students should be acquiring a firm footing in the basic vocabulary and grammar of the subject, teachers find themselves embarrassedly exposing what they take to be confusion and uncertainty on basic matters of doctrine and language. What is worse, it is very hard to explain why the law is in the state that it is. Why, for example — and most prominently in those early weeks — do we have so much trouble with states of mind? Whatever our doctrinal camp, we do have to talk about states of mind; and so do the judges. The essay that follows may be seen as a small part of an attempt to understand what is wrong. Its topic is judicial discourse; its particular focus is on the relationship in such discourse between states of mind and their proof. The relationship is of crucial historical and continuing importance.

1 Presumptions

(a) THE PRESUMPTION OF INTENTION

In *R v Cox*[1] in 1859, a case of alleged wounding with intent, Bramwell B told the jury that, although 'a man is generally supposed, by law, to intend the natural consequence of his act', yet in the case before them they had to be 'satisfied of the existence of the actual intent to wound.' Glanville Williams has based upon this direction the conclusion that the so-called presumption of intention 'was not applied to crimes of specific intent like the crime of wounding with intent . . . '[2] That is perhaps a large conclusion from one direction. But the direction is certainly interesting. Normally, though intention might be said to be required, it was an intention imputed from the circumstances of the act. But it was, according to this direction, an 'actual intent' where the requirement was expressed in the statute creating the offence ('with intent to wound'). Compare this with Brett J's view, in *R v Prince*,[3] of the effect of the word 'knowingly' in the statutory definition of an offence: it merely 'alters the burden of proof.' Brett J went on to explain that even where such a word was not used, so that 'proof of the committal of the acts may prima facie . . . import the proof of the mens rea', it is still 'open to the prisoner to rebut the prima facie evidence, so that if, in the end, the jury are satisfied that there was no criminal mind, or mens rea, there cannot be a conviction . . .'[4] For Brett, therefore, the question resolved by the presence or absence of the mens rea adverb was as to the location of the burden of proof (in our modern sense, I believe[5]): by whom are the jury to be 'satisfied' as to whether the defendant acted with a 'criminal mind'? The requirement of a 'criminal mind' exists in either case; in one, proof of the act is prima facie proof of knowledge, in the other it is not. The accuracy of this analysis is not here in question. Its relevance lies in the difference between Brett J's conception and that expressed by Bramwell B. For Bramwell, so far as his language shows, the distinction is not as to burden of proof but is that between 'an actual intent' and one merely 'supposed' to exist.

The truth is that any attempt to understand the history of English criminal law in a systematic way runs foul of a number of complex confusions. Three relevant matters that have tended to be tangled together over a long period are: the 'guilty mind' or 'criminal intent', if any, substantively required for liability; evidence of such guilty mind or intention; and the burden of proof. The 'duty of the prosecution to prove the prisoner's guilt' was seen in 1935 as a 'golden thread' running '[t]hroughout the web of English criminal law.'[6] But it appears to be too generous to the subject to characterise it as a web rather than as a complex of knots. By 1955 Professor Edwards felt able to rely upon 'the irrefragable rule that the legal burden' (that is, the persuasive burden) 'of proving the guilt of the accused rests upon the prosecution' as sufficient ground for asserting that there was 'no justification for the introduction' of a doctrine that 'the absence of the word "knowingly" ' affects that burden.[7] But this was to treat the treasured rule as having been 'irrefragable' long before such a status could be claimed for it.

Little, certainly, relating to mens rea or its proof in the nineteenth century is consistent and clear. But there was at least a general understanding that a 'sane adult is presumed to intend the natural consequences of his conduct'[8] — where 'natural' sometimes meant 'which must necessarily follow'[9] and more often 'which was probable' (whence the customary pleonasm, 'natural and probable'). Evidence of insanity could rebut the presumption; although every man is presumed to be sane, the contrary could be proved. Or there might be 'evidence of a state of intoxication rendering the accused incapable of forming' the intent required for the offence.[10] Such qualifications apart, however, proof of an act that caused a 'natural' consequence is in most cases proof that the actor intended that consequence. And where the law speaks the language of 'malice', it is proof that the actor brought about the relevant harm 'maliciously'.[11]

Stephen did not think that this was:

> ' . . . really a rule of law, further or otherwise than it is a rule of common sense. The only possible way of discovering a man's intention is by looking at what he actually did, and by considering what must have appeared to him at the time the natural consequence of his conduct.'[12]

But if there is indeed no other way of 'discovering a man's intention', the rule, in its relation to the responsible agent, becomes effectively one of law. Now it was not, of course, entirely true that there was never any other way. Positive proof of intention might be found in a confession. And indications of an intention inconsistent with that sought to be imputed to the defendant might be given by him when charged or in a statement to the court. But self-serving statements by the defendant to the police or from the dock or through counsel are not compelling evidence, especially if the prosecution is not conceived as having a burden of proof in the modern sense. The evidence crucially unavailable in most cases before 1898 is that of the defendant himself as a witness; he cannot explain, under oath and subject to cross-examination, that indeed he did not realise the harm his act might cause or intend that harm.[13] In the absence of such evidence the conclusion that he 'must as a reasonable man have contemplated'[14] what people generally would have foreseen — nay, that he intended the obvious consequence — is treated as in most cases inexorable. Madness, serious intoxication and biological immaturity (the grounds of irresponsibility) are features observable by others. Evidence of a sane sober adult's failure to appreciate, or of his not having intended, the probable consequence must almost inevitably come from him and must be tested. This could not be.

(b) THE PRESUMPTION AND THE CRIMINAL EVIDENCE ACT 1898

We realise now that the establishment of the accused person as a competent witness in 1898 had an enormous potential for changing ways of thinking about the proof of fault and the burden of proof. But it is unreasonable to think that that potential ought to have been immediately realised (in either sense of the word). Familiar ways of thinking and talking naturally go on. Advocates and judges practising in the first half of the twentieth century were trained in the late nineteenth — and trained on the job, not by academic systematisers. Even quite modern judges in their turn were taught by, studied introductory books written by, and took their criminal law first and foremost from judgments delivered by, those so trained. It ought not therefore to be surprising that, though the Criminal Evidence Act was seen as radically affecting the course and the tactics of the criminal trial, its full implications were not at first perceived. The relation of the accused's competence to the presumption of intention provides ample suggestive evidence. It was not until 1935 that the House of Lords made clear that the prosecution bore the burden of proving fault as well as act; until then the presumption played its double or ambiguous role — as variously expressing the notion of imputed fault or as casting the burden of proof upon the defendant. Again, once the defendant can give evidence, there will be many cases in which it cannot be said that intention must be inferred from the objective circumstances (or is to be imputed) on the ground that his actual state of mind cannot be discovered. Yet in 1912, when a jury were 'unanimously and emphatically of opinon that . . . the prisoner did not realise the consequences of what he was doing' (that is, that he was strangling his wife), they were told that a man is held to intend the consequences of his act; and his conviction was affirmed on appeal.[15] The case is among those relied upon by the House of Lords in *DPP v Smith*[16] as late as 1960 for a similar conclusion. And there is the related point that once we are able to entertain, and critically test, the defendant's own evidence about his state of mind, it becomes less appropriate than formerly to say that evidence of intoxication goes to *capacity* to form a required intent. That way of talking derives from the time when the presumption took effect more or less inexorably in relation to responsible agents. What the defendant had to do was to show that he was not responsible, that he lacked capacity. We can now say, as we do when we are concerned with a 'specific intent' offence, that the question is whether the defendant was so drunk that he *did not* form the intent.[17] In 1920, however, Lord Birkenhead LC expressed it in terms of incapacity. One of his famous conclusions in *DPP v Beard*[18] was:

> 'That evidence of drunkenness falling short of a proved incapacity in the accused to form the intent necessary to constitute the crime . . . does not rebut the presumption that a man intends the natural consequences of his acts.'

Though later criticised,[19] this in 1920 was perhaps understandable. Lord Birkenhead, himself reared in the law before the 1898 Act, was relying on the cases of that earlier time.[20] And *Woolmington* was still fifteen years in the future. Twenty-five years after *Woolmington*, however, and in a different intellectual climate, the same language is less forgivable and has disastrous implications. In *DPP v Smith*[21] the presumption is being expressed as one which determines the guilt of a person who is 'in law responsible and accountable for his actions, that is, . . . *capable of forming an intent*, not insane . . . and' (in the light of the Homicide Act 1957, s 2, then recently passed) 'not suffering from diminished responsibility.' This by 1960 was a hopeless anachronism. But the combination in English criminal law of continuity (the march of old precedents and the influence of old practical teaching) and of discontinuity (the passing of landmark statutes and the emergence of new modes of thought) makes the concept of an anachronism a somewhat relative one.

Seven years later, of course, s 8 of the Criminal Justice Act 1967 was enacted to correct the error in *DPP v Smith*. As there will be occasion to refer to the section in a little detail later, it will be convenient to set it out in full:

> 'A court or jury, in determining whether a person has committed an offence, —
>
> (a) shall not be bound in law to infer that he intended or foresaw a result of his actions by reason only of its being a natural and probable result of those actions; but
>
> (b) shall decide whether he did intend or foresee that result by reference to all the evidence, drawing such inferences from the evidence as appear proper in the circumstances.'

The substantive requirement of intention (or of foresight) has been separated from its proof. There is no longer a presumption of intention (or of foresight); in its place is an invitation to the court or jury to use common sense.

(c) PRESUMED KNOWLEDGE AND REASONABLE MISTAKE

I wish now to relate the foregoing to a difficulty that many modern criminal lawyers are inclined to see in authorities which require a defendant's mistake of fact to be a reasonable one if it is to secure him an acquittal. Many cases can be cited for the relationship between the requirement of mens rea and the defence of mistake. I concentrate on *R v Tolson*.[22]

The judgment of Stephen J in that case has remained for generations of students a locus classicus on the requirement of a guilty state of mind: 'the full definition of every crime contains expressly or by implication a proposition as to a state of mind.'[23] Of course the judges did not all express this notion in the language that we would now use. Wills J required 'at least the intention to do something wrong';[24] Hawkins J understood the word 'feloniously' to denote 'that [the] act was done with a mind bent on doing that which is wrong.'[25] But Stephen J at least seemed to speak in modern terms when he said that 'it may, I think, be maintained that in every case knowledge of fact is to some extent an element of criminality as much as age or sanity.'[26]

What, in the instant context of bigamy, emerges from these affirmations of the requirement of a 'state of mind', of 'an intention to do something wrong', of 'knowledge of fact'? They are, for all the majority judges in *Tolson*, reflected in the proposition that a reasonable mistake as to the non-existence of the former marriage, because of the death of the spouse, will excuse. For Cave J, indeed, 'the somewhat uncouth maxim, "actus non facit reum, nisi mens sit rea" ' actually 'embodies' the doctrine that 'an honest and reasonable belief in the existence of circumstances which, if true, would make the act for which the prisoner is indicted an innocent act has always been held to be a good defence.'[27] We may nowadays be divided on the question whether, or when, unreasonable mistakes ought to entail acquittal. But we ought to be able to agree on the oddity of asserting that a 'state of mind', 'intention' or 'knowledge' is required and of then directly translating that requirement into a doctrine that there is a defence of reasonable mistake. Yet none among a group of distinguished judges questions either the logic or the requirement of reasonableness.

We are left asking: what *is* the mens rea of bigamy? It hardly suffices to say, as Lord Fraser does in *DPP v Morgan*, that 'bigamy does not involve any intention except the intention to go through the ceremony of marriage.'[28] That in itself is not a guilty state of mind. Nor ought we, employing late twentieth century categories, to explain *Tolson* as deciding that bigamy is a crime of negligence. That may be the effect of the case; but none of the judges who decided it identified the 'state of mind' required as negligence or referred to the care that a person embarking on a second marriage ought to take in order to avoid the sanctions of the criminal law.[29] We have, I think, to conclude that bigamy is being understood in *Tolson* as, in effect, an offence requiring knowledge of the crucial fact (survival of the spouse) although that requirement is not expressly stated in the statute. Just such a requirement, after all, was read into other statutes. But the cases show no consistency in the way the implications of the requirement were worked out. In *R v Sleep*[30], in 1861, the jury found that the defendant had 'reasonable means of knowing' that the copper of which he was found in possession was marked with a broad arrow. But, probably because of his statement to the police as reported to them, they felt unable to find that he knew that it was so marked. The court held that guilty knowledge was essential, although not mentioned in the statute, and that the jury's findings entailed an acquittal. In *Tolson*, on the other hand, the defendant is regarded as bearing a significant burden in relation to the vital issue. Knowledge would be presumed if there were no evidence of mistaken belief to disprove it.

Although one should not be dogmatic as to the nature of the burden borne by the defendant,[31] Brett J in *R v Prince* seemed to mean a persuasive burden,[32] and probably Cave J in *Tolson* also.[33] But whether a persuasive burden or a burden of introducing credible evidence, it can be discharged only by evidence of reasonable mistake. Why 'reasonable'? A part at least of the answer may be that there is unlikely to be anything that can count as impressive, still less as persuasive, evidence of an unreasonable mistake. Where the mistake is one that everyone would have made, or even one that anyone might have made, there is no problem. *Tolson*'s case is an example. It was a matter of 'general report' that Mr Tolson's ship had sunk with the loss of all hands. Mrs Tolson's mistake is acceptable because there is persuasive evidence of it — evidence of circumstances that persuaded others to make it themselves. But a defendant cannot without difficulty be supposed to have made an unreasonable mistake. In general she cannot offer the only evidence that might satisfy the jury that she did — that is, her own testimony of incomprehension, credulity or venial folly. So the defence burden and the exclusion of the accused from the witness box combine to demand that the mistake relied upon be a shared mistake. And that hard fact of the law of proof becomes enshrined — before *Tolson*, in *Tolson* and for generations after *Tolson*[34] — in a statement of the substantive law.

Thus, in one strand of the case law at least, the presumption of intention has its analogue in a presumption of knowledge. The former, it will be recalled, assumed a responsible agent. It is interesting to notice the analogy drawn by Cave J in *R v Tolson*[35]: 'Honest and reasonable mistake stands in fact on the same footing as absence of the reasoning faculty, as in infancy, or perversion of that faculty, as in lunacy.'

(d) TWENTIETH CENTURY DEVELOPMENTS

The generalisations in *Tolson* about mens rea and about the effect of mistaken belief make it a leading case. But it should also have been recognised a long while ago as a misleading one. For by the middle of the present century the legal context and climate in which states of mind were discussed and investigated had undergone important relevant changes. Firstly, because a defendant could now give evidence (from 1898), the best evidence of her state of mind, short of a confession, would in most cases be available. She could explain that she did indeed make a mistake that others (more intelligent, less tired or stressed, even simply less careless) would not have made. If she did not give evidence, or if her evidence was found quite implausible, the common-sense conclusion that she knew what others would have known remained available and might be expected to be reached. But there was no need now for, in effect, a presumption, having substantive force, that she knew obvious things or made only reasonable mistakes. Secondly, the burden of proof had shifted — or its correct location was acknowledged (in 1935). All that the defendant's evidence need do was to induce the tribunal of fact to think it possible that she made the mistake she claimed to have made. Thirdly, the scholars were at last expounding a 'general part' of the criminal law, providing practitioners, for the first time, with an adequate intellectual basis for the elimination of old inconsistencies and confusions. The landmark event, of course, was the publication of Glanville Williams' treatise, *Criminal Law — The General Part*, in 1953. Yet in spite of these and other changes, and in spite of contradictions apparent on its face, *Tolson* has continued for nearly one hundred years to be cited as current authority almost without critical comment. The latest citation (contemporary with the writing of this essay in the summer of 1986) is that by the House of Lords in *Pharmaceutical Society of Great Britain v Storkwain Ltd.*[36] A submission that 'words appropriate to require mens rea in accordance with *R v Tolson*' must be read into the statutory provision under consideration in that case is still treated as being, 'in other words', the submission that:

> '. . . the subsection must be read subject to the implication that a necessary element in the . . . offence . . . is the absence of belief, held honestly and on reasonable grounds, in the existence of facts which, if true, would make the act innocent.'[37]

Tolson therefore stands as my exemplar of an inappropriately operating system of precedent.

The events of 1898 and 1935 and the change in the intellectual climate ought to have produced similar effects on the presumption of intention and the presumption of knowledge (as I have dared to re-label the requirement that a mistake be reasonable). But their twentieth-century histories have been instructively different.

The presumption of intention was belatedly killed off in 1967. It may be claimed that it has gone on to haunt us since then; for s 8 of the Criminal Justice Act has been undermined or sidestepped in important appellate cases.[38] But the enactment of s 8 deserves to be treated as very plainly an act of execution. The interesting point for present purposes is the manner of that execution. The gist of s 8 is that a state of mind (in respect of consequences) required for liability is not to be imputed; it is to be found as a fact. The section assumes that a state of mind is required. By implication the pre-existing presumption is allowed the status only of a rule of evidence; and by a rule of evidence that ought to be a truism it is replaced. But s 8 does not deal with knowledge, or awareness of the possible existence, of circumstances. And there remains no general enactment about the proof of such states of mind.[39]

Two features distinguish the presumption of knowledge from the presumption of intention. One is the fact that the former was more consistently expressed in the form of a substantive rule: that mistaken beliefs must be held 'on reasonable grounds' if they are to protect from criminal liability. The other is that mistake of fact may be held to have analytically different functions in the different contexts in which it is relied on. So there need be no surprise that the presumption of knowledge has a separate latter-day history, and indeed a history with a number of strands.

First, eight years after s 8 was enacted the House of Lords insisted in *DPP v Morgan*[40] that a rule of law requiring a mistaken belief in a fact to be reasonably held could not co-exist with a substantive requirement of knowledge, or of awareness of the possibility, of the contrary. Rape required knowledge of, or recklessness as to, the woman's not consenting; it could not also be demanded that a mistaken belief in her consent be a reasonable one. The equivalent of the truistic proposition of evidence in s 8, then, was an assertion of a point of elementary logic as though it were a point of law. Some subsequent cases, indeed, bade fair to confine the point to rape[41] — as though it were truly a specialised point of law and not of mere logic; but that danger seems to have passed.[42] Meanwhile, when rape achieved a statutory definition in the aftermath of *Morgan*, the proposition was rightly restated as one of evidence: the presence or absence of reasonable grounds for a belief that the woman was consenting was declared to be merely 'a matter to which the jury is to have regard' in considering his claim to have held the belief.[43]

It is of interest to refer to the judgment of the Court of Appeal in *Morgan*, which was reversed by the House of Lords. A crucial part of the reasoning in the Court of Appeal, to be found in one paragraph of the judgment,[44] may be summarised in two propositions. One relates to the incidence of the supposed requirement of reasonable grounds for a mistaken belief. The requirement is said to exist 'where the definition of the crime includes no specific mental element beyond the intention to do the prohibited act'; for in such cases the defendant bears an evidential burden in relation to a defence of mistake. The other proposition concerns the discharge of that burden:

> 'The rationale of requiring reasonable grounds for the mistaken belief must lie in the law's consideration that a bald assertion of belief for which the accused can assert no reasonable ground is evidence of insufficient substance to raise any issue requiring the jury's consideration.'

This reasoning, which has not prevailed, is significant. The first proposition shows the attenuated survival, even as late as 1975, of the notion that the presence or absence of a 'specific mental element' affects the burden of proof.[45] The attenuation is dictated by *Woolmington*; the burden *of proof* can no longer be regarded as affected. But the substituted reference to the burden of introducing evidence was, with respect, misconceived. Even where knowledge of a fact is expressly required as an element of an offence, there must be an evidential burden on the defendant in respect of any special belief that would entail ignorance of that fact. If there is no evidence of such a belief, how can the jury consider it? But the other proposition is the more interesting. It appears to concede that the issue, if properly raised, will be: Did he believe . . . ? The non-existence of reasonable grounds, however, is treated as of such crucial significance that the jury ought not to be seized of that issue. The jury are therefore not to have a chance of saying whether in their opinion this defendant (perhaps credulous, thoughtless or mentally impaired) may have entertained a belief for which there were no reasonable grounds. The evidential consideration is given substantive effect. We thus had a striking late example of the perennial confusion of matters of substance with matters of proof that is one of the themes of this essay.

The second strand in the recent history concerns mistakes forming the basis of pleas of excuse or justification. The defendant admits that he caused the harm and that he intended to cause it. He explains that he acted as he did only because he believed that he was threatened by another person, X, with death or serious injury if he did not so act (duress), or because he thought that he or another person whom he was acting to protect was under attack from Y, the victim (private defence). It turned out that he was wrong. May he rely on a mistake that others would not have made? A similar answer might be expected for both defences. But the defences have diverged on this issue in two important judgments given by the Lord Chief Justice.

In *R v Graham*[46] in 1981 Lord Lane CJ held the view that '. . . in general, if a mistake is to excuse what would otherwise be criminal, the mistake must be a reasonable one'; and he applied this generalisation to duress. The correct question was whether the defendant may have been impelled to act as he did 'because, as a result of what he reasonably believed [X] had said or done, he had good cause to fear' death or serious injury at X's hands if he did not so act.

In *R v Gladstone Williams*[47] in 1983, on the other hand, the Court of Appeal took the bold step of announcing the contrary rule for private defence. The reasonableness or otherwise of a belief that Y was attacking the defendant or a third person was relevant to the question whether as a matter of fact the defendant held that belief. If he may have done so, it was not proved that he intentionally or recklessly applied 'unlawful' force, as the definition of an assault requires. Unlawfulness — here, the absence of an occasion for legitimate private defence — is treated as a 'definitional element' of the offence; and the requirement of intention or recklessness in respect of such an element cannot, under the logic of *DPP v Morgan*, co-exist with a requirement that a belief excluding that state of mind be reasonable.

In *Albert v Lavin*,[48] only three years before, Hodgson J for the Divisional Court had cited, and felt bound by, a mass of dicta (from the late nineteenth century to the House of Lords in *DPP v Morgan*) requiring a belief in the existence of an occasion for private defence to be reasonable. The rule was otherwise for belief in the victim's consent; but that was because non-consent was a 'definitional element' of an assault offence, as of rape. But the distinction between consent and other grounds for the lawful use of force was rejected by the Court of Appeal in *R v Kimber*[49] (a case on belief in consent); and *Gladstone Williams* followed *Kimber* in that rejection.

Even a friend of the outcome of *Gladstone Williams* may regret the method used to achieve it. The case appears to turn on the fact that the word 'unlawful' occurs in the definition of assault. And it appears to treat an occasion for private defence (or prevention of crime), like victim's consent, as excluding 'unlawfulness' in a way that duress, on the evidence of *Graham*, does not. Assault could equally well be defined as the use of force without consent, all grounds of justification or excuse being available to exclude liability as with other offences.[50] As it is we are left with an uncertain and unrationalised distinction between different defences. What was needed was a frontal assault on the dicta which had hauled the 'honest and reasonable belief' formula all the way from its nineteenth century point of origin, rather than a side-stepping of them by the rejection of a distinction (between definitional and defence elements) on which, before *Morgan*, they had not been based. What was needed, in short, was the renunciation of a formula derived from a bygone legal environment.

It was the environment of *Tolson*. The third strand in the recent history of mistaken belief concerns the kind of belief relied on in *Tolson* itself — the belief of a person going through a ceremony of marriage that he is not currently married. The requirement that such a belief be 'honest and reasonable' has been repeated without fail in all the English bigamy cases since *Tolson*. And in one case, *R v King*[51] in 1963, it has constituted the ratio decidendi. But even in that case the point was not debated or justified; it was simply taken for granted. Such is the power of oft-repeated expressions of earlier times. In *DPP v Morgan* the correctness of the requirement in bigamy was not doubted. But it remains open to the House of Lords to hold that bigamy requires knowledge or recklessness in respect of the defendant's marital status and not mere negligence. The interpretation of *Tolson* offered in this essay is only one of the grounds on which it might properly do so.

2 Inferences

(a) SECTION 8 OF THE CRIMINAL JUSTICE ACT 1967

'The various acts constituting the outward part of a crime are sometimes said to constitute a presumption of *malice* or *criminal intent*. But most of those instances

> are today understood to be either "conclusive presumptions," ie rules of substantive law defining the criminal act, or else mere inferences of fact not affecting the accused with a duty to produce evidence.'[52]

With the enactment of s 8 of the Criminal Justice Act 1967 English law renounced a 'conclusive presumption' to be derived from *DPP v Smith* — that a sane, sober adult intends the plainly foreseeable result of his acts — in favour of a 'mere inference of fact'. A court or jury, having to decide whether a person 'intended or foresaw a result of his actions', is to decide that question 'by reference to all the evidence, drawing such inferences from the evidence as appear proper in the circumstances.'

The main proposition in s 8 is that the court or jury must decide whether the defendant before them actually had the state of mind required for the offence charged. But you cannot have direct evidence of a state of mind; so, in the absence of a confession, you have to decide whether other proved facts justify the confident conclusion that it existed. Section 8 calls the reaching of that conclusion 'drawing an inference.' It is highly unsatisfactory language, the more so because advocates and judges are given to using the language of relevant statutory provisions when they address juries. If they use the language of s 8, they must surely mystify many jurors to whom it is unfamiliar. It must be puzzling enough to be told that you may, but are not bound to, 'draw the inference' that the defendant intended (or foresaw) the harm he caused; and the more puzzling if 'drawing an inference' is an operation of whose nature you are not entirely sure. It is submitted, on the contrary, that s 8, to the extent that it contains a message for juries, requires translation by judges into words that their lay hearers will be sure to know.

Paragraph (a) of s 8 declares that juries are not to be told that they must infer that the defendant intended or foresaw a result from the fact that it was 'natural and probable'. This decision is an instruction to the judge, not to the jury, who obviously need not be told what it is that they are not to be told. But para (b) points the way to some advice to the jury. There are, of course, ways of advising them without using the language of 'inferences'. Where foresight of a result is in issue, they may be told that the fact that the result was one that was plainly likely to occur is something that may help them to decide whether the defendant foresaw it. For a jury must obviously be entitled, and will often feel driven, to say: 'Somebody who does that can hardly fail to realise that such a result may occur (or is very likely to occur; or is a near certainty). We see no reason to doubt that this person realised what would be obvious to others.' Where the issue is whether the defendant intended to cause a harm that he did in fact cause, it may be useful to invite the jury to consider whether the case is one in which they find themselves saying: 'A person is hardly likely to do as the defendant did unless he intends to cause just such a harm. Why should we doubt that the defendant intended to cause this harm?'[53] Such reactions to the evidence will often be 'proper' because they are reactions of common sense. But of course the jury must consider all the evidence, including any explanation the defendant may have given, before deciding that the reaction is the right one in the case before them.

Juries are, however, invited to 'draw inferences'. Moreover, just as the word 'presumption' has been misused in the past, so (I believe) the notion of an 'inference' is now being misused. Some very troubling passages, certainly, are to be found in important recent murder cases.

(b) THE RECENT MURDER CASES

A question with which the House of Lords was concerned in *R v Moloney*[54] may be put thus: is foresight of the probability (in any degree) of death or serious injury a form of the mental element of murder? In the words of Lord Bridge, is such foresight 'equivalent or alternative to the necessary intention'?[55] But his Lordship had earlier identified as an 'uncertainty' for resolution, the degree of probability required 'if foresight of probable consequences is to be treated either as equivalent to intent *or as evidence from which* intent may (or must?) be inferred.'[56] Now the notion of foresight as 'alternative to' intention is plain enough; it is the notion that murder requires either intention, in a narrow sense, to cause death or serious injury, or foresight of the likelihood or probability (in some degree) that death or serious injury will occur. But the notion of foresight as 'evidence from which intent may (or must?) be inferred' is puzzling. If intent *must* be inferred, the words 'evidence' and 'inferred' are both being misused; what we should have would be a substantive rule treating foresight as a case of intention. And the conception of foresight as evidence from which intention *may* be inferred is a very different one from foresight as 'alternative to' intention. The difference is sufficient to justify the supposition that this earlier passage in the opinion is a casual error to which Lord Bridge will not return.

When the vital question is legitimately posed — is foresight 'equivalent or alternative' to intention? — it is at once answered in the negative. But Lord Bridge then proceeds to state the opinion '. . . that foresight of consequences, as an element bearing on the issue of intention in murder, or indeed any other crime of specific intent, belongs not to the substantive law but to the law of evidence.'[57] It must be objected that what 'belongs to the law of evidence' is not foresight of consequences; it is a consequence's foreseeability — the fact that a result was 'natural and probable,' not the fact that it was seen by the defendant to be so. As Lord Bridge at this point in his opinion rehearses the modern history of the presumption of intention (mentioning the 'irrebuttable presumption' or 'rule of substantive law' in *DPP v Smith* and the corrective enactment of s 8),[58] he might have been expected to say precisely that. But he does not. He acknowledges that 'we should now no longer speak of presumptions in this context but rather of inferences.' But he then goes on to suggest that there are cases in which the jury may be invited to say whether the relevant consquence was, and whether it was foreseen by the defendant as being, a natural consequence of his act; and he concludes: 'The jury should then be told that if they answer Yes to both questions it is a proper inference for them to draw that he intended that consequence.'[59]

The idea of foresight as evidence of intention was repeated in *R v Hancock and Shankland*[60] in two slightly different versions. The Court of Appeal version[61] assumes as a first stage a finding by the jury 'that the defendant appreciated that what he did was highly likely to cause death or really serious bodily injury.' This finding will have been based '[o]n the evidence considered as a whole', including 'the defendant's evidence and that of his witnesses.' The jury may be told, says Lord Lane CJ, that if they make this finding:

> '. . . there is evidence before [them] from which [they] can infer that the defendant intended to cause death or really serious bodily injury, but [they] must not find him guilty of murder unless [they] feel sure that he so intended.'

The conception here (as in the Lord Chief Justice's subsequent judgment in *R v Nedrick*[62]) is of foresight as 'evidence' from which alone intention can be inferred; the other evidence in the case has been used in finding foresight. The other version occurs in a passage in Lord Scarman's opinion in the House of Lords which seems to contemplate the aggregation of foresight with the very evidence from which it has itself been inferred, as the basis of an inference of intention. Commenting on *R v Moloney*, his Lordship says[63] that in that case:

> '. . . the House made it absolutely clear that the foresight of consequences is no more than evidence of the existence of the intent; it must be considered, and its weight assessed, together with all the evidence in the case. Foresight does not necessarily imply the existence of intention, though it may be a fact from which when considered with all the other evidence a jury may think it right to infer the necessary intent.'

Later, however,[64] he may be interpreted as returning to the idea of the inference of intention from foresight alone. During a critique of the *Moloney* 'guidelines' for a direction to the jury he says that those guidelines require a reference to the probability of the consequence in question (not just to its being 'natural'), together with an explanation:

> '. . . that the greater the probability of a consequence the more likely it is that the consequence was foreseen and that if that consequence was foreseen the greater the probability is that that consequence was also intended.'

It does not, with respect, appear to make sense to suggest that, having used all the evidence in the case to arrive at a finding that the defendant foresaw the relevant harm, the jury may then use that evidence a second time, together with their conclusion from it, for the purpose of (as it were) upgrading their finding to one of intention. On the other hand, the suggestion that one state of mind may simply be inferred from another is strange enough to require explanation.[65] To determine its meaning, it is necessary to see what the recent cases decide about intention as the crucial ingredient in murder. What is it that is to be inferred?

The essential substantive proposition that the two House of Lords decisions yield is that murder is a crime of intention: it requires an intention to cause death or serious bodily harm and no other state of mind in relation to any consequence of the fatal act will suffice. Granted this premise, the question arises: what is 'intention' for this purpose? As to this Lord Bridge insisted that 'intention is something quite distinct from motive or desire.'[66] He gave as an example the case of a man boarding a plane bound for Manchester 'even though Manchester is the last place he wants to be and his motive for boarding the plane is simply to escape pursuit.' Such a man 'clearly intends to travel to Manchester.'[67] So he does. But he can also be said to 'desire' to fly to Manchester rather than be caught by his pursuers. Arrival in Manchester is not, to use Lord Lane CJ's expression, his 'primary desire or motive';[68] but under the circumstances he desires it nevertheless. Mr Moloney himself, in one statement attributed to him, said that he 'didn't want to kill [the deceased]. It was kill or be killed. I loved him, I adored him.'[69] But 'not wanting' to kill (preferring the continuation of the life that is taken) is consistent with 'wanting' to kill (rather than be killed). One may aim to achieve, and in this sense 'intend', what he would much prefer not to have to bring about.

Lord Bridge also said that the possibility that the Manchester plane may have to be diverted to Luton during its flight 'does not affect the matter'; the traveller intends to go to Manchester 'because it is a moral certainty that that is where he will arrive.'[70] This anticipates his Lordship's later reference to foresight of a natural consequence of an act, in the sense of a consequence that the act will cause 'unless something unexpected supervenes to prevent it.'[71] But the reluctant traveller does not seem to be a good example of a person's intending a virtually certain consequence. For even one who boards a horse-drawn conveyance that will go wherever it pleases the horse to take it can be said to intend to arrive wherever the horse arrives; yet arrival at the actual destination was never 'a moral certainty' in Lord Bridge's sense.

The example of the Manchester plane is cited again by Lord Lane CJ in *R v Nedrick*[72] as an illustration of how 'a man may intend to achieve a . . . result while at the same time not desiring it to come about.' But it seems to be an unhappy example for the purpose of cases such as *Hancock and Shankland* and *Nedrick* themselves. The question in those cases is: if a person drops a lump of concrete from a road bridge so that it kills someone in a car passing below (*Hancock*) or sets fire to a house so that someone in the house is killed (*Nedrick*), can he — or on what further facts can he — be found to have intended to cause death or at least serious bodily harm, given that causing death or serious harm was not his 'primary desire or motive'? In the course of a helpful attempt 'to crystallise the effect of their Lordships' speeches in . . . *Moloney* and . . . *Hancock*', the Court of Appeal in *Nedrick*[73] have made two negative contributions to an answer. First, 'If he did not appreciate that death or serious harm was likely to result from his act, he cannot have intended to bring it about.' That, in context, is clear. Secondly:

> '. . . the jury should be directed that they are not entitled to infer the necessary intention, unless they feel sure that death or serious bodily harm was a virtual certainty (barring some unforeseen intervention) as a result of the defendant's actions and that the defendant appreciated that such was the case.'[74]

What the Court of Appeal was able to derive from *Moloney* and *Hancock* by way of a positive answer was the proposition that:

> '. . . if . . . the defendant recognised that death or serious harm would be virtually certain . . . to result from his voluntary act, then that is a fact from which [the jury] may find it easy to infer that he intended to kill or do serious bodily harm, even though he may not have had any desire to achieve that result.'

This becomes slightly stronger in the final paragraph of the Lord Chief Justice's judgment. From a person's realisation that death or serious harm is 'for all practical purposes inevitable' the inference that he intended that result 'may be irresistible.' But his Lordship is careful to add: 'The decision is one for the jury to reach upon a consideration of all the evidence.'

It is clear, then, that the defendant's foresight of death or serious harm — even his realisation that either result was a virtual certainty — is not being offered as evidence of his having acted with 'any desire to achieve' such a result. Lord Lane, indeed, appears in both *Hancock and Shankland* and *Nedrick* to have interpreted the House of Lords as proposing a direction to the jury about the relevance of foresight in a case 'in which the defendant's motive or purpose was not primarily to kill or injure.'[75] That avoids at least one difficulty that would otherwise attend an invitation to 'infer' intention. The suggestion that a person's having aimed to cause a particular harm may be derived from a prior conclusion that he foresaw it, would seem to envisage a superfluous step in the fact-finder's reasoning. Realising that a result is highly likely to occur is not a step on the way to, or an element in, having the purpose of achieving it. By the same token, it is the fact that the result *was* highly likely, not the actor's having realised that fact, that draws from us the exclamation: 'Why did he do that if not to cause that result?' It is, indeed, when we are not persuaded, despite the high likelihood of the result, that the actor was aiming to achieve it, that we may nevertheless be interested in our natural conclusion that he realised how dangerous his act was. We want to know from the recent cases what state of mind, other than a desire to cause death or serious bodily harm, can be 'inferred' as 'intention' from that realisation.

The cases do not provide an answer. The jury are not being told that the defendant's recognition of death as a virtual certainty *is* an intention to cause death. For it is precisely from such recognition that his having intended death may be 'easy to infer' or from which 'the inference may be irresistible.' The recognition and the intention are different things; if the former were a case of the latter it would be neither meaningful to describe the latter as 'inferred from' the former nor accurate to offer the 'inference' as permissible rather than compelled. And there is no hint of any other sense in which the word 'intention' is to be understood — no suggestion, for example, that the defendant's appreciation of the great danger created by his act entitles the jury to conclude that he was 'willing to kill'[76] or indifferent to the risk of death.

'The inference may be irresistible . . . The decision is one for the jury . . .' This is entirely faithful to the speeches in the House of Lords cases. It stops short of declaring that realising a result to be 'for all practical purposes inevitable' is as a matter of law a case of intending that result; and it does not suggest what (if any) additional finding would convert the finding of such a realisation into a finding of intention. Any state of mind short of a desire to cause the result is (at best) left to the jury as material relevant to their 'inferring' the existence of an element that is not further specified. This use of the word 'infer', which is surely a misuse, has the effect of concealing the nature of the decision that is left to the jury. The jury are to say whether realising death or serious bodily harm to be a virtual certainty is a case of intending either result within the meaning of an offence requiring proof of such an intention. It is suggested in *Nedrick*, of course, that they be offered a strong hint that the right answer is 'Yes'; but it is a hint, not an instruction.

(c) DEEP-SEATED ENGLISH VICES

Two of the themes of the earlier part of this essay are again illustrated by these recent cases.

Firstly, we have a new example of the failure to disentangle substance from proof, though a failure different in kind from that corrected by s 8. What we needed was a plain statement of the law relating to the fault element in murder. If this was to be expressed in terms only of intention, but not limited to intention in the sense of a desire to cause death or serious harm, the cases cried out for a clear explanation of what the word 'intention' was meant to convey. Instead, the focus of the leading opinion in *Moloney* was on the business of deciding whether the fault element had been proved; and *Hancock and Shankland*, on appeal from convictions based on the defective model direction in *Moloney*, followed suit. 'The golden rule', insisted Lord Bridge,[77] is that 'the judge should avoid any elaboration or paraphrase of what is meant by intent.' He acknowledged, however, that there are some cases where 'some further explanation or elaboration' is necessary. But when he, Lord Lane CJ and Lord Scarman, came, one after the other in *Moloney* and *Hancock and Shankland*, to suggest what explanation or elaboration would be helpful, all that any of them offered was advice on how intent may be sought, not on 'what is meant' by it. English law still fights shy of definition and dwells upon process. And it does so in such a way that many are persuaded that the law is actually being clarified. One of the remarkable, and significant, things about the House of Lords cases was the professional reaction to them. Observations about ways in which juries may be helped to *find* intention were, I believe, quite widely perceived as statements about what intention *is*. Such a misreading would tend to confirm that the failure to separate substance and proof remains a flaw deeply embedded in our legal culture.

Secondly, the cases reveal, once again, a subservience to the rhetoric of the past. I do not believe that it would now occur to us to advise a jury in any of the ways suggested in *Moloney, Hancock and Shankland* or *Nedrick* if the old presumption of intention had never existed. It is because for so long it was said that a sane person is presumed to have intended the natural and probable result of his acts that we now feel obliged to say that the fact that the result was probable or virtually certain is 'evidence' from which foresight of it, or intention to cause it, may be 'inferred'. But this is a most unnatural way to talk and we ought to give it up. I have already presumed to suggest the kind of way in which a jury might preferably be addressed.

The new proposition that intention may, but need not, be inferred from the fact that the result was recognised as probable or virtually certain is, I believe, obscurantist and strictly nonsensical. But this kind of language will no doubt continue to be found convenient so long as it is desired to avoid instructing the jury about the meaning of 'ordinary words' in their legal contexts. If the jury are not to be clearly told what for purposes of murder 'intention' is, the phrase 'You may infer intention' will serve as a way of saying, without seeming to say, 'You may, if you see fit, declare that the case is one of murder.'[78] A tendency, by one device or another, to leave it to the jury to determine for themselves the limits of the criminal offence with which they are dealing is, of course, another familiar feature of English judicial behaviour. But it is not the subject of this essay, which has not undertaken to illustrate all the bad habits of thought and discourse to which our criminal law is prone.[79]

NOTES

1 (1859) 1 F & F 664.
2 *The Mental Element in Crime* (1965), pp 63–64, 68.
3 (1875) LR 2 CCR 154 at 162.
4 Ibid at 163.
5 See further, below, at n 32.
6 Per Viscount Sankey LC in *Woolmington v DPP* [1935] AC 462 at 481, HL.
7 J Ll J Edwards *Mens Rea in Statutory Offences* (1955), p 97 (after an elaborate review of the cases, beginning with the dictum in *R v Prince*, relating to ' "knowingly" and the burden of proof': pp 90 et seq).

8 CS Kenny, *Outlines of Criminal Law* (1902), p 41.
9 The version of Alderson B in *R v Gathercole* (1838) 2 Lew CC, 237 cited by WTS Stallybrass in L Radinowicz and JWC Turner (eds), *Modern Approach to Criminal Law* (1945), p 406.
10 Stephen J in *R v Doherty* (1887) 16 Cox CC 306 at 308; cf Coleridge J in *R v Monkhouse* (1849) 4 Cox CC 55 at 56; Brett J in *R v Stopford* (1870) 11 Cox CC 643: all referred to by Lord Birkenhead LC in *DPP v Beard* [1920] AC 479 at 497–499, HL.
11 See eg *R v Martin* (1881) 8 QBD 54 ('maliciously' in the Offences against the Person Act 1861).
12 2 *History of the Criminal Law*, p 111. There seems here to be the germ of an error — that of suggesting that intention can be inferred from foresight — that I shall have occasion to criticise below (p 81). But Stephen may have been treating that which is foreseen as probable as 'intended'; and if so, he is not making the error that I shall complain of.
13 Cf per Lord Diplock in *Hyam v DPP* [1975] AC 55 at 90, 94, HL.
14 In *R v Ward* [1956] 1 QB 351 at 355–356 Lord Goddard CJ approved of this language as 'unimpeachable' in a summing-up; and it was employed by the trial judge in *DPP v Smith* [1961] AC 290.
15 *R v Philpot* (1912) 7 Cr App Rep 140, CCA.
16 [1961] AC 290, HL.
17 *R v Sheehan, R v Moore* (1975) 60 Cr App Rep 308, CA; *R v Garlick* (1980) 72 Cr App Rep 291, CA.
18 [1920] AC 479 at 502, HL.
19 *Broadhurst v R* [1964] AC 441 at 461, PC.
20 See n 10, above.
21 [1961] AC 290 at 327, HL.
22 (1889) 23 QBD 168.
23 Ibid at 187.
24 Ibid at 172.
25 Ibid at 193–194.
26 Ibid at 187.
27 Ibid at 181. Cf *Bank of New South Wales v Piper* [1897] AC 383 at 389, PC.
28 [1976] AC 182 at 238.
29 Contrast Lord Diplock in *Sweet v Parsley* [1970] AC 132 at 163, HL.
30 (1861) Le & Ca 44.
31 Viscount Sankey LC in *Woolmington v DPP* [1935] AC 462, HL, insisted that in many early authorities in which the language of persuasion is used, one is entitled to doubt whether the burden of proof was under consideration or whether the reference is not to 'a stage in the trial' (as we would now say, an evidential burden) rather than to the burden of persuasion.
32 (1875) LR 2 CCR 154 at 162 (using the verb 'satisfy').
33 (1889) 23 QBD 168 at 181–184.
34 See text at n 36, below.
35 (1889) 23 QBD 168 at 181.
36 [1986] 2 All ER 635 at 638, HL.
37 Adopting the language of Lord Diplock in *Sweet v Parsley* [1970] AC 132 at 163, HL. (The statutory provision was s 58(2)(a) of the Medicines Act 1968, contravention of which is an offence under s 67(2).)
38 By *DPP v Majewski* [1977] AC 443, HL, and *Metropolitan Police Comr v Caldwell* [1982] AC 341, HL; a proposition about proof of foresight of a harm is rendered irrelevant by a rule that the recklessness required for an offence is supplied by the act of getting drunk or, more generally, by a denial that recklessness requires foresight of the harm.
39 For legislative proposals, see the Law Commission's draft Criminal Liability (Mental Element) Bill, cl 7 (Law Com no 89; 1978); and the draft Criminal Code Bill, cl 18 (Law Com no 143; 1985).
40 [1976] AC 182.
41 See especially *R v Phekoo* (1981) 73 Cr App Rep 107, CA; and generally David Cowley [1982] Crim LR 198.
42 See *R v Kimber* (1983) 77 Cr App Rep 225, CA; *R v Williams* (1983) 78 Cr App Rep 276. See also *R v Taaffe* [1984] AC 539, HL; *Westminster City Council v Croyalgrange Ltd* [1986] 2 All ER 353, HL.
43 Sexual Offences (Amendment) Act 1976, s 1(2).
44 [1976] AC at 191; see also at 192.
45 Cf above, p 68. See also the dissenting opinion of Lord Simon in the House of Lords ([1976] AC at 217–218) for a different kind of echo either of the same notion or of the non-application of the presumption of intention to crimes of specific intent (cf p 68, above), or of both.
46 (1981) 74 Cr App Rep 235.

47 (1983) 78 Cr App Rep 276; and see *R v Jackson* [1985] RTR 257, CA. In *R v Asbury* [1986] Crim LR 258 the Court of Appeal (obiter), while sympathetic towards its view in *Gladstone Williams*, appeared not to regard that view as *ratio decidendi* in the latter case.
48 (1980) 72 Cr App Rep 178.
49 (1983) 77 Cr App Rep 225.
50 In *Gladstone Williams* Lord Lane CJ felt that the qualification 'unlawfully' was essential to deal with casual, non-harmful touchings incidental to life in society. Sed quaere; see Codification of the Criminal Law (Law Com No 143), paras 13.13, 13.14 (as to the use of 'unlawfully' and 'without lawful excuse' in the specification of offences); and draft Criminal Code Bill, cl 49 (act justified or excused by law) and cl 77 (assault). For recent elaborate discussions of assault, which cannot be said to resolve the problem of classifying 'definitional' and 'defence' elements, see *Collins v Wilcock* [1984] 3 All ER 374 (crime); *Wilson v Pringle* [1986] 2 All ER 440, CA (tort).
51 [1964] 1 QB 285.
52 9 Wigmore *Evidence*, 2511a (Chadbourn rev 1981).
53 If realising that the result is 'for all practical purposes inevitable' (cf below, p 80) or 'almost certain' (cf Law Com no 143, draft Criminal Code Bill, cl 22(a)) were acknowledged to be a case of intending the result, both kinds of advice to the jury would sometimes be appropriate as offering different routes to the vital finding.
54 [1985] AC 905.
55 Ibid at 928.
56 Ibid at 925. (My italics).
57 Ibid at 928, referring for support to Lord Hailsham in *Hyam v DPP* [1975] AC 55 at 65: 'Knowledge or foresight is at the best material which entitles or compels a jury to draw the necessary inference as to intention.' This (as to foresight) is open to the same objections as the passages in *R v Moloney* and *R v Hancock and Shankland* (below) criticised in the text.
58 He also cites a familiar passage from the judgment of Lord Goddard CJ in *R v Steane* [1947] 1 KB 997 at 1004, which anticipates s 8 but provides no basis for the conception questioned in the text.
59 [1985] AC 905 at 929. If the defendant foresaw the consequence as natural — that is, as virtually certain, why is it also necessary that it should actually have been so?
60 [1986] AC 455.
61 Ibid at 461.
62 [1986] 1 WLR 1025; see text following n 74, below.
63 [1986] AC 455 at 471–2.
64 Ibid at 473.
65 Compare the proposition, which I have questioned elsewhere, that an alleged handler's 'wilful blindness' may be evidence, but cannot be more than evidence, of his having believed the goods to be stolen: *R v Griffiths* (1974) 60 Cr App Rep 14. See also M Wasik and MP Thompson (1981) 32 NILQ 328 at 333–4.
66 [1985] AC 905 at 926.
67 Ibid.
68 *R v Nedrick* [1986] 1 WLR 1025 at 1027.
69 [1985] AC 905 at 915.
70 Ibid at 926.
71 Ibid at 929.
72 [1986] 1 WLR 1025 at 1027.
73 Ibid at 1027–1028.
74 It is said a few lines earlier that if the defendant thought the risk to which he was exposing the deceased was only slight, 'it may be easy for the jury to conclude that he did not intend to bring about' death or serious harm. But the passage quoted in the text seems to oblige them so to conclude.
75 *R v Hancock and Shankland* [1986] AC 455 at 461; less clearly in *R v Nedrick* [1986] 1 WLR 1025 at 1027.
76 Cf Law Commission, *Imputed Criminal Intent* (*DPP v Smith*) (1967), para 17.
77 [1985] AC 905 at 926.
78 A Briggs (1985) 5 LS 314 at 319; JC Smith [1986] Crim LR 402–3, where Professor Smith reveals that he too is baffled by the notion of awareness of probability as evidence of intention.
79 I am grateful to Mark Thompson for helpful discussions both before I began to write this essay and after his careful reading of an earlier draft.

Omissions and the duty myth

Brian Hogan

When a child, even of tender years, is caught out in some minor peccadillo, such as breaking the teapot, drowning the cat or setting fire to his grandmother, his common reaction will be to say, 'I wasn't doing anything.' He knows he is hardly likely to be believed and that condign chastisement lies ahead, but he says it on the off chance that he will be believed because he knows that *if* he is believed he has a cast-iron excuse. At a very early age children grasp the notion that if you do not cause a consequence you cannot incur liability for it.

Quite right of course. The notion is so simple to understand that even the lawyer can grasp it. But the lawyer, you know, will not let any proposition slip by without qualification or exception. After all, he will say, circumstances might arise where either it can be said that the defendant caused a particular consequence by his failure to prevent it; or, if we cannot say that, we can say that his failure to prevent the consequence was so patently unforgivable that we ought to hold the defendant accountable.

But when you think about it, my delinquent child has got hold of a fundamental truth; there is no way you can *cause* an event by doing nothing (or is it, more precisely, by not doing anything?) to prevent it. If grandma's skirts are ignited by her careless proximity to the gas oven, the delinquent grandson cannot be said to have killed her by his failure to dowse her. No sensible doctor would enter as the cause of her death, say, failure to telephone the fire brigade.

But we immediately encounter the problem of what is meant by doing nothing, or, rather, not doing anything. The vexing problem of the distinction between act and omission. And 'although my difference between act and omission is often denied,' wrote Mr Peter Glazebrook,[1] 'the distinction is deeply embedded in the law.' True enough, but my own view is that the distinction is at best unhelpful and at worst misleading. It is, however, well entrenched, has found its way into the Draft Criminal Code Bill and, whatever I say, is likely to stay entrenched for some time yet. But that does not deter me from putting another view which I believe to be more logically attractive and even to express more accurately the common law.

It may be helpful if I begin with my general conclusion before I adduce the arguments. This is that it would be much more conducive to clarity of thought if we spoke of conduct and causation. If any proposition is self-evident (and, arguably, none is) it is that a person cannot be held to have caused an event which he did not cause. Hence my delinquent child cannot sensibly be said to have caused the death of his grandmother simply by a failure to take steps (which may or may not have been successful anyway) to prevent that death. To say to the child, 'You have killed your grandmother' would simply be untrue.

This is not to say that I am against liability for omissions. There would be nothing in principle objectionable in Parliament enacting a law which made it an offence for a member of a household to fail to take steps reasonably available to him to prevent or minimise harm to other members of the household. There are of course numerous instances where Parliament (and a handful where the common law) has penalised omissions[2] but what is noteworthy is that the defendant is penalised for the omission but not visited with liability for the consequences of that omission. Thus it is an offence under s 6(1) of the Maritime Conventions Act 1911, punishable with two years' imprisonment on indictment, for the master of a vessel to fail to render assistance to anyone in danger of being lost at sea. Fair enough, but it is to be noted that the master is made liable in respect of the omission; he is not, rightly enough, made liable in respect of any death or injury for any such death or injury is not of his doing. Exceptionally a statute may punish an omission as severely as the completed offence. A well-known example arises under the Road Traffic Act 1972, as amended, under which the punishment for a failure to provide a specimen is the same as for driving with an excessive blood-alcohol concentration. The driver is, however, convicted and punished in respect of the omission; he is not convicted and punished for the separate offence of driving etc since this has not been proved. In these circumstances it is entirely acceptable to punish the motorist for his omission as severely as for the driving offence but it would be wrong to convict him for the driving offence and unnecessarily grotesque to deem him to have driven over the prescribed limit.

A common law horse from the same stable is the offence of failing without reasonable excuse to assist a constable to quell a breach of the peace when called upon by the constable to do so.[3]

The person so failing does not thereby become a party to the breach of the peace, nor a party to any assault which may be committed on the constable. Quite rightly again. The law may properly take the view that able-bodied citizens have an interest in the maintenance of order and may be punished for an unreasonable failure to assist in keeping the peace. But it would be ludicrous to make the shirker a party to the crimes involved for he has played no part in their commission. He is to be punished for an omission to prevent harm; he is not to be artificially treated as its cause. Similarly public officers who neglect, without reasonable cause, to perform the obligations of their offices may be convicted of an offence but the offence lies in the neglect and the office holder does not become a party to the harm he might have prevented. Thus in *R v Dytham*[4] the police officer who decided not to go to the aid of a citizen obviously being subjected to a violent assault was held to have been properly convicted as a public officer of failing, without reasonable excuse, to perform a duty (namely, to preserve the peace) he was bound by law to perform. There was, inevitably, no suggestion that he was a party to the murder or manslaughter of the citizen. The police officer was fined £150 for his dereliction; a penalty of an altogether different order would surely have been appropriate could his dereliction have been regarded as a contribution to (as aiding or abetting) the 'murderous assault' on the citizen.

So in no sense am I against liability for omissions. I would ask only two conditions of a law punishing omissions. One is that it be clearly articulated and the other is that it seeks to punish the defendant for his dereliction and does not artificially treat him as a cause of the event he has not brought about by his conduct.

As to the first condition it would seem to me that any further development of the law is best left to Parliament. Some Canadian Provinces have, for example, enacted laws[5] making it an offence for any person (Alberta), or any person in the course of his professional duties (Ontario), having reasonable cause for believing that a child is being ill-treated to fail to report the same to the relevant authorities. Such a law might lead to officious interference in the lives of others but given the scale of child abuse (or, perhaps, given our growing intolerance of it) such a law might be enacted here. You would not find me going to the barricades against it so long as it aimed at encouraging the citizen to prevent harm and did not seek to make the citizen a party to the harm caused by another. There is a clear difference between the two.

I would be much less happy if the courts, out of the blue, were to declare that such a failure was a criminal offence. There are precedents in the sense that the common law has created offences of failing unreasonably to assist a constable to quell a breach of the peace or for a public officer unreasonably to fail to carry out the duties of his office but it would surely be unacceptable for the judges suddenly to expand this limited range of precedents. The temptation may arise when a social worker (not, presumably, a public officer, but one who is paid by the taxpayer to perform tasks on our behalf) has lamentably failed to take steps which might have avoided appalling harm to a child, to recognise (or create) a duty and hold him or her liable for its dereliction. I doubt whether any court would be (or even should be) so bold as to pluck from the ether of the common law new duties of this kind. Even if a court were so bold, it would surely see the gravamen of the offence in the dereliction and would stop short of artificially treating the social worker as a party to the harm merely because of a failure to take steps which *might* have prevented it.

It follows that if the facts of *R v Smith*[6] were to recur, I would favour precisely the same result. There, it will be recalled, a mother died leaving a daughter and three sons, one of whom was incapable of looking after himself and who (it may be assumed callously for the purposes of the argument) was ignored by the others so that he suffered in health. Since he did not die the prosecution was strapped for an appropriate charge and lighted on assault and false imprisonment. Burrough J wondered whether there was an appropriate indictment for the case but was clear that the charges of assault and false imprisonment could not be made out. Some might accuse Burrough J of being behind the times (assuming our times recognise higher standards of selflessness than his) but there would appear to be no evidence which either then or now would support the charges preferred. No hurt was done to the helpless son; nor was he made to apprehend any, which disposes of assault; and since there was no evidence that he was prevented from going where he liked, nothing to support the charge of false imprisonment either.

Some may accordingly see me as callous, as indifferent to suffering, as Burrough J. Actually Burrough J doesn't seem to have been too bad an old stick. He was, it is said,[7] esteemed for the kindness and simplicity of his demeanour. Not even my best friends would say anything quite so nice of me but I am prepared roundly to condemn such conduct as was shown in *R v Smith*. What I am not prepared to assent to is that they might be properly convicted of assault or false imprisonment. Manifestly, on the evidence tendered by the prosecution, they could not. Let me repeat, I am not against the enactment of a statute (though I am very much against the judges finding such a rule in the bran-tub of the common law) making it an offence for a member of a household to fail to take reasonable steps to prevent or minimise harm to another member of that household provided the gravamen of the offence lies in the dereliction of the duty and the law does not seek to visit him with liability for consequences which he does not cause.

Thus far I have discussed cases where by no stretch of the imagination can it be said that the defendant has caused a result by his inaction. The question then arises whether a result may ever be caused by inaction. My answer is: No. On the other hand a result may be caused by the defendant's *conduct* and the totality of the defendant's conduct causing a result may properly include what he has not done as well as done. In such cases I doubt whether it is very, or at all, helpful to analyse each phase of the defendant's conduct as one of omission or commission. The question is simply: did the defendant's *conduct* cause the result?

Take a simple example. X, driving his car, sees Y beginning to cross the road ahead. X realises that unless he takes some action, such as removing his foot from the accelerator to the brakes or turning to left or right, he will run down Y. In fact he takes no action whatsoever and runs down Y. Charged with an offence in relation to the harm done to Y, X would surely be laughed out of court if he said: I did not do anything to cause harm to Y. We would not have the slightest difficulty in saying that X ran down Y and was the cause of the harm to Y. *R v Miller*[8] holds, and with respect rightly, that one who inadvertently (or otherwise faultlessly, presumably) starts a chain of events causing harm may be properly held liable if, having become aware that he was the cause, he fails to take steps reasonably available to him to prevent or minimise the damage that will ensue. A fortiori the driver X. There is nothing inadvertent about his causing of harm to Y. X chooses to stay with a course of conduct which he knows will cause harm to Y.

Miller is interesting. One analysis of the case is to say[9] that when the defendant became aware that he had caused (albeit inadvertently) the fire he was under a duty to take steps reasonably available to him to prevent or minimise further harm. Lord Diplock, with whom all their lordships agreed, expressed some support for the duty theory as having the merit of being easier to explain to the jury but then added that he would prefer 'responsibility' instead of duty. He thought that 'duty' was:

> '. . . more appropriate to civil than to criminal law since it suggests an obligation owed to another person, ie the person to whom the endangered property belongs, whereas a criminal statute defines combinations of conduct and states of mind which render a person liable to punishment by the state itself.'

Quite what Lord Diplock is getting at here is not perhaps as clear as crystal, but two things may be said. The first is that he was right to say, if this is what he was saying, that there is no general duty to intervene to prevent or minimise harm to another's property. The second is, in the context of his speech read as a whole, that, having addressed his mind to the question whether it could be said that the defendant caused the fire and inevitably concluding that he did, he sees that it can make no sensible difference that mens rea was formed after the first event in the chain of events leading to the damage. Nor, with respect, can I. The defendant's causal contribution did not end when he inadvertently dropped the lighted cigarette. The fire was causally attributable to him from start to finish; he can hardly be heard sensibly to say that the only damage he caused was the scorch hole in the mattress. When he became aware that steps reasonably available to him would prevent further harm he was still causing the damage. The only difference between the damage caused before and after his awareness was that he was not criminally liable for the damage occurring before his awareness since he lacked mens rea but was liable for the damage he caused after his awareness since he now had mens rea.

Miller to my mind is not in principle distinguishable from the illustration concerning the motorist, X, given above. At one stage X is driving in a perfectly lawful manner; his driving becomes unlawful only when he realises that if he continues to drive in that manner he will cause harm to Y which it is open to him to avoid. It is unrealistic and unnecessary to look only at the last item in the chain (the failure to remove the foot from the accelerator or to turn away) and, if it is characterised as an omission, to talk of a duty to take action. X's *conduct* causes the harm to Y; X ran Y down.

So in *R v Pittwood*[10] it becomes fruitless to debate whether leaving open the level-crossing gates is to be characterised as omission or commission. The court characterised the conduct as misfeasance and in so doing, though the report is brief, appears to have looked at the totality of the defendant's conduct. And looking at the totality of his conduct it can easily be said that he created a situation of danger which caused harm to the victim.

It is true that in *R v Pittwood* the court also said that a duty might arise out of a contract and the cases on 'omissions' are certainly littered with references to 'duty'. In my view these references to duty are unhelpful. The issue in *R v Pittwood* was simply whether the defendant had *caused* the deaths of the victims with the relevant mens rea. Most assuredly he had no duty to take employment as a level-crossing keeper but once he did so he must not perform the office (in the same way as one must not drive a car or handle a gun) in such a way as to cause harm to others. No one has a duty to buy a car or a gun, or to obtain employment as a level-crossing keeper, or even to walk down the road to post a letter. But if they choose to do any of these things they must so conduct themselves so as not to cause harm, and if their conduct causes harm with the relevant mens rea they will fall foul of the criminal law. There is no need to complicate such cases by the search for duty.

There is perhaps a stronger case for imputing the duty concept in connection with domestic and similar relationships. So in *R v Instan*[11] where the niece failed to summon medical assistance for her aunt who died of gangrene, the court talks of a duty founded in moral obligation. In law, of course, and now as much as then, the niece had no duty whatever to look after her aunt. Had she been paying a casual visit to her aunt, noticed that her aunt would die without prompt medical attention, but had left without taking any measures of assistance then surely the case would have been decided differently. What was determinative in *R v Instan* was that the niece had taken it upon herself to look after her aunt. She had no duty to do so, any more than the defendant in *R v Pittwood* had any duty to take the job of level-crossing keeper, but having undertaken a certain task (and it is essentially on all fours with driving a car or using a gun or walking down the road to post a letter) it must be performed properly. If it is performed improperly and, with the relevant mens rea, causes harm to another, then criminal liability follows.

It might be said that in the 'omission' area it does no harm to use the duty concept. In *Miller* Lord Diplock did say that reference to duty was something that juries might find helpful. In my view, however, it may be positively misleading in that it suggests that the category of 'duty' is never closed and that it is open to judges (I am confining myself to criminal liability, for civil liability is something else) to recognise new duties.

Consider *People v Beardsley*.[12] The defendant had, in the absence of his wife, invited a woman to spend a weekend with him in his apartment. They drank heavily and at one stage the woman, having procured some morphine tablets, was trying to take some when the defendant knocked the box from her hand. However she picked up two tablets from the floor and swallowed these. She soon fell into a coma but though she was evidently ill the defendant did no more than put her to bed. When a doctor was eventually called by a friend of the defendant, the woman was dead. The defendant's conviction for manslaughter was quashed on the grounds that he was neither under nor had assumed any duty towards her. The defendant, said the court, 'had assumed either in fact or by implication no care or control over his companion.'

The result is soundly condemned by Professor Hughes. 'To be temperate about such a decision,' he says,[13] 'is difficult. In its savage proclamation that the wages of sin is death, it ignores any impulse of charity and compassion. It proclaims a morality which is smug, ignorant and vindictive. In a civilised society, a man who finds himself with a helplessly ill person who has no other source of aid should be under a duty to summon help whether the person is his wife, his mistress, a prostitute or a Chief Justice.'

Let me say again that I have no objection in principle against the statutory creation of such a duty though there would, I think, be immense practical difficulties in identifying who is required to play the good samaritan and what he would be required to do to discharge his duty. But the last thing I would want is for such a law to make guilty of manslaughter one who has not causally contributed to the death. However one looks at *Beardsley* it is really quite impossible to say that the defendant killed his mistress.

The court in *Beardsley* recognised, properly enough, that it is possible for someone to assume the care and control of another so as to render that someone liable for improperly conducting his care and control. The court cited *Instan* with evident approval. But the court declined to say that one who invites another to his house for a drink thereby assumes the care and control of his guest so as to be liable for homicide if he fails to summon help when his guest has a heart attack.

Mind, *R v Stone, R v Dobinson*[14] comes perilously close to saying that the host might incur liability for homicide in just such a situation. This was the case where a man and his mistress, both elderly and not very competent, allowed the sister of the man to live with them and gave her the use of a room. The sister also seems to have been somewhat lacking in competence, was morbidly anxious about putting on weight, clearly neglected herself and was eventually found dead in her bed from toxaemia caused by infected bed sores and prolonged immobilisation. Both the man and the mistress were aware of the sister's deteriorating condition but failed to take any effective steps to summon help. Obviously they were under no duty whatsoever to have taken in the sister in the first place and had the sister lived next door to them they could not have incurred any liability if, well aware of her perilous condition, they had proffered no assistance. But they had taken in the sister and what was regarded as even more significant was that the mistress had from time to time supplied the sister with food, and on one occasion helped a neighbour to give her a bed bath, and on another the man and the mistress had made ineffectual efforts to get a doctor. On these slender threads the Court of Appeal, upholding their conviction for manslaughter, held that the jury was entitled to infer that they had assumed the care and control of the sister.

I see nothing wrong with the principle in *R v Stone* which I take to be that if one chooses to assume the care and control of another then the self-imposed responsibility must be carried out with reasonable care and skill and that liability for manslaughter (or even murder[15]) may be incurred if that responsibility is discharged in a grossly negligent (now reckless) manner. What is disturbing about *R v Stone* is that the evidence hardly supported the inference that these two elderly incompetents had taken it upon themselves to discharge the onerous task of looking after the sister. Did they really *kill* the sister?

I am unhappy about the duty concept in the context of 'omission'. It is likely to mislead a jury into thinking of duties in other than legal terms; into a consideration of the immorality of particular conduct; into convicting the defendant merely for his callousness. Better to put the issue as simply one of causation. For this purpose it is proper to look not merely at the last link in the causal chain, be it commission or omission, but all the relevant conduct of the defendant. The quesions then become whether the *conduct* of the defendant caused the actus reus and whether he did so with mens rea. To introduce an imprecise, ill-defined concept of 'duty' into the equation only serves to confuse the issue.

NOTES

1 'Criminal Omissions' (1960) 76 LQR 386.
2 See Graham Hughes 'Criminal Omissions' (1958) 67 Yale LJ 590.
3 *R v Brown* (1841) Car & M 314.
4 [1979] 3 All ER 641, CA.
5 See the Alberta Child Welfare Act, RSA 1980, c C-8 and the Ontario Child Welfare Act, RSO 1980, c 66. Cf Stuart *Canadian Criminal Law*, p 72.
6 (1826) 2 C & P 449.
7 Foss *Judges of England* Vol 9, p 14.
8 [1983] 1 All ER 978, HL.
9 See Professor JC Smith's commentary on *R v Miller* [1982] Crim LR 526 at 528. Cf Professor Glanville Williams [1982] Crim LR 773.
10 (1902) 19 TLR 37.
11 [1893] 1 QB 450.
12 (1907) 113 NSW 1128.
13 67 Yale LJ 590, 624.
14 [1977] 2 All ER 341, CA.
15 *R v Gibbins and Proctor* (1918) 13 Cr App Rep 134.

Bribery and corruption

David Lanham

I was extremely pleased to be asked to contribute an essay in honour of John Smith, to whom I owe so much both as a criminal lawyer and as a law teacher generally and from whose massive fund of ideas I draw so freely, so frequently and so unashamedly. One reason for choosing bribery and corruption as my essay was that so far John had not given the subject detailed consideration, so leaving me with something arguably original to say. It was accordingly a great relief, from a purely selfish point of view, to find that John's Criminal Code Team had deferred consideration of this topic to Pt II of the Code.[1] That left me still with a reasonably untilled field.

The law of bribery and corruption in England is the product of a hesitant common law and piecemeal and overlapping statutory development. The common law offence of bribery, which was for a long time widely underestimated[2] was supplemented in 1889 by the Public Bodies Corrupt Practices Act which covers the corruption of agents of public bodies as there defined and the Prevention of Corruption Act 1906 which punishes the corruption of private agents and those of certain public authorities. Then in 1916 the various kinds of corruption were brought together by the Prevention of Corruption Act of that year but the common law offence was left intact. In addition to these relatively general offences of corruption there is a number of special offences covering such matters as bribery at elections.[3]

The degree of overlap between the common law and the legislation makes it undesirable to deal with the law in totally watertight compartments, but as the legislation raises particular problems of its own, it will be convenient to examine the common law and the legislation under separate heads, though with a certain amount of cross-fertilization. Accordingly section 1 below, though dealing with the common law offence, will draw on cases decided under the legislation as appropriate. The discussion will also attempt to take account of cases decided in other jurisdictions whether at common law or under analogous legislation. Section 2 will be concerned with the general offences of corruption under the 1889, 1906 and 1916 Acts. No attempt will be made to discuss the specialised offences except where they throw light on the more general ones.

1 Bribery at common law

It is difficult to find a satisfactory definition of bribery at common law as the offence underwent a development over the centuries and is often described in terms of a number of individual offences rather than a single offence. *Russell on Crime* came close to stating a general principle and a precis of his definition will serve as a useful starting point:

> 'Bribery is the receiving or offering of any undue reward by or to any person whatsoever . . . in order to influence his behaviour in [an official situation] and incline him to act contrary to the known rules of honesty and integrity.'[4]

Four aspects of the law of bribery will be examined in detail.

(a) THE POSITION OF THE PERSON BRIBED

Bribery is concerned with influencing those who exercise public rather than private functions. While Russell describes the offence as extending to gifts to anyone in an official situation, Coke and Hawkins, upon whom Russell relies, state an exception in the case of the King. For Coke[5] and Hawkins[6] bribery consists of the taking rather than the giving of a bribe and the exception seems to be based on the notion that the king can do no wrong and so cannot act corruptly. As there can be no question of trying the monarch in any case, the more practical result of the exception would seem to be that a person attempting to bribe the sovereign would also not be guilty as there can be no intention to corrupt a person who is legally incorruptible.

Apart from the monarch there is no official too high to be criminally liable for receiving a bribe. Bribery proceedings have been brought against Lord Chancellors,[7] a Chief Justice[8] and a First Lord of the Treasury.[9] While originally bribery was considered to be the taking of rewards by judicial officers,[10] it has long been regarded as extending to both judicial and ministerial officers. This covers all public officers. In *R v Whitaker*,[11] the colonel of a regiment accepted money from a firm of caterers to induce him to accept their representative as tenant of the regimental canteen. His counsel conceded that bribery extended to judicial and ministerial officers but argued that the colonel of a regiment was not a ministerial officer. The Court of Criminal Appeal held that every public officer who was not a judicial officer was a ministerial officer and dismissed the colonel's appeal against conviction.

In *Whitaker*,[12] Lawrence J defined a public officer as one 'who discharges any duty in the discharge of which the public are interested, more clearly so if he is paid out of a fund provided by the public.'[13] This suggests that governmental payment is an important but not a necessary factor in determining who is a public officer. A West Indian case raises the issue directly. In *Stewart v R*[14] the defendant was an unpaid liaison officer whose duty it was to recommend to the Minister of Labour the names of agricultural workers for farm work in the United States. He received £7 for showing favour to an applicant. The Jamaican Court of Appeal held that he was guilty of bribery and that it made no difference that he was not a paid official or that he was not appointed under any regulation. But the law is even wider. While some stress is laid in a number of cases on the fact that the recipient of the bribe was a public officer, there is no requirement that the recipient should hold any kind of continuing position. In *R v Pitt and Mead*[15] the bribing of electors at a Parliamentary election was held to be an offence at common law. Furthermore it is an offence to bribe jurors.[16] Though this offence is called embracery[17] and appears to be obsolescent[18] it is a species of bribery and supports the view that no continuing office is necessary for the crime to be committed. For these reasons it is better to describe the recipient as a person acting in an official capacity[19] or performing a public function rather than as a public officer. The main limitation is that bribery at common law does not extend to persons performing private functions.[20]

It is not necessary that, at the time of the receipt of the bribe, the receiver is in a position to exercise an official function. In *H M Advocate v Dick*[21] Lord Young recognised that a person might be guilty of taking a bribe in anticipation of his appointment as a magistrate for services to be performed after the appointment.

It seems that the law also covers cases where the person bribed purports to exercise public powers. In *Ex p Winters*,[22] the defendant held himself out as a police officer and took a bribe. His defence was that he was not in fact a police officer. The court held against him and observed that if he was officer enough to accept a bribe he was officer enough to go to the penitentiary for so doing.

(b) REWARD

Russell defines the bribe itself in terms of 'reward'.[23] This suggests that it covers anything which is regarded or intended to be regarded as of value to the person bribed. While money or tangible objects are the most obvious form of bribe there is no reason why the bribe should not take the form of intangibles like services. Nor, where the bribe takes the form of a promise, need the promise be legally enforceable. In *Scott v State*,[24] D told a woman that he would assist her father to get a licence to sell soft drink if she went riding with him and showed him a good time. The Supreme Court of Ohio held that sexual favours constituted a 'valuable thing' within the meaning of the local bribery statute.

Rewards, treats, and triviality

Russell places no qualitative or quantitative limit on the notion of reward except that it should be 'undue'. Coke,[25] on the other hand, refers to a limitation on the notion of reward in these terms: 'unless it be meat and drink and that of small value'. The same exception was recognised by Willes J in the *Bodmin Case*.[26]

The distinction between a bribe and a treat has arisen in more modern times in a South African case, *S v Deal Enterprises (Pty) Ltd*,[27] where D gave a state employee substantial sums of money and on a charge of bribery contended that they were a Christmas gift. Nicholas J rejected this defence and observed that it would be unfortunate if the season of goodwill were to be regarded as a legitimate cloak for the giving of bribes.[28] The learned judge recognised that in some circumstances entertainment might be legitimate but that that did not mean that gifts in lieu of entertainment could be treated on the same basis.[29] It seems that the courts will construe this exception very narrowly and rightly so. In the context of election law treating is a crime in its own right[30] but the general law of bribery has not been extended in this way, so that within narrow bounds the defence of 'treating' is still open.

Quite apart from treating, the benefit given may be so trivial that it does not amount to a 'reward' at all. In *Woodward v Maltby*[31] a gift of a book of matches containing an exhortation to vote for a candidate was held to be neither treating (because it was not meat, drink, entertainment or provisions) nor bribery because the value was so small that it could not be inferred that it was given in order, as a gift, to influence the recipient voter. From this it appears that the triviality of the gift is not a defence in its own right but a factor in determining whether it was given as a reward.

(c) THE MENS REA OF BRIBERY

As bribery involves two parties it is difficult to define the mens rea in brief terms. Russell's definition of bribery includes the phrases 'in order to influence his behaviour' and 'to incline him to act contrary to the known rules of honesty and integrity.'[32] An alternative way of describing this mental element is in terms of corrupt purpose or corrupt intent,[33] in other words an intent to seduce the recipient of the bribe into taking a price for action in an official capacity.[34] None of these formulae captures the full flavour of the mental element in bribery and further elaboration is necessary.

The most obvious case of corruption is one in which a reward is given or received to induce the recipient to act in breach of duty, eg to exercise a discretion in a way he would not otherwise exercise it.

More difficult is the case where the reward is offered or received as an inducement to the recipient to perform his duty, eg to exercise a discretion in the right direction. In *Williams v R*,[35] a charge of attempted bribery was brought under the Australian Commonwealth Crimes Act 1914, s 73. Blackburn J[36] took the view that the requirement of corruption at common law implied an intention to procure a breach of duty on the part of the official bribed but that no such limitation applied to the statutory offence. This is too narrow a view of the common law. In *R v Gurney*[37] D was charged with attempting to bribe and corrupt a JP. The common serjeant told the jury that if D sent the money with the intention of producing any effect on the JP's decision that was an attempt to corrupt. There is no suggestion that the intent must be to induce the JP to come to the wrong decision. In this kind of case it can either be said that there is no requirement that the gift is intended to cause a breach of duty or that taking the gift into consideration is itself a breach of duty. Whichever way the law is stated it is not necessary to show that the discretion would have been properly exercised differently in the absence of the gift.

Another problem is how close a connection there must be between the bribe and the official function of the recipient. A narrow view was taken in a Scottish case, *HM Advocate v Dick*.[38] D, a councillor, obtained £600 as a bribe for undertaking to procure the granting of a licensing certificate by a magistrate. The court held that D was not guilty of bribery because the reward did not relate to the exercise by the councillor of his official functions but was merely an inducement to D to use his influence as a councillor to procure the granting of the certificate. A more extreme case is *R v David*[39] where D gave a constable a travelling rug to destroy evidence found on D's premises. The court held that D was not guilty of corruption under s 87 of the Queensland Code because it was no part of the constable's duty to destroy evidence. The court observed that the charge should have been brought under s 121 of the Code (interference with the due administration of justice). The case is of little authority on the common law, but so far as it goes it provides some support for the narrow view taken in *HM Advocate v Dick*.

A wider view of the relationship between bribery and discharge of duty was taken by the Privy Council in *A-G of Hong Kong v Ip Chiu*.[40] A suspect with a past history of drug offences gave the defendant police officers $2000 to avoid being beaten up or having evidence planted upon him. The defendants were charged under the Prevention of Bribery Ordinance with accepting an advantage on account of abstaining from performing an act in their capacity as public servants. The Hong Kong Court of Appeal held that they were not guilty because it was no part of their duty to fabricate evidence. The Privy Council adopted a wider test of liability. The question did not turn on duty but whether the gift could have been effectively solicited if the person in question were not the kind of public servant he in fact was. Applying that test, however, the Privy Council held that the defendants were not guilty since beating a suspect or planting evidence could have been perpetrated equally well by a stranger as by a member of the police force. While the principle adopted by the Privy Council is a welcome antidote to the narrow view taken in *HM Advocate v Dick* and *R v David*, the application of that principle to the facts of the case looks more questionable. By virtue of their duties with regard to the investigation of crime, police officers are in a much stronger position to fabricate evidence than private citizens are. The case could be justified on a different basis that it cannot be illegal to give a person a reward to induce him not to commit a criminal offence.

If the Privy Council approach is projected on to the cases of *HM Advocate v Dick* and *R v David* a different result would follow. A councillor, representing the interests of the local public might quite effectively influence the decision of a licensing magistrate and it must be the duty of a police officer to make decisions about the retention and safeguarding of evidence. Accordingly a conviction would have been appropriate in both *HM Advocate v Dick* and *R v David*.

The next question is whether the receiver can plead as a defence that he had no intention of allowing the bribe to influence him. In *S v Van Der Westhuizen*[41] Baker J said that if the receiver takes money from the giver intended by the giver as a consideration for pushing the giver's interest with no intention of doing anything for the giver, he would still be guilty of bribery. This seems correct. In those circumstances the giver would be guilty of bribery and the receiver would be an accomplice to that offence. The fact that he might be guilty of defrauding the giver should be no defence to the bribery charge. On the other hand if the receiver accepts something not in order to influence him but for some quite different purpose the crime is not made out. In *S v Ernst*,[42] D received money from a person who had been dismissed from his employment. The money changed hands openly and D contended that he regarded it as a fine and intended to return it. Galgut J held that D would not be guilty on these facts and that even if the giver thought he was paying the money as an inducement to D to give him back his job, D would not be guilty unless he knew that this was the giver's motive.

Entrapment

What then is the position if the giver offers or the receiver accepts or solicits the bribe in order to trap the other party? In *S v Ernst*,[43] Galgut J implies that the receiver would have a good defence if he accepted the bribe in order to trap the giver or if he intended to report the matter to the police. Similarly in *S v Pillay*,[44] the giver of a bribe offered it in order to trap the receiver. The court held that the giver was not guilty of bribery. A different view of the law was taken in *R v Smith*.[45] D was charged under the Public Bodies Corrupt Practices Act 1889 with corruptly offering a gift to a mayor to induce him to influence the sale of land by the council to D. D's defence was that he made the offer in order to expose corruption on the part of the mayor. The Court of Criminal Appeal held that the judge was right to withdraw that defence from the jury. Though the case was decided under a statutory provision its reasoning is applicable to common law bribery.

There is accordingly a degree of conflict between the South African cases and *R v Smith*. The latter case has been criticised by Gordon,[46] who has suggested that it should not be followed in Scotland. However there is room for a sensible middle view based on a distinction between instigation and acquiescence. Where the trapper does no more than pretend to respond to an approach by the other party, there is no intention to corrupt anyone whether for a good or bad motive. But if the trapper takes the initiative and offers a bribe in the hope of trapping the recipient there is an intention to corrupt even though it may be for the purpose of bringing a prosecution. The law should not countenance gratuitous temptation, though where corruption is already reasonably suspected in an agency it may be permissible to take positive steps to flush out the corrupt official. Such steps however should be taken only as a well-planned exercise with appropriate safeguards against oppression and abuse. This suggests that any such operation should be conducted by the police or a law enforcement agency. It should not be left to private enterprise. *R v Smith* is consistent with this position. There is a similar element of corruption when the trapper is the recipient who solicits a bribe in order to trap a potential giver. Though the common law is not directly concerned with punishing corruption of private individuals it is concerned to prevent such individuals from taking part in corrupting those exercising public functions. If it is sought to trap a private individual suspected of offering bribes some police or other law enforcement agency should be involved.

(d) THE PROBLEM OF MUTUALITY

In the paradigm case of bribery there are two guilty parties: the giver and the receiver of the bribe. This feature of the crime has led some courts to take the view that an innocent intent on the part of one party may provide a defence to the other even if the latter has a guilty intent. A number of different situations must be considered.

First it is an offence at common law not only to give or receive a bribe but also to offer or solicit a bribe. It is not clear whether offering or solicitation amounts to the substantive offence of bribery or merely to an attempt to bribe. Russell,[47] for instance, defines the crime in terms of 'offering or receiving' but there seems no good reason to distinguish the briber and person bribed in this way. The question is of little practical importance as bribery and attempted bribery are both common law misdemeanours punishable in the same way. What is important is that both offer and solicitation, whether regarded as bribery or attempt, are unilateral acts and do not depend on any act or state of mind on the part of the offeree or person solicited. This point was considered directly in *S v Kok.*[48] D, a police officer asked X for money as an inducement not to report an incident. The court held that D was guilty of attempt irrespective of the state of mind of X and that the fact that X later paid the money as part of a police trap did not affect D's liability for attempt.

A more difficult situation is that where D does not initiate the transaction but acts in response to an initiative from the other party. What is the position if D accepts an apparent bribe where the initiator has no corrupt motive? It seems that D will be guilty if he believes the other has a corrupt motive. In *Sims v State*[49] X gave D, a member of the legislature, a bribe in order to trap him.[50] The court held that at common law the receiver of the bribe was guilty even though the giver had no corrupt motive. That leaves the question whether D can be found guilty if he knows that the other party has no corrupt intention. A number of South African cases have held that in these circumstances D must be acquitted of bribery. The leading case is *R v Geel*[51] where D, a municipal officer, was charged under statute with corruptly accepting £20 from X as an inducement to obtain a site licence. X believed that the £20 was payable by law to the municipality and did not intend any part of that sum as an inducement to D to issue a site permit. The Appellate Division held that D could not be convicted of the offence on the ground that a recipient cannot induce himself to do or refrain from doing. Though the case was decided on a statutory offence the reasoning appears equally applicable to bribery. The court recognised however that D might have been guilty of an offence involving fraud.

A different view on the liability for bribery in these circumstances was taken by the Jamaican Court of Appeal in *Stewart v R.*[52] X had paid D, an official, £7 for selection for agricultural work. D contended he was not guilty inter alia because it had not been shown that X paid the money in bad faith. The court held that both a receiver and an offeror could be guilty of an offence within the definition of bribery and so there was no substance in D's contention.[53] The question was dealt with briefly and it is not clear how far the court intended to go. If the decision means that the actual innocence of the giver is no defence to the receiver it is in line with the South African cases. But if it means that D is liable even if he knows or believes that X has an innocent motive the case conflicts with *R v Geel* and like cases. The West Indian solution is attractive in that it punishes recipients who intend to act corruptly in the sense of dishonesty, but if the essence of the offence is inducement it is difficult to resist the logic of the South African cases.

While the recipient who knows that the giver is innocent may not be guilty of bribery, the apparent gap in the common law is closed by the existence of the offence of misconduct in a public office. The leading case is *R v Bembridge.*[54] D was charged as an accountant in the office of receiver and paymaster general of fraudulently concealing the omission of certain charges from accounts delivered to an auditor. D argued that he was guilty only of a civil wrong. Lord Mansfield, with whom Willes and Buller JJ agreed, held that where there was a breach of trust, fraud or imposition in a matter concerning the public a criminal offence was committed even though as between individuals only a civil wrong would have taken place.

In addition, depending on the nature of the benefit and the conduct of the defendant there may be liability for such offences as theft, obtaining by deception or blackmail.

2 Statutory offences of corruption

The Public Bodies Corrupt Practices Act 1889[55] creates offences of corruption in relation to public bodies. The offences are generally punishable by up to two years' imprisonment and a fine and other penalties such as civil reparation, disqualification from public office and forfeiture of pension rights.[56] Prosecutions can be brought only with the consent of the Attorney-General or Solicitor-General or, in Scotland, the Lord Advocate.[57] It is specifically provided that the invalidity of the appointment or election of a person to a public office shall be no defence[58] and an interpretation section defines various of the terms used in creating the offence.

The principal gap left by both the common law of bribery and the 1889 Act was the corruption of private agents. This gap was filled by the Prevention of Corruption Act 1906 which created offences punishable by up to two years' imprisonment and a fine.[59] While the main point of the 1906 Act is to cover corruption of private agents, there is an overlap with the 1889 Act as the agents of certain kinds of public authorities are also covered.[60] Prosecution may be brought in England[61] only with the consent of the Attorney-General or Solicitor-General. Information must be on oath.[62]

The third Act, the Prevention of Corruption Act 1916, creates no new substantive offence but increases the maximum penalty under the two earlier Acts where the corruption relates to contracts with the Crown, a government department or a public body[63] and creates a presumption of corruption in certain cases.[64] A time limit of six months is placed on summary proceedings under the 1906 Act[65] and the definitions of 'agent' and 'public body' under the earlier Acts are expanded. The result is that the overlap between the 1889 and 1906 Acts is expressly recognised and formalised.

While the overlap between the two earlier Acts is considerable it is not complete and so it is desirable to set out at least part of the definition of the offences under each of the Acts.

The Public Bodies Corrupt Practices Act 1889, s 1(1) provides that:

> 'Every person who shall by himself or by or in conjunction with any other person, corruptly solicit or receive or agree to receive for himself, or for any other person, any gift, loan, fee, reward, or advantage whatever as an inducement to, or reward for, or otherwise on account of any member, officer or servant of a public body as in this act defined, doing or forbearing to do anything in respect of any matter or transaction whatsoever, actual or proposed, in which the said public body is concerned, shall be guilty of a misdemeanour.'

Section 1(2) covers the converse case of the giver or offeror of the bribe.

The Prevention of Corruption Act 1906, s 1(1) provides that:

> 'If any agent corruptly accepts or obtains, or agrees to accept or attempts to obtain, from any person, for himself or for any other person, any gift or consideration as an inducement or reward for doing or forbearing to do, or for having after the passing of this Act done or forborne to do any act in relation to his principal's affairs or business, or for showing or forbearing to show favour or disfavour to any person in relation to his affairs or business . . . he shall be guilty of a misdemeanour.'

The subsection goes on to provide for the punishment of those who corruptly give, agree to give or offer any gift or consideration to agents in such circumstances.

These provisions raise questions of interpretation similar to those which arise from the common law definition of bribery. The same four matters discussed above will be examined in the context of these statutory offences.

(a) THE PERSON BRIBED

In the 1889 Act there is no limit on the nature of the person bribed but the bribe must relate to the conduct of a member, officer or servant of a public body. In the 1906 Act the person bribed must be an agent. As the 1906 provision is the wider one in most respects and the word 'agent' has received more judicial attention than the corresponding phrase in the 1889 Act, the meaning of 'agent' will be examined first and then the additional questions raised by the formulation in the 1889 Act will be discussed.

(i) The meaning of 'agent'

For the offence to be made out the recipient or intended recipient must be an agent. This term is in part defined in the Act itself. By s 1(2) 'agent' includes any person employed by or acting for another. Section 1(3) goes on to provide that:

> 'A person serving under the Crown or under any corporation or any [municipal],[66] borough, county or district council, or any board of guardians is an agent within the meaning of this Act.'

In 1916 the term 'agent' was widened to include a person serving under a public body.[67] The term 'public body' is defined in part by reference to the definition in the Public Bodies Corrupt Practices Act 1889 and includes in addition local and public authorities of all descriptions.[68] A quick whip through the statute book reveals that the 1889 Act[69] provides that public body:

> '. . . means any council of a county or county of a city or town, any council of a municipal borough, also any board, commissioners, select vestry or other body which has power to act under and for the purposes of any Act relating to local government, or the public health or to a poor law or otherwise to administer money raised by rates in pursuance of any public general Act[70] but does not include any public body as above defined existing elsewhere than in the United Kingdom.'

Finally, 'public body' includes the Civil Aviation Authority, by virtue of the Civil Aviation Act 1971, s 62(2).

The purpose of this complex and tortuous body of legislation seems to be to make it as clear as constant repetition can make it that those who serve under public authorities are to be regarded as agents. Section 4(2) of the 1916 Act had a rather higgledy-piggledy legislative history and emerged in its final form only after an amendment in the House of Lords,[71] introduced with little by way of explanation, was accepted without discussion by the House of Commons.[72] The 1916 provision gives the impression of having been rushed through rather than thought through. In the debate in the House of Lords on what became s 4(2) Lord Buckmaster, Lord Chancellor, pointed out that the reason for adding 'local and public authorities of all descriptions' to the list was to include such institutions as the Port of London Authority and the Water Board which were not strictly 'public bodies' as defined in the original 1889 Act. It would have been better to have left the reference to the 1889 Act out of s 4(2) altogether, not only for the sake of simplicity of expression and ease of reference, but also to foreclose any appeal to the eiusdem generis principle to cut down the scope of the Act. Such an appeal was successfully made in *R v Newbould*[73] where Winn J ruled at the Sheffield Assizes that the National Coal Board was not a public authority within the meaning of s 4(2). Happily this interpretation did not survive for long. Other trial judges[74] refused to follow it and in *DPP v Manners*[75] the House of Lords overruled *R v Newbould* and held that the North Thames Gas Board was a public authority within s 4(2). Lord Edmund Davies in particular endorsed the view that it was difficult to imagine wording that could have been wider than that in s 4(2).[76]

Though the spectre of the eiusdem generis rule has been exorcised from s 4(2), other questions remain. What for example is the position with regard to public bodies which exist outside the United Kingdom? Suppose an officer of an Australian local authority visits England in order to place a contract for materials required by the authority. Would a company which sought to gain the contract by bribery be liable under the Prevention of Corruption Act? The original definition of agent in s 1(3) of the 1906 Act seems wide enough to cover this situation. The incorporation of the definition of public body from the 1889 Act, however, though widening the definition of public authorities in some respects appears to have cut it down in relation to some kinds of authorities existing outside the United Kingdom, especially local authorities. But s 4(2) of the 1916 Act went on to add 'local and public authorities of all descriptions.' Since a foreign local authority is on the face of it within this part of the definition, there is an internal inconsistency. Did Parliament in 1916 intend to retain the exception relating to non-United Kingdom authorities or did it intend to remove it? No attention was paid to this matter when the Bill was debated.

As the exception works in favour of the liberty of the subject it will probably be held to have survived the addition of the wide words at the end of the definition but it stands as a singular anomaly, when neither private agents nor Crown servants enjoy any similar exemption.

While the complex definition of agency raises its own problems it also manages to leave a number of others unresolved.

First, does the definition extend to ex-agents? A reward given to a current agent is within the legislation but what if the agent has retired, resigned or been dismissed before the reward is given? This question has received the attention of the High Court of Australia in the context of the Secret Commissions Act 1905 (Cth) which provides inter alia that agent 'includes a person serving under the Crown.' By a majority the High Court in *R v Brewer*[77] held that the definition did not extend to ex-servants of the Crown. The differences between the United Kingdom and Australian definitions make it difficult to place much reliance on this case. However there is a sufficient similarity of wording between the Australian definition and that of the British provision to make the decision at least relevant in the United Kingdom. The presumption in favour of the liberty of the subject supports the majority view, but as even ex post facto rewards to ex-agents may have a potentially corrupting effect on the agents concerned in their later conduct or on other agents who may get to know of the rewards, there is something to be said for interpreting the legislation to include ex-agents.

Another problem left unresolved by the legislation is whether officials exercising independent functions can be regarded as agents. In *R v Barrett*,[78] D, an additional superintendent registrar of births, received money for arranging a marriage ceremony at an early date. He was charged with corruptly receiving money as a servant of the Crown. He argued that he was not a servant of the Crown because he was a person exercising an independent office, was paid not by the Crown but by a local authority and was not dismissible by the Crown. The Court of Appeal held that none of these considerations prevented D's being in the service of the Crown. The celebration of marriage was a matter of concern to the state and the duties of assistant superintendent registrar were performed on behalf of the Crown. The question was not whether D was employed by the Crown or employed by any other body but whether he was serving under the Crown.

Once 'serving under the Crown' is divorced from 'employed by the Crown', there seems no reason to require that the recipient should hold any continuing office. In other words, the fact that the recipient is performing an ad hoc single duty for the Crown should be enough to bring him within the definition of 'serving under the Crown' and thus of 'agent' for the purposes of s 1(3). This is fully in line with the common law position discussed above.[79]

Another important question is whether a police officer is an agent for the purpose of this legislation. The matter was considered in a Scottish case. In *Graham v Hart*,[80] D was charged with corruptly offering a consideration to a police officer. The case for the prosecution was that the officer was an agent of the Chief Constable. The Court of Justiciary held that this was correct. The fact that the conduct might have been bribery at common law or under another Act was not to the point, and the court refused to be influenced by civil law cases holding that a police officer is not a servant for the purpose of vicarious liability. A different view has been taken obiter in New South Wales[81] but the Scottish case seems correct in principle.

If, as seems appropriate, a police officer is to be considered an agent for the purpose of this legislation, the question arises whether a judge is also to come within the definition. In another Scottish case, *Copeland v Johnson*,[82] sheriff substitute Dickson held that a member of a licensing court was not an agent in this context. In favour of this view it can be argued that judges are agents of the law rather than of any identifiable principal and that their independence distinguishes them from other servants or agents. Whatever the force of these arguments in other contexts, however, it does not seem desirable that judges or those who bribe them should be protected from this legislation. For the purpose of the law of corruption a judge should be regarded as in the service of the Crown. As in the case of a policeman the fact that a judge is not a servant for other branches of the law should not influence the question whether he is an agent for the purpose of this offence.

An agent may have more than one principal and the fact that he may be acting predominantly for one does not mean that he may not be charged with an offence in relation to another principal. In *Morgan v DPP*,[83] D was both an inspector in a car company and a trade union official. In the latter role he solicited money from a person who had been blacked by the union and who wished to resume work for the car company. D was charged with the offence as agent of the car company. He appealed against conviction on the ground that he was acting as agent of the union. The Divisional Court held that the words 'in relation to his principal's affairs' were to be widely construed[84] and that though the act was done in relation to the union's affairs it was also done in relation to the company's. Similarly in *R v Gallagher*,[85] the Victorian Full Court held that an official of an incorporated trade union could be an agent both of the union and of all or some of its members.

The reference to persons in the definition makes it clear that both corporations and unincorporated bodies like partnerships or firms are capable of being agents.[86] What is less clear is whether a member of the governing body of a corporation or other institution is an agent of that body. Under New South Wales, Victorian, Queensland and Western Australian legislation,[87] it is expressly provided that a member of the governing body of a corporation is such an agent. In *Leary v Cohan*[88] it was held that local government aldermen were agents under the New South Wales Secret Commissions Prohibition Act but Studdart AD, CJ took the view obiter that members of a governing body were not agents within the usual meaning of the word.

The legislation does not expressly deal with purported agents but these are probably impliedly covered. There is some authority to suggest that if A purports to act as the agent of P, A is estopped from denying the agency.[89] The cases are not entirely clear on the point but the principle is firmly established in American law.[90] In *State v Pohlmeyer*,[91] D was charged with embezzlement as agent of a corporation. He claimed that his appointment was invalid. The Supreme Court of Ohio held that one who receives money in the assumed exercise of authority as agent is estopped from denying the agency in both civil and criminal proceedings.

(ii) Any member, officer or servant of a public body

Though there is no limit on the kind of person who may be the recipient of the bribe, the bribe must relate to the conduct of a member, officer or servant of a public body. As a person serving under a public body is also an agent most cases of bribery under the 1889 Act will be covered by the 1906 Act offence, which also extends to agents or private individuals or bodies. But it is possible that the 1889 Act is wider than the 1906 one in some respects and may fill some of the gaps left by the definition of 'agent'. The problem relating to the agents of foreign authorities is the same under both Acts but other problems may receive a different solution. First there should be no difficulty in convicting for rewards given after an agency has terminated.[92] Suppose D1, an officer of a local authority, influences a decision which creates a large financial gain for D2. If after D1 retires, resigns or is dismissed from his post, D2 pays D1 a substantial sum of money as a reward for his part in the decision, the crime would appear to have been committed. D1 would have received and D2 have given a reward for doing something in which the public body is concerned.[93] There is no requirement that at the time the reward is paid the recipient should be a current officer (or member or servant) of the public body.

The second gap partly closed by the formulation in the 1889 Act is that relating to members of governing bodies. There is a suggestion that these are not agents[94] but so far as public bodies are concerned, members, eg councillors, are expressly covered.

The other possible gap in the meaning of 'agent', that relating to judges, is not filled by the 1889 formulation. If a judge is not an agent of the Crown[95] he is certainly not a member, officer or servant of a public body, wide though the latter concept may be. Finally it would seem that police officers,[96] people exercising independent judgment[97] and those acting in more than one capacity[98] are capable of falling within the formulation of the 1889 offence.

(b) THE NATURE OF THE BRIBE

Under the 1906 Act the bribe must take the form of 'gift or consideration'. Consideration is defined as including valuable consideration of any kind.[99] There is something of a contractual flavour about the word 'consideration'[100] and it could be argued that the phrase 'valuable consideration' has its whole contractual meaning so that an illegal, void or unenforceable promise would not be sufficient.[101] But the better view is that the phrase 'gift or consideration' as a whole simply means something of value (or assumed to be of value) to the person bribed so that, for example, a promise of sexual favours or criminal services would be within the phrase.[102] The word 'includes' in the definition also supports this view.

There is no reason why the term valuable consideration should be restricted to substantial consideration in the sense used in bankruptcy matters.[103] The smaller the gift or consideration, however, the more difficult it is to prove the link between the gift and the favour.[104]

The bribe is also described in wide terms in the 1889 Act. It may take the form of a gift, loan, fee, reward or advantage.[105] This seems to cover much the same ground as that in the 1906 Act.

(c) THE MEANING OF 'CORRUPTION'

The most difficult question under the 1889 and 1906 Acts is the meaning of 'corruption'. The main questions are whether the word adds anything to the remainder of the formulation of the offence, and if so, what it is that it adds. The cases on these questions are in impressive disarray.

The problem has arisen under corruption legislation in England and similar legislation in the Australian States. This legislation was designed to cover the same kind of conduct though in each State it was given the name 'Secret Commissions Prohibition Act'.[106]

Inspiration will accordingly be sought from both English and Australian law.

The starting point is *Cooper v Slade*.[107] The Corrupt Practices Prevention Act 1854, s 2, declared guilty of bribery 'every person who shall . . . give or promise money . . . to any voter in order to induce any voter to vote or refrain from voting . . . or shall corruptly do any such act as aforesaid on account of any voter having voted or refrained from voting.' The meaning of 'corruptly' was considered by the House of Lords. In the course of advice to the House, Willes J[108] stated his opinion that the word 'corruptly' did not mean dishonestly but purposely doing an act which the law forbids as tending to corrupt voters whether by giving a pecuniary inducement to vote or a reward for having voted in a particular manner. His Lordship further observed that the word 'corruptly' was used as a designation of the act of rewarding a man for having voted in a particular way rather than as part of the definition of the offence. Coleridge J dissented.[109] In the House of Lords itself, Lord Cranworth[110] said that he could not give the word 'corruptly', as used in the statute, referring to a payment after voting, any other meaning than a payment in violation of that which the statute was passed to prohibit. Lord Wensleydale[111] found difficulty in understanding the meaning of 'corruptly' as used in the statute. He took the view that the statute was not limited to payment after a promise previously made but covered a payment without previous promise. With some hesitation his Lordship put forward the view that if a man gave money to a voter as a reward for having voted for him, that being the moving cause of the vote, it must be a corrupt payment.

It seems then that while Lord Cranworth supported the view of Willes J in regarding the word 'corruptly' as a description rather than an ingredient, Lord Wensleydale did attempt to give the word some independent content. The whole discussion is obiter, however, because on the facts there was an antecedent promise to pay and any payment made afterwards was clearly a corrupt payment.

Willes J's view in *Cooper v Slade* was followed without further elucidation by Blackburn J in the *Bewdley Case*.[112] But in the same year in the *Bradford Case (No 2)*,[113] Martin B held that some meaning had to be given to the word 'corruptly' and that it involved an evil mind. This suggests that some additional element, like dishonesty, is involved.

The last three cases were concerned with offences in the context of elections. A link between dishonesty and secret commissions was forged by the Court of Appeal in a civil case, *Bulfield v Fournier*.[114] An agent unsuccessfully sued his principal for breach of contract. The principal had dismissed the agent for receiving secret commissions. In dismissing the agent's application for a new trial, the Court of Appeal held that the taking of a secret commission was dishonest and absolutely contrary to law.[115] A somewhat different approach was taken by the Court of Criminal Appeal in *R v Evans-Jones, R v Jenkins*.[116] In proceedings under the Prevention of Corruption Acts 1906 and 1916, the judge told the jury that if they were satisfied that the payments were honestly made they should acquit. The main question for the Court of Criminal Appeal was the correctness of the direction on the burden of proof. The court upheld the direction on that point but made no suggestion that the reference to dishonesty was too favourable to the accused.

A case which raised the question of dishonesty more squarely and gave 'corruptly' some content is *R v Lindley*.[117] L was charged with corruptly giving gifts of money to servants of a company contrary to s 1(1) of the Prevention of Corruption Act 1906. Pearce J told the jury that L must have dishonestly intended to weaken the loyalty of the servants to their master and transfer that loyalty from the master to the giver. While this case establishes a link between corruption and dishonesty it raises the question of what is meant by 'dishonesty'. It is apparently not all intentions to weaken loyalty which are to be regarded as corrupt. What then is the additional factor which enables a line to be drawn? Is it to be left to the unfettered discretion of the jury or magistrates' court? Despite these difficulties Pearce J's approach was followed by Veale J in *R v Calland*.[118] C, an inspector of a life assurance company, was charged with corruptly offering an agent of the Ministry of Social Security a reward of £30 per month for information about the parents of new born children. Veale J directed the jury that corruption meant dishonestly trying to wheedle an agent away from his loyalty to his employer. The learned judge distinguished between sharp practice and dishonesty. The jury acquitted the accused.

Yet another view was taken by the Court of Appeal in *R v Smith.*[119] The court referred to the division of opinion between Willes J and Coleridge J in *Cooper v Slade*[120] and observed that the wording of the Prevention of Corruption Act was different from that in the Corrupt Practices Prevention Act 1854. The court held that it was wrong to say that the word 'corruptly' could not be given some meaning additional to what was provided by the words of the section without it.[121] On the other hand the court approved the view of Willes J that 'corruptly' did not mean dishonestly but purposely doing an act which the law forbids as tending to corrupt. Corruption meant putting public servants into a position where they were subject to temptation. This case was followed in *R v Wellburn*[122] where the Court of Appeal expressly disapproved *R v Lindley* and *R v Calland* and approved the direction of the recorder that corruptly did not mean dishonestly but purposely doing an act which the law forbids as tend to corrupt. Though the court said that the mischief aimed at by the legislation was to prevent agents and public servants from being put into positions of temptation, it did not insist that this aim should be explained to juries.

The position in English law is hardly satisfactory. Despite the constant approval given to passages in the judgment of Willes J in *Cooper v Slade*, the word 'corruptly' is not seen as merely descriptive but as having an independent role to play. On the other hand it does not mean dishonestly and judges are not to give further guidance on the content of the expression. In *R v Wellburn* the Court of Appeal took the view that juries would have no difficulty in deciding whether a gift had been received corruptly.[123] Given the divergence of opinion on whether it means anything at all, this assessment seems unduly optimistic.

In Australia some cases have taken a different direction. In *R v Stevenson*,[124] S, the representative of a firm which supplied paint, gave sums of money to the foreman of a hospital to induce him to recommend the firm's paint to other hospitals. S pointed out that it was a rule with his firm to pay gratuities but conceded that this was not reputable. Hood J asked the Crown Prosecutor what he thought 'corruptly' meant. The Crown Prosecutor adopted the definition of Blackburn J in the *Bewdley Case* and added 'an act is corrupt if it is one which violates the prohibition of the Act.' In reply Hood J observed that this would make the word meaningless, which could not be correct, and that 'corrupt' must mean some wrongful intention. When it came to directing the jury, however, the learned judge equated corruption with an intent to influence the agent to show favour. But the Secret Commissions Prohibition Act 1906 (Vic) contained the words 'as an inducement or reward' in addition to the word 'corruptly'. The words 'as an inducement' are sufficient in themselves to require an intention to influence. If the word 'corruptly' adds anything it must be an element beyond the intention to influence. On the facts of the case some defence of mistake of law might have been open to the accused S. He appears to have been aware of the dubious morality[125] of the gifts but the general tenor of his remarks is that he did not regard the practice as illegal. While mistake of law is not generally a defence it may negative a mens rea involving dishonesty, and in his dissenting opinion in *Cooper v Slade*[126] Coleridge J seems to have recognised that mistake of law would negative corruption. Again, if Hood J had been prepared to go as far as the judges in *R v Lindley*[127] and *R v Calland*,[128] S might have expected a more favourable direction since it was arguable that he did not intend to wheedle the agent away from his loyalty to his employer beyond such wheedling as is implicit in the attempt to influence. In the event the jury acquitted S which suggests that they may have taken a different view of corruption from Hood J since the facts were not in dispute.[129]

The problem arose again in a different way in *C v Johnson.*[130] C, a land salesman, was convicted of an offence under s 5 of the Secret Commissions Prohibition Act 1920 (SA) and was disqualified by the Land Agents Board on the ground that he had been convicted of an offence involving dishonesty. The question was thus directly raised whether corruption in the 1920 Act involved dishonesty. The Supreme Court of South Australia (in banco) unanimously held that it did. Bray CJ[131] said '. . . an offence against section 5(a) of the Secret Commissions Prohibition Act 1920 necessarily involves dishonesty and . . . a man who acts corruptly within the meaning of that section necessarily acts dishonestly.' The learned Chief Justice then defined dishonesty to mean 'dishonesty according to normally received standards of honest conduct.' A defendant's belief that the conduct was honest would not be enough.[132] Chamberlain J agreed that corruption involved dishonesty but saw dishonesty as the intention of an agent to take advantage of his relationship with his principal to secure some benefit to himself or some other person without the knowledge of his principal.[133] Hogarth J agreed that corruption involved dishonesty but did not indicate what he understood by this latter term.[134]

Finally, there was some discussion of the meaning of 'corruption' in a repealed version of s 73 of the Crimes Act 1914 (Cth) by the Federal Court of Australia in *Williams v R.*[135] That section was concerned with bribery rather than secret commissions but the court took the view that 'corruption' had strong connotations of misconduct and dereliction of duty and implied an intention to procure breach of duty on the part of the official bribed.[136] This approach could be adopted in the Prevention of Corruption legislation but it was based on a view of the common law which was probably too narrow.[137]

Not all Australian cases attempt to find an additional element of dishonesty in the requirement of corruption. In *R v Dillon,*[138] Brooking J followed the approach in *R v Wellburn*[139] and held that an agent acts corruptly if he receives a benefit in the belief that the giver intends that it should influence him to show favour in relation to the principal's affairs. This view was endorsed by the Full Court of Victoria in *R v Gallagher.*[140] The Court accepted the view in *C v Johnson*[141] that corruption involved dishonesty but observed that the quality of the act did not ipso facto determine the elements necessary to constitute the criminal offence. This comes close to Willes J's treatment of corruption in *Cooper v Slade,*[142] and denies any independent role for the word 'corruptly'.

The result is that Australian courts are just as divided on the meaning of corruptly as those in England. They do however provide some pointers towards a solution. Some of the difficulties of finding an independent part for the word 'corruption' to play can be overcome if the purpose of the legislation is considered. While the 1906 statute is called the *Prevention of Corruption Act* it is clear that it was intended to be directed against secret commissions. When the legislation was first presented to Parliament it had the title 'Illicit Secret Commissions Bill 1899'[143] and even when the later versions of the Bill were renamed, the debates made constant reference to secret commissions.[144] Then in the 1906 debates on the Bill, the Attorney-General, Sir John Walton, expressly linked corruption with the element of secrecy.[145] It has also been noted that the Australian legislation passed at much the same time and in largely similar terms with a deep interest in the progress of the British legislation was passed under the title *Secret Commissions Prohibition Act.*[146] Though the word 'secret' appears in the title, headnotes and sidenotes it does not feature in the body of the section where its place is taken by the word 'corruptly'.

In the Australian context the link between secrecy and corruption has been expressly recognised in *C v Johnson*[147] where Bray CJ observed that if the word 'corruptly' were not in s 5 of the Secret Commissions Prohibition Act 1920 (SA) it might be an offence for an agent to solicit a commission even with the consent and approval of the principal.[148] This at least partly solves the problem of giving the word 'corruptly' an independent part to play, though it opens up a range of other questions.

If the principal knows about and consents to the transaction and the giver and receiver know of that consent, the transaction is not corrupt. But as corruption is part of the mens rea it should be enough that the defendant believes the facts to be such that the transaction is not secret, in other words that the transaction has the consent of the principal. If corruption involves dishonesty, a mistake of fact which negatives dishonesty is a good defence.[149] Even if the narrower view of Willes J in *Cooper v Slade*[150] is adopted, in this instance the result will be the same. If 'corruptly' means 'purposely doing an act which the law forbids as tending to corrupt', then in the context of secret commissions legislation that means purposely offering or accepting a secret commission, as opposed to an open commission which is not regarded as unlawful or corrupting.

More troublesome is the question whether mistake of law negatives corruption. The general rule is that mistake of law is no defence.[151] But where dishonesty is an element of the offence a claim of right is a good defence even if based on mistake of law.[152] If therefore corruption involves dishonesty mistake of law is arguably a good defence. The problem could arise in a number of ways, eg the defendant may believe that the consent obtained from a director of a company is in law the consent of the company. Alternatively the defendant may believe that it is lawful to reward agents who have helped him. While the insistence of the Australian courts that corruption involves dishonesty might provide a defence, the courts have not pushed the logic that far. As noted earlier in *R v Stevenson*[153] Hood J made no attempt to put the defence of mistake of law to the jury, though that course would have been consistent with his approach to the meaning of 'corruptly'. In a case decided the same year, *R v Scott*,[154] the defendant was charged under the Secret Commissions Prohibition Act 1905 (Vic) with corruptly giving a valuable consideration. He asserted that he was quite unconscious of having committed any offence. Cussen J told the jury that mistake of law was no defence. It seems however from the discussion during argument that Cussen J was influenced by the view of Blackburn J in the *Bewdley Case*,[155] that corruption did not involve wickedness. For this reason the relationship between dishonesty and mistake of law did not fall to be decided.[156]

Entrapment presents problems under the relationship between corruption and dishonesty. In *R v Smith*[157] a would be trapper was found guilty of corruption under the Public Bodies Corrupt Practices Act. In that case the court rejected the view that corruption involved dishonesty. But if a trapper attempts to influence a public servant in order to bring him to justice and succeeds in the attempt, the public servant has been corrupted. Is it entirely clear that the trapper is not dishonest in these circumstances? Does it make any difference in the case of a private agent that the trapper acts with the consent of the principal, or in either case that the trapper is a police officer or acts under the direction of the police. The substitution of the word 'dishonestly' for 'corruption' gives no clear guidance on these problems. Instead of asking whether entrapment is honest or not it is better to confront the problem directly and as in the case of bribery[158] recognise that active[159] instigation is unlawful unless carried out by the police or other enforcement agencies with due regard for the need to avoid oppression.

The Prevention of Corruption Act 1916, s 2, raises a presumption of corruption where the money, gift or other consideration has been paid or given to or received by a person employed by the Crown or a public body by or from a person holding or seeking to obtain a contract with the Crown or public body. While a useful evidentiary tool for the prosecution this provision does not solve the problems of the meaning of corruption. The presumption, unlike its civil law counterpart,[160] is not conclusive.[161] Any substantive role which recognises that a commission may not be corrupt is left intact.

As in the case of bribery, it is no defence for the agent to assert that he did not intend to act in consequence of the secret commission. In *R v Dillon*,[162] the agent argued that, as he had no intention of showing any favour to the giver, he was not acting corruptly. Brooking J held that this was no defence and that if the defendant believed that the giver intended to influence him to show favour in relation to the principal's affairs or business, he acted corruptly.

(d) MUTUALITY

The discussion of this problem under 'Bribery'[163] is applicable here.

Conclusion

The above examination of the law of bribery and corruption reveals a considerable degree of complexity and overlap. The inclusion of this subject in the list proposed for Pt II of the Criminal Code[164] makes the area ripe for restatement. While there are a few matters to resolve, the common law offence is relatively straightforward and could perhaps be left to develop at common law under the rubric of a fairly general provision in the Code. The main doubt relates to entrapment which could be met by giving a chief officer of police a power to authorise the offer of an inducement where there is reasonable ground to believe that the offeree has been guilty of accepting bribes in the past.

The main need for reform or at least restatement is in the area of statutory corruption. There is no good reason for having two separate statutory schemes. Most of the 1889 Act is now superfluous. Secondly, the definition of 'agent' cries out for simplification. It may be questioned whether the statute should cover governmental agents at all as the law of bribery covers this field. If it is desirable to include agents of public authorities this could be done by a vastly simpler provision than those which set out the present law. The other aspect of statutory corruption which requires treatment is the definition of corruption itself. There is a good case for saying that the central element of corruption in the case of private agents is the absence of the consent (or possibly the knowledge) of the principal. If this is made explicit many of the problems should melt away.

NOTES

1 Codification of the Criminal Law. A Report of the Law Commission (Law Com no 143), p 162.
2 See Archbold *Pleading and Evidence in Criminal Cases* (19th edn, 1878), p 891 and (20th edn, 1886), p 945.
3 Representation of the People Act 1983, s 113.
4 *A Treatise of Crimes and Misdemeanours*, Vol 1, p 223 (4th edn, 1865). The 12th edition states the definition more narrowly and less satisfactorily: Vol 1, p 381; see also *Hawkins* 1 PC, Chap 67, s 1; *Coke* 3 Inst 145.
5 3 Inst 145.
6 1 PC, Chap 67, s 1.
7 *R v Bacon* (1620) 2 State Tr 1087; *R v Earl of Macclesfield* (1725) 16 State Tr 767.
8 *Thorpe's Case Coke* 3 Inst 145.
9 *R v Vaughan* (1769) 4 Burr 2494. See also *R v Pollman* (1809) 2 Camp 229.
10 See *Coke* 3 Inst 145; *R v White* (1875) 13 SCR (NSW) 322.
11 [1914] 3 KB 1283. See also *R v White* (1875) 13 SCR (NSW) 322 (bribing an MP) and *R v Boston* (1923) 33 CLR 386.
12 [1914] 3 K B 1283.
13 Ibid at 1296.
14 (1960) 2 WIR 450. See also *R v Gurney* (1867) 10 Cox CC 550 (bribery of a JP).
15 (1762) 3 Burr 1335. See also *R v Lancaster and Worrall* (1890) 16 Cox CC 737 (bribery of local government electors).
16 Eg *Pomfriet v Brownsal* (1600) Cro Eliz 735; *Bradley and Jones' Case* (1613) Godb 240; *Jepps v Turnbridge and Wiseman* (1611) Moore KB 815.
17 Ibid.
18 *R v Owen* [1976] 1 WLR 840, CA.
19 Cf Russell (n 4 above), 'official situation'.
20 *HM Advocate v Dick* 1901 3 F (Ct of Sess) 59.
21 1901 3 F (Ct of Sess) 59 at 64.
22 140 P 164 (1914) (Criminal Court of Appeals of Oklahoma).
23 See n 4 above.
24 141 NE 19 (1923); see also *US v Girard* 601 F 2d 69 (1979) at 71. *Zalla v State* 61 So 2d 649 (1952) (promise of illegal lottery tickets).
25 3 Inst 145.
26 (1869) 1 O'M & H 117 *Election Cases* 124–5.
27 1978 (3) SA 302.
28 Ibid at 311.
29 Ibid.
30 See Representation of the People Act 1983, s 114.
31 [1959] VR 794.
32 Above, n 4.
33 *S v Deal Enterprises (Pty) Ltd* 1978 (3) SA 302, 308 (per Nicholas J).
34 Ibid.
35 (1979) 23 ALR 369.
36 At 373.
37 (1867) 10 Cox CC 550. See also *R v Wellburn* (1979) 69 Cr App Rep 254 (on the meaning of corruption under s 1 of the Prevention of Corruption Act 1906); *R v Boston* (1923) 33 CLR 386; *R v Patel* 1944 AD 511; *S v Deal Enterprises (Pty) Ltd* 1978 (3) SA 302; *S v Van Der Westhuizen* 1974 (4) SA 61.
38 1901 3 F (Ct of Sess) 59. See also *R v Botile* 1960 (1) SA 862.

39 [1931] QWN 2.
40 [1980] AC 663, PC. See also *R v Patel* 1944 AD 511.
41 1974 (4) SA 61. See also *R v Dillon* [1982] VR 434 (secret commission).
42 1963 (3) SA 666.
43 1963 (3) SA 666.
44 1964 (2) SA 385. See also *S v Nkadimeng* 1962 (4) SA 564.
45 [1960] 2 QB 423.
46 *Criminal Law* (2nd edn 1978), p 1012.
47 Above, n 4. See also *Gorman v R* (1944) 45 WALR 80.
48 1960 (4) SA 638.
49 198 SW 883 (1917); see also *People v Lyons* 122 NE 2d 809 (1954); *S v Nkadimeng* 1962 (4) SA 564; *S v Gouws* 1975 (1) SA 1.
50 If the trapper is himself guilty of an offence the problem does not arise.
51 1953 (2) SA 398. See also *R v Durga* 1952 (4) SA 619; *R v Mithi* 1959 (4) SA 287; *S v Pillay* 1964 (2) SA 385; *S v Mbokatwane* 1970 (3) SA 64.
52 (1960) 2 WIR 450.
53 Ibid at 453.
54 (1783) 3 Doug KB 327. See also *R v Llewellyn-Jones* [1968] 1 QB 429; *R v Jones* [1946] VLR 300.
55 S 1.
56 S 2, as amended: see Criminal Justice Act 1967, s 92(8).
57 S 4.
58 S 3.
59 S 1, as amended: see Criminal Justice Act 1967, s 92(8).
60 S 1(3).
61 S 2(1).
62 S 2(3).
63 S 1.
64 S 2.
65 S 3.
66 The word 'municipal' was removed in 1974: Local Authorities Miscellaneous Provisions (No 2) Order 1974 (SI 1974 No 595) Sch 1, Pt 1.
67 Prevention of Corruption Act 1916, s 4(3).
68 Ibid, s 4(2).
69 S 7.
70 See *R v Gilbertson* (1899) 129 CC Ct Cas 372.
71 See 23 Official Report (5th series) Col 987.
72 88 Official Report (5th series) Col 1566.
73 [1962] 2 QB 102.
74 See *R v Joy and Emmony* (1974) 60 Cr App Rep 132 (Judge Rigg QC) and *R v Hirst and McNamee* (1975) 64 Cr App Rep 151.
75 [1978] AC 43.
76 Ibid at 54.
77 (1942) 66 CLR 535.
78 [1976] 1 WLR 946, CA.
79 NS 15–19.
80 1908 SC (J) 26. See also *R v Harris* (1927) 48 NLR 330 at 347.
81 *R v Keane* (1929) 30 SR (NSW) 63 at 65, per Ferguson ACJ: *Hole v Gibb* (1943) 60 WN (NSW) 130 at 132, per Maxwell J.
82 1967 SLT (Sh Ct) 28.
83 [1970] 3 All ER 1053.
84 Following *R v Dickinson* (1948) 33 Cr App Rep 5 at 9.
85 [1986] VR 219. G's appeal was allowed on other grounds.
86 Interpretation Act 1978, Sch 1.
87 Secret Commissions Prohibition Act 1919 (NSW), s 2; Crimes Act 1958 (Vic), s 175; Queensland Code, s 442A; WA Code, s 546.
88 (1940) 14 LGR 142 (NSW).
89 1 Halsbury's *Laws of England* (4th edn) p 434.
90 CJS Vol 2A, pp 637–8.
91 52 NE 1027 (1899). See also *State v Kearne* 129 NE 2d 547 (1955).
92 Cf n 77, above.
93 See *R v Andrews Wetherfoil Ltd* [1972] 1 All ER 65, CA.

94 See n 87, above.
95 Cf n 82, above.
96 Cf ns 80–81, above.
97 Cf n 78, above.
98 Cf n 83, above.
99 1906 Act, s 1(2).
100 *R v Braithwaite* [1983] 1 WLR 385 and 973, CA.
101 See *State v Walls* (1876) 54 Ind 561; *Nerot v Wallace* (1789) 3 Term Rep 17 at 23.
102 Cf *State v Scott* 141 NE 19 (1923) and discussion of the common law above.
103 As to which see Cavanough 'Dispositions before bankruptcy: meaning of "valuable consideration" ' (1984) 58 Law Inst J 492; Fletcher *Law of Bankruptcy* (1978), p 203.
104 Cf *Woodward v Maltby* [1959] VR 794.
105 As defined in s 7.
106 Victoria enacted such legislation in 1905 (see now Crimes Act 1958, s 176); Western Australia followed Victoria's lead in the same year (see now Code ss 529 and 530). Tasmania came third in 1906 (see now Code, s 266). The other states came into line rather later: New South Wales in 1919, South Australia in 1920 and Queensland in 1931 (see now Code, S 1 442B).
107 (1858) 6 HL Cas 746.
108 Ibid at 773.
109 Ibid at 785.
110 Ibid at 788.
111 Ibid at 790.
112 (1869) 19 LT 676 at 678. See also *S v Deal Enterprises (Pty) Ltd* 1978 3 SA 302; affd 1981 (4) SA 29.
113 (1869) 19 LT 723 at 728.
114 (1895) 11 TLR 282. See also *R v Brown* (1956) 116 CCC 287; *87; R v Gross* [1946] OR 1.
115 See also the view expressed by Isaacs AG during the debate on the Secret Commissions Bill (Cth) 1905 Australian Official Report, Vol XXVII, p 3290.
116 (1923) 17 Cr App Rep 121.
117 [1957] Crim LR 321.
118 [1967] Crim LR 236.
119 [1960] 2 QB 423.
120 Above, ns 42–44.
121 Ibid at 429.
122 (1979) 69 Cr App Rep 254. The approach in *R v Wellburn* was followed by Brooking J in *R v Dillon* [1982] VR 434. See also *R v Parker* [1985] Crim LR 589, CA (reward for past favour).
123 Ibid at 265. See also *US v Pommerening* 500 F 2d 92 (1974).
124 [1907] VLR 475.
125 Compare Veale J's reference to sharp practice in *R v Calland* [1967] Crim LR 236.
126 (1857) 6 HL Cas 746 at 785.
127 [1957] Crim LR 321.
128 [1967] Crim LR 236.
129 [1907] VLR 475 at 476.
130 [1967] SASR 279.
131 Ibid at 291.
132 Ibid.
133 Ibid at 301.
134 Ibid at 302.
135 (1979) 23 ALR 369.
136 Ibid at 373.
137 See ns 36–37, above.
138 [1982] VR 434.
139 (1979) 69 Cr App Rep 254, above, n 57.
140 [1986] VR 219. G's appeal was allowed on other grounds.
141 [1967] SASR 279, above, ns 65–69.
142 (1858) 6 HL Cas 746, above, ns 42–3.
143 70 Official Report (4th series) col 13.
144 See eg 109 Official Report (4th series) col 224; 119 Official Report (4th series) col 237; 161 Official Report (4th series) cols 149 and 152. See also 152 Official Report (4th series) col 1319 (Parliamentary question).
145 161 Official Report (4th series) cols 152 et seq.
146 See n 105, above.

147 [1967] SASR 279 at 291.

148 A further point of interest if not direct influence is that the Commonwealth Secret Commissions Act 1905, s 4, avoids the word 'corruptly' and contains instead the phrase 'without the knowledge and full consent of the principal.'

149 *R v Bernhard* [1938] 2 KB 264, CCA.

150 (1858) 6 HL Cas 746 at 773.

151 *R v Esop* (1836) 7 C & P 456; *Thomas v R* (1937) 59 CLR 279; *Iannella v French* (1968) 119 CLR 84.

152 Eg *R v Hall* (1828) 2 C & P 409; *R v Bernhard* [1938] 2 KB 264; *Wilson v Inyang* [1951] 2 KB 799.

153 [1907] VLR 475.

154 [1907] VLR 471.

155 (1869) 19 LT 676.

156 See also the conflicts of opinion on claim of right in *R v Brown* (1956) 116 CCC 287; for Canadian law generally, see Read 'Secret Commissions' (1984) 26 Crim LQ 182.

157 [1960] 2 QB 423.

158 See section I(c) above.

159 Merely pretending to take part in response to an initiative by the other party does not corrupt and so is not illegal: *Leary v Cohan* (1940) 14 LGR 142 (NSW); *R v Cobcroft* (1966) 85 WN (Pt 1) NSW 608. In both cases the legality of the entrapment was assumed sub silentio.

160 See *Industries and General Mortgage Co Ltd v Lewis* [1949] 2 All ER 573.

161 The defendant must disprove corruption on a preponderance of probability: *R v Carr-Briant* [1943] KB 607.

162 [1982] VR 434. See also *R v Mills* (1978) 68 Cr App Rep 154 at 158–9; *R v Carr* (1956) 40 Cr App Rep 188 at 189.

163 Above, section I(d).

164 See n 1, above.

The defence of absence of fault in Australasia and Canada

Gerald Orchard

It has long been a theme of critics of strict liability that it should be replaced by liability for negligence.[1] This would avoid the conviction of those who are blameless, while giving as much effect as is practicable to the apparent object of the legislation, that care be taken to ensure the prevention or avoidance of the proscribed conduct, events or situations.

Of course, in many instances the law gives effect to such a principle. In respect of particular offences legislation often provides a defence in the nature of absence of fault, although it is sometimes confined to particular kinds of case (for example, when the offence was caused by a third person), and some of these provisions have invited and have received a strict construction.[2] Even in the absence of a relevant statutory defence, the courts have recognised that liability for the breach of unqualified duties or prohibitions imposed by regulatory legislation might be excluded if the prohibited event is caused by the act of a third person, or some other occurrence which D could not reasonably foresee or control, and in respect of which D was not at fault.[3] There have also been occasional cases where such legislation has been held to impose no liability if D's conduct contravened the statute only because of circumstances resulting from the unknown conduct of another over whom D had no control,[4] or, more generally, if D was not negligent.[5] Moreover, the likelihood that holding an offence to be one of strict liability would lead to liability on the part of a class of persons who are unable to take effective steps to prevent offences is an important factor suggesting that strict liability was probably not intended.[6]

In addition, on a number of occasions judges have acknowledged the undesirability of imposing liability on those who were without fault, and have attributed the need for strict liability to the difficulty of proving subjective mens rea, or the inadequacy of that as a measure of responsibility. Possible alternatives which have been alluded to have included placing the burden of proving absence of mens rea on D, and the imposition of liability for negligence (with or without a reversal of the burden of proof).[7] English courts, however, have not developed a general principle allowing absence of negligence as a ground of exculpation, and the possibility was ignored when the House of Lords had the opportunity of reviewing this area of the law in *Pharmaceutical Society of Great Britain v Storkwain Ltd*.[8]

Courts in some other common law jurisdictions have gone further in fashioning general principles designed to minimise the incidence of criminal liability without fault, and it is the purpose of this essay to examine the position which has been reached in Australia, Canada and New Zealand. Although there are some important differences, the principles developed in these three countries are similar. In particular, in each jurisdiction the courts have recognised that, although the legislation may be ambiguous or silent as to any requirement of mens rea or fault, an offence may fall within one of three categories: it may be an offence for which the prosecution is required to prove mens rea, it may be an offence in relation to which due diligence or reasonable mistake may exculpate D, or it may be an offence of 'absolute' liability. These categories provide a convenient framework for considering the law, which will be used here, but in one respect they may be misleading. The courts commonly assign offences to one category or another, but in reality an offence will often belong to more than one of the categories: mens rea may have to be proved in respect of some of the physical ingredients of the offence, but in respect of others there may be the possibility of a defence of absence of negligence, or there may be absolute liability.[9] As to terminology, offences in the first of these classes are commonly called mens rea offences, those in the intermediate class, offences of strict liability, and those in the third class, offences of absolute liability.

1 Offences requiring proof of mens rea

In *R v City of Sault Ste Marie*,[10] the leading Canadian authority, Dickson J described the first category of offence as consisting of:

> 'Offences in which mens rea, consisting of some positive state of mind such as intent, knowledge, or recklessness, must be proved by the prosecution either as an inference from the nature of the act committed, or by additional evidence.'

This includes all offences where a positive state of mind is an ingredient because the statutory definition includes a term such as 'wilfully', 'knowingly', or 'intentionally', and, in the absence of some clear statutory indication to the contrary, the rule in Canada is that it also includes every offence which is 'criminal in the true sense'. In these cases there is a presumption that negligence is not sufficient, and that it is an essential ingredient of the offence that the prohibited act was done ' . . . intentionally or recklessly, with knowledge of the facts constituting the offence, or with wilful blindness towards them.'[11] In New Zealand and Australia it is also now accepted that such a state of mind is ordinarily required for serious crime, unless there is good reason for supposing that the contrary was intended.[12] Where such a state of mind is an ingredient of an offence D will be entitled to acquittal if it was absent, even if this was the result of some mistake or ignorance for which there were no reasonable grounds.[13]

As it is an ingredient of the offence, the relevant state of mind must be proved by the prosecution beyond reasonable doubt, unless there is a statutory provision to the contrary. In most cases, however, proof of the prohibited conduct will provide sufficient evidence from which the requisite mens rea may be inferred, although this must depend on the nature of the conduct and the circumstances of each case.[14] But in New Zealand there is also an anomalous rule that if the statute is silent as to mens rea the required state of mind is to be presumed upon proof of the prohibited conduct, although if there is evidence that it was absent D should be acquitted if the jury is left in reasonable doubt on the question. This rule was laid down in *R v Strawbridge*[15] where the Court of Appeal accepted that an earlier decision[16] placing the persuasive burden on D could not be maintained after *Woolmington v DPP*,[17] but thought that Lord Diplock's speech in *Sweet v Parsley*[18] supported the modified rebuttable presumption. It seems wrong that the applicable evidential principles should vary according to whether an ingredient of the offence is specified in the statute or is implied by the common law, and in principle there should be no rule that in the absence of evidence to the contrary mens rea must be presumed upon proof of the prohibited conduct.[19] On the other hand, if there is evidence from which the required mental element may be inferred it may well be that the tribunal of fact should not be required to consider any particular reason why it might have been absent unless there is some evidence of it.[20] Lord Diplock (who did not distinguish between offences according to whether the statute specified the mental element) does not seem to have gone further than this.

Two further points should be mentioned. First, although Dickson J confined this category to truly criminal offences and offences where the statute expressly requires mens rea, it is clear that the same rule as to the burden of proof applies to any element of fault which may be expressly required by the terms of the statute, unless the statute provides otherwise.[21] Second, if the terms of the statute implicitly make an element of intention or fault an ingredient of the offence, it is equally clear in principle that this must be proved by the prosecution. In one Canadian decision a majority of the Supreme Court held that this was not so in the case of a regulatory offence in respect of which such proof would be difficult,[22] but the better view is that in the absence of a statutory provision to the contrary the prosecution must prove all the elements of an offence, whether they are required expressly or impliedly by the terms of the statute, or are implied by the common law, and whether the offence be truly criminal or regulatory.[23]

2 Offences where reasonable mistake or absence of negligence may exculpate

Where the legislation does not positively import an element of mens rea or fault and the offence is a 'regulatory' or 'public welfare' offence — where the proscribed acts 'are not criminal in any real sense, but are acts which in the public interest are prohibited under penalty'[24] — it is held, at least as a general rule, that to require subjective mens rea would give insufficient effect to the object of the legislation. It is in this context, however, that general principles have been developed which restrict the scope of absolute liability, although significant differences have emerged between the law in Canada and New Zealand on the one hand, and Australia on the other.

(a) THE CONTENT OF THE DEFENCE

In Canada and New Zealand a person responsible for the proscribed conduct or state of affairs may be able to rely on a defence which is variously described as 'due diligence', absence of fault, or absence of negligence. In many cases the basis of this defence will be an honest and reasonable belief in facts which, if true, would make the conduct innocent, or reasonable failure to know of facts constituting an offence, but even if the relevant facts were known the defence is available if D was not negligent in bringing about the forbidden event, had done what a reasonable person would have done in the circumstances, or had taken all reasonable care to prevent the proscribed conduct or state of affairs.[25]

This principle subsumes a number of circumstances which are commonly regarded as distinct grounds of exculpation. In addition to reasonable mistake of fact, it includes cases where a prohibited event or circumstance resulted from an act of a stranger or an event which D was unable to prevent (an 'Act of God', or 'inevitable accident'), cases where it was impossible for D to comply with the law, cases where D's conduct was involuntary, and cases where D acted under compulsion or in circumstances of necessity.[26] In every case, however, it will be essential that the exculpatory circumstance was not attributable to earlier fault on D's part, although for the defence to be defeated on this ground it seems that the kind of event which occurred will have to have been 'clearly foreseeable', and that it will not necessarily suffice that D was acting illegally or 'negligently'.[27]

The general nature of the defence avoids the difficult and somewhat arbitrary distinctions that might be drawn between, for example, mistake, ignorance and impossibility,[28] and it also allows the possibility of a defence of 'reasonable care' or 'reasonable conduct' even though there may be some doubt whether the requirements of any of the more particular defences have been satisfied.[29] On the other hand, the defence does not extend to error of law made after reasonable inquiry,[30] although there have been suggestions that, at least in relation to minor offences, it might be a defence that 'a public official charged with responsibility in the matter' led D to believe that proposed conduct was lawful.[31]

It is also well established in Canada that, when the defence is available, due diligence may relieve D of vicarious liability for the conduct of another.[32]

In *Sault Ste Marie*[33] Dickson J said that 'the due diligence which must be established is that of the accused alone', and that when an employer is charged in respect of an act of an employee in the course of employment the success of the defence will depend on 'whether the accused exercised all reasonable care by establishing a proper system to prevent commission of the offence and by taking reasonable steps to ensure the effective operation of the system.' He added that the availability of the defence to a corporation 'will depend on whether such due diligence was taken by those who are the directing mind and will of the corporation.'[34] These principles have been applied in a number of cases,[35] including some where D sought to excuse an omission to perform a statutory duty by evidence that another was employed to discharge it.[36] But two qualifications appear to be necessary. First, even if there is no evidence that D (or the directing mind of a corporation) exercised due diligence it seems the defence may still succeed if the actual offender acted with all reasonable care.[37] Second, although it will often be necessary to establish a preventive system and positively attempt to enforce it, something less may sometimes suffice to satisfy the real test, whether D did all that could reasonably be expected in view of the nature of the offence and the circumstances.[38]

Whether the standard of reasonable care or 'due diligence' is met in a particular case will be a question of fact, in respect of which a number of factors will commonly have to be considered: for example, the existence of any general standard or practice commonly accepted as appropriate in respect of the activity in question,[39] the gravity and likelihood of the relevant harm, the nature, cost and practicability of alternative courses of action open to D, and the extent to which causes beyond D's control contributed to the offence.[40] In New Zealand it is said that, although liability is not absolute, the defence is not easy to establish and that a high standard of care is required. This is emphasised by a tendency to describe the defence as 'total absence of fault'.[41] Breach of this standard need not involve moral blame and, at least when the object of the legislation is the protection of public safety or welfare, the objective standard is not be reduced by reference to the particular characteristics of D.[42]

The Australian authorities do not yet support a general defence of absence of negligence, although in many cases the imposition of liability without fault is avoided by the recognition of one or more narrower grounds of exculpation. The most important of these is reasonable mistake of fact: it has been held in numerous cases that although the ingredients of a statutory offence do not include a 'specific state of mind', nevertheless there is a general rule, or prima facie presumption, that an honest and reasonable belief in a state of facts which, if they existed, would make conduct innocent is a ground of exculpation. This is commonly called the *Proudman v Dayman* defence, that being the case where Dixon J provided a full statement of the principle.[43] Although it has been disputed whether there are two distinct principles pursuant to which a mistake might excuse,[44] it is now well established in Australia that when intention, knowledge or advertence is an ingredient of an offence D may be excused because of some honest mistake (or ignorance), even though there were no reasonable grounds for it,[45] but for the *Proudman v Dayman* defence the existence of such reasonable grounds is a substantive requirement.[46] Exculpation on the ground of reasonable mistake of fact is recognised as a 'middle course' between imposing absolute liability and requiring mens rea, in the sense of intention, knowledge or advertence.[47]

The standard description of the defence requires a reasonable belief in facts which would make D's conduct innocent.

As a general rule a mistake of law does not suffice, and although there have been suggestions that the question is whether D had a belief in facts taking conduct outside the offence charged,[48] that is probably appropriate only when actual advertence is required. The predominant view is that for a defence of reasonable mistake D must believe in facts which would make the conduct no offence at all.[49] More questionably it has been suggested that if statute provides that certain facts constitute a defence, the court cannot extend the effect of this by allowing a reasonable but mistaken belief in such facts to have the same effect.[50] In the context of a codified defence of reasonable mistake it has been held that for a corporation to have the defence the relevant belief must be held by a 'directing mind'.[51] This, however, can result in liability when the offence is not the result of fault on the part of anyone and it seems to be arguable that for the common law defence it will suffice if a reasonable mistake can be attributed to the corporation via its 'directing mind', or if the actual offender was reasonably mistaken, and there was no senior officer of the corporation who either knew or should have known the relevant facts.[52]

It is sometimes said that the defence requires a positive belief in exculpatory facts, and that simple ignorance cannot suffice,[53] but it is doubtful whether there is any such general rule. Although there have been cases where it has apparently been thought that such a positive belief is essential,[54] in most of these (and perhaps all of them) D's ignorance was not regarded as reasonable, or D had taken inadequate precautions to prevent the offence. In most cases it will not be possible for anyone to prove D's state of mind with precision, and even if it can be it may be disputable whether it is properly classified as 'simple ignorance' of facts making conduct criminal, or as a 'positive belief' in their absence, as when D might not consciously think about the matter but apparently acts upon an assumption that conduct is innocent.[55] Where D may be liable in respect of recurring acts it has been held that it is not necessary that he apply his mind to each act, provided he has a 'general' and reasonable belief in the continued efficacy of an adequate system designed to prevent offending,[56] although it seems unlikely that such a case will involve more than an assumption on D's part. Moreover, the distinction between simple ignorance and positive mistake may be quite arbitrary, for if there was nothing to put a reasonable person on inquiry the person who remains unaware of a fact because he does not think about it may be no more blameworthy than one who makes a conscious and reasonable mistake.[57] In *Maher v Musson*[58] D had made a positive inquiry and the defence was described in the usual way, but it was also said that it should suffice if there was 'ignorance upon reasonable grounds', or if D 'neither believed nor had reason to believe' that the circumstances were such as made the conduct an offence.[59] There appears to be no reason to confine this to cases where the act of a third person was responsible for the existence of the proscribed circumstances,[60] and it is thought that the better view is that the defence of reasonable mistake extends to every case where D is reasonably unaware of essential facts, provided that a defence of this scope is consistent with the object of the legislation.[61]

On the other hand, in *Boucher v GJ Coles & Co Ltd*[62] Wells J said that although a defence is recognised when D holds a reasonable belief in exculpatory facts, because it is presumed that the legislature did not intend to demand 'the impossible or the impracticable', nevertheless there is no justification for importing a more general exemption 'in favour of a defendant who has acted without negligence . . . unless the language of the enactment contains a clear reference to it.' In *R v He Kaw Teh*[63] Brennan J appears to support this when he treats absence of reasonable mistake as a form of mens rea and says that it is wrong to equate it with responsibility for negligence: in these cases, he reasoned, criminal liability is imposed for intentionally doing the physical act when there are no reasonable grounds for believing it is innocent, and not for 'failing to take care in inquiring into the circumstances.' Where a mistake, or inadvertence, does not excuse simply because it is not supported by reasonable grounds it is fair to say that to that extent liability is imposed for negligence,[64] but these judgments indicate that although strict liability will often be subject to a defence of reasonable mistake (which might or might not require a conscious belief in exculpatory facts), Australian courts have yet to recognise a more general defence of due diligence.

The practical effect of this restricted view of the *Proudman v Dayman* defence may not be great because it is supplemented by other possible grounds of excuse. In particular, it has been held that even when reasonable mistake is not a defence D will not be liable if he was unable to prevent the proscribed event or state of affairs, and it can be attributed to an 'act of a stranger', or an 'Act of God' — the unauthorised act of a person over whom D had no control, or a natural event which could not be prevented.[65] This defence has been extended to a case where the prohibited act was done by D, or his employee, but circumstances making it unlawful arose from the act of another and, although D remains vicariously liable for acts of employees, it appears that the defence may be available even though the act of the 'stranger' was purportedly done pursuant to a contract with D.[66] The intervening act must be of a kind which D could not reasonably foresee or guard against, and it will not suffice if it was foreseeable as an 'ordinary chance' of the activity D was engaged in.[67] In addition, whether or not the offence is one in respect of which reasonable mistake may be a defence, it appears that other grounds of exculpation will usually be available: for example, impossibility,[68] necessity,[69] duress or physical compulsion, or the fact that D acted involuntarily.[70]

(b) THE BURDEN OF PROOF

In Australia, doubts as to the burden of proof have been associated with doubts as to the true conceptual basis of exculpation in cases of reasonable mistake. On one view reasonable mistake is a defence which exculpates D notwithstanding that every element of the offence is established, while on another it excuses D because it negates mens rea, an essential ingredient of the offence. Howard regards it as a defence, which D should have the persuasive burden of establishing,[71] although the English authorities which are the source of the principle treat reasonable mistake as exculpatory because it negates mens rea, or hold that the absence of such a mistake is a form of mens rea.[72] This issue has not been finally resolved,[73] and in *R v He Kaw Teh*[74] Gibbs CJ thought that it may be that little turns on the question, which 'is largely one of words'. No doubt the courts would have more difficulty justifying placing the burden of proof on D in respect of an ingredient of an offence, but classifying reasonable mistake as a defence would not mean that the persuasive burden must rest on D, as is apparent from the established rule that D has an evidential burden only in respect of such defences as self-defence, duress and provocation.[75]

In any event, in Australia D is not now required affirmatively to prove reasonable mistake. In *Maher v Musson*[76] Dixon J had no doubt that D had the persuasive burden, but that was before *Woolmington*[77] and, subsequently, in *Proudman v Dayman*[78] he indicated that the position was uncertain. Later decisions at first placed the persuasive burden on D,[79] but more recent authorities have reduced this to a mere evidential burden, so that the defence must be considered if there is evidence before the court which is capable of raising a reasonable doubt on the issue, and D should be acquitted if the tribunal of fact is left in such doubt.[80] This view appears to receive decisive confirmation from the High Court in *R v He Kaw Teh*,[81] where all the judges support it, and only one contemplates the possibility of the contrary rule surviving 'in the case of some minor statutory offences of a strict liability kind which carry a modest penalty.'[28]

The position is otherwise in Canada and New Zealand where the rule governing the burden of proof varies according to whether the offence is 'truly criminal' or is a 'public welfare' or 'regulatory' offence only. In the absence of a statutory provision to the contrary, if an offence is truly criminal the prosecution must prove the mens rea which is expressly or presumptively required, and D is entitled to acquittal if there is a reasonable doubt on this issue. But if it is a regulatory offence and the terms of the legislation do not make mens rea or fault an essential element of it,[83] the prosecution need only prove that D committed the prohibited act, or was responsible for the actus reus (although it must prove this beyond reasonable doubt), and D has the burden of proving the defence of absence of fault on the balance of probabilities. In Canada this rule was established by the Supreme Court in *Sault Ste Marie*[84] and, although it had previously accepted that the persuasive burden did not shift to D in relation to either truly criminal or regulatory offences,[85] in *Civil Aviation Department v MacKenzie*[86] the New Zealand Court of Appeal adopted the Canadian rule. In these cases *Woolmington* is held to be concerned only with truly criminal offences and the reversal of the burden of proof is justified on the basis that D will usually know far better than the prosecution how the breach occurred and what had been done to avoid it. Although it is not made explicit, it seems that there is concern that a mere evidential burden would make it too easy to secure unwarranted acquittals and if this is correct the judicial reversal of the persuasive burden may be justified as a necessary prerequisite to the amelioration of strict liability by a general defence of absence of fault.[87] On the other hand, in the case of many offences mens rea or fault can be readily inferred from the conduct or events which the prosecution will be required to prove,[88] and whenever this is the case the special rule is unnecessary. In *MacKenzie* McMullin J concluded that the courts should continue to leave it to Parliament to impose the persuasive burden on D in particular instances when this is thought to be necessary, and expressed his 'emphatic dissent' from the judicial creation of a general rule to this effect. Apart from authority, he found support for this view in the fact that in the context of 'true' crime the courts have not thought it necessary to impose the persuasive burden on D merely because relevant facts were peculiarly within his knowledge; and in the imprecision of the key concept of 'public welfare' or 'regulatory' offences, which may include offences where the available penalties are such that they cannot be regarded as other than 'serious'.[89]

(c) THE AVAILABILITY OF THE DEFENCE

It is accepted in each jurisdiction that legislation may exclude the defence by implication and the inevitable result of this is a degree of uncertainty as to when it might be available. The principles appear to have been most clearly worked out in Canada.

The judgment in *Sault Ste Marie* suggests that offences of absolute liability — where neither absence of mens rea nor absence of fault excuses — will be rare. It was said that the arguments against absolute liability have greater force than those in favour of it, and that it 'violates fundamental principles of penal liability.'[90] There is no presumption that 'full mens rea' is an ingredient of a public welfare offence, but 'in general' absence of fault is a defence, offences of absolute liability being those where the legislature has 'made it clear that guilt would follow proof merely of the proscribed act.' The court added that primary considerations determining whether this is intended were 'the over-all regulatory pattern adopted by the legislature, the subject-matter of the legislation, the importance of the penalty, and the precision of the language used.'[91]

The vagueness of these criteria might suggest that the position is no more predictable than the traditional choice between requiring mens rea and imposing strict liability, but it is alleviated by the general reluctance of Canadian courts to find that the defence of absence of fault has been excluded. Thus, the Supreme Court has affirmed that 'the clearest intendment' is needed for absolute liability,[92] and in other courts it has been said that the creation of such an offence 'must be considered to be an extraordinary undertaking',[93] which will occur 'only in the rarest of situations.'[94] The presumption against absolute liability is strengthened if the court regards the possible penalty as severe or as involving serious consequences, which it usually will if imprisonment is possible,[95] and there have even been cases where the imposition of absolute liability for such an offence has been held to be invalid as violating the principles of fundamental justice guaranteed by s 7 of the Canadian Charter of Rights and Freedoms.[96] The language or 'over-all regulatory pattern' of the legislation has been held to support the due diligence defence if the language is broad and imprecise,[97] if the relevant activity is permitted in specified circumstances rather than being prohibited without qualification,[98] or if absolute liability is more clearly imposed by other provisions in the statute.[99] The nature of the offence may tell against absolute liability if it is not practicable to ensure the absence of proscribed circumstances,[100] if it consists of an omission,[101] if it can be committed in ways involving no serious harm,[102] or if the defence of due diligence is rarely likely to succeed;[103] on the other hand the Supreme Court has held that the mere fact that availability of the defence might 'considerably weaken' the legislation will not justify interpreting it as imposing absolute liability, at least when reasonably substantial penalties are possible.[104]

The clearest examples of implied exclusion of the defence are cases where the statute expressly allows a defence of due diligence, but imposes some additional requirement, or allows it only in specified circumstances.[105] Where the statute allows a defence of absence of fault for some offences, but not the one charged, it is sometimes (but not always) inferred that absolute liability is intended, especially if earlier legislation allowed the defence,[106] and the same inference may be drawn if D is 'deemed' to be guilty in specified circumstances.[107]

Although the subject matter and object of the legislation are relevant considerations, they are unlikely to justify absolute liability in the absence of textual support for the inference that this was intended. The leading Supreme Court decisions allow the defence in respect of offences designed to prevent pollution and to preserve wildlife, and later cases allow it in respect of a wide variety of regulatory offences of a kind typically associated with strict liability. For example, traffic offences designed to preserve public safety, rights to compensation, or law enforcement;[108] offences designed to promote industrial safety, compliance with revenue or liquor laws, or free competition;[109] offences aimed at preventing unlicensed trading in securities, or practice in a profession;[110] and immigration offences.[111] On the other hand, there have been occasional cases where in terms the legislation has merely provided an unqualified prohibition but an intention to impose absolute liability has been found, having regard to the importance of the public interest in question (for example, road safety or conservation of wildlife), the provision of relatively minor non-custodial penalties, and the absence of stigma attaching to conviction.[112]

The weight of Canadian authority supports the conclusion that after *Sault Ste Marie* it will be very unusual for it to be found that it is not a defence to a public welfare offence that there was no negligence on D's part.[113] In New Zealand there is not the same bulk of confirmatory case law, but the position there will presumably be similar after the adoption of the broad Canadian principles in *Civil Aviation Department v MacKenzie*.[114] It is true that there the Court of Appeal found that the availability of the defences was positively supported by the serious nature of the 'public welfare regulatory' offence alleged in that case (which consisted of dangerous flying, punishable by up to 12 months' imprisonment, with mandatory suspension of the pilot's licence in the absence of special reasons), and was cautious in describing the effect of its decision.[115] There is, however, good reason for believing that criminal liability without fault will be a rare phenomenon. The Court of Appeal has said that New Zealand courts 'subscribe strongly' to the 'cardinal requirement' of the criminal law that for liability there must normally be mens rea, in the sense of 'true moral blameworthiness', although the degree of required blameworthiness varies with the subject matter and wording of the legislation.[116] This was said with particular (although not exclusive) reference to serious crime, but in recent years New Zealand courts have not only insisted on mens rea for truly criminal offences,[117] but have also generally required at least negligence when a regulatory offence is charged.[118] The placing of the burden of proof on D should further encourage this and, although there will continue to be cases where the defence is excluded,[119] these will probably be rare.[120]

Australian courts have not yet recognised a broad defence of absence of fault, nor have they adopted the rather firm Canadian rules for determining when liability should depend on reasonable mistake rather than subjective mens rea. However, their approach to the interpretation of offences will usually result in the *Proudman v Dayman* defence being available to regulatory offences. Although some earlier judgments had suggested otherwise, in *R v He Kaw Teh*[121] it was held that mens rea is an essential element of every statutory offence unless the language and subject matter of the legislation excludes it, expressly or by necessary implication. The factors identified as relevant to this question are familiar: for example, it is unlikely that mens rea will be unnecessary if the offence is 'truly criminal', if it attracts significant stigma, if the possible penalties are severe, or if those subject to the legislation are unable to take effective precautions to avoid the risk of offending; conversely it is less likely that mens rea is essential if the offence is 'regulatory', is designed to preserve public welfare or safety, if the penalties are relatively light, or when mens rea would often be difficult to prove.[122] But it is also acknowledged that mens rea is an ambiguous concept, and in particular it may either require actual advertence to external elements, or absence of honest and reasonable mistake may suffice. The choice between these also depends on the true construction of the legislation, the relevant factors being much the same as those to be considered in determining whether any requirement of mens rea has been excluded. Ordinarily the criminal law requires actual advertence and it is unlikely that something less will do if the offence is serious, if the penalties are severe, if it is doubtful whether liability for negligence will make the legislation more effective, and if intent or knowledge could usually be inferred from the proscribed conduct.[123] On the other hand, it seems that even in the case of a truly criminal offence the court might sometimes find that absence of a reasonable mistake is the appropriate degree of fault, at least in relation to circumstances which are not 'integral parts' of the proscribed conduct, if it is thought that the policy of the legislation is to prohibit the conduct unless the circumstances can reasonably be thought to be absent.[124]

In *R v He Kaw Teh* the court recognises the possibility of an objective test of fault being applicable to some truly criminal statutory offences, but it does not give particular attention to how readily the reasonable mistake defence might be excluded from regulatory offences. Nevertheless, it is accepted that some form of mens rea is required unless it is excluded expressly or by necessary implication, and reasonable mistake is recognised as being established as a possible alternative to full mens rea or absolute liability. Although it has been suggested that it should be confined to statutes which explicitly refer to some undertaking or conduct by a person required to abide by specified 'standards',[125] there have been numerous Australian cases holding that such a defence is available to regulatory offences which do not require subjective mens rea.[126] It is commonly said that a 'clear' or 'necessary' implication will be required to exclude the defence,[127] and it has been suggested that this will be an 'extraordinary and unusual' case.[128] *R v He Kaw Teh* is at least consistent with such an approach. Cases will continue to arise where absolute liability is held to be impliedly imposed, but it is probably correct to say that this will be unusual and for the most part it will be confined to 'minor statutory offences of a regulatory kind.'[129]

3 Offences of absolute liability

These are offences where the prosecution is not required to prove mens rea or fault, nor does reasonable mistake or absence of fault excuse. In *Sault Ste Marie*[130] Dickson J said that absolute liability:

> '. . . entails conviction on proof merely that the defendant committed the prohibited act constituting the *actus reus* of the offence. There is no relevant mental element. It is no defence that the accused was entirely without fault. He may be morally innocent in every sense . . . '

Of course, some modification of this is necessary to take account of offences which are defined in terms of an omission or state of affairs, and as a description of the concept of absolute liability it needs to be qualified in three respects. First, if the statutory definition of an offence expressly or impliedly requires conscious or intentional conduct absence of such a mental element excuses D even if in respect of other elements the offence is absolute.[131] Second, it is possible for an offence to require mens rea or fault in respect of some circumstances, but to impose absolute liability in respect of others.[132] Third, the terms, subject-matter and object of the legislation might make it clear that it was not intended that lack of negligence should always excuse, and to that extent liability is absolute, but it may be found that narrower grounds of exculpation have not been excluded, provided they are not attributable to fault on D's part.[133] For example, it was suggested earlier that in Australia there may be no general rule that simple ignorance cannot suffice for a defence of 'reasonable mistake'. Some offences, however, may be of such a nature that although a defence requiring a positive belief would be consistent with the legislative object a defence of reasonable ignorance would not be. In *Boucher v GJ Coles and Co Ltd*[134] it was accepted that D might have a defence to a charge of keeping unsound food for sale if, as a result of making all practicable inquiries, tests and inspections, it was believed that all the cans were sound, but reasonable ignorance was not sufficient. Modern methods of packaging mean that to allow the latter as a defence would defeat the legislature's object that liability should be borne by retailers. In Australia it has also often been said that even when the defence of reasonable mistake is excluded it is likely to remain a defence that D was unable to prevent the proscribed event because of an act of a stranger, an Act of God, compulsion or automatism.[135] Similarly, in Canada it is established that there is a common law defence of necessity which is available to any offence unless this is inconsistent with the legislation,[136] and there seems little doubt that it will usually be available even if the general defence of due diligence is excluded;[137] and in New Zealand the common law defence of impossibility may excuse overstaying a temporary residence permit, although it has been held that an amendment to the legislation has the effect of removing the defence of reasonable mistake which had previously been allowed.[138]

As to the burden of proof, in Australia it seems clear that, as with reasonable mistake, other grounds of excuse (apart from insanity) will be made out if there is evidence raising the issue which leaves the court in reasonable doubt. In Canada and New Zealand where a public welfare offence is charged it appears that D must have the burden of proof whenever absence of fault is essential to the defence relied upon; the authorities indicate that this rule applies in all such cases, and it would be absurd to apply a less demanding rule when the general defence is excluded but some particular instances of absence of fault are nevertheless allowed to excuse. In *Perka v R*[139] however, the Supreme Court of Canada held that in relation to necessity D had only an evidential burden, upon the theory that necessity creates 'moral or normative involuntariness' and thus negates an essential ingredient of the offence — voluntary conduct. But in the analysis of offences the concept of involuntary conduct has not been regarded as extending to cases where D was able to make a conscious choice, and a more satisfactory explanation of *Perka* may be that it concerned a truly criminal offence to which the rule in *Woolmington* applied, regardless of whether excusing circumstances were thought of as negating an essential ingredient or as a defence. When the legislation does not expressly or impliedly make fault an ingredient of a public welfare offence, conceptual notions of what is or is not an element of an offence do not provide adequate reasons for departing from the rule that D must prove the no-fault defence.[140]

To allow absence of fault to excuse in some circumstances but not others can produce arbitrary distinctions,[141] but it is consistent with principle in allowing absolute liability no more scope than is required by the terms or object of the legislation.

4 Conclusion

The scope of strict liability has been circumscribed by the common legislative practice of providing defences for those who are not negligent, and by the not uncommon judicial practice of insisting on a degree of mens rea. Nevertheless the principles which have been considered here have real value in achieving a significant further reduction in criminal liability without fault. In Australia reasonable mistake as a ground of exculpation has evolved from authorities concerned with mens rea in traditional crime but, although it has been extended to offences generally, the courts have yet to enlarge its content, although other no-fault defences are recognised. The Canadian and New Zealand courts have recognised a broader defence and, once a distinction is clearly drawn between mens rea in the sense of actual advertence and unreasonable mistake or ignorance, the most coherent view appears to be that adopted in these jurisdictions, that when liability is imposed in the latter case its basis is the failure to take reasonable care, or negligence.[142]

Of course, there are areas of doubt and difficulty. Absolute liability may be unusual, but the factors which may be found to imply it remain imprecise, and the classification of offences in *Sault Ste Marie* is inherently problematic because of the difficulty in sensibly and consistently distinguishing 'truly criminal' offences from mere 'regulatory' or 'public welfare' offences. Some offences assigned to the latter category carry severe maximum penalties, and there is a real possibility that it will be held to include some offences which would previously have been held to require proof of mens rea. The High Court of Australia does not place quite the same importance on classifying offences as truly criminal or merely regulatory, and it seems to be rather more ready to allow that the nature and object of a serious crime might justify requiring reasonable grounds for an excusing mistake,[143] although in the absence of a statutory provision it does not require D to prove this in any case. The reversal of the burden of proof in Canada and New Zealand is controversial. In addition to the problem of uncertainty, the difficulty the prosecution might have in rebutting an unjustified plea of due diligence will arise from the physical nature of the particular offence, or the absence of evidence, rather than the classification of the offence as being other than 'truly criminal'. It may well be that in the case of most regulatory offences the object of the legislation would be sufficiently secured by imposing only an evidential burden on D, and by requiring a high standard of care.

NOTES

1 Eg JC Smith 'The Guilty Mind in the Criminal Law' (1960) 76 LQR 78, 98; Glanville Williams *Criminal Law: The General Part* (2nd edn, 1961), p 262.

2 Most notoriously in *Smedleys Ltd v Breed* [1974] AC 839; contrast *Tesco Supermarkets Ltd v Nattrass* [1972] AC 153.

3 Eg *Burns v Bidder* [1967] 2 QB 227; cp *Alphacell Ltd v Woodward* [1972] AC 824 at 834, 845, 847; LH Leigh *Strict and Vicarious Liability* (1982), pp 3–5.

4 Eg *Reynolds v GH Austin & Sons Ltd* [1951] 2 KB 135.

5 Eg *Leicester v Pearson* [1952] 2 QB 668; *R v Gosney* [1971] 2 QB 674, CA.

6 *Lim Chin Aik v R* [1963] AC 160 at 174–175; *Sweet v Parsley* [1970] AC 132 at 163; *Gammon (Hong Kong) Ltd v A-G of Hong Kong* [1985] AC 1 at 13–14.

7 Eg *Tesco Supermarkets Ltd v Nattrass* [1972] AC 153 at 169, per Lord Reid; *Sweet v Parsley* [1970] AC 132 at 150, per Lord Reid, at 157–158, per Lord Pearce; cp *Warner v Metropolitan Police Comr* [1969] 2 AC 256 at 280, per Lord Reid.

8 [1986] 2 All ER 635; cp *Gammon (Hong Kong) Ltd v A-G of Hong Kong* [1985] AC 1.
9 Eg *R v Charterways Transportation Ltd* (1981) 60 CCC (2d) 510; *R v Dilorenzo* (1984) 11 CCC (3d) 13; cp *R v He Kaw Teh* (1985) 60 ALR 449 at 454, 455, 491–492, 502–503; and see generally the discussion of 'possession' in this case.
10 (1978) 85 DLR (3d) 161 at 181.
11 Ibid at 170.
12 Eg *R v Meek* [1981] 1 NZLR 499 at 502–503; *R v Howe* [1982] 1 NZLR 618 at 623; *R v He Kaw Teh* (1985) 60 ALR 449 at 457, 491–492, 502.
13 *R v City of Sault Ste Marie* (1978) 85 DLR (3d) 161, 170; *R v Pappajohn* (1980) 111 DLR (3d)1; *R v He Kaw Teh* (1985) 60 ALR 449 at 456, 487, 499; *Welsh v Donnelly* [1983] 2 VR 173 at 180–181; *R v Brown* (1975) 10 SASR 139 at 147–148, 164; in *R v Strawbridge* [1970] NZLR 909, 916 it was implied that reasonable grounds were needed if the statute was silent as to mens rea, but the Court of Appeal abandoned this in *R v Wood* [1982] 2 NZLR 233 at 237.
14 Cp *R v He Kaw Teh* (1985) 60 ALR 449 at 458, 490–491, 502.
15 [1970] NZLR 909; cp *R v Somers* (1984) 16 CCC (3d) 357; this is more fully considered in Orchard 'The Judicial Categorisation of Offences' (1983) 2 Canterbury Law Review 81, 87–91.
16 *R v Ewart* (1905) 25 NZLR 709; cp *R v Prince* (1875) LR 2 CCR 154 at 163, per Brett J.
17 *Woolmington v DPP* [1935] AC 462, HL.
18 [1970] AC 132 at 164.
19 *R v He Kaw Teh* (1985) 60 ALR 449 at 491, per Brennan J.
20 Cross *Evidence* (6th edn, 1985), pp 111–112; this is well established in respect of automatism, and see, eg, *R v Pappajohn* (1980) 111 DLR (3d) 1 (mistake), and *R v Kamipeli* [1975] 1 NZLR 610 at 619 (intoxication).
21 *Civil Aviation Department v MacKenzie* [1983] NZLR 78 at 85; *R v Z-H Paper Products Ltd* (1979) 52 CCC(2d) 91 at 97.
22 *Strasser v Roberge* (1979) 103 DLR (3d) 193; cp *R v Brown and Ballman* (1982) 69 CCC (2d) 301; *R v Rogo Forming Ltd* (1980) 56 CCC (2d) 31 at 40–41.
23 Cp *R v He Kaw Teh* (1985) 60 ALR 449 at 490, 489–499; but in regulatory contexts the legislation is sometimes narrowly construed to exclude an implicit requirement of mens rea; see, eg, the interpretation of 'permits' in *R v City of Sault Ste Marie* (1978) 85 DLR (3d) 161 and *Proudman v Dayman* (1941) 67 CLR 536.
24 *Sherras v De Rutzen* [1895] 1 QB 918 at 922, per Wright J; 'regulatory' and 'public welfare' appear to be synonymous, and the New Zealand Court of Appeal combines them in the phrase 'public welfare regulatory offences': *Civil Aviation Department v MacKenzie* [1983] NZLR 78.
25 *R v City of Sault Ste Marie* (1978) 85 DLR (3d) 161 at 174, 181–182; *Civil Aviation Department v MacKenzie* [1983] NZLR 78 at 85–86.
26 For impossibility, see, eg: *R v Maidment* (1984) 10 CCC (3d) 512; *Tifaga v Department of Labour* [1980] 2 NZLR 235; *Finau v Department of Labour* [1984] 2 NZLR 396; cp *Kilbride v Lake* [1962] NZLR 590; and for an instance of necessity: *R v Slovack* [1980] 1 WWR 368.
27 *Perka v R* (1984) 13 DLR (4th) 1, 19–20; cp *Tifaga v Department of Labour* [1980] 2 NZLR 235, 245–246; Howard *Strict Responsibility* (1963), pp 193–199; when an offence requires a particular state of mind it will be necessary that such a state of mind accompanied conduct to which the proscribed event can be attributed; *R v Bailey* [1983] 1 WLR 760 at 764–765; cp *Sione v Labour Department* [1972] NZLR 278.
28 Cp *Police v Creedon* [1976] 1 NZLR 571, 580–582.
29 Cp *R v Gonder* (1981) 62 CCC (2d) 326; and for the possibility of a defence of 'commercial necessity', see *The Generous* (1818) 2 Dods 322 at 327.
30 Eg *Molis v R* (1980) 116 DLR (3d) 291, 298; *R v MacDonald* (1983) 3 CCC (3d) 419; *R v Bouchard* (1984) 15 CCC (3d) 282; but it is probably a defence that D was ignorant of an unpublished law: *Lim Chin Aik v R*[1963] AC 160; *R v Catholique* (1979) 104 DLR (3d) 161.
31 *R v Walker* (1980) 51 CCC (2d) 423, 429; *R v MacDougall* (1982) 1 CCC (3d) 65 at 71; *R v Gruber* [1982] 1 WWR 197; cp *R v Gallinger* [1980] 1 WWR 628; *R v Richardson* (1981) 62 CCC (2d) 417.
32 In *R v Watch* (1983) 10 CCC (3d) 521 at 530 it was said that 'the clearest possible language' would be needed to establish vicarious liability in the absence of fault.
33 (1978) 85 DLR (3d) 161 at 185.
34 Citing the decision on the statutory defence in *Tesco Supermarkets Ltd v Nattrass* [1972] AC 153, HL.
35 Eg *R v Gulf of Georgia Towing Co Ltd* [1979] 3 WWR 84; *R v Z-H Paper Products Ltd* (1979) 52 CCC (2d) 91 at 95; *Ministry of Environment v Exolon Co of Canada Ltd* (1981) 36 OR (2d)

530; *Aurora Quarrying Ltd v Catherwood* [1982] 6 WWR 517.
36 *R v Merkle* [1980] 1 WWR 361; *R v Highland Enterprise Ltd* (1981) 60 CCC (2d) 78.
37 Cp *R v Westfair Foods Ltd* (1985) 18 CCC (3d) 178; *R v Consumers Distributing Co Ltd* (1980) 57 CCC (2d) 317; but D would be liable if he intentionally procured commission of the offence by an innocent agent or, no doubt, if reasonable care by D would have prevented the offence.
38 *R v Watch* (1983) 10 CCC (3d) 521; cp *Tesco Supermarkets Ltd v Nattrass* [1972] AC 153 at 194, HL.
39 *R v Consumers Distributing Co Ltd* (1980) 57 CCC (2d) 317 at 324.
40 *R v Slovack* [1980] 1 WWR 368; cp *Sweet v Parsley* [1970] AC 132 at 163, HL.
41 *Hastings City Council v Simons* [1984] 2 NZLR 502 at 506; *Ministry of Transport v Burnetts Motors Ltd* [1980] 1 NZLR 51 at 57; *Police v Creedon* [1976] 1 NZLR 571 at 575, 582, 586–587; a more lenient approach was perhaps taken in *Finau v Department of Labour* [1984] 2 NZLR 396.
42 *Civil Aviation Department v MacKenzie* [1983] NZLR 78 at 85.
43 (1941) 67 CLR 536 at 540–541; cp *Maher v Musson* (1934) 52 CLR 100; *Thomas v R* (1937) 59 CLR 279; an influential account of the early authorities was given by Colin Howard 'Strict Responsibility in the High Court of Australia' (1960) 76 LQR 547; cp Howard *Strict Responsibility* (1963), ch 6; Howard *Criminal Law* (4th edn, 1982), pp 363–379.
44 Peter Brett, 'Strict Liability: Possible Solutions' (1974) 37 MLR 417.
45 See the Australian cases cited above in n 13.
46 Eg *Dimella Construction Pty Ltd v Stocker* (1976) 14 SASR 215 at 219; *Mayer v Marchant* (1973) 5 SASR 567 at 571; *Kidd v Reeves* [1972] VR 563 at 567–569; *Handmer v Taylor* [1971] VR 308 at 315; *Gherashe v Boase* [1959] VR 1; for doubts on this question see *Kain & Shelton Pty Ltd v McDonald* (1971) 1 SASR 39 at 45; *Ianella v French* (1968) 119 CLR 84 at 110–111; *Samuels v Centofanti* [1967] SASR 251 at 269–270.
47 *R v He Kaw Teh* (1985) 60 ALR 449 at 455–456, per Gibbs CJ, at 486–487, per Brennan J, at 498–499, per Dawson J. It is generally assumed that a 'reasonable' ground is one which might deceive a reasonable person, although in *GJ Coles & Co Ltd v Goldsworthy* [1985] WAR 183 at 187–188 Burt CJ suggested that the test is whether the mistake is based on D's 'appreciation of primary objective fact which is in reason capable of sustaining the belief'; sed quaere as this adds very little to the subjective test; inadequate inquiry did not suffice in *Handmer v Taylor* [1971] VR 308.
48 *McCrae v Downey* [1947] VLR 194 at 202–203; *Welsh v Donnelly* [1983] 2 VR 173 at 184.
49 *Bergin v Stack* (1953) 88 CLR 248; *R v Reynhoudt* (1962) 107 CLR 381 at 385–386; it might once have been enough for liability that D adverted to facts making conduct immoral or tortious, but this is unlikely to be accepted today: Howard *Criminal Law* (4th edn, 1982), pp 373–376; O'Connor and Fairall *Criminal Defences* (1983), pp 46–47.
50 *R v Iannazzone* [1983] 1 VR 649 at 655–656.
51 *GJ Coles & Co Ltd v Goldsworthy* [1985] WAR 183.
52 Cp *Brambles Holdings Ltd v Carey* (1976) 15 SASR 270 at 279; *Mayer v Marchant* (1973) 5 SASR 567 at 588–589; the question did not arise in *Burnett v L F Jeffries Nominees Pty Ltd* (1983) 33 SASR 124 because the innocent driver was also the managing director.
53 Eg O'Connor and Fairall *Criminal Defences* (1983), p 44.
54 *Proudman v Dayman* (1941) 67 CLR 536 at 538–539, 541; *Green v Sargeant* [1951] VLR 500; *Gherashe v Boase* [1959] VR 1; cp *Brown v Green* (1951) 84 CLR 285 at 294; *Cameron v Holt* (1980) 142 CLR 342 at 346–347; *GJ Coles & Co Ltd v Goldsworthy* [1985] WAR 183 at 187–188, 191.
55 Brett 'Strict Liability: Possible Solutions' (1974) 37 MLR 417, 435; Howard *Criminal Law* (4th edn, 1982) p 367; cp JC Smith [1982] Crim LR at 448.
56 *Mayer v Marchant* (1973) 5 SASR 567 at 570, 576, 588; *Pearce v Stanton* [1984] WAR 359; cp *Boucher v GJ Coles & Co Ltd* (1974) 9 SASR 495 at 498, 504; *GJ Coles & Co Ltd v Goldsworthy* [1985] WAR 183.
57 *Kain & Shelton Pty Ltd v MacDonald* (1971) 1 SASR 39 at 45.
58 (1934) 52 CLR 100.
59 Ibid at 105, per Dixon J at 109, per Evatt and McTiernan JJ; cp *R v He Kaw Teh* (1985) 60 ALR 449 at 475.
60 Cp *Mayer v Marchant* (1973) 5 SASR 567 at 574, 590.
61 This qualification is considered later, in the section on 'Absolute Liability'.
62 (1974) 9 SASR 495 at 504.
63 (1985) 60 ALR 449 at 489; and at 499 Dawson J said that it is not 'a defence based solely or even primarily upon the absence of negligence'.

64 Ibid at 457, per Gibbs J; cp *R v City of Sault Ste Marie* (1978) 85 DLR (3d) 161 at 174.
65 *Snell v Ryan* [1951] SASR 59; *Norcock v Bowey* [1966] SASR 250.
66 *Mayer v Marchant* (1973) 5 SASR 567; cp *Reynolds v GH Austin & Sons Ltd* [1951] 2 KB 135; *Brambles Holdings Ltd v Carey* (1976) 15 SASR 270; the possibility of the defence when the act was done pursuant to a contract was left open in *Burnett v LF Jeffries Nominees Pty Ltd* (1983) 33 SASR 124.
67 *Boucher v GJ Coles & Co Ltd* (1974) 9 SASR 495 at 497–498.
68 Cp *Narrandera Pastures Protection Board v Coote* (1961) 78 WN (NSW) 697; *Brew v Cox* [1964] SASR 90.
69 Cp *R v Loughnan* [1981] VR 443.
70 Cp *Hearn v McCann* (1982) 29 SASR 448 at 452; as to compulsion, see *O'Sullivan v Fisher* [1954] SASR 33, and Howard *Strict Responsibility* (1963), pp 193–199; *R v Larsonneur* (1933) 24 Cr App Rep 74 was doubted in *Kain & Shelton Pty Ltd v McDonald* (1971) 1 SASR 39 at 51–52, and *Tifaga v Department of Labour* [1980] 2 NZLR 235 at 239.
71 Howard *Criminal Law* (4th edn, 1982), pp 363–364.
72 *R v Prince* (1875) LR 2 CCR 154 at 169–170, per Brett J; *R v Tolson* (1889) 23 QBD 168 at 181, per Cave J; *Bank of New South Wales v Piper* [1897] AC 383 at 389–390, PC; cp *Sweet v Parsley* [1970] AC 132 at 163, per Lord Diplock.
73 *Welsh v Donnelly* [1983] 2 VR 173 at 180; *Handmer v Taylor* [1971] VR 308 at 311.
74 (1985) 60 ALR 449, 456; at 485–486 Brennan J adopted the mens rea theory; cp 498–499, per Dawson J.
75 Cp *Police v Creedon* [1976] 1 NZLR 571 at 586, per Cooke J.
76 (1934) 52 CLR 100 at 105–106.
77 *Woolmington v DPP* [1935] AC 462.
78 (1941) 67 CLR 536 at 541.
79 Eg *O'Sullivan v Harford* [1956] SASR 109 at 114; *R v Bonner* [1957] VR 227; *Gherashe v Boase* [1959] VR 1; *Hann v Butcher* [1963] SASR 197.
80 Eg *Mayer v Marchant* (1973) 5 SASR 567 at 570–571, 587–588; *Boucher v GJ Coles & Co Ltd* (1974) 9 SASR 495 at 501; *Power v Huffa* (1976) 14 SASR 337 at 344; *Holt v Cameron* (1979) 22 SASR 321 at 323; *Franklin v Stacey* (1981) 27 SASR 490 at 491; *Kidd v Reeves* [1972] VR 563; cp *Lyver v State of Victoria* [1983] 2 VR 475 at 485.
81 (1985) 60 ALR 449 at 457, per Gibbs CJ, at 486, 491, per Brennan J, at 499, per Dawson J; cp *Sweet v Parsley* [1970] AC 132 at 164, per Lord Diplock.
82 Ibid at 474, per Wilson J.
83 As to this, see the doubts raised by *Strasser v Roberge* (1979) 103 DLR (3d) 193, n 22, above.
84 (1978) 85 DLR (3d) 161.
85 *R v Strawbridge* [1970] NZLR 909; *Police v Creedon* [1976] 1 NZLR 571.
86 [1983] NZLR 78.
87 Cp *Sweet v Parsley* [1970] AC 132 at 157–158, per Lord Pearce; *Tesco Supermarkets Ltd v Nattrass* [1972] AC 153 at 169, per Lord Reid.
88 Cp *R v He Kaw Teh* (1983) 60 ALR 449 at 458, 491, 502; *Police v Creedon* [1976] 1 NZLR 571 at 575–576.
89 Cp *R v Gonder* (1981) 62 CCC (2d) 326 at 329.
90 (1978) 85 DLR (3d) 161 at 171.
91 Ibid at 182.
92 *Canadian Dredge and Dock Co Ltd v R* (1985) 19 CCC (3d) 1 at 8.
93 *R v Richardson* (1981) 62 CCC (2d) 417 at 430.
94 *R v Cummins* [1979] 3 WWR 593 at 606.
95 In *R v Chapin* (1979) 95 DLR (3d) 13, the possibility of up to 6 months' imprisonment, prohibition from hunting, and confiscation of a weapon were cited as reinforcing the presumption; cp *R v Z-H Paper Products Ltd* (1979) 52 CCC (2d) 91; *R v Merkle* [1980] 1 WWR 361; *R v Blackburn* (1980) 57 CCC (2d) 7; *R v Higgins* (1981) 60 CCC (2d) 246; *R v Watch* (1983) 10 CCC (3d) 521; contrast *R v Trophic Canada Ltd* (1980) 57 CCC (2d) 1.
96 *Reference Re s 94(2) of Motor Vehicle Act* (1983) 4 CCC (3d) 243; *R v Westfair Foods Ltd* (1985) 18 CCC (3d) 178.
97 *R v Watch* (1983) 10 CCC (3d) 521; *R v Merkle* [1980] 1 WWR 361.
98 *R v Chapin* (1979) 95 DLR (3d) 13 at 21; *R v Slovack* [1980] 1 WWR 368.
99 *R v Watch* (1983) 10 CCC (3d) 521; *R v Higgins* (1981) 60 CCC (2d) 246.
100 *R v Chapin* (1979) 95 DLR (3d) 13 at 23.
101 *R v Rohan's Rockpile Ltd* (1981) 57 CCC (2d) 388.
102 *R v Slovack* [1980] 1 WWR 368.
103 *R v Cummins* [1979] 3 WWR 593.

104 *R v Chapin* (1979) 95 DLR (3d) 13 at 22.
105 Eg *R v Grottoli* (1978) 43 CCC (2d) 158; *R v Consumers Distributing Co Ltd* (1980) 57 CCC (2d) 317; *R v The Star Luzon* [1984] 1 WWR 527.
106 Compare *R v Naugler* (1981) 65 CCC (2d) 25 and *R v Richardson* (1981) 62 CCC (2d) 417; *R v Maginnis* (1981) 64 CCC (2d) 430 seems to go too far in regarding the provision of a defence of 'lawful excuse' for related offences as supporting absolute liability for a serious offence for which no such defence was provided.
107 *R v Capozzi Enterprises Ltd* (1981) 60 CCC (2d) 385; *R v Z-H Paper Products Ltd* (1979) 52 CCC (2d) 91 (although in both these cases there is a contrary minority view).
108 Eg *R v Higgins* (1981) 60 CCC (2d) 246; *R v Blackburn* (1980) 57 CCC (2d) 7; *R v Watch* (1983) 10 CCC (3d) 521; *R v Dilorenzo* (1984) 11 CCC (3d) 13.
109 Eg *R v Z-H Paper Products Ltd* (1979) 52 CCC (2d) 91; *Aurora Quarrying Ltd v Catherwood* [1982] 6 WWR 517; *R v Rohan's Rockpile Ltd* (1981) 57 CCC (2d) 388; *R v McNeney* (1984) 11 CCC (3d) 557; *R v Boardman* (1979) 47 CCC (2d) 334; *R v Charterways Transportation Ltd* (1981) 60 CCC (2d) 510.
110 *R v Richardson* (1981) 62 CCC (2d) 417; *Re Ghilzon and Royal College of Dental Surgeons* (1979) 22 OR (2d) 756.
111 *R v Singh* (1981) 63 CCC (2d) 156; cp *R v Malhotra* (1980) 57 CCC (2d) 539.
112 Eg *R v Walker* (1979) 48 CCC (2d) 126; *R v Maidment* (1984) 10 CCC (3d) 512; similarly if compensation is the primary remedy: *Re Pasqua Hospital and Harmatiuk* (1983) 149 DLR (3d) 237; although sometimes the defence will be held available in criminal but not civil proceedings: *R v Saskatchewan Wheat Pool* (1979) 104 DLR (3d) 392.
113 *R v Trophic Canada Ltd* (1980) 57 CCC (2d) 1 is a rare example of such a case; cp Peiris 'Strict Liability in Commonwealth Criminal Law' (1983) 3 Legal Studies 117, 127–131, where many of the cited cases pre-date the fundamental restatement of principle in *Sault Ste Marie*.
114 [1983] NZLR 78.
115 Ibid at 85: 'In practice, the recognition of such a defence, with the onus of establishing it on the defendant, may well diminish the number of statutory offences which the courts feel compelled to hold to be absolute.'
116 *R v Howe* [1982] 1 NZLR 618 at 623.
117 Eg *R v Strawbridge* [1970] NZLR 909; *R v Meek* [1981] 1 NZLR 499 at 501–502; *R v Wood* [1982] 2 NZLR 233 at 237; *Police v Rowles* [1974] 2 NZLR 756.
118 Eg *Police v Creedon* [1976] 1 NZLR 571 (failing to comply with traffic sign); *Auckland City Council v King* [1977] 1 NZLR 429 (driving while disqualified); *Flyger v Auckland County Council* [1979] 1 NZLR 161 and *Rooke v Auckland County Council* [1980] 1 NZLR 680 (driving with excess blood-alcohol content); *Labour Department v Alouha* [1975] 1 NZLR 507 (overstaying an immigration permit); *MacKenzie v Hawkins* [1975] 1 NZLR 165 (omitting to provide animals with proper shelter).
119 For example, when a civil remedy or forfeiture of prohibited goods is held to depend on guilt of an offence: *Fraser v Beckett and Stirling Ltd* [1963] NZLR 480; cp *Police v Taylor* [1965] NZLR 87; or when special procedures are provided for the relief of those unable to fulfil statutory obligations: *Dobson v Wairewa County* [1968] NZLR 284.
120 In *Hastings City Council v Simons* [1984] 2 NZLR 502 at 506, a case concerning pollution, it was said without qualification that *R v MacKenzie* applied to offences 'within the public welfare category' recognised in that case.
121 (1985) 60 ALR 449; cp *Proudman v Dayman* (1941) 67 CLR 536.
122 Ibid at 452–454, per Gibbs CJ, at 480–481, per Brennan J, at 500–502, per Dawson J.
123 Ibid at 457–458, per Gibbs CJ, at 502, per Dawson J; applying this approach it was held that knowledge of the nature of the goods was an implicit ingredient of importing narcotics, which carried a maximum penalty of life imprisonment; cp *Samuels v Centofanti* [1967] SASR 251 at 269–270.
124 Ibid at 489, 491–492, per Brennan J, who treated as open the issue in *DPP v Morgan* [1976] AC 182; cp 457, per Gibbs CJ.
125 *Boucher v GJ Coles & Co Ltd* (1974) 9 SASR 495 at 504.
126 *Maher v Musson* (1934) 52 CLR 100 (a 'revenue' offence); *McCrae v Downey* [1947] VLR 194 (moving goods without a permit); *Gherashe v Boase* [1959] 1 VR 1 and *Handmer v Taylor* [1971] VR 308 (unauthorised logging); *Kidd v Reeves* [1972] VR 563 (driving while disqualified); *Boucher v G J Coles & Co Ltd* (1974) 9 SASR 495 at 508 (keeping unsound food for sale); *Burnett v LF Jeffries Nominees Pty Ltd* (1983) 33 SASR 124 (operating overloaded vehicle).
127 Eg *Bergin v Stack* (1953) 88 CLR 248 at 261.
128 *Kain & Shelton Pty Ltd v McDonald* (1971) 1 SASR 39 at 44, per Bray CJ.

129 Howard *Criminal Law* (4th edn, 1982), p 377; see eg *Welsh v Donnelly* [1983] 2 VR 173 (operating overloaded vehicle); *Hearn v McCann* (1982) 29 SASR 448 (speeding); *Franklin v Stacey* (1981) 27 SASR 490 (driving unregistered vehicle); *Norcock v Bowey* [1966] SASR 250 (owning straying cattle); *Lipshut v McKay* [1950] VLR 57 (breach of price controls); some serious sexual offences continue to involve liability notwithstanding reasonable mistake: *R v Kennedy* [1981] VR 565.
130 (1978) 85 DLR (3d) 161 at 170.
131 Cp *Hearn v McCann* (1982) 29 SASR 448 at 454 (but although it may be right to say that an automaton does not 'drive', it may be wrong to extend this to cases of duress).
132 Cp *R v Kennedy* [1981] VR 565.
133 Cp *Civil Aviation Department v MacKenzie* [1983] NZLR 78 at 81; *Tifaga v Department of Labour* [1980] 2 NZLR 235 at 241.
134 (1974) 9 SASR 495 at 498, 508; cp *GJ Coles & Co Ltd v Goldsworthy* [1985] WAR 183 at 187–188.
135 Eg *Sullivan v Fisher* [1954] SASR 33; *Norcock v Bowey* [1966] SASR 250; *Kain & Shelton Pty Ltd v McDonald* (1971) 1 SASR 39 at 51–52; *Mayer v Marchant* (1973) 5 SASR 567 at 572; *Boucher v GJ Coles & Co Ltd* (1974) 9 SASR 495 at 504–505; *Hearn v McCann* (1982) 29 SASR 448 at 452.
136 *Perka v R* (1984) 13 DLR (4th) 1.
137 *R v Walker* (1979) 48 CCC (2d) 126; Stuart *Canadian Criminal Law* (1982); pp 167–168.
138 Note [1986] New Zealand Law Journal 66.
139 (1984) 13 DLR (4th) 1, 21–22.
140 *Strasser v Roberge* (1979) 103 DLR (3d) 193 applied it even when the statute implicitly made fault an ingredient, but that is questionable; a rule that D had a mere evidential burden in relation to some aspects of the defence (eg the fact of necessity), but the persuasive burden in relation to preceding fault, would be unduly complex.
141 Budd and Lynch 'Voluntariness, Causation and Strict Liability' [1978] Crim LR 74.
142 Which in *Sweet v Parsley* [1970] AC 132 at 162–165 was the mens rea which Lord Diplock regarded as normally to be implied when the statute is silent on the question.
143 *R v He Kaw Teh* (1985) 60 ALR 449 at 457, per Gibbs CJ, at 489, per Brennan J, at 498–499, per Dawson J; nor does the New Zealand Court of Appeal exclude this possibility: *R v Howe* [1982] 1 NZLR 618 at 623–624.

Clarifying the criminal law: declarations in criminal proceedings

ATH Smith

Introduction

In a recent article, I explored some of the implications of the fact that English criminal law can operate in a way that is inherently offensive to the principle of legality.[1] Based as it is on the common law methodology, it is essentially retrospective in its operation, and since this is at variance with the objectives of due notice and fair warning to which a system of criminal justice should aspire,[2] ways must be sought of minimising this unhappy feature of our criminal justice system. One obvious method of pursuing this objective is through the enactment of a criminal code, a project to which John Smith has turned his formidable energies recently, chairing the team that has produced a report and draft Bill that might yet form the basis of such a code.[3] This is a logical development of his work in synthesising and rationalising the criminal law both in his writings and in his work for the Criminal Law Revision Committee.

A code, even when it is enacted, cannot be expected to resolve all the problems that will inevitably arise over the precise scope of criminal liability. There will continue to be difficulties of interpretation and construction; gaps in the law will emerge because of unforeseen manifestations of human wickedness, and the inherently ambiguous nature of language must mean that the courts will still have to resolve the doubts from time to time. The common law tradition is that such doubts should be settled piecemeal, as they arise for decision in each case, with an immediate impact on the case out of which the problem arises. Even though the courts recognise that their decision-making has the dual purposes of dispute resolution and the articulation of legal rules, they are by tradition hostile to any attempt to have them resolve disputed legal questions in the abstract.[4] Departures from that tradition have been grudging and infrequent, especially in the criminal law field. Yet the declaration is in many respects admirably suited to clarifying doubts about the scope of the criminal law. The process has the least adverse impact from a rule of law perspective; it enables the citizen to ascertain in advance precisely what he may or may not do without subjecting him to the threat of retrospective sanction. Yet until comparatively recently, it has been relatively little used for this purpose. As recently as 1962, I Zamir[5] summarised what he took to be the legal position governing the availability of declarations as follows:

> 'Where a person acts or intends to act in a certain way, which is not malum in se, and is confronted with the threat of criminal prosecution, he may bring an action for a declaration to the effect that that act is not illegal. The court will not generally be inhibited from making such a declaration by the mere fact that the matter could be criminally adjudicated. Where, however, the criminal jurisdiction has been vested in another tribunal, the court may examine whether that tribunal is more appropriate than the High Court for the determination of the issue. When the answer is in the affirmative, the court will be reluctant to exercise its declaratory power.'

The purpose of this contribution is to examine some recent developments in which the English courts have shown themselves more readily prepared to lend their declaratory jurisdiction to the purpose of achieving greater clarity in the criminal law. I am delighted to have been given an opportunity to write it in appreciation of John Smith's unfailing encouragement to me.

Whereas Zamir hints that the process has been used only in those cases where the conduct concerned is not 'truly criminal', we are currently witnessing the secondary phase in the development of the declaratory process in the criminal law, the end result of which may well mean that genuine doubts about the scope of criminal liability can be resolved in the abstract, without the need to resort to the blunderbuss techniques of prosecution and conviction. As is the way with our essentially pragmatic English system, we have already begun to evolve a mechanism for the resolution of semi-hypothetical disputes, with the development of the Attorney-General's Reference procedure.[6] Many of the arguments that can be invoked against hypothetical dispute resolution inherent in the action for a declaration might equally be levelled at that procedure; yet for all that it appears, that mechanism has worked tolerably well since provision was first made for it in 1972.[7]

In developing the declaratory remedy, the courts have been moving tentatively and cautiously. This article will urge that in making the declaration more readily available, the courts are moving in the right direction; the undoubted difficulties and obstacles should be confronted and overcome, for reasons both of principle and practice. It may well be that the need to seek declaratory relief will not often arise. If the criminal will not often, in Mr Justice Holmes' droll description, 'carefully consider the text of the law before he murders or steals',[8] he is even less likely to ask a court just how far he can go in some nefarious enterprise before he starts to run foul of the law. But sometimes we use the criminal law for purposes to which it is not naturally suited, as when it is an adjunct to administration. And at other times, there is genuine doubt as to the meaning of a statute and the individual needs to know where he stands. If our system cannot be perfect, it can be better than it is at present.

1 The problem illustrated

No better illustration of the potential usefulness of a declaratory process can be given than by contrasting two recent incidents involving the Attorney-General. In January 1981, the Attorney-General brought what was described in court as a 'test prosecution' against a leading firm of antique dealers to ascertain the scope of s1(1) of the Auction (Bidding Agreements) Act 1927. It was common practice for antique dealers to bid for valuable items at auction collectively, and there was an argument that this contravened the provisions of the Act.[9] The auction houses objected to the practice, since it might result in items being sold at auction for much less than their true worth. The dealers countered by saying that if they did not act collectively, they would not be able to buy at all, since the items would be too expensive for them individually, and what they were doing was not caught either by the terms of the Act or by its spirit. The Attorney-General was faced with a dilemma. He could have sought to resolve it by making his own judgment about the scope of the Act, and indicating that he would (or would not) consider bringing prosecutions under the Act.[10] On the other hand, to bring a prosecution when it was accepted on all sides that the dealers were acting in good faith and in the belief that their conduct was within the law might seem oppressive. No defence of mistake of law would be available to the dealers, and the Attorney-General could offer no guarantee that the court would not take an extremely dim view of the way in which the dealers were acting, and impose a more severe penalty than he might have wished. Nor could the Attorney-General offer any post-conviction balm if the court did the unexpected, since that, constitutionally, is a matter for the Home Secretary.[11] On balance, however, he decided to institute a prosecution. In the event, the court decided that the conduct was not caught by the terms of the Act, and the defendants were acquitted. A letter in the Times[12] lamented the fact that there was no declaratory process that might have achieved the same result without having placed in jeopardy the good reputation of the particular defendants, and asked rhetorically whether it was right that the good name, property and even liberty of individuals should be jeopardised for the sake of clarifying inadequately-drafted laws. The letter went on to suggest that an alternative declaratory judgment procedure should be available.

Whether or not and in what circumstances such a procedure was already available had been the subject of discussion in the House of Lords shortly before, in *Imperial Tobacco Ltd v A-G*.[13] The decision is of considerable importance in the development of the declaratory process in criminal law matters, since the House of Lords expressly invited the Attorney-General to address them on the procedural aspects of the case. The tobacco company, having been prosecuted for a breach of the Lotteries and Amusements Act 1976, ss 2 and 14, sought a declaration in the Commercial Court to the effect that the scheme that they had devised did not contravene the provisions of the Act. The House came to the conclusion, contrary to the decision of the Court of Appeal, that the conduct engaged in by the plaintiff tobacco company was indeed an offence, and a declaration to the opposite effect could not have been granted. Many of the remarks in the speeches are, therefore, technically obiter, and the law governing precisely when a declaration can or cannot issue is left to some extent uncertain. In the course of his speech, Viscount Dilhorne said:

> 'I can well see the advantages of persons being able to obtain rulings on whether or not certain conduct on which they wish to embark will be criminal and it may well be a defect in our present system that it does not provide for that.'

The suggestion that the declaratory process is never available in such situations surely goes too far, and Viscount Dilhorne was uttering his remarks in a context where a prosecution had already been instituted when the application for a declaration was made. There may be a defect in the law, but it is not so large as the learned Lord's remarks would lead us to believe.

The second illustration that may be offered of the utility of a clarificatory process arises out of the incident in which the Attorney-General sought guidance in the form of a declaration in *A-G v Able*,[14] on the question whether the distribution of a booklet by the Society for Voluntary Euthanasia (Exit) constituted the offence of aiding and abetting the commission of suicide under s2(1) of the Suicide Act 1961. His reasons for proceeding in this form rather than by bringing a prosecution were fully explained in an affidavit presented to the court by the Attorney-General's legal secretary. They indicate a considerable sympathy on the part of the prosecuting authorities for the predicament in which the prospective defendants were placed, and display a willingness to resolve legal disputes otherwise than by prosecution and conviction. The secretary might have made the point that to proceed by way of prosecution would not necessarily have clarified the law because of the inscrutability of the jury's verdict, especially if the result was an acquittal. The sequence of events was that, when the existence of the booklet was brought to his attention, the Attorney-General contacted the Society and indicated that he considered that the distribution was criminal. However, the Society obtained legal advice to the contrary. In the words of the affidavit:

> 'It is accepted that the members of that committee are respectable persons who chose to issue the booklet out of genuine and strongly-held beliefs and who would not follow a course of action which they know to be criminal. In view of the existence of a genuine dispute as to the precise ambit of the law it was considered desirable to seek a declaration from this Honourable Court to resolve that dispute quickly and authoritatively without exposing respectable people to prosecution for an offence carrying a maximum of 14 years imprisonment.'

In the event, Woolf J (as he then was) declined to grant the declaration sought, largely because he felt that the question would turn in each case on the intention with which the booklet was distributed, and this was pre-eminently a matter for the jury in each case. Nevertheless, the learned judge conducted an extensive examination of the law of complicity, and offered a considerable amount of guidance as to the scope of the law in the course of his judgment. As he put it:

> 'Having examined the facts and the law, I am satisfied that there is no form of declaration that it would be appropriate to grant. That it is desirable for the law to be clarified, I accept, but if there is to be any clarification as a result of the proceedings before this court, it must come not as a result of my granting the declaration, but from the limited assistance which I have been able to give in the course of this judgment.'

But that assistance was, in spite of his Lordship's diffidence, considerable. It put the members of the Society on notice that if they continued to distribute the booklet, there was a real risk that a jury might draw adverse inferences of culpable intent against them, and they could therefore mould their conduct accordingly. Of course, they could have gone on to take the risk that they would encounter a sympathetic jury; but the declaratory process had, in this situation, already proved its worth.

My principal concern in this essay is with the defendant who seeks to invoke the jurisdiction and assistance of the court to enable himself to ascertain the legality of his own proposed conduct. It is a process of which the Attorney-General might also usefully avail himself. A related but different problem arises when a person who is injuriously affected by the doubtfully lawful conduct of another wishes to use the civil declaratory processes to have the conduct terminated, or as a buttress in a suit for damages. There have been a number of recent decisions in this area too,[15] but since they raise issues of only tangential relevance to the particular problems that I wish to air, especially difficulties of locus standi, they will not be examined here.

2 The scope of the declaration

One of the problems of coming to firm conclusions about the exact state of the law is, as Professor HWR Wade observed in his comments on *Gillick*[16] 'the amorphous character of the declaratory judgment, which lacks a precise area of application.' A declaration of right is an authoritative statement of the law as it applies to the parties.[17] A familiar remedy in modern times, especially in the administrative law context,[18] the declaration is of comparatively modern origin, being little more than a century old. The power to make a declaration is inherent, and originally it was available only in the Court of Chancery, but was extended to afford general relief by the Judicature Acts of 1873 and 1875, and the Rules of the Supreme Court of 1883[19] made thereunder. These left the courts considerable discretion to develop the remedy as they saw fit, and at least some of the early cases and decisions on the rules relating to the availability of the declaratory judgment can be traced to judicial unfamiliarity with (if not antipathy to) declaratory proceedings generally.[20]

The jurisdiction to grant a declaration is extremely broad. 'Anyone is on principle entitled to apply to the court for a declaration as to their rights[21] unless statutorily prohibited expressly or by necessary implication.'[22] It is still the case that 'the scope of the declaratory jurisdiction can be defined only in a negative way, that is, by stating the cases in which the courts have no power to grant declaratory relief.'[23] In practice, the courts have exhibited most sympathy towards applications emanating from persons in brushes with officialdom over such relatively minor regulatory matters as the validity of a defective premises repair order,[24] the validity of by-laws regulating street construction,[25] liability to taxation under a questionable assessment,[26] the common law right to continue to conduct auctions where this had been purportedly taken away by by-laws,[27] and various rights under the town planning legislation.[28] Although the sanction to penalise a failure to comply with the law was in each case criminal in character, in most cases the penalties threatened were relatively trivial, but not invariably so. In *London and Country Commercial Investments Ltd v A-G*,[29] for example, a failure to secure the necessary Treasury approval for a particular financial transaction could result in imprisonment for a period of two years, which might be imposed not simply on the plaintiff company, but also on a large group of its directors and officers.

The distinction between offences malum in se and prohibita which underlies the traditional accounts of the law,[30] and which will not in any event withstand very rigorous critical scrutiny, is breaking down in practice. Recent applications have concerned the scope of the law of abortion,[31] aiding and abetting suicide,[32] and the giving of contraceptive advice by doctors to sexually under-age girls.[33] These are some of the most highly controversial social, legal and moral issues of recent times, and can hardly be regarded as offences mala prohibita. It is true that since the regulatory offences tend to be offences of strict liability, there is not the mens rea complication that inhibited Woolf J in *Able*, and the declaration is to that extent easier to formulate than it may be for the more serious crimes. More significant than the subject matter of the application, it would seem, is the fact that the applicant exhibits a willingness to comply with the law, whatever it may be, so long as he knows what it enjoins or prohibits. As Professor Wade puts it, 'everything depends on the merits of his motives for seeking the remedy.'[34] In appropriate circumstances, the courts do appear to be taking an increasingly helpful attitude towards those in a genuine quandary about their legal positions, even though it may be that a breach of the law would result in a serious social wrong.

3 The jurisprudential status of the declaration

One of the areas of uncertainty surrounding declaratory relief is the status of the decision of a civil court in criminal proceedings. To what extent can the declaration bind the parties subsequently? In the civil law it cannot, of course, be enforced, but it does in appropriate circumstances create a res judicata between the parties to it.[35] But so far as the criminal law is concerned, the law is in a state of considerable confusion on the point. There are dicta to the effect that a decision would not be binding on a criminal court.[36] Lord Denning MR in the *Royal College of Nursing v DHSS* case[37] said that 'if there should ever be a case in the courts, the decision would ultimately be that of the jury', which suggests that a declaration could not be decisive. It has also been suggested that a declaration would not give rise to a plea of autrefois acquit.[38] Against this, however, Zamir[39] suggests that a declaration 'will probably create a res judicata', and an American note says that the characteristic feature of the declaratory judgment is precisely that the issue does become res judicata.[40]

Some light may be shed on the point by turning to first principles. A declaration is available only to resolve points of law,[41] and is only available where the facts are not in dispute.[42] Even though the application of the law to the facts of the case in hand may be a matter for a jury, it is difficult to see how a declaration establishing a point of law can avoid the ordinary rules of precedent in so far as it relates to the state of the law. This is not the same as issue estoppel, which the House of Lords has held cannot apply in criminal law,[43] which is principally concerned with findings of fact. Suppose for the sake of argument[44] that a prosecution were brought against a nurse in the face of the ruling by the House of Lords in the *DHSS* case that abortions performed by nurses under the instructions of doctors cannot be regarded as unlawful. The trial judge would be bound to accede to a submission of no case were the facts such that they could not possibly give rise to a conviction.

Even if the declaration does not technically create a res judicata, this would not seem to be a reason why the declaration should not issue at all. The beauty of the remedy is precisely that the courts are able to state what rights are, and what the law is, even though there may be no enforcement mechanism available. And in any event, there are other mechanisms available to the courts to prevent the abuse of their proceedings.[45] For example, where an application for a declaration has been instituted, the courts have regarded that as a reason to stay subsequent prosecutions on the grounds that this amounts to an abuse of the court's processes.[46]

4 The case for affording declaratory relief

Essentially, the case for affording the individual declaratory relief is one of principle. The criminal law is the system of rules by which he must live under pain of opprobrium and penalty should he fail to conform to its dictates. It follows as a matter of principle that he should be able to know in advance precisely what it enjoins him to do or abstain from doing. As an American court pithily put it, 'the right to test a statute by submitting to arrest is not a remedy.'[47] Where a citizen wishes to know the limits of the permissible, some mechanism ought to be available to enable him to ascertain them. Sometimes, too, as in the *Imperial Tobacco* case,[48] considerable amounts of money are at stake. The advertising gambit impugned in that case was to cost several million pounds to mount, and it cannot be right that the subject should be obliged to risk all in the face of vague laws.

To this simple (if not simplistic) line of reasoning, there are two possible counters. There is, first, the thin-ice principle enunciated by Lord Morris in *Knuller (Publishing, Printing and Promotions) Ltd v DPP*:[49]:

> 'In many cases there can be no certainty what the decision will be. But none of this is a reflection on the law. Nor do I know of any procedure under which someone could be told with precision just how far he may go before he may incur some civil or some criminal liability. Those who skate on thin ice can hardly expect to find a sign which will denote the precise spot where he (sic) will fall in.'

What Lord Morris appears to be saying is that an imprecise criminal law has a valuable deterrent effect where the activity in which the individual is engaging is in any event of doubtful social utility (for example selling pornography).[50] Quite apart from the value–judgment inherent in such a stance, and the difficulties of knowing how to assess what is or is not of social value, there is the objection that if the conduct happens to fall on the right side of the proscription, the individual is entitled to engage in it, however morally or socially disreputable his conduct may be. But in any event, this response runs entirely counter to the principle of legality on which our system is based.

A second, related response to the rule of law argument was explicitly stated by Brightman LJ in the *DHSS* decision[51] when he said:

> 'I decline to express a view as to precisely what does or does not need to be done by, or to be personally and immediately supervised by, the doctor in order to satisfy the stringent requirements of section 1. It is not the function of the court to decide how close to dangerous waters it is possible to sail without actually being shipwrecked.'

The doctors who would be subject to such a law might be forgiven for thinking that such an attitude is, to put it mildly, unhelpful. If it is the function of a criminal court to say after the event that the doctor has sailed too close to the wind, what is to prevent it from saying in advance where the line is to be drawn? The danger here is that the doctor confronted by such an uncertain law is bound to err on the side of caution, and where he is engaging in what Parliament has deemed to be socially valuable (or at least socially neutral) conduct, the state of the law has an improperly inhibiting effect. If he proceeds in the face of uncertainty, he puts at risk his career, and may well find himself subjected to all the informal sanctions that the pre-trial procedure inflicts. A determination that conduct is not criminal dissolves the inhibiting effect of such uncertainty.

But Brightman LJ may have been making a rather different point, which is that it is not part of the court's function to assist those who are predisposed to engage in unlawful conduct. That is, constitutionally, the courts should not lend themselves to a process whereby they assist a rogue to escape the law. This is echoed in the remarks of du Parq LJ, who said that the individual was not entitled to know what the penalty would be if he were acting illegally:[52]

> 'In effect, therefore, the appellant is asking the court to inform him how he would stand if he should do an unlawful act. If he intends to act unlawfully, the question is merely academic. If he has it in mind to act illegally and wrongfully, it is no doubt convenient for him to know how severe the penalty is likely to be, or how easily he is likely to escape, but it seems strange that a court of law should be asked to expend time and trouble providing him with this information.'

But it does not follow that conduct that is on the borderline of criminality is necessarily of no social utility, which seems to be the premise underlying this objection. The abortion case affords a good example of the point.[53] Parliament had decided that, for a variety of social reasons outlined in the Abortion Act 1967, abortions could in future be lawfully performed. The only difficulty was that it was unclear under the Act who should be permitted to perform them. That was the issue that the courts were invited to decide, and on which the House ultimately provided an extremely helpful answer. What is critical, it is suggested, is that the applicant should exhibit a willingness to comply with the law, whatever the law might be.

A number of subsidiary arguments of varying strengths can be given to buttress the case from the standpoint of principle.[54] The case in favour of making the declaration available is even stronger in this country than it is in America, since we have no defence of due warning and fair notice. In this country, the constitutionality of legislation is unimpeachable, so that the individual has no opportunity to argue that the legislation was invalid, although regulations and other forms of subordinate legislation, or administrative orders, can be challenged by acting in breach of them and then contending at prosecution that they were ultra vires.[55] Furthermore, we have no mistake of law defence[56] permitting the individual to argue that he acted in good faith on what he believed the law to be. Without a declaratory process, therefore, the individual would be forced to take the risk and then run foul of the ignorantia juris maxim.

There are some additional arguments. An individual who takes trouble to bring the legality of the conduct in question before the court will almost invariably be law-abiding. A declaration will therefore have a uniquely deterrent effect, especially individual, but quite possibly general too. The declaratory process may have the advantages of speed, especially where the criminal process is by way of indictment,[57] and the issue may be too complex for the lower courts.[58] One might also mention here the position of the Attorney-General. The readiness with which successive incumbents have resorted to the Attorney-General's Reference procedure suggests that they find it a most valuable device. It must often be the case that they have some doubts about a particular point of law arising out of some questionable course of conduct of which they are aware. A greater resort to the declaratory jurisdiction of the courts is surely to be preferred to the blunt instrument that the prosecution process represents.

5 The objections to declaratory relief

The objections to the granting of declaratory relief would appear to be of two kinds — considerations of institutional principle and, reflecting them, problems of procedure and practice.

There is a strong sense in the judgments that too ready a grant of declarations would clutter the courts. This 'floodgates' argument was advanced, for example, by the Solicitor General in the *Imperial Tobacco*[59] decision. Once the initiative for the invocation of the criminal law no longer rests with the responsible prosecuting authorities, there is a risk that the process will run out of control. This was advanced in one of the earliest and most critical decisions, *Dyson v A-G*,[60] where it was devastatingly rejected by Farwell LJ:

> 'if "inconvenience" is a legitimate consideration at all, the convenience in the public interest is all in favour of providing a speedy and easy access to the courts.'

Underlying this objection may be the fear that judges might be asked to rule on, for example, the legality of publishing arguably pornographic literature.[61] If so, the fear would seem to be groundless, since the procedure is not available where the facts are in dispute.[62] A further screening device is the fact that the declaration is a discretionary remedy; this is perhaps a less sound response, since the discretion ought to be exercised in accordance with some principles, and mere distaste for the applicant who happens to be acting just on the right side of legality does not, without more, appear to be a particularly worthy reason.[63]

A second objection of principle is that of hypotheticality. Constitutionally, it is for the judges to decide disputed issues between subject and subject, or between the individual and the state. If there is no real issue, the courts have no business to be expressing opinions, and have no jurisdiction to do so. The point is seen even more starkly in American law. By virtue of the American constitution, the courts have authority to take jurisdiction only where there is a genuine 'case or controversy'.[64] Where a person has not yet embarked on a criminal course of conduct, the argument may run, there is no issue on which the court can fasten; the issue is not yet ripe. The difficulty is that if the actor pushes ahead too far with his proposed course of conduct in order to create a justiciable issue, he may run into the rule that an offence may already have been committed and therefore prosecution is the most appropriate form of adjudication. Yet on occasion, the courts have been prepared to overlook the difficulty. In *Gillick*,[65] for example, it was accepted that there was no danger that any of the applicant's own children either had received contraceptive advice or was likely to be in any need of it. Counsel in the House of Lords sought to argue that the issue was indeed moot, but the House held that Mrs Gillick's private rights were sufficiently threatened by the circular impugned. This is a wholly different attitude from that displayed in *Tindall v Wright*[66] where the court said that:

> 'The court will not decide a point of law which has become academic, even though both parties are anxious to have it determined, and though it is a matter of public importance on which a Government Department desires the guidance of the court with a view to introducing amending legislation if necessary.'

Allied to this objection is the notion that if the court does take jurisdiction when it should not have done so, the resulting judgment may have no value as a precedent. Indeed, some critics would go so far as to argue that such opinions have no value as precedents even where jurisdiction is properly assumed.[67] I confess that, so far as declarations are concerned, I find the argument hard to follow, although I would concede that there may be something in the point when the case presented is wholly hypothetical. But where a person intends to engage in a particular course of conduct so long as it is lawful, I cannot see that what he proposes is hypothetical even though it may relate to the future, or that the resulting judgment as to his rights to engage in that conduct should not operate as a precedent in similar future cases.

The third objection is that judicial restraint is desirable in matters of criminal law, and the conditions that dictate this may be absent when the courts decide issues in the abstract. When the courts are deciding prospectively, they are freed from the constraints that the position of the individual defendant imposes. Put another way, the judges are freer to make law in an inclusionary way when they are not confronted by a real defendant who may suffer as a result of the decision that they take. For example, in *Neale v RMJE (a minor)*[68] the court was confronted with the question whether a person was 'drunk' in a public place for the purposes of s12 of the Licensing Act 1872 when he had reduced himself to a state of intoxication through solvent abuse. There can be little doubt that the mischief at which Parliament was striking in the legislation was very similar to that presented by the new social phenomenon of glue-sniffing, and had the court been permitted to proceed analogically, it might well have been tempted to short circuit the legislative process by saying that solvent abuse came within the mischief of the legislation. But the fact that a particular defendant stands to suffer as a result of their decision constrains the courts to apply such rule of law conventions as the strict construction of statutes when they are confronted with ambiguous legislation. A declaratory process would release them from such constraints. In his comment on *A-G's Reference (No 3 of 1983)*,[69] in which the court gave an extended definition to the law of affray, John Smith observes that 'the judges may have renounced any power to create new offences, but their ability and inclination to extend old ones seems to be flourishing.' In doing this on the reference procedure, the judges can perhaps be criticised for acting in breach of the separation of powers notion underlying our constitution; they are legislating and not judging. But they do not thereby ignore the constraints of due notice and fair warning, since the liberty of no particular individual is involved. Whether the risk of such a breach is so serious that it should be allowed to weigh against the otherwise valuable declaratory procedure is a difficult point to assess.

The second type of objection to the declaratory process is more procedural than principled. The obstacles may well be the more concrete applications of some of the institutional objections, and the mechanisms by which they are effected. It is said, for example, that equity and hence the civil courts will not interfere in criminal matters. The objection was stated very clearly in *Watt v McLaughlin*:[70]

> 'The existence of those (the criminal) courts has always been held a sufficient ground for the Chancery Court to refuse a declaration or an injunction to restrain such alleged criminal acts where no damage to property is alleged or threatened.'

This view of the law was outdated even when it was uttered, although it still manifests itself in the rule that the remedy will not be available where the statute expressly or impliedly decrees that another tribunal should determine the matter.[71] In *Flint v A-G*,[72] for example, where a conscript wished to establish by way of declaration in the Chancery Court that he had been improperly conscripted, it was held that the action must be decided (by way of prosecution) in the High Court, and that the Chancery Court had no jurisdiction to decide the matter (although Neville J added for good measure that had it been a matter of discretion, he would have exercised that against the applicant in any case). In the *Pyx Granite* case[73] by contrast, the House of Lords was quite undeterred by the fact that the relevant legislation established a mechanism for resolving the disputed issue. The remedies that it gave were cumulative rather than exclusive, and the courts can grant a stay of the other proceedings pending the outcome of the declaration application should they choose to do so.[74] The objection on this count may then be a matter that the court should take into account in deciding whether or not it should exercise its discretion in favour of the applicant, but it should not be decisive.

This leads to a related objection that the civil courts should not decide matters of criminal law or, conversely, that the criminal courts are best equipped to resolve questions of criminal law.[75] This objection has a superficial plausibility, but it is undercut by the fact that the declaration is available only to resolve disputed questions of law, and can be issued only where the facts are not in dispute. Those features that make the criminal courts singularly well-equipped to resolve criminal law disputes are not really deployed at all when the only dispute is as to the law. There is, perhaps, a burden of proof point. It may be rare that disputes in criminal law can be emptied of all their factual content, if only because a defendant may wish to reserve his position should the legal argument be lost. But where that can be done, the criminal courts have no obvious superiority over the civil. Indeed, where the issue is complex, it may be altogether more appropriately settled in the High Court rather than before a bench of magistrates or the Crown Court. Since rights of appeal exist as far as the House of Lords no matter where the process begins, it is to some extent artificial to think in terms of civil and criminal courts in any event.

That the civil courts can decide disputed questions about the scope of the criminal law is well illustrated by *Grundy (Teddington) Ltd v Fulton*[76] which contains one of the best analyses of problems raised by the concept of appropriation under the Theft Act 1968 which it was necessary to resolve for the purposes of interpreting an insurance contract. Similarly, the leading definitions in the common law of riot are all taken from decisions in actions for damages under the Riot (Damages) Act 1886.[77] Furthermore, it is clearly the law that, even where there has been a clear breach of the criminal law, the civil courts can intervene to prevent continuing breaches of the criminal law if that rather than a criminal prosecution is the more appropriate way of preventing the miscreant from continuing his unlawful activities.[78]

Another facet of this objection is that not only are disputes as to fact the essence of most criminal trials, but there are different kinds of fact.[79] That is, even where it is known or agreed precisely what happened, the jury has a role in deciding what the significance of the 'facts' should be. It is for the jury (or other tribunal of fact) to decide whether admitted conduct is 'dishonest' for the purposes of the law of theft,[80] or 'insulting' within s 5 of the Public Order Act 1936,[81] or 'obscene' for the purposes of the Obscene Publications Act 1959.[82] For that reason too, the civil courts must be slow to intervene with declarations, since they might thereby usurp the functions of the jury.[83] This cannot be countered by the simple argument that the declaration is available for legal disputes only, but it prompts a suggestion. Since the jury is the most appropriate tribunal to determine these disputed questions of value, would it not be possible in appropriate cases to summon a jury to assist with the application for the declaration ?

A formidable obstacle apparently erected in the *Imperial Tobacco* decision[84] is that if criminal proceedings have already been instituted when the application for the declaration is made, the applicant should not be permitted to forestall a prosecution by going belatedly onto the attack. In that case, Viscount Dilhorne, having observed that no case had been cited to their Lordships where a civil court had after the commencement of a prosecution granted a declaration that no offence had been committed, said:

> 'In my opinion, it cannot be right to grant a declaration that an accused is innocent after a prosecution has started.'

A similar view was expressed by Lord Lane, who said:

> 'Where there are concurrent proceedings in different courts between parties who for practical purposes are the same in each, and the same issue will have to be determined in each, the court has jurisdiction to stay one set of proceedings if it is just and convenient to do so or if the circumstances are such that one set of proceedings is vexatious and an abuse of the process of the court. Where however criminal proceedings have been properly instituted and are not vexatious or an abuse of the process of the court it is not a proper exercise of the court's discretion to grant the defendant in those proceedings a declaration that the facts to be alleged by the prosecution do not in law prove the offence charged.'

By contrast in the Court of Appeal in the same case, Ormrod and Browne LJJ clearly thought that the objection was not decisive,[85] and the other members of the House of Lords came to no clear conclusions on the point. Since the decision of the House was obiter, the way is still open to argue that although this may be a reason for not affording discretionary relief, it should not be a conclusive objection.[86] Of course, the defendant should not be permitted to employ the declaratory process to challenge a conviction vexatiously.[87] But there may in exceptional cases be reasons why it should be right to proceed by the civil rather than the criminal process even after the criminal proceedings have been activated. There is, too, an argument from principle. Once the conduct to be challenged has already occurred, the choice of procedure by which its legality is to be established is largely a matter of determining what consequences should flow; the distinction between the civil and the criminal law is essentially procedural and consequential.[88] In other words, whether or not the conduct is in practice to be regarded as criminal rests on the decision of a prosecutor. It would be most consistent, and in accordance with principle to say that, once the allegedly criminal conduct has already taken place, the courts should not grant declarations at all. That is, the real objection ought to be that the individual has already committed a criminal offence and should take the consequences, whatever they might be. But if that stance is not adopted, it becomes a matter of discretion for the court. It would look extremely odd to say that the discretion of the court exists when the putative defendant gets in first, but not where the prosecutor happens to be first off the mark. It would then be the choice of the prosecutor that defeats the court's discretion, and it is by no means obvious why that should be so. The better course, it is suggested, is to treat the availability of a declaration as a matter for discretion even when the criminal proceedings have begun. What one can say is that, once the wrongful conduct has taken place, it should not depend on whether it is the prosecutor or the applicant who happens to strike the first blow, which may be entirely a matter of chance. Liability to criminal penalties ought to turn on matters of principle and not, as John Smith has so persuasively argued, on matters of chance.[89]

NOTES

1 'Judicial Law Making in the Criminal Law' (1984) 100 LQR 46.
2 For an excellent discussion of the principle of legality in its application to the substantive criminal law, see PW Low, JC Jeffries Jnr and RJ Bonnie *Criminal Law: Cases and Materials* (1982), ch1.
3 Codification of the Criminal Law: A Report to the Law Commission (1985), HC 270. For commentaries, see [1986] Crim LR 285 ff.
4 For a recent study, see J Jaconelli 'Hypothetical Disputes, Moot Points of Law and Advisory Opinions' (1985) 101 LQR 587.
5 *The Declaratory Judgment* (1962), p 224. The classic treatise is E Borchard *Declaratory Judgments* (2nd edn, 1941); see also PW Young *Declaratory Orders* (1975).
6 Criminal Justice Act 1972, s 36. For a discussion, see J Jaconelli 'The Attorney-General's Reference: A Problematic Device' [1981] Crim LR 543.
7 J Ll J Edwards *The Attorney-General, Politics and the Public Interest* (1984), p159.
8 Holmes J in *McBoyle v United States* 283 US (1931).
9 Some of the possible interpretations of the Act were canvassed in my 'Auction Rings' [1981] Crim LR 87.
10 As he did, for example, in the case of the legality of the post-coital pill, the use of which he ruled to be lawful. See 42 HC Official Report (5th series) cols 238, 239.
11 'The Prerogative of Mercy, the Power of Pardon and Criminal Justice' [1983] PL 389.
12 12 January 1981. I fear that I must acknowledge its authorship.
13 [1981] AC 718. For an extended discussion, see J Ll J Edwards *The Attorney-General, Politics and the Public Interest* (1984), p 150. And see D Feldman 'Declarations and the Control of Prosecutions' [1981] Crim LR 25.
14 [1984] QB 795. For discussion, see KHM Smith 'Assisting in Suicide — The Attorney-General and the Voluntary Euthanasia Society' [1983] Crim LR 597.
15 Constitutionally, the most important of these is undoubtedly *Gouriet v Union of Post Office Workers* [1978] AC 435, HL. See J Ll J Edwards *op cit* at 129. *Amstrad Consumer Electronics plc v British Phonographic Industry Ltd* [1986] FSR 159.
16 [1984] QB 581; revsd [1986] AC 112. See the comment by HWR Wade in (1986) 102 LQR 173.
17 B Kercher and M Noone *Remedies* (1983), p 154.
18 See SA de Smith *Judicial Review of Administrative Action* (4th edn, 1980), pp 504–509. HWR Wade *Administrative Law* (5th edn, 1982), pp 522 et seq. And see I Zamir 'The Declaratory

Judgment Revisited' (1974) CLP 43. The decision of the House of Lords in *O'Reilly v Mackman* [1983] 2 AC 237 may very well have reversed this trend, since in public law matters the proper course is now to proceed by way of application for judicial review. See HWR Wade (1986) 102 LQR 173. See the same author's 'Procedure and Prerogative in Public Law' (1985) 101 LQR 180, 182–3.

19 In particular, Ord 25, r 5. See now Ord 15, r 16. See generally *Supreme Court Practice* (1985), p 217.

20 See for example *Grand Junction Waterworks Co v Hampton Urban Council* [1898] 2 Ch 331. See also *Flint v A-G* [1918] 1 Ch 216.

21 'Rights' in this context includes obligations and liabilities.

22 Per Lord Lane in *Imperial Tobacco v A-G* [1981] AC 718 at 750.

23 Zamir *op cit*, p 31.

24 *St James Hall Ltd v LCC* (1900) 83 LT 98, CA.

25 *A-G v Ashborne Recreation Ground Co* [1903] 1 Ch 101.

26 *Dyson v A-G* [1911] 1 KB 410; *Dyson v A-G* [1912] 1 Ch 158. See also *Grant v Knaresborough UDC* [1928] Ch 310.

27 *Nicholls v Tavistock UDC* [1923] 2 Ch 18.

28 *Swallow and Pearson (a firm) v Middlesex County Council* [1953] 1 All ER 580, [1953] 1 WLR 422; *Hamilton v West Sussex County Council* [1958] 2 QB 286; *Marshall v Nottingham Corpn* [1960] 1 WLR 707; *Pyx Granite Co Ltd v Ministry of Housing and Local Government* [1960] AC 260.

29 [1953] 1 All ER 436, [1953] 1 WLR 312.

30 Zamir *op cit*, who quotes Borchard, to the same effect; *op cit* n 5 above.

31 *Royal College of Nursing of the United Kingdom v Department of Health and Social Security* [1981] AC 800 (CA and HL).

32 *A-G v Able* [1984] QB 795. Perhaps the novelty of this should not be exaggerated. The leading decision on the law of blackmail before the passing of the Theft Act 1968 was *Thorne v Motor Trade Association* [1937] AC 797 HL. Lord Wright expressed some reservations about the propriety of the proceedings which were collusive in nature, but issued the declaration nevertheless.

33 *Gillick v West Norfolk and Wisbech Area Health Authority* [1986] AC 112.

34 Wade *op cit*, p 525. Cf the discussion below, n 52 (text thereat) on the courts as allies of rogues.

35 See generally Wade *op cit*, p 245.

36 *London and Country Commercial Properties Investments Ltd v A-G* [1953] 1 WLR 312 at 317. In *Imperial Tobacco*, Lord Lane asks: 'What effect in law upon the criminal proceedings would any pronouncement from the High Court in these circumstances have? The criminal courts would not be bound by the decision.'

37 Above, n31.

38 Viscount Dilhorne in *Imperial Tobacco*, at 741.

39 Zamir *op cit*, p 225. And see Morris and Howard *Studies in Criminal Law* (1964), Ch VII and M Friedland *Double Jeopardy* (1969).

40 Note, 'Declaratory Relief in the Criminal Law' (1967) 80 Harv LR 1490, at 1510.

41 See Ormrod LJ in *Imperial Tobacco* [1979] QB at 581, 582.

42 See Ormrod LJ [1979] QB at 581, Browne LJ at 592.

43 *DPP v Humphrys* [1977] AC 1, HL. See P Mirfield 'Shedding a Tear for Issue Estoppel' [1980] Crim LR 336.

44 The argument is very much in the hypothetical, since the consent of the Attorney-General is required for a prosecution for abortion.

45 They are fully canvassed by D Feldman 'Declarations and the Control of Prosecutions' [1981] Crim LR 25.

46 *Thames Launches Ltd v Trinity House Corpn (Deptford Strond)* [1961] Ch 197. And see Feldman, last note.

47 *Aerated Products Co v Godfrey* 263 App Div 685 at 687 (1942), 35 NYS 2d 124 at 126. The point was recognised by the House of Lords in *Ealing London Borough Council v Race Relations Board* [1972] AC 342. Cf however *Smeeton v A-G* [1920] 1 Ch 85.

48 Above, n 22.

49 [1973] AC 435 at 463.

50 The example is given by Viscount Dilhorne in *Imperial Tobacco* at 741. 'Publishers may be tempted to seek declarations that what they propose to publish is not a criminal libel or blasphemous or obscene.'

51 [1981] AC 800 at 810.

52 *Marshall v English Electric Co Ltd* [1945] 1 All ER 653.

53 Above, n 31.

54 Dr Jaconelli says that the justification for permitting the courts to decide hypothetical cases is that it would be decided in the abstract, 'divorced from sympathy or hostility'; (1985) 101 LQR 587. But in the criminal law context, this is a welcome by-product rather than a justification for engaging in the practice at all.

55 In *R v Jenner* [1983] 2 All ER 46, [1983] 1 WLR 873, where the defendant sought to defend his failure to comply with a stop notice with the argument that the notice was invalid, it was held at first instance that he should have applied for judicial review, following *O'Reilly v Mackman* [1983] 2 AC 237, and had left his challenge too late. Better sense prevailed in the Court of Appeal.

56 The point is made by Glanville Williams *Textbook of Criminal Law* (2nd edn, 1983) pp 452–3.

57 As it was, for example, in the *Imperial Tobacco* case.

58 In the *Imperial Tobacco* case, the question whether the spot cash scheme was an 'unlawful competition' and 'lottery' occupied five days in their Lordships House, and was the subject of disagreement between the House and the Court of Appeal. What would the poor magistrates have done?

59 [1979] QB 555 at 592.

60 [1911] 1 KB 410; *Dyson v A-G* [1912] 1 Ch 158.

61 This fear was voiced by Viscount Dilhorne in the *Imperial Tobacco* case. Jurisdiction was assumed in *Chance International Pty Ltd v Forbes* (1968) 89 WN (NSW) 19, 3 NSWR 487, where the question was whether certain magazines had been properly forfeited as obscene under the Customs legislation. The judge held that it was for him to decide whether they were in truth obscene. They were, and no declaration was given.

62 See Ormrod LJ [1979] QB 555 at 581 and Browne LJ at 592.

63 The point is developed further below.

64 Brilmayer 'The Jurisprudence of Article III: Perspectives on the "Case or Controversy" Requirement' (1979) 93 Harv L Rev 297. Zamir *op cit*, p 45, makes the point that the English cases are equivocal on the question whether the denial of relief in the face of hypotheticality is a matter of jurisdiction or one of the exercise of discretion.

65 Above, n33.

66 (1922) 38 TLR 521.

67 See for example J Jaconelli, (1985) 101 LQR 587 at 617, who says that 'on the most persuasive rationale of the doctrine of precedent advisory opinions by the courts lack binding effect.' This is because, so the argument runs, they defeat the expectations of formal justice that like cases should be treated alike. There is not space here to develop a full refutation of the point, but if the explanation for the maxim is itself one of legitimate expectation, the actor can have little complaint if there has been a formal warning by way of declaration that the previous precedent is regarded as unreliable. To put it another way, the cases are not 'like', since the person who acts after the declaration is in a position to know that the law has been changed.

68 (1984) 80 Cr App Rep 20, and see *Lanham v Rickwood* (1984) 148 JP 737.

69 [1985] Crim LR 207 at 209, CA.

70 [1923] 1 IR 112.

71 See generally HWR Wade *Administrative Law* (5th edn, 1982), p 595. The declaration shares this feature with other remedies available against administrative authorities.

72 [1918] 1 Ch 216. See also *Smeeton v A-G* [1920] 1 Ch 85.

73 [1960] AC 260.

74 As in *St James Hall Ltd v LCC* (1900) 83 LT 98.

75 Per Ormrod LJ in *Imperial Tobacco* [1979] QB 555 at 581.

76 [1981] 2 Lloyd's Rep 666; affd [1983] 1 Lloyd's Rep 16, CA.

77 In particular *Field v Metropolitan Police Receiver* [1907] 2 KB 853.

78 *Stoke-on-Trent City Council v B and Q (Retail) Ltd* [1984] AC 754; *Runnymede Borough Council v Ball* [1986] 1 All ER 629, [1986] 1 WLR 353, CA.

79 Glanville Williams 'Law and Fact' [1976] Crim LR 472 and 532.

80 *R v Feely* [1973] QB 530. This has its critics; see E Griew 'Dishonesty: The Objections to Feely and Ghosh' [1984] Crim LR 341.

81 *Brutus v Cozens* [1983] AC 854, HL.

82 *R v Anderson* [1972] 1 QB 304, CA.

83 Viscount Dilhorne in *Imperial Tobacco*.

84 Above, n 22.

85 [1979] QB at 582 and 592 respectively.

86 See *IXL Timbers Pty Ltd v A-G (Tas)* (1963) 109 CLR 574, where a prosecution had in fact been instituted when the action for the declaration was sought. Windeyer J in the High Court gave the declaration notwithstanding, saying that although he should have preferred the matter to have come

before him by way of appeal, he would not regard the fact that the prosecution had been initiated as a conclusive bar. The decision was not cited to their Lordships in *Imperial Tobacco.*

87 *Munnich v Godstone RDC* [1966] 1 All ER 930, [1966] 1 WLR 427, CA. See also *Williams v Weston-Super-Mare UDC* (1909) 74 JP 52.

88 Glanville Williams *Textbook of Criminal Law* (2nd edn, 1983), p 28; Smith and Hogan *Criminal Law* (5th edn, 1983), Ch 2.

89 'The Element of Chance in Criminal Liability' [1971] Crim LR 63.

Trying to help another person commit a crime

JR Spencer

If I urge you to rob a bank, burn down a house or maim an enemy I am in serious trouble whether or not you do so, because my behaviour amounts to the inchoate offence of incitement. In addition, if you do commit the crime I encouraged I am likely to find myself guilty of your offence as an accessory. But if I furnish help rather than give encouragement it is a different story. If I merely lend you my car for the robbery, or give you the keys to the house, or sell you a handy cosh, or show you how to use it, or discover for you where you will be able to belabour your intended victim alone and unsuspecting, I may or may not be in trouble. If you commit the crime I knew you intended with my help to commit, I am likely to be an accessory, but if you do not, I may well commit no offence at all. I may be guilty of some specific offence of supplying equipment for a particular criminal purpose, for instance, under s 59 of the Offences Against the Person Act 1861, which penalises the supply of drugs or instruments intended to cause abortion. Sometimes the courts will bend the facts, or law, or both, to turn what I have done into incitement, conspiracy or obstructing the police. Failing any of these, however, I am guilty of no offence at all. This is very strange. In either case, I have done all that I have to do to incur criminal liability. It is no fault of mine — or to be accurate, it is not due to any lack of fault on my part — that the crime was never committed. If my behaviour was bad enough to punish where you actually made use of the help I gave you, it was surely bad enough to punish where I fully expected you to use it but you got caught before you had the chance. If you do eventually commit your crime, there seems to be no good reason why the police should have to wait until you have done so before they can proceed against me. In a number of legal systems, including some which derive from English common law, facilitation, like incitement, is generally punished, and is punished as an inchoate offence. The purpose of this essay is to argue that it ought to be so punished in England as well.

I cannot claim that this proposal is entirely original. Wider liability for abetment was one of Richard Buxton's proposals in his interesting paper in 1969,[1] and the idea of a general inchoate offence of abetment is much older, appearing in Macaulay's Indian Penal Code of 1860. But I think the idea is worth dusting off and re-examining, now that there is a renewed possibility that we may get a criminal code in England too. My main argument for the proposal is, I believe, a new one. It is the effect that the absence of such an offence has on other parts of the criminal law. I shall try to show that the lack of an inchoate offence of facilitation creates a theoretical gap in the criminal law through which undeserving rogues threaten to escape, and that the courts regularly plug it by bending other offences, with baleful side-effects. It seems a particularly suitable topic for an essay written in honour of John Smith, because inchoate offences and the liability of accessories are areas which have been much illuminated by what he has written in honour of other people.[2]

1 Four inept ways to penalise facilitation

(a) BY MAKING THE FACILITATOR AN ACCESSORY TO THE CRIME HE SEEKS TO HELP

If the person to whom the help was supplied succeeds in committing the offence with it, it is black-letter law that the facilitator can be convicted of committing the offence as an accessory; and it is as a secondary party to a completed offence that those who facilitate crimes usually seem to be prosecuted. The most obvious drawback to dealing with facilitators as secondary parties, however, is that a secondary party presupposes a principal offender who has committed a crime, or, at the very least, the actus reus of one. If the intended principal tries to commit the offence and fails, the facilitator may be convicted as a secondary party to an attempt, provided the principal's behaviour came near enough to success to amount to a criminal attempt. Thus in *R v Dunnington*[3] a man was convicted as an accessory to an attempted robbery where he drove a pair of would-be robbers to a shop, the owner of which promptly put them to flight empty-handed with a barrage of empty milk-bottles. But where the person whose crime he tried to facilitate never even got as far as an attempt, there is no way of convicting a facilitator as a secondary party; because although one may be an accessory to an attempt, it is not a criminal offence, as such, to attempt to be an accessory. This was almost certainly the position at common law,[4] and it is put beyond doubt by the Criminal Attempts Act 1981, s1(4), which makes it the crime of attempt to try to commit any offence except, inter alia, 'aiding, abetting, counselling, procuring or suborning the commission of an offence'. This seriously limits the usefulness of complicity as a means of catching facilitators.

But this is not the only way in which treating a facilitator as a secondary party is an inept way of dealing with him. It also causes difficulties when the person he facilitates does go on to commit the offence. This is particularly so where the facilitator knew little of the offence for which his advice or equipment were wanted.

At one time it seems to have been the law that a person who furnished help or advice in advance of a crime could only be convicted as a secondary party where he knew the details of the crime which the principal was planning. Thus in *R v Lomas*[5] a man was convicted as an accessory before the fact to a burglary because he had provided the burglar, a man called King, with a jemmy. The Court of Criminal Appeal quashed his conviction, in the light of a special verdict from the jury '. . . that he handed the jemmy to King with the knowledge that it was wanted for a burglary. He did not know that it was wanted for this particular burglary.' The short judgment of the Court of Criminal Appeal contains no reasons, but in argument Lush J said 'If the verdict merely means the appellant handed King's jemmy to him with the knowledge that he would commit some burglary with it, it is not enough', and for many years the case was taken as deciding exactly that. There was more than a grain of sense in such a rule, bearing in mind both the theory that an accessory is another person who has also committed the crime of which the principal is guilty, and the practice when it comes to drafting indictments and recording convictions. A person who provides a jemmy for use in a burglary will not be convicted of being an accessory to burglary in general, but to a given burglary in a given building on a given date. If the Cambridge Fagin provides the local Bill Sykes with a jemmy which he then uses for burgling inter alia Selwyn College, the particulars in the indictment will not say 'Fagin on a date unknown made himself an accessory to various burglaries later committed by Bill Sykes', but 'Fagin, on 1st January 1986, aided and abetted, counselled and procured Bill Sykes to enter Selwyn College as a trespasser and there steal money and other valuables, the property of the Master and Fellows.' Since the Accessories and Abettors Act 1861 permits an accessory to be indicted as a principal, it could even aver that '*Fagin*, on the 1st January 1986, having entered Selwyn College as a trespasser, there stole money and other valuables the property of the Master and Fellows.' If a jemmy-provider is to be prosecuted for participating in a particular burglary, and is liable on conviction to have participation in that particular burglary hung around his neck for ever, it makes sense that he should be guilty only where he had that particular burglary in mind. The practical problem with the rule that a person was only an accessory where he knew the details of the crime to be committed is, of course, that it makes it impossible to convict the person who makes such a habit of equipping burglars with jemmies that he is not interested in what crime they propose to commit or where. If there is nothing except complicity in the burglary of which such a person can be convicted then a serious gap in the law is exposed. And so it was that in *R v Bullock*[6] and in *R v Bainbridge*[7] the Court of Criminal Appeal departed from *Lomas* and decided that the supplier of a criminal's equipment could indeed be convicted as an accessory whether or not he knew the time and place where the burglary was to be committed, as long as he knew the general type of crime which was afoot. This approach was approved by the House of Lords in *DPP for Northern Ireland v Maxwell*.[8]

This shift of approach certainly enables a number of people who deserve punishment to get it. But it leads to an obvious problem of 'fair labelling', and other problems besides. Professors Smith and Hogan explain one of these as follows:

> 'Where D has supplied E with the means of committing or information on how to commit a crime of a particular type, is he to be held liable for all the crimes of that type which E may thereafter commit? What if the Midland at Stoke Newington was the second, third or fourth bank which E had feloniously broken and entered with Bainbridge's apparatus? . . . Yet once it is conceded that D need not know the details of any specific crime, it is difficult to see why he should be liable for any one crime of the type contemplated and not for others.'[9]

This point can be pressed further. Older readers will remember the successful London burglar whom the newspapers nick-named 'Flannel-Foot' because of the soft shoes he used to wear. When after a long career he was eventually caught, he was sentenced for several hundred burglaries. If his shoe-maker knew he wanted soft shoes for burglary, he was presumably guilty of the several hundred burglaries as well; and if the shoe-maker had been caught and punished for the first hundred or so while Flannel-Foot was still at large, it is hard to see why he could not in theory be prosecuted for the remaining burglaries which Flannel-Foot committed while he was in prison. Only the uncertain doctrine of abuse of process could stop it. This particularly difficulty was noticed by a Law Commission working party on accessories in 1972[10] which approved of the *R v Bainbridge* rule, but proposed a statutory qualification that such a supplier could only be prosecuted once. This proposal was not of course enacted, nor has it found its way into the Law Commission's Draft Criminal Code, although this also affirms the *Bainbridge* approach. The problem would never have arisen in the first place if the courts had stuck to the sensible rule that a person is an accomplice to a particular crime only where he knows the details of what is planned — a rule which they would have adhered to, one suspects, if facilitation had been a crime as such, and there was no need to disguise it as a way of being a party to a particular crime.

There is also the problem of squaring the *Bainbridge* rule with the rules about accomplices and transferred malice.

In *R v Saunders and Archer*,[11] as everyone will remember, Archer gave Saunders, a discontented husband, a poisoned apple with which to kill his wife. After one unsuspecting bite, she passed it over to their child, and Saunders, not caring to admit what he had tried to do, sat there and let the child eat it, with fatal results. On these facts, Saunders was convicted of murdering the child, but Archer was acquitted as accessory, because Saunders' deliberate failure to intervene to save his child made the outcome 'a distinct thing' from what Archer had in contemplation — which was the death of the wife and not the child. The rule deduced from this case is that if E supplies D with equipment or information to commit one particular crime, he does not become an accessory if D then deliberately uses it to commit another. It seems to be universally accepted by the writers, it was approved by the Law Commission working party in 1972,[12] and it now appears in the Law Commission's Draft Code.[13] But if in the light of *Bainbridge* Archer would have been guilty if he had given Saunders the apple in order to poison he knew not whom, why on earth should it matter that Archer gave it to him to kill one person and he used it to kill another? To this there is surely no sensible answer. It could be said that E, although willing to help kill X, might have refused his help had he known the victim would in fact be Y; but so might the poisoner of apples who was ignorant of the name of the intended victim, had he actually known it was Y who would be killed. Furthermore, where the supplier did know the identity of the intended victim, it is never suggested that we need enquire whether this made any difference to his willingness to supply; all that is needed to get him off, apparently, is the bare fact that the principal used the equipment on someone else. Taken with the rule derived from *Saunders and Archer*, the *Bainbridge* rule produces the absurd paradox that the less a supplier knows, the greater his potential liability — a paradox which would not arise, of course, if the supplier was not an accessory at all unless he knew the details, which Plowden's commentary upon the case suggests was the rule at the back of the court's mind when it decided *Saunders and Archer*.

Thus prosecuting facilitators as accessories is inept not only because it fails to catch many of those who should be caught, but also because the attempt to make it catch them has distorted the law relating to accessories. A general offence of facilitation would make it possible to restore the rule in *Lomas* that a facilitator is an accessory only where he has a specific crime in view, and with it some internal consistency to the law of accessories.[14]

(b) BY BENDING THE LAW OF INCITEMENT

In *Invicta Plastics Ltd v Clare*[15] the defendant manufactured a device called 'Radatec' which detected police speed traps by giving out a high-pitched whine whenever it came near one. This he then advertised in the motoring press with pictures which made its capabilities plain to the most moronic driver. For this the defendant was prosecuted for inciting others to use unlicensed apparatus for wireless telegraphy contrary to s1(1) of the Wireless Telegraphy Act 1949. The prosecution showed that it was almost impossible for Radatec to be used without committing this offence, because it worked by receiving the radio waves which police speed traps emitted; it was illegal to receive these radio waves without a licence from the Secretary of State to do so, and the Secretary of State, as might be expected, was not in the habit of issuing licences to enable motorists to evade police speed-traps. The defendant was convicted, and the Divisional Court upheld his conviction on appeal. In doing so it rejected the defence argument that what he had done was not capable of amounting to incitement.

Like bending the law of accessories, this approach procured the conviction of someone who was a definite social menace and who clearly deserved to be convicted of something. And like bending the law of accessories, this approach is open to a number of criticisms.

The most obvious is that a prosecution of this particular malefactor for inciting people to receive radio waves was highly artificial. Contravening the Wireless Telegraphy Act is behaviour which does nobody any obvious harm, and must rank as one of the most trivial offences which it is possible for a person to commit. The real gravamen of the defendant's behaviour was not that he was encouraging people to receive illicit radio waves, but that he was trying to supply motorists with equipment to enable them to disregard the speed limits with impunity, and so commit offences which risk the lives and limbs of innocent people. The radio waves were morally irrelevant: his behaviour would have been just as bad, and the need to convict him just as great, if it had been legal to receive these radio waves without a licence, or if the device had detected police speed traps without incidentally receiving radio waves. It is as if a person who had agreed to drive a get-away car for a murder or a bank robbery were to be convicted for parking it on a double yellow line. Presumably the reason why Invicta Plastics were prosecuted for inciting the wireless telegraphy offence rather than for inciting drivers to break the speed limit was that Radatec could easily be used without the user breaking the speed limit, whereas it was almost impossible to use it without breaking the Wireless Telegraphy Act. Incitement involves an element of persuasion, and whereas it is plausible to argue that selling someone equipment amounts to persuading him to commit a crime when he cannot use the equipment without committing it, the argument is much less plausible if the equipment can be used without committing the offence.

This leads to the second criticism of the decision, which is that as a weapon against facilitation it is either too narrow to be of much use, or else it is dangerously too wide.

In principle, incitement involves urging or persuading people to commit crimes. The decision in *Invicta Plastics Ltd v Clare* is based on the idea that supplying equipment can be deemed to be urging or persuading people to use it. But if one act can be deemed to be another act, from which it is distinct, the question arises whether the two things are deemed to be the same in every case, or only in certain cases. At the narrowest, it could be argued that supplying equipment only amounts to persuading people to commit crimes with it when all those features are present which were present in *Invicta Plastics Ltd v Clare*. Thus it is open to argument that supply amounts to incitement only where the equipment, like Radatec, was virtually incapable of any legal use.[16] This would make it difficult to use incitement against someone who knowingly supplied burglars with neutral items of equipment like cars, crowbars or pairs of gloves. It may also be the case that incitement can only be used where the equipment is advertised directly to the people who are actually likely to use it. Thus in *R v James and Ashford*[17] the Court of Appeal thought that incitement could be used against those who supply dishonest householders with 'black boxes' to fit to electricity meters to make them under-record, and thereby commit the offence of dishonestly abstracting electricity; but doubted whether it could be used against the manufacturer who made them for a supplier, because there was 'no advertisement or open persuasion to others to use these devices.' Thirdly, in *Invicta Plastics Ltd v Clare*, as is usual in incitement prosecutions, the defendant took the initiative in stirring up the mischief, in that case by offering his wares for sale; and there might be problems in prosecuting D for incitement where it is the person supplied who took the initiative in the matter. It may be acceptable to convict D of incitement to abstract electricity where he advertises 'black boxes' and supplies them to dishonest householders on demand, but it looks very strained to convict D of incitement when his neighbour E asks to borrow some tools to fix up the black box which E has bought, and D, ever the good neighbour, complies with the request.[18]

But if the law of incitement was stretched to cover these types of case, then there would be a real danger that incitement would be too wide, because within the decision in *Invicta Plastics Ltd v Clare* there lurks the germ of something rather dangerous. Before that decision, it was implicit in the crime of incitement that the defendant desired that the person he encouraged should commit the offence. The person who supplies equipment or information will have this state of mind where, for example, he thrusts a gun into another's hand and says 'Shoot P with it', but often he will be quite indifferent, particularly where he supplies the equipment or information for money, when his only concern is likely to be that he gets paid. This was almost certainly the case with Invicta Plastics, which presumably knew that their Radatec sets were likely to be used in breach of the Wireless Telegraphy Act, but would have been equally happy if their customers had bought them for paperweights or mantelpiece ornaments. The decision accepts the idea that it is enough to make a person guilty of incitement that he knows his behaviour makes it more likely that someone else will commit an offence. If this is limited to the case where D takes the initiative by directly advertising equipment which is incapable of being used without committing the offence this extension is not likely to be dangerous. But if it is not so limited, then we are left with the proposition that *any* behaviour can amount to incitement where the actor knows it is more likely that a crime will be committed as a result. This would create some bizarre possibilities: like a prosecution for incitement to burgle against the interior decorator who, like the defendant in *Stansbie v Troman*[19] leaves a house unlocked, thereby creating a risk of burglary, or a prosecution for riot against a television camera team which films a demonstration knowing the demonstrators are more likely to cause trouble if they know they have a wider audience. The beginnings of this are already noticeable in the *Amstrad* case,[20] where the Court of Appeal (Civil Division) suggested that a manufacturer who marketed a cassette recorder which, although capable of lawful use, was likely to be very useful to those who wished to copy tapes in breach of copyright, might be guilty of incitement to commit an offence under the Copyright Act. These problems would be avoided if the courts limited the widened crime of incitement to the case where equipment, information or other assistance was supplied or offered to those who were believed to want it to enable them to commit a criminal offence, and where this was done without any reasonable excuse for doing it. But if those limits were imposed, we should have a crime of facilitation, purpose-made but deemed to be a form of incitement; and it would be simpler, surely, to call it 'facilitation' and get rid of the legal fiction that it is a form of incitement.

(c) BY BENDING THE LAW OF CONSPIRACY

(i) To commit a crime

Conspiracy charges are clearly appropriate for some people who supply criminals with equipment, or agree to do so. There would be no difficulty where, for example, D1 says to D2 'Let us kill our enemy, P. You stab him, and I'll lend you my knife', and D2 agrees. By the Criminal Law Act 1977, a conspiracy is committed where: 'a person agrees with any other person or persons that a course of conduct shall be pursued which, if the agreement is carried out in accordance with their intentions . . . will necessarily amount to or involve the commission of any offence or offences by one or more of the parties to the agreement', and what D1 and D2 have done fits this definition exactly. But in many cases of facilitation a conspiracy charge is not so obviously appropriate. Take the case, for example, where D1 asks D2 to supply a car, and D2 hires him one knowing full well that D1 wants it to commit a bank robbery. Can it really be said that D2 has 'agreed that a course of conduct shall be pursued' when all that he has done is to lend something to somebody knowing that he intends to pursue it? As Glanville Williams says, 'It would be going too far to say that a person has agreed that a crime should be committed if he merely supplies the instrument of crime upon request.'[21] Secondly, there is the part of the statutory definition which says 'if the agreement is carried out in accordance with their intentions.' On the face of it, this suggests that even if an agreement to supply equipment for an offence can properly be seen as an agreement for that offence to be committed, at least two parties to the agreement must *intend* the crime to be committed, and if the defendant is one of only two parties to the agreement, then he must so intend. If the car-owner is paid in advance he is unlikely to care whether or not the robbery is committed, and may even hope that it is not. Can it fairly be said that he then 'intends' the robbery to take place?

Yet despite these difficulties, in *R v Anderson*[22] the House of Lords was willing to bend the definition of conspiracy to fit this sort of case; and as with the inflation of complicity and incitement, various undesirable side-effects are the result. D1 had agreed to help D2 escape from prison by furnishing him with tools, equipment and a get-away car for a fee of £20,000. In his defence,

D 1 said that he did not intend to carry out his part of the bargain: all he meant to do was to supply a token part of the equipment, get his hands on D2's money, and disappear. To make him guilty of conspiracy it was necessary, he argued, that he should intend the plan to go through, and as he did not so intend he was not guilty. The House of Lords rejected this. They held that the phrase 'if the agreement is carried out in accordance with their intentions' must be taken to mean 'if the agreement is carried out in accordance with its terms', and it was thus irrelevant whether or not D1 really meant D2 to escape. Otherwise, said Lord Bridge, the consequences would be mischievous:

> 'The proprietor of a car hire firm agrees for a substantial payment to make available a hire car to a gang for use in a robbery . . . Making his car available for use in the robbery is as much a part of the relevant agreed course of conduct as the robbery itself. Yet once he has been paid, it will be a matter of complete indifference to him whether the robbery is in fact committed or not . . . Parliament cannot have intended that such parties should escape conviction on the basis that it cannot be proved against them that they intended that the relevant offence or offences should be committed.'

The decision enables some very naughty men to get their just deserts, but what it does to the law of conspiracy is distinctly unsatisfactory.

In the first place, it does obvious violence to the words of the statute. The sentence 'if the agreement is carried out in accordance with their intentions' has a literal meaning which is perfectly clear, and although it is narrower than the House of Lords wanted, that meaning is not absurd, and it is contrary to every rule of statutory construction for a court to take words in a criminal statute which are neither obscure nor absurd and replace them with other words which extend the ambit of the offence. Furthermore, the phrase which the House of Lords construed was drafted by the Law Commission, and it is clear from the relevant Law Commission Report[23] that the draftsman meant them to convey the notion that a defendant is only guilty of conspiracy if he wanted the plot to succeed; and as Parliament knew that it was enacting the Law Commission's proposals, presumably Parliament did indeed want people to escape convictions for conspiracy where they did not wish the plot to succeed. Secondly, there is a strong practical objection to the construction it was given in *R v Anderson*, which is that whilst it enables some people to be convicted who clearly deserve to be convicted of something, it also enables other people to be convicted of conspiracy who surely deserve to be guilty of nothing at all. For example, if a person is guilty of conspiracy where he merely purports to agree, it is difficult to see why the policeman who has infiltrated the conspiracy with a view to catching the real villains is not guilty of conspiracy. In *Anderson* Lord Bridge said that he would not be, but it is difficult to see how this can be so. He was not guilty of conspiracy at common law, it is true, but there is no loophole for him in the words of the Criminal Law Act as the House of Lords has interpreted it. Similarly, the reluctant participant who secretly intends to frustrate the conspiracy at the earliest possible moment would also appear to be guilty.

Without strongly advocating either of them, Professor Smith has mapped two routes by which those who supply equipment to criminals might be brought within the scope of conspiracy, doing less damage to legal principle in the process.[24] One, which would only be open where the defendant agreed to supply two or more criminals who had earlier conspired to commit a crime, is a prosecution for aiding and abetting a conspiracy. The other, which would avail even where the defendant agreed to supply a single intending criminal, is a prosecution for conspiracy to aid and abet an offence. As the authorities stand, nobody knows whether either or both of these charges are possible, and there is room for two opinions as to whether either is desirable on principle.[25] But what is clear is that some bad — if unlikely — cases of deliberate facilitation would still remain unpunished even if both these developments of conspiracy took place: for example, where D2 hears that D1 intends to maim P and sends him the instrument to do it with unasked. And both methods, surely, are complicated and convoluted ways of striking at behaviour which, if we want to punish it, could much more easily be criminalised directly by creating a special offence of facilitation.

(ii) *To defraud*

In *R v Hollinshead*[26] three men manufactured and marketed 'black boxes' — devices to be fitted to electricity meters to make them under-record — and then foolishly agreed to supply a consignment of them to a 'plain clothes' policeman. For this they were prosecuted and convicted for conspiracy to defraud. The Court of Appeal quashed their convictions.[27] Although it is well established[28] that 'fraud' in this context includes any behaviour by which the victim is dishonestly deprived of something, whether or not he is actually deceived in the process, the Court of Appeal felt that for conspiracy to defraud the defendants must themselves agree to do something which cheats him. It was not enough, they felt, that the conspirators should merely agree to furnish someone else with the means by which he could do so if he felt like it. The House of Lords reversed the Court of Appeal and reinstated the conviction. By doing so, they made it possible to punish those who facilitate others to commit electricity meter frauds, which are a serious problem, being estimated to cost the electricity supply industry over £50m in revenue each year.[29] But — despite Lord Roskill's protests to the contrary — in the process they undoubtedly made an offence which was already vague and amorphous even more so.

Had there been a general inchoate offence of facilitation, this would have been unnecessary.

(d) BY EXTENDING THE SCOPE OF OBSTRUCTING THE POLICE

A common type of assistance to criminals is warning them when a witness or a policeman comes along.

If the lookout is there by agreement with the principal he is guilty of conspiracy. He is guilty of the crime as an accomplice if the principal commits it, or guilty of the attempt as an accomplice if the principal gets no further than an attempt. But there is a problem in the case where D2 unquestionably warned D1, and the prosecution can show neither that he did so by agreement, nor that D1 got as far as committing or attempting to commit the crime.

This difficulty arose in acute form in the early days of motoring, when pioneer motorists were as little inclined to obey the speed limit as their successors, and the police were considerably more anxious to catch them. When the police set up speed traps, the Automobile Association counter-attacked by hiring a team of scouts to warn motorists when they were approaching one. The police wished to prosecute the scouts, but they had committed no obvious offence. Conspiracy to exceed the speed limit was no use because although the scouts were present by agreement, the agreement was with the Automobile Association rather than the motorist concerned.[30] It was difficult to prove the scouts were guilty of complicity in the offence of exceeding the speed limit, because by making the speeding motorists slow down as they went through the trap they deprived the police of any reliable evidence that the speed limit had in fact been broken. So the police hit upon wilfully obstructing a constable in the execution of his duty, an offence then contained in the Prevention of Crime Act 1885, and now appearing in the Police Act 1964, s 51.

Assaulting a constable in the execution of his duty was an offence by s 12 of the Prevention of Crimes Act 1871, and obstructing the police became an offence when the Prevention of Crimes Amendment Act 1885 amended s 12 by tacking 'resisting or wilfully obstructing' onto the end. For this reason it is generally assumed that Parliament only meant the new offence to cover obstruction in its literal physical sense: behaviour such as holding a door shut against a constable trying to enter when he has statutory authority to do so, or hindering an arrest by snatching the malefactor out of the policeman's grasp as an alternative to the usual method of hitting the policeman over the head. It is most unlikely that anyone foresaw or intended that the offence of obstruction should cover non-physical interference, particularly when such behaviour was directed at third parties rather than at the police. This point was taken by the courts in Scotland, where the offence was, and still is, limited to obstruction in the physical sense.[31] In *Bastable v Little*,[32] the first of the speed-trap cases to reach the Divisional Court, the scout's behaviour was held not to amount to the offence of obstructing the police for various reasons, including that the offence is limited to physical obstruction[33] and that the behaviour must be directed at the police rather than at a third party.[34] But both of these limitations were unanimously rejected in the next speed-trap case, *Betts v Stevens*,[35] where the Divisional Court said that warning an offender was indeed obstructing the police in the execution of their duty, provided it could be shown — as, surprisingly, it was shown in that case — that he was actually offending at the time that he was warned. Finally in *Green v Moore*[36] even this limitation was discarded, when it was held to be obstruction to warn those who are merely about to commit an offence.

Those who have written upon the subject all agree that it was a bad move to extend the offence of wilful obstruction from physical obstruction to obstruction in the moral sense. The effect was to remove any clear limit from the offence, so enabling it to grow in all sorts of unexpected directions, some of which are quite alarming. Thus in *Ricketts v Cox*,[37] for example, it was held to cover the person who would not co-operate with the police by answering their questions, at any rate where the refusal was hostile and accompanied by bad language. The first steps down this slippery slope were taken in cases where, in essence, D had been trying to help another person to commit a criminal offence. Would they have been taken, one wonders, if there had been an explicit offence of trying to help another person to commit a crime?

2 ARE SPECIFIC OFFENCES OF FACILITATION AN ANSWER TO THE PROBLEM?

A number of specific offences already penalise particular types of facilitation. Section 59 of the Offences Against the Person Act, which has already been mentioned, makes it a crime to supply drugs or instruments intended to procure an abortion. The Misuse of Drugs Act 1971 penalises not only the possession of controlled drugs, but, by s 4, their manufacture and supply. Section 15(1) of the Forgery and Counterfeiting Act 1981 makes it an offence to pass counterfeit money, and s 15(2) then makes it an offence 'to deliver to another any thing which is, and which he knows or believes to be, such a counterfeit, intending that the person to whom it is delivered or another shall pass or tender it as genuine.' The Firearms Act 1968 forbids the possession of firearms by various people — minors, convicted criminals, and those who do not hold a firearms certificate — and prohibits the possession of machine-guns and gas-pistols by anyone outside the armed forces; other sections of the Act then ban the supply of weapons to those who commit crimes by possessing them. In addition there are other statutory offences which, although primarily aimed at something else, incidentally make it criminal in certain circumstances to facilitate the commission of crimes by others. Section 64 of the Offences Against the Person Act makes it an offence to possess or manufacture any explosive, 'or dangerous or noxious thing, or any machine, engine, instrument or thing, with intent by means thereof to commit, *or for the purpose of enabling any other person to commit*' any offence which is triable only on indictment.[38] Similarly, s 3 of the Criminal Damage Act 1971 makes it an offence to possess anything with the intent either to use it to commit criminal damage oneself, 'or cause or permit another to use it.' The first of these offences would be apt to catch the man who sets up as a wholesale dealer in murder-weapons or instruments of torture, and either would apply to the unofficial manufacturer or retailer of bombs or incendiary devices; although neither, presumably, would cover the person who agrees to give or lend for a criminal purpose some item which he normally uses for lawful purposes — the DIY enthusiast who lends his electric drill for a knee-capping, for example, or his blow-lamp to fire a barn.[39] And the offences of forgery,[40] false accounting[41] and suppression and destruction of documents,[42] although mainly aimed at those who plan to obtain something by criminal deception for themselves, also catch some who furnish, or plan to furnish, other people with the means of obtaining property or services by deception.

The present range of offences is quite inadequate to cover all the cases which ought to be covered, and the gaps between them produce some anomalies which suggest the criminal law has a very odd set of values. It is an offence under s 59 of the Offences Against the Person Act to lend a knitting-needle for an abortion, for example, but no offence at all to lend a knife to commit a murder — unless of course the murder is attempted or committed. Section 64 of the Offences Against the Person Act and s 3 of the Criminal Damage Act would seem to make it an offence to store a pair of pliers for someone like Mr Whybrow,[43] knowing he intends to use them to wire up his bath to electrocute his wife; but it would not cover lending him a pair extempore for this purpose, or even giving him a lesson if he is uncertain how to do it. Nor, I suggest, can these difficulties be sensibly overcome by the creation of more and more specific offences. Each new offence would give rise to a new anomaly because of a piece of similar behaviour which it did not cover. Facilitation is a general problem, and it needs a general solution. It is no less blameworthy intentionally to facilitate one offence rather than another equally serious one, nor is it better to do so by giving equipment rather than advice, or vice versa.

Of course, some of the existing specific offences do useful work in punishing certain types of facilitation, and some would still be needed even if a general offence of facilitation were created. Specific offences would be particularly useful in cases like the supply of controlled drugs, for example, where it is the supplier who is the major villain rather than the person he supplies.

3 OBJECTIONS TO A GENERAL OFFENCE OF FACILITATION

The first objection is that general liability for facilitation would be curiously out of proportion with the liability of the person who is helped. Take the following example. A, wishing to commit a burglary, asks B to lend him a jemmy, and B does so in full knowledge of A's purpose. That night, the police arrest A as he is about to leave his house on burglary bent. A has not yet committed his burglary, nor does his behaviour, which is purely preparatory, amount to an attempt. As he is still 'at his place of abode', he has not even committed the offence under s25 of the Theft Act of going equipped. Except for the dubious possibility of a charge of conspiracy to burgle based on an extended reading of *Anderson*[44] A has committed no offence by acquiring the jemmy. So how can we justify convicting B for supplying it?

This is a considerable difficulty, but I think it can be answered by enquiring why, as a matter of policy, the law does not wish to penalize A. The reason, surely, is that he is still a long way from his objective, and has a number of psychological barriers to cross before he reaches it, at any one of which he may change his mind and abandon his wicked plan. It seems unduly harsh to punish someone who may yet decide to behave himself, and it is practically unwise as well, because if a man stands to be punished as soon as he has begun to carry out his plan, having begun he may think he has nothing to lose by going on. But this reasoning does not apply to B who has knowingly supplied him with help such as advice or equipment. B has done the last act that he is able to do. He has passed his final psychological barrier. There is no question of his changing his mind and simply not doing it: as far as B is concerned the deed is done. So it is neither unjust nor foolish to punish B for helping A when we do not punish A.

To this, B's would-be defender may fairly reply: 'It is true that B, unlike A, has reached the point where he can no longer stop the mischief by merely deciding not to go on with it. He can no longer be defeated by his own inertia. But it is still possible for him to change his mind and take positive action to undo the help that he has given. For example, after listening to a particularly spirited sermon B might repossess his jemmy, warn B's intended victim or even frustrate the venture by going to the police. Indeed, the law already takes account of this possibility where A commits or attempts to commit the burglary, and B is prosecuted as an accomplice. An accomplice is not guilty if, before the crime was committed, he took appropriate steps to withdraw his help. But this could not apply to your new-fangled crime of facilitation, because it would be committed as soon as the help was offered.' The reply to this, I suggest, is that withdrawal *could* be made a defence to a charge of facilitation, and in my view it should be.[45] The policy reasons for allowing such a defence to an accessory — the need to encourage withdrawal, and the need to give the accomplice a let-out which is available to the principal — apply to the general offence of facilitation just as strongly. The only objection, surely, is that it looks odd that someone who has already committed a crime should have the power to 'uncommit' it, as it were, by something he does afterwards. Odd or not, however, this is something which occurs in a number of other legal systems. In some countries, for example, a conspirator's criminal liability is wiped out if he then frustrates the venture or informs the police.[46] Even in English criminal law there is at least one precedent for 'uncommission', although it is not a very attractive one. An Act of George II against smuggling[47] provided that if, before conviction, a smuggler named two or more accomplices who were then brought to justice, he should be 'clearly acquitted and discharged of his . . . offence.'

An alternative and harsher way of tackling the imbalance between the liability of A and B is to stretch A's liability backwards in time so that he too commits an inchoate offence when he acquires his tools. RS Wright proposed this course for the most serious crimes in s 31 of his Jamaica Code:

> 'Whoever prepares or supplies, or has in his possession, custody, or control, or in the possession, custody or control of any other person on his behalf, any instruments, materials or means with a purpose that such instruments, materials or means may be used by him or by any other person in committing any crime by which life is likely to be endangered, or any forgery or any crime relating to coin, or any felony punishable with penal servitude for ten years or upwards, shall be liable to punishment in like manner as if he had attempted to commit that crime . . .'

Apart from its severity, this sort of provision would cause a problem in English criminal law because it would outflank the proximity requirement in the law of attempt. (And in this connection, it is worth pointing out that if a crime of facilitation were created, it would be necessary to provide that the person who received help was not an accessory to the facilitation, or else the law of attempt would be outflanked even without a provision like s 31 of the Jamaica Code.)

The second objection to a general crime of facilitation is that it would be over-broad and thus oppressive.

Whether or not this is so depends, obviously, on the precise scope of the offence. I am certainly not proposing an offence which would cover a wider range of behaviour than is already caught by the existing law of accessories when the person helped gets as far as committing or attempting the crime for which the help was provided. The proposed offence of facilitation would be wider, of course, but only because it would occur whether or not the ultimate crime was committed or attempted. Thus it would not make the helper guilty where *he* had done any less than he has to do at present. It would only be broader than the existing liability of accessories because there would be no need for any further behaviour by somebody else over whom the helper, once he has helped, has no further control. For anyone who does not find

Bainbridge and the related case law oppressive, it is hard to see what would be harsh or oppressive in a general offence of facilitation. Of course, for those who feel that the law on accessories is already too much, a second helping of the same dish would obviously be unwelcome.

The offence of facilitation which I am proposing would cover two things — provided they are done with an appropriately guilty mind, a difficult point which I shall try to deal with later. The first is actually providing another with equipment, advice or other help for use in the commission of a crime. This would make a person guilty in the *Bainbridge* type of case, but irrespective of whether a burglary took place. The second is offering equipment, advice or other assistance which is intended to be helpful in the commission of a crime. This would cover the person who has agreed to supply a particular would-be criminal with equipment, but has not yet done so: the sort of behaviour which the House of Lords pressed into the mould of conspiracy in *Anderson*. It would also cover those who hold themselves out as generally willing to provide equipment, advice or other help to anyone who wants it: like the person who made and marketed the radar-trap detector in *Invicta Plastics Ltd v Clare*, and the 'black box' manufacturer in *Hollinshead*.

The real difficulty about a crime of facilitation is the appropriate mental element for the offence. There is no problem with direct intention to help. Unless he can claim some general defence, I do not think it would be in the least oppressive to convict anyone of an offence of facilitation who acted with the direct intention of helping another to commit an offence — that is to say, actually desiring him to commit it. If his intention can be proved, no tears need be shed for the man who lends his car to a burglar for the night, in return for a promise of a percentage of his takings; or who gives his knife to a would-be assassin, hoping and believing that he will use it to stab a common enemy; or who lends his flat to a friend, hoping he will there seduce the girl whom they both know to be 13; or the man who lends his Harley Davidson motor cycle to a friend to see if he can make it to 100 mph in a residential street with a 30 mph limit; or even the man who lends his copier to another to enable him to make pirate copies of books or tapes in breach of copyright. But possible harshness begins when the offence starts to bite upon acts of facilitation done with something less than a desire that an offence should be committed: the man who hires his car to someone believing that he will use it for a burglary, although he would rather he did not; the man who sells a knife to someone whom he believes to be a would-be assassin, notwithstanding his protestations that he only wants it to trim his grandmother's toenails; the hotelier who lets a room to a man with a girl who is allegedly his daughter, a couple whom the hotelier believes to be a dirty old man and a runaway girl whom he has picked up for sex; and the dealer who sells a powerful motorcycle to a youth whom he firmly expects to exceed the speed limit on it. If we substitute mere suspicion for belief in the examples just given, then liability for facilitation does begin to look distinctly harsh. The first harshness — which already troubles Glanville Williams over the present law of accessories[48] — is that it threatens to make crimes out of normal commercial activities. There must be few motor-dealers who fail to foresee an impending breach of the speed limit when they sell a young man a powerful motorcycle, and few publicans who never suspect that one of their customers will drive home with above the permitted level of alcohol in his body. Is it fair to make the seller his buyer's keeper in this type of case? And the second harshness is that liability for facilitation then begins to threaten — as the existing law of accessories already threatens — to punish people for acts done in good faith for some higher social purpose: the doctor who puts a promiscuous girl of 13 on the pill, knowing that he is increasing the risk of further unlawful sexual intercourse taking place, but feeling he would be increasing the chance of unwanted pregnancy if he refused; the scientist who publicises the fatal and undetectable effects of some household product, hoping that this will cause it to be withdrawn from the market, but realising that the publicity may lead to the odd murder or two first; the newspaper editor, who reports the trial of a criminal for some particularly clever and simple fraud, realising that he is thereby passing the idea on to a lot of people who are equally dishonest although considerably less ingenious;[49] and the manufacturer who markets a copying machine which has a number of legitimate uses, but which he knows will be used by some people to pirate copyright books or tapes.[50]

Various suggestions could be made to limit the possible over-breadth of an offence of facilitation, several of which have already been proposed as possible limits to the liability of helpers as accessories to the completed offence. Unfortunately, there are difficulties with all of them.

The first not-so-bright idea is that liability for facilitation should be limited to those who furnish help desiring the crime to be committed, leaving out all those who do not so desire.[51] The difficulty, however, is that where someone supplies tools or equipment to a criminal in return for cash it is most unlikely that he will actually *desire* any crime to be committed. Such a person is unlikely to care whether the offence is committed or not as long as he gets his money. Indeed, as his part in the affair is less likely to be detected if the crime he tried to help is not committed, he may well hope that it is not. Thus a crime of facilitation so limited would miss many of the cases where it is particularly needed.

The second suggestion is to limit liability to facilitating the more serious offences — a course for which there is a precedent. Under the Criminal Attempts Act 1981 liability for attempt is limited to attempting indictable offences, and Glanville Williams advocates limiting in the same way the liability of accessories.[52] It might be thought wise to limit an offence of facilitation to facilitating indictable offences. This would certainly get rid of a number of ludicrous and footling possibilities — like, for example, a prosecution for facilitating an offence of Sunday trading by giving a shop assistant a lift to the illegally open DIY on a rainy Sunday. However, there is a difficulty in so limiting a general offence of facilitation which does not apply to limiting either attempt or accessorial liability in this way. This is that there could be cases of facilitating offences on a grand scale which are significantly more serious matters than actually committing them, and large-scale facilitation of summary offences could be a serious matter. *Invicta Plastics Ltd v Clare*[53] and the other cases where people tried to help motorists in general to flout the speed limit are clear examples. Being an accessory, and attempting a crime, involve crimes which are necessarily committed one at a time, as each offence is attempted in the case of attempt, and in the case of being an accessory, as each person who is helped or encouraged commits each crime. There cannot be a single offence which relates to more than one other offence. But facilitation would be like incitement and conspiracy: it would be possible for there to be one offence of facilitation which related to a whole range of crimes by others. So, on reflection, it does not look so wise to limit the proposed offence of facilitation to trying to help others to commit indictable offences. If there is to be any limitation of this sort, perhaps it would be better to borrow from s 4(1) of the Criminal Law Act 1977, which requires the Director of Public Prosecutions to consent to a prosecution for conspiracy to commit a summary offence.

The third suggestion might be to limit an offence of facilitation to the case where the person who helps another has a specific crime by the other in view. This is contrary, as we have seen, to the usual position which the courts take up when dealing with the accessorial liability of those who have furnished criminals with tools and equipment. But Woolf J recently took this line in two cases where, in civil proceedings, one of the questions to be decided was how far a person is liable as an accessory for more minor acts of assistance. In *A-G v Able*[54] the point was whether a person committed the offence of attempting to aid, abet, counsel or procure suicide contrary to s 2(1) of the Suicide Act 1961[55] when he distributed a booklet entitled 'A Guide to Self-Deliverance', containing explicit instructions as to how to take one's life. He was not guilty, said Woolf J, where he merely distributed the book generally, but he might be where he meant a particular copy to reach someone who was actually contemplating suicide, intending that he should make use of it. And in *Gillick v West Norfolk and Wisbech Area Health Authority*[56] one of the questions was whether a doctor who prescribed contraceptives to a girl under 16 could be guilty as an accessory to her boyfriend's offence of unlawful sexual intercourse. Not usually, he thought, because:

> 'In order to be an accessory, you normally have to know the material circumstances. In such a situation the doctor would know no more than that there was a risk of sexual intercourse taking place with an unidentified man at an unidentified place on an unidentified date — hardly the state of knowledge which is normally associated with an accessory before the fact.'

It has already been argued that this is the right approach where the question is whether someone is guilty as an accessory, because an accessory is prosecuted and punished for taking part in a specific offence. But if this approach were taken to limit a general offence of facilitation, a number of cases within the intended mischief of the offence would unfortunately escape. The most serious example would be the general offer to supply criminals with tools and equipment — like jemmies, or coshes, or duplicate keys, or knuckle-dusters, or poisons, or 'black boxes', or even radar-trap detectors as in *Invicta Plastics Ltd v Clare*.

The problem of mens rea in facilitation is a thorny one, and there is no easy solution to it. However, the following two limits would, I think, go some way to solve it. The first would be to provide that the general offence of facilitation was only committed by someone who *knew* or *believed* that what he did or offered to do would help another person to commit a crime: near certainty should be required, mere suspicion should never be enough. This ought to keep outside the criminal law most ordinary commercial transactions. The ordinary shopkeeper may occasionally suspect that someone is buying his goods with an unlawful purpose in view, but he is most unlikely to be more positively aware. Where he does know, however, or as good as knows, then I for one do not see any hardship in convicting him. This, however, would not help the person who knows, or is as good as certain that what he does will help another to commit an offence, but who acts from a desire to cause a more-than-compensating good, or to avoid a different and, as he sees it, a worse evil: the manufacturer who markets a copier excellent for a number of legitimate purposes, but incidentally excellent for making pirate copies; the doctor who puts the promiscuous 13-year old on the pill; the scientist who publicly exposes the lethal qualities of a freely-available household product; and the newspaper editor who reports the clever but simple fraud. What is needed here, I suggest, is some means of persuading the courts to accept a defence of necessity which operates when the act was done in the belief that it was necessary to avoid a greater harm or evil, or that it would bring about a more-than-compensating good.[57] Until recently, this suggestion would have looked completely hopeless in the light of the English case law. However, we now have the *Gillick* case in the House of Lords.[58] One of the points at issue, it will be recalled, was whether a doctor who prescribed contraceptives to an under-age girl made himself criminally liable as an accessory to any man who then had unlawful sexual intercourse with her. At first instance Woolf J, as we have seen, said the answer was generally 'No'. In his view the doctor would be guilty if, as is most unlikely, he gave the advice with the measured intention of encouraging sexual intercourse; but if he merely foresaw that this would be the general effect of his advice, he would not be guilty, at any rate if he did not know the details of when, who with, and where. His views were mentioned with approval by the three judges who formed the majority when the case reached the House of Lords. Woolf J's view on the liability of accessories, however sensible, squares ill with *Bainbridge* and the rest of the case law on the subject. Lord Brandon, who in his dissenting opinion took the clear view that the doctor would be guilty even if he did not desire to encourage sexual intercourse and only knew the general effect his advice was likely to have, has the case law firmly on his side. Professor Smith's view on the decision is that the courts really decided the case by accepting 'a concealed defence of necessity'.[59] It is difficult to dissent from this — except to say that as both Lord Scarman and Lord Bridge reinforced their views on complicity with arguments on social policy, the defence of necessity was hardly very much concealed. Said Lord Scarman:

> 'If the prescription is the bona fide exercise of his clinical judgment as to what is best for his patient's health, he has nothing to fear from the criminal law or from any public policy based on the criminality of a man having sexual intercourse with her.'

What is needed in the definition of an offence of facilitation is some signal to persuade the courts to take this sort of approach. Perhaps the well-worn but useful phrase 'without reasonable excuse' would enable the courts to distinguish between the person who publishes for gain a manual of instruction for burglars, and the newspaper editor who publishes some information useful to burglars which happens to come out in the evidence at an important criminal trial.

4 TRYING TO HELP CRIMINALS: OTHER LANDS AND OTHER LAWS

It is instructive to see how the problem was tackled in earlier attempts to draft penal codes based on English common law.

It was not directly faced by the Commissioners who produced the abortive Draft Code of 1843.[60] This contained provisions which approach the matter in much the same way as modern English law: there were sections which made a person liable as an accessory to a completed crime, and which applied to those who helped as well as those who incited; and there was a separate inchoate offence of incitement, which consisted of attempted persuasion rather than attempted help.[61] A similar approach was taken by Stephen and his associates with the slightly less abortive Draft Code of 1879.[62] Although this never reached the statute book in England it became the basis of the Penal Codes of Canada, Queensland, Western Australia, Tasmania and New Zealand. These, like their model, use a basic framework much like the present English law: liability as an accessory based on either help or encouragement[63] and an inchoate offence, called different names in different codes, but basically covering incitement only.[64] In some of these jurisdictions, as in England, problems have arisen with defendants who offered help rather than encouragement, and judges have sometimes managed to interpret the local 'incitement' provision to cover what was done; as in the Canadian case where an underground newspaper carried instructions for horticulturally-minded hippies on how to grow their own pot.[65]

Macaulay's Indian Penal Code of 1860, however, confronts the problem head-on by creating an inchoate offence of abetment which covers both incitement and attempting to help. The relevant provisions are as follows:

> 's107 *Abetment of a thing*. — A person abets the doing of a thing, who
> *First* — Instigates any person to do that thing; or
> *Secondly* — Engages with one or more other person or persons in any conspiracy for the doing of that thing, if an act or illegal omission takes place in pursuance of that conspiracy, and in order to the doing of that thing; or
> *Thirdly* — Intentionally aids, by any act or illegal omission, the doing of that thing
> . . .
> s 108 *Abettor*. — A person abets an offence, who abets either the commission of an offence, or the commission of an act which would be an offence, if committed by a person capable by law of committing an offence with the same intention or knowledge as that of the abettor.
> . . .
> *Explanation 2*. To constitute the offence of abetment, it is not necessary that the act abetted, should be committed or that the effect requisite to constitute the offence should be caused.'

This seems to make it quite clear that a person who tries to help by providing assistance in advance is guilty of abetment, whether or not the crime is then committed. So it is surprising to read in a current textbook of Indian criminal law that where the crime is never committed, there can be abetment consisting of instigation but not help.[66] The cases cited in support of this[67] were cases where the prosecution case was that A had committed a crime with B's active assistance at the time of commission, A was acquitted, and B's conviction was quashed as inconsistent with A's acquittal; so they hardly cover the case where B furnished help in advance of a crime which was never in fact committed.

RS Wright's Jamaica Code of 1877, which never actually became law in Jamaica but was adopted in various places in the West Indies and in Africa,[68] strikes at facilitation with even greater determination. Section 31, which has already been quoted,[69] creates a general offence of preparation for crime, which covers both getting together the equipment to commit a serious crime and supplying it to others. And s 32 contains a general provision on abetment which is as follows:

> '(i) Whoever, directly or indirectly, instigates, commands, counsels, procures, solicits, or in any manner purposely aids, facilitates, encourages, or promotes, whether by his act, presence, or otherwise, and whoever does any act for the purpose of aiding, facilitating, encouraging or promoting the commission of a crime by any other person, whether known or unknown, certain or uncertain, is guilty of abetting that crime and of abetting the other person in respect of that crime;
>
> (ii) Whoever abets a crime shall, if the crime be actually committed in pursuance or during the continuance of the abetment, he deemed guilty of that crime;
>
> (iii) Whoever abets a crime shall, if the crime be not actually committed, be punishable as follows . . .'

The American Law Institute's *Model Penal Code* also punishes those who try to help another person to commit a crime, but it reaches them by a rather different route, namely by stretching the crime of attempt to cover attempting to be an accessory. Article 5.01(3) provides:

> '*Conduct designed to aid another in commission of a crime*. A person who engages in conduct designed to aid another to commit a crime which would establish his complicity under art 2.06 if the crime were committed by such other person, is guilty of an attempt to commit the crime, although the crime is not committed or attempted by such other person.'

This provision has been incorporated into the penal codes of various States, including Hawaii, Pennsylvania and Texas.[70] I have not made any extensive study of how this problem is approached in systems other than those derived from English common law, but it is clear that some do contrive to punish facilitation irrespective of any crime committed by the person facilitated. Neither France, West Germany nor Scotland do this.[71] But the Swedish Penal Code, if I understand it correctly, contains a provision rather similar to s 31 of Wright's Jamaica Code which punishes both preparing to commit a crime and equipping others to do so.[72] And s 97 of the Penal Code of the Cameroons, which is both elegant and neat, is as follows:

> '(1) An accessory shall mean a person who abets the commission of a felony or misdemeanour, that is:
>
> (a) who orders or in any manner causes the commission of an act or omission so defined; or
>
> (b) who aids or facilitates the preparation or the commission of such an offence.
>
> (2) Attempted abetment shall be treated as abetment.'

Conclusion

The Law Commission's excellent Draft Code, in which John Smith has played such an honourable part, contains inchoate offences of incitement and conspiracy but no offence of facilitation. This is hardly surprising, since the codifiers were anxious to codify English common law as it is, without proposing major changes other than those which had already been put forward by the Criminal Law Revision Committee and other official law reform bodies.

I hope, however, that this essay shows that such an offence would not really be such a major change, because the courts generally manage to catch facilitation already, although at the cost of straining other parts of the criminal law beyond their elastic limit. I hope that what has been done about the problem in certain other penal codes shows that it is a proposal which should at least be taken seriously.[73]

NOTES

1 'Complicity in the Criminal Code' (1969) 85 LQR 252, 268, et seq.
2 'Secondary Participation and Inchoate Offences' in *Crime, Proof and Punishment* (Essays in Memory of Sir Rupert Cross) (1981), and 'Aid, Abet, Counsel, or Procure' in *Reshaping the Criminal Law* (*Festschrift* for Glanville Williams) (1978).
3 [1984] QB 472, CA. Cf *R v Hapgood and Wyatt* (1870) LR 1 CCR 221, 11 Cox CC 471.
4 See Smith 'Secondary Participation and Inchoate Offences' in *Crime, Proof and punishment* (1981) 21–44; and Glanville Williams, *Textbook of Criminal Law* (2nd edn, 1983) 417–418.
5 (1913) 9 Cr App Rep 220, CCA.
6 [1955] 1 WLR 1, CCA.
7 [1960] 1 QB 129, CCA.
8 [1978] 1 WLR 1350. The case was different in that the defendant did not know the time and place where the crime was to be committed, although similar in that he was not sure precisely what crime it was to be.
9 *Criminal Law* (5th edn, 1983) p 132.
10 Law Commission Working Paper no. 43.
11 (1573) 2 Plowd 473.
12 Working Paper no 43.
13 Section 31(6): '. . . a person who assists or encourages a principal in pursuance of an agreement between them that an offence shall be committed in relation to a particular person or thing is not guilty as an accessory to an offence intentionally committed by the principal in relation to some other person or thing.'
14 In a case like *Maxwell*, I think the helper could still be guilty as an accessory. Although he did not know precisely which of several crimes of violence was planned, he knew precise details of the time and place and that his conduct would facilitate only one single offence.
15 [1976] RTR 251, [1976] Crim LR 131.
16 Although this seems unlikely in the light of *Amstrad Consumer Electronics plc v British Phonographic Industry Ltd* [1986] FSR 159. See below.
17 (1985) 82 Cr App Rep 226.
18 In the South Australian case of *R v Crichton* [1915] SALR 1, however, it was accepted that someone who supplied an abortifacient to a woman at her request could be convicted of inciting her to procure an abortion.
19 [1948] 2 KB 48.
20 Note 16, above. It should be noticed, however, that the manufacturer did advertise that the equipment would make it 'possible to copy your favourite cassette'.
21 *Textbook of Criminal Law* (2nd edn, 1983) 422.
22 [1986] AC 27, HL.
23 *Conspiracy and Criminal Law Reform* (Law Com no 76, 1976).
24 [1985] Crim LR 651–657.
25 See Smith (n 24, above): Smith in *Crime, Proof and Punishment* (n 2, above, 35–36, 40–41: Williams *Textbook of Criminal Law* (2nd edn, 1983) 424–425. The Court of Appeal rejected the idea of conspiracy to aid and abet in *R v Hollinshead* [1985] 2 WLR 761, CA, but the House of Lords [1985] AC 975 left it open.
26 [1985] AC 975, HL.
27 [1985] 2 WLR 761, CA.

28 *Scott v Metropolitan Police Comr* [1975] AC 819, HL.
29 See Jarman 'Electricity Meter Fraud and "The Black Box"' (1985) 149 JP 103.
30 The organisers of the Automobile Association would undoubtedly have been prosecuted for conspiracy if its members had not included five members of the Government, the leader of the opposition, several judges, both Archbishops and a number of prominent policemen. See W Plowden *The Motor Car and Politics 1896–1970* (1971), ch 4, n 35.
31 *Curlett v M'Kechnie* 1938 JC 176, 1939 SLT 11.
32 [1907] 1 KB 59.
33 Per Ridley J; Lord Alverstone CJ expressly disagreed with him on this.
34 A reason given by Lord Alverstone CJ, who, with Darling J, also said there must be evidence that the person warned was actually committing a criminal offence.
35 [1910] 1 KB 1.
36 [1982] QB 1044.
37 (1981) 74 Cr App Rep 298.
38 The Act itself says 'any felony in this Act mentioned', but this was amended by the Criminal Law Act 1967, s10 and Sch 2 Para 8.
39 Compare the cases which hold that the *use* of an ordinary article as an offensive weapon does not amount to an offence of *possessing* an offensive weapon unless the assailant was earlier in possession of it with a premeditated intention of so using it: *Ohlson v Hylton* [1975] 1 WLR 724; *Wood v Metropolitan Police Comr* [1986] 1 WLR 796.
40 Forgery and Counterfeiting Act 1981, s1.
41 Theft Act 1968, s 17.
42 Theft Act 1968, s 20.
43 *R v Whybrow* (1951) 35 Cr App Rep 141.
44 [1986] AC 27; above.
45 I once thought otherwise. I am grateful to Dr Leonard Leigh for converting me. Buxton takes the opposite view in his paper, n 1, above.
46 This is so in the case of incitement and conspiracy in German law: *Strafgeseztbuch* art 49(a)(3). By art 50 of the Norwegian Penal Code, liability for attempt is extinguished where the defendant voluntarily desists after reaching the stage of an attempt. Section 95(5) of the Penal Code of the Cameroons provides that 'no penalty may be imposed upon a conspirator who prevents the execution of the offence resolved or who before any attempt at execution informs the administrative or judicial authorities of the conspiracy.'
47 (1736) 9 Geo II c 35, s XII.
48 *Criminal Law, The General Part*, p 124; *Textbook of Criminal Law* (2nd edn, 1983) 341 et seq.
49 Cf Lord Roskill's opinion in *R v Hollinshead* [1985] AC 975, which contains full details of how to make and fit 'black boxes'.
50 *Cf Amstrad Consumer Electronics plc v British Phonographic Industry Ltd* [1986] FSR 159, above, n 16.
51 This seems to be Buxton's suggestion, at least in the case of help offered generally rather than to a particular individual: see his article (n 1 above), Appendix 1 (iii).
52 *Textbook of Criminal Law* (2nd edn, 1983) 343.
53 [1976] RTR 251, [1976] Crim LR 131.
54 [1984] QB 795.
55 Although it looks like a form of being an accessory, it is in fact a substantive offence, and there can therefore be an attempt to commit it: *R v McShane* (1977) 66 Cr App Rep 97, CA.
56 [1984] QB 581.
57 Article 3.02 of the American Law Institute's Model Penal Code provides a general defence where behaviour otherwise criminal is done in the belief that it is necessary to avoid a greater harm or evil to the actor or to another; but even that would only half solve the problem, which also arises with those who believe their behaviour will promote some greater good.
58 [1986] AC 112.
59 [1986] Crim LR 113.
60 Parl Pap (1843), vol XIX.
61 But the incitement provision, if enacted, might have covered certain cases of help. Article 1 of Chapter XXII was as follows: 'Whosoever shall, by solicitation, *advice*, force, threat or otherwise endeavour to procure, *promote*, or compel the commission of a crime by any other person, shall [incur various penalties].'
62 Parl Pap (1878/9), vol XX.
63 Canadian Criminal Code, s 21; Queensland Criminal Code, s 7; Western Australian Criminal Code, s 7; Tasmanian Criminal Code, s 3; New Zealand Crimes Act 1961, s 66.
64 Canadian Criminal Code, s 22 ('Counselling', which was originally undefined, but is now

defined by s 22(3) to include procurement, solicitation and incitement). Queensland Criminal Code, s 539 (attempting to procure another to commit a crime); cf Western Australian Criminal Code, s 556, Tasmanian Criminal Code, s 298, and New Zealand Crimes Act, s 311(2) ('Everyone who incites, counsels or attempts to procure any person to commit any offence . . .').

65 *R v McLeod and Georgia Straight Publishing Co Ltd* (1970) 75 WWR 161 (British Columbia CA). Conveniently, the article did end with the exhortation 'Plant your seeds.' In *R v Baker* (1909) 28 NZLR 536 the New Zealand Court of Appeal held that a man who gave a would-be safe-breaker a lesson was guilty as an accessory to his subsequent burglary because he had 'counselled' its commission. As the New Zealand equivalent of incitement covers 'counselling' as well as inciting (see the previous note), Baker could presumably be prosecuted even if his pupil never put into practice what he had learnt.

66 *Nelson's Penal Code of India* (7th edn), p265.

67 *Faguna Kantha Nath v State of Assam* (1959) 22 S Ct Jo 643; *Jamuna Singh v State of Bihar* (1967) S Ct Jo 175.

68 See Friedland 'RS Wright's Model Criminal Code: A forgotten Chapter in the History of the Criminal Law' (1981) 1 OJLS 307. The code is to be found in Parl Pap. 1877, vol III.

69 See p 160, above.

70 See GP Fletcher *Rethinking the Criminal Law* (1978) 679.

71 Article 60 French Penal Code punishes accessories to crimes which are actually committed, and supplements this with specific provisions concerned with particular forms of facilitation, eg ss398/399 (making or supplying picklocks or skeleton keys). Sections 48, 49 and 49a of the West German *Strafgeseztbuch* punish accessories, incitement and conspiracy, but not mere facilitation, which as in France is caught (if at all) by specific offences, eg s 311a concerning explosives, and the *Ordnungswidrigkeiten* of 2 January 1975, which punishes making forgeries or supplying them to others. Scottish common law penalises incitement, conspiracy and also being an accessory ('art and part'), but it seems that one cannot be art and part of a crime which is not committed. Whether one can attempt to be an accessory is a problem which does not seem to have been discussed in Scotland.

72 Chapter 23, s 2 (translated by Thorsten Sellin): 'A person who with the intention of committing or promoting a crime, presents or receives money or something else as prepayment or payment for the crime, or who procures, constructs, gives, receives, keeps, conveys or engages in any such activity with poison, explosive, weapon, picklock, falsification tool or other such ancillary means, shall, in cases where specific provisions have been made governing this, be sentenced for preparation of the crime, unless he is punishable for the completed crime or attempt.'

73 I should like to thank Professor Glanville Williams, Mr Peter Glazebrook, Dr Leonard Leigh, Professor Kurt Lipstein and Professor ATH Smith, all of whom helped me in various ways with this paper; which does not of course mean that they agree with any or all of it.

Criminal law and administrative law: problems of procedure and reasonableness

DGT Williams

Introduction

> 'Judicial review has I think developed to a stage today when, without reiterating any analysis of the steps by which the development has come about, one can conveniently classify under three heads the grounds on which administrative action is subject to control by judicial review. The first ground I would call "illegality", the second "irrationality" and the third "procedural impropriety".'[1]

After making that statement Lord Diplock, who was delivering his speech in the well-known *GCHQ* case in 1984, proceeded to give a brief explanation of each of the three heads. His condensation of the scope of judicial review is not without difficulties, terminological and otherwise, but it is a reminder of the potentially wide range of controls exercised by the courts. These controls extend beyond central and local government to a variety of bodies at the fringe of government, and the principles of administrative law inevitably impinge upon or draw from other areas such as tort, contract, company law, labour law, and criminal law. Moreover, the application of the principles of administrative law can sensibly be considered only with proper regard for the statutory, institutional and broader social or political context of a particular case.[2]

The problem of making statements of general principle, while at the same time allowing for particular qualifications in application, is evident in the impact of administrative law on criminal law, criminal procedure, and the exercise of police powers. The impact is seen in a variety of situations: for instance, in the procedure of the lower criminal courts; in the interpretation of byelaws and departmental legislation; in prosecution policy; in the utilisation of civil proceedings in aid of the criminal law; in the law of arrest and search; and in the exercise of common law powers used to prevent breaches of the peace. Nevertheless a linking factor is provided by the wide rules of judicial review which have evolved over many years as a means of ensuring that administrators and others act within the four corners of their authority (usually statutory).[3] Lord Diplock's identification of illegality, irrationality and procedural impropriety was an attempt to provide well-lit signposts in an area where the cases and the complexities have increased dramatically of late, especially since a streamlining of the available remedies from 1977.[4]

The interaction of criminal law and administrative law, however, is not new. Challenges based on the ultra vires rule were familiar in response to subordinate legislation long before modern 'administrative law' was recognised by commentators or practitioners; and the considerable case law associated with subordinate legislation is a useful reminder even now of the difficulties of statutory interpretation which underline so much of administrative law.

Byelaws were once a regular source of challenge in the courts,[5] though it would be unwise to rely on the authority of cases prior to the mid-nineteenth century.[6] Judicial control was such that byelaws were questioned both on straightforward grounds of ultra vires[7] and on the basis (within a wider concept of ultra vires) of standards of uncertainty, repugnancy, and unreasonableness.[8] The latter standards were applied with 'a jealous eye' to old railway byelaws,[9] but they became diluted with regard to the newly emerging local authorities of the nineteenth century and beyond by the so-called rule of 'benevolent interpretation' expressed in the leading case of *Kruse v Johnson.*[10] The courts have not been keen, for instance, to strike down local byelaws on grounds of uncertainty;[11] and in an Australian case alleging repugnancy Griffith C J in the High Court confessed that he found it difficult to decide the case 'with sufficient gravity.'[12] Even so, allegations of uncertainty and repugnancy can and do succeed;[13] and, more commonly, they can be employed to shore up allegations of unreasonableness.

The concept of unreasonableness is undoubtedly the most important legacy inherited from the old case law on byelaws. As examples of unreasonableness as a ground of invalidity, Lord Russell of Killowen CJ said in *Kruse v Johnson* that if byelaws

> '. . . were found to be partial and unequal in their operation as between different classes; if they were manifestly unjust; if they disclosed bad faith; if they involved such oppressive or gratuitous interference with the rights of those subject to them as could find no justification in the minds of reasonable men, the court might well say, "Parliament never intended to give authority to make such rules; they are unreasonable and ultra vires." '[14]

Allegations of unreasonableness had been made in numerous cases before the end of the nineteenth century: these included instances where the Salvation Army ran foul of byelaws directed against singing or the playing of musical instruments in the street,[15] and some of the later model byelaws dealing with noise nuisance have their origins in the nineteenth century.[16] Cases subsequent to *Kruse v Johnson* have raised issues of public order,[17] the use of profane or obscene language,[18] street betting,[19] the regulation of traffic,[20] the duties of landlords,[21] and public health.[22]

Challenges to byelaws are much rarer nowadays. One reason for this decline is the increased use of model byelaws. Model byelaws are not immune from judicial challenge; but, emerging as a by-product of the confirming power as to byelaws exercised by the Department of the Environment or the Home Office, they are available for local authorities to adopt with both the assurance of confirmation and greater confidence in their validity.[23] The Home Office and other departments will sometimes produce model byelaws to meet new conditions, as in response some years ago to the playing of radios on seafronts and beaches.[24] A striking example concerned the emergence in public places of slot machines for the sale of contraceptives; it 'was felt that that was unseemly and socially undesirable, and the Home Secretary suggested that towns should deal with the situation by making a byelaw and he circulated a draft of what he thought would be a suitable provision. It was an effective step, and such machines disappeared from public places.'[25] The adoption of a model byelaw remains a discretionary step for each local authority, but in practice model byelaws pre-empt the relevant fields and secure an impressive measure of uniformity throughout the country.[26] Uniformity in its turn often prepares the ground for national legislation, and a further reason for the decline in byelaw cases in the courts is that some of the most controversial subject-matter — in such areas as planning and public health and environmental safeguards — would now be directly catered for in Acts of Parliament. Criminal and regulatory law on a national level has often evolved from local experimentation, through private Acts of Parliament (which, of course, are not open to challenge in the courts[27]) and through local byelaws; and the erosion of local initiative through centralised control or replacement has been a marked feature of governmental developments of the past century. Paradoxically, the 'democratic' element in local law-making — which is recognised in the 'benevolent interpretation' doctrine — should be regarded as weaker in view of the extent of departmental influence.

The doctrine of 'unreasonableness' explained in *Kruse v Johnson* has, however, survived the decline of byelaw challenges in the English courts. This is in part because it continues to flourish in countries (such as Canada) where much is still done through the mechanism of byelaws.[28] Secondly, the grounds of uncertainty, repugnancy and unreasonableness have been extended to local authority action akin to that of making byelaws.[29] Thirdly, there is the possibility — despite discouraging words in the war-time case of *Sparks v Edward Ash Ltd*[30] — that unreasonableness could be invoked with regard to departmental subordinate legislation. In South Africa, for instance, it appears that the '*Kruse* test of reasonableness not only applies to byelaws but to *all* kinds of delegated legislation.'[31] Some would argue that the *Kruse v Johnson* test of unreasonableness is 'essentially similar' to the *Wednesbury* test applied to all forms of administrative action.[32] Nevertheless the 'identifiable and specific meaning'[33] given to unreasonableness in *Kruse v Johnson* seems peculiarly appropriate for providing standards in the formal expression of legislation. Under English law there is at present no review of Parliamentary legislation,[34] but a distinction between departmental subordinate legislation and local byelaws is surely unacceptable for purposes of judicial review. There may in particular contexts be strong arguments for judicial restraint, but in cases involving the criminal law and allied powers and procedures there is every ground for reinforcing traditional common law presumptions in favour of personal freedom and freedom of speech.[35] Such reinforcement should, perhaps as compensation for the absence of the familiar procedures of law-making in departmental legislation, be based on the *Kruse v Johnson* concept of unreasonableness.

The interaction of criminal law and administrative law can be observed in a variety of other contexts. A good example is the area of 'Crown privilege' or public interest immunity, where the Crown or the police directly seek to withhold — on grounds of public interest — the production of documentary or other evidence in a court of law. Claims of immunity are not often made in criminal proceedings themselves, a point emphasised as a result of an apparent refusal by the prosecution to disclose copies of army medical reports about a man accused of murder: the trial judge threatened at one stage to issue a subpoena to 'the whole Army Council if you like.'[36] However, a series of interesting cases at the periphery of criminal law have occurred over the years. These include the pre-1968 instances where the Home Office withheld police reports and other material relevant to an assault in a prison hospital; where the Home Secretary objected to the production of various police reports and communications in a civil action for conspiracy to defraud; and where, even in the context of habeas corpus, non-disclosure was allowed for diplomatic communications.[37] The law on 'Crown privilege' was reassessed and amended in the leading case of *Conway v Rimmer* in 1968,[38] establishing the 'vital principle' that the last word in determining the public interest 'lies not with a minister but with the courts.'[39] *Conway v Rimmer* itself arose from an action for malicious prosecution brought by a former probationary police officer, and many of the later cases exploring the limits of judicial supervision in this area have involved the police or aspects of criminal law and procedure. In the *Rossminster* case, for instance, the House of Lords touched upon 'the public interest immunity which covers investigations into possible criminal offences';[40] in the *Malone* case there was a possible reserve argument of 'Crown privilege' to use against a subpoena seeking production of telephone tapping warrants;[41] in the *Gaming Board* case the House of Lords ruled against disclosure (for the purpose of a criminal libel action) of certain correspondence between the Board and an assistant chief constable;[42] in the *Wakefield Prison* case a claim of public interest immunity, made by the Home Secretary with regard to certain documents on prison control units, was rejected;[43] and there have been difficult cases arising from investigations of complaints against the police.[44] That the English courts have yet to face additional problems in the area of public interest immunity is indicated by important decisions of the High Court of Australia in *Sankey v Whitlam*[45] (where a private prosecutor succeeded in securing access to several high-level governmental documents for which immunity had been claimed) and *Alister v R*[46] (involving attempted access, for the purposes of a criminal appeal, to documents belonging to the Australian Security Intelligence Organisation).

Other facets or principles of administrative law can be observed in cases where the courts have explored issues of policy in the investigation and prosecution of offences;[47] where civil proceedings (through injunctions and declarations) have been instituted in aid of the enforcement of the criminal law;[48] where the exercise of the power of pardon[49] and of powers of parole[50] has been challenged; and where the limits of the jurisdiction of magistrates' courts and other bodies are in issue.[51] In the course of the varied case law in such areas, the courts have had to wrestle with some of the most troublesome rules or principles of administrative law. These include issues of locus standi or standing, particularly in the context of the Attorney-General's discretion whether or not to authorise relator proceedings;[52] the control of discretionary power whether under statute or the prerogative;[53] the fettering of discretionary power through the adoption of rigid policies or otherwise;[54] the appropriateness of the remedy sought;[55] and the elusive concept of jurisdiction. Questions of jurisdiction have given rise to particular controversy (in administrative law generally) since the decision of the House of Lords in *Anisminic Ltd v Foreign Compensation Commission* in 1968,[56] and some indication of the difficulties can be seen in the case of *Thelander v Woodward*[57] in the Court of Appeal of New South Wales. A Royal Commission (consisting of one judge) investigating drug trafficking was held to have travelled outside 'the remitted jurisdictional area' in adjudging a witness to be in contempt by refusing to answer certain questions. No appeal on fact or law lay from the Commissioner; in investigating an alleged contempt he had 'embarked upon an inquiry in respect of which he had jurisdiction'; but, in determining the 'fine line' between a false answer (perjury) and no answer at all, he had taken 'into account matters he had no right to take into account. Whilst this is not a matter of jurisdiction in the narrow sense, it is within the wider sense as expounded by Lord Reid in *Anisminic* . . .'[58]

In two areas in particular, the interaction of criminal law and administrative law is clearly demonstrated. The first of these, not surprisingly, is the area of procedure. Procedural requirements can be expressly set out in statutory form or they can be implied by virtue of the rules of natural justice (or fairness). The second area in which administrative law is prominent is that of reasonableness, which provides an important (if elusive) standard in numerous contexts relevant to criminal law. Any foray into the realms of unreasonableness is handicapped by terminological and other problems, but an attempt should be made to separate different emphases and assumptions adhered to in the courts.

Criminal law: procedure

Express procedural requirements, set out in a primary or subordinate legislative instrument, bring into play the well-known mandatory-directory distinction. The courts have produced 'a multiplicity of irreconcilable decisions making it impossible to assert with any certainty that a provision will be held either mandatory or directory in a particular context.'[59] The case law is not unlike that relating to strict liability in criminal law: various presumptions have emerged over the years but, even when armed with a check-list of factors which a court might deem to be relevant, the decision may be difficult to predict. The judges have of late recognised the need to avoid artificial and rigid distinctions and they have sought to tailor the law to meet the circumstances.[60] Nevertheless one of the presumptions which is bound to affect procedural requirements in the area of the criminal law is that in favour of the liberty of the person. Hence very many of the rules of procedure in magistrates' courts and in wider areas of law enforcement are likely to be seen as obligatory. Failure to secure a consent (required by statute) for the institution of criminal proceedings can be fatal;[61] the courts have insisted on strict observance of the requirement that an accused should be informed of his right to trial by jury;[62] and equally the courts have not been disposed to interpret narrowly statutory provisions about notice of proceedings.[63]

The importance of notice has, of course, been widely recognised as an important ingredient of the right to be heard (audi alteram partem) under the implied rules of natural justice. In the context of police disciplinary proceedings there have been several important cases on audi alteram partem, and these include the landmark decision of *Ridge v Baldwin* in 1963.[64] The impact of the rules, however, has been much wider and sometimes unexpected — as in the case where it was held that certiorari lay to quash a conviction because of the failure of the prosecution to notify the applicant of the existence of two witnesses.[65] Insistence on the 'elementary' and 'basic' need to give an accused 'a reasonable chance' to prepare and present his case is seen in *R v*

Thames Magistrates' Court, ex p Polemis in 1974;[66] but it is nevertheless not uncommon for there to be breaches of natural justice where criminal courts are perhaps tempted to act too swiftly.[67] At the same time, the application of the rules of natural justice may vary according to the circumstances, and it is not always an easy task to determine in advance the procedural protections available to someone facing a criminal charge or other serious penalty.

Consider, for instance, the sphere of binding-over orders. Binding over, in its most commonly understood sense, involves the making of an order by a criminal court (usually a magistrates' court) that someone shall enter into a recognisance, with or without sureties, to keep the peace and be of good behaviour. Refusal to enter into such a recognisance can lead to a term of imprisonment, and default in observing the terms of a recognisance duly sworn can lead to forfeiture, by the recognisor and by any sureties, of all or part of the sums stated in the recognisance. An important aspect of preventive justice and sitting uneasily at the borderline of civil and criminal proceedings,[68] the power to bind over has to be exercised in accordance with natural justice. But as recently as 1964, it was argued in the Divisional Court that a court could without more ado conclude a trial by dismissing a charge of assault and then bind over both the accused and two prosecution witnesses. 'I must say,' said Lord Parker CJ, 'that I shudder at the idea that that can be done, although it is said that it is done quite generally. It seems to me to be elementary justice that particularly a mere witness before justices should at any rate be told what is passing through the justices' minds, and should have an opportunity of dealing with it.'[69] There is more uncertainty as to binding over an acquitted or convicted defendant after a criminal trial, but it seems that the courts are now prepared to adopt a special rule of proportionality. In *R v Central Criminal Court, ex p Boulding*,[70] the applicant — who had been convicted of insulting words or behaviour during a demonstration outside the premises of a fur-manufacturing company — had, in addition to being fined, been bound over for two years in the sum of £500 (with the alternative of three months' jail). This was done without any inquiry into the applicant's means and without any opportunity for representations; and it was held, given the severity of the binding-over order, that there had been a breach of natural justice. In an earlier decision (in 1973) the Divisional Court had been less sympathetic to an acquitted defendant who had been bound over in the sum of £100.[71]

An additional (and unsuccessful) argument raised in *R v Central Criminal Court, ex p Boulding* concerned the rule against bias (nemo iudex in causa sua). It was argued that the judge, in commenting that democracy is 'a delicate plant' and that some minorities in asserting their views were 'no different from the adherents of Hitler', had given an appearance of bias.[72] This view was rejected, but it is a reminder of yet another facet of natural justice which can impinge upon criminal proceedings. The test for bias has been variously expressed, and an effort to provide an acceptable formula was made by Ackner LJ in a case in 1982 concerning information made available to magistrates through computerised court sheets: '. . . would a reasonable and fair-minded person sitting in court and knowing all the relevant facts have a reasonable suspicion that a fair trial for the applicant was not possible?'[73] This is a somewhat more cautious formulation than the claim that 'justice should both be done and be manifestly seen to be done'[74] but it allows for a wide range of circumstances where allegations of bias may be raised.

Cases in this century include challenges to the impartiality of a justice of the peace in Ireland who had allegedly said with reference to three members of one family who had appeared before him in binding-over proceedings, that 'as sure as I'm living I will not leave any member of the Feheens in Bohonagh';[75] complaints about the role or behaviour of a justices' clerk;[76] allegations that someone has participated in an appeal against his own decision;[77] claims that the conduct of proceedings may have shown a partisan attitude on the part of the person conducting the proceedings;[78] a series of arguments as to bias raised against a coroner in a particularly controversial case;[79] and a submission that the chairman of a bench had, as the defendant's former headmaster, written an adverse report on him only months earlier.[80] Those responsible for the conduct of judicial proceedings must take account of possible allegations of bias as an important aspect of wider allegations of a breach of natural justice or a denial of procedural fairness.

2 Reasonableness

The term 'reasonableness' appears frequently and confusingly in administrative law. We have seen how it has emerged as a test or standard with regard to subordinate legislation;[81] and 'reasonableness' has also been relevant in the formulation of a test for bias.[82] More generally it can be employed as the broad standard for challenges to the exercise of discretion, or it can be seen as one of the particular grounds of challenge to the exercise of discretion, in each case under the broad umbrella of the ultra vires rule.[83] A different approach is adopted by the courts where a *statute* requires 'reasonable grounds' or 'reasonable cause to believe' or 'reasonable suspicion' as a precondition for the exercise of discretionary power; and likewise a different approach is or should be adopted where the *common law* requires reasonableness or reasonable grounds or reasonable cause as a precondition for the exercise of discretionary power. In precondition cases the judicial approach should be much stricter, largely because the courts (in the exercise of powers of review under the ultra vires rule) are more at ease in determining whether there is prior authority to act at all than in examining the actual exercise of discretionary power through the application of wide standards of unreasonableness.

A statutory requirement of 'reasonable cause to believe' or one of its variants was dramatised in the case of *Liversidge v Anderson*,[84] but the main body of case law relates to statutory and common law powers of arrest. Early on in his dissenting speech in *Liversidge v Anderson*, for instance, Lord Atkin spoke of the power of arrest without warrant 'confided by the common law both to constables and to private individuals';[85] and in a later Privy Council case Lord Devlin said that the relevant test of reasonable suspicion in the Criminal Procedure Code (of Malaysia) 'is one that has existed in the common law for many years.'[86] That the determination of the reasonableness of suspicion may involve considerations of policy is illustrated in *Wright v Sharp*, a postwar case where a taxicab driver — who had become entangled in a bizarre series of events centred on a 'cops and robbers' fight in Shaftesbury Avenue — lost his case for false imprisonment. The trial judge spoke of a wave of crime sweeping the country and of motor vehicles being used for escape; and he insisted that the liberty of the subject must be balanced against the need to aid the detention and apprehension of criminals.[87] In a case in 1984, by contrast, where 'a typical, ordinary respectable Englishman' ('well dressed, articulate and not over-assertive') had been arrested, damages were awarded because of the absence of reasonable grounds for arrest, even though the trial judge accepted that the court should not adopt 'a harsh approach' as to what constituted reasonable suspicion in the officer's mind.[88] The effect of such cases is to confirm that the person making the arrest must be ready to justify the reasonableness of his suspicion in a court of law.[89]

The only surviving powers of arrest without warrant at common law are those relating to breach of the peace. In the words of Watkins LJ in the Court of Appeal, there is power to arrest for breach of the peace:

> '. . . where (1) a breach of the peace is committed in the presence of the person making the arrest, or (2) the arrestor believes that such a breach will be committed in the immediate future by the person arrested although he has not yet committed any breach, or (3) where a breach has been committed and it is reasonably believed that a renewal of it is threatened.'[90]

The preconditions for the exercise of the power of arrest in the second and third situations consist both of establishing that a 'breach of the peace' properly understood was anticipated and that there were reasonable grounds for the anticipation. A good example of the latter is provided by the New Zealand case of *Allen v Police* where the appellant, even assuming that he was quiet when the police arrived at a coffee-bar, had by his previous conduct given the officer reasonable cause to believe that a breach of the peace might be committed.[91]

The law on arrest for breach of the peace provides a bridge between police powers (as commonly understood by reference, for instance, to the Police and Criminal Evidence Act 1984) and preventive powers of the police in the area of public order. The government took the view in 1985 that new legislation on public order need not extend to any codification or strengthening of common law powers. This was because, in the government's view, the police 'have not sought codification and see no benefit in it' and also because 'there is advantage in the flexibility of common law powers which are defined and controlled by the courts.'[92] The word 'flexibility' may, of course, be used as an alternative to 'uncertainty', and indeed Lord Scarman in the Brixton Report commented on 'a degree of uncertainty in the case law' relating to the common law duty of the police to take reasonable steps, short of arrest, by, for example, 'moving people on or dispersing a crowd, to prevent or quell disorder.'[93] A similar element of 'flexibility' or 'uncertainty' attaches to the common law powers of the police to enter private property to prevent breaches of the peace.[94] Once again the exercise of the powers depends upon certain preconditions. In *Duncan v Jones*, for instance, it was 'found as a fact that the respondent reasonably apprehended a breach of the peace'[95] and in *Thomas v Sawkins* the comment was made judicially 'that the justices had before them material on which they could properly hold that the police officers in question had reasonable grounds for believing that, if they were not present, seditious speeches would be made and/or that a breach of the peace would take place.'[96] The authority of the police to take preventive action is, in Lord Atkin's words, 'a conditional authority',[97] and presumably it is for the courts — as under the law of arrest — to insist on a proper showing of reasonable anticipation of a threat to the peace. In the words of de Smith:

> 'This is not to say that the courts will readily interfere with the exercise of

discretion if, from the nature of the subject-matter or the surrounding circumstances (eg the necessity for taking swift action for the preservation of public order), it would be difficult for anyone but the repository of the power to form an opinion as to the occasion for its exercise, or if it would be unfair to penalise the authority for a possible error of judgment in a doubtful case.'[98]

Despite that eloquent reminder of the factors encouraging judicial restraint in some circumstances, it would seem desirable for the courts to adopt a consistently strict approach towards preconditions in public order cases. With reference to the power to impose conditions on processions, for instance, the government in its White Paper of 1985 — in proposing new tests — spoke of its determination 'to ensure that demonstrators have an effective means of challenging any decision by the police to impose conditions which is not justified by a real risk of serious disorder, disruption or coercion.'[99] Likewise, the initial question in a standard *Duncan v Jones* case is 'whether, on the particular facts, there were reasonable grounds on which a constable, charged with the duty of preserving the peace, reasonably anticipated that a breach of the peace might occur.'[100] The issue is whether the courts demand enough of a showing, bearing in mind Lord Parker CJ's words that there 'must exist proved facts from which a constable could reasonably have anticipated' a breach of the peace and that 'it is not enough that his contemplation is that there is a remote possibility but there must be a reasonable possibility of a breach of the peace.'[101] The disturbing feature of *Duncan v Jones* is not so much the principle which was stated on the preventive powers of the police as the application of the principle to the facts; and some of the police actions allegedly taken during the miners' strike of 1984–85 were likewise open to question on the issue as to whether the preconditions were satisfied.[102] In *Moss v McLachlan* in 1984, Skinner J stressed that the conditions for reasonable preventive action exist only if the police 'honestly and reasonably form the opinion that there is a real risk of a breach of the peace in the sense that it is in close proximity both in place and time.'[103] There is still much to be done to identify the sorts of criteria which the police might legitimately take into account, but what is clear is that in the law of public order, as in the law of arrest, the courts need to attach special significance to the *conditional* authority allowed to the police.

Once the preconditions have been satisfied, however, the courts are entitled to switch their approach in examining the legality of particular action. This is demonstrated in *Holgate-Mohammed v Duke*,[104] a decision of the House of Lords in the context of arrest. The appellant had been arrested on suspicion of theft, and the lower courts were satisfied that the police officer who made the arrest had reasonable cause for his suspicion. So the 'condition precedent' to his power to take the appellant into custody was fulfilled, noted Lord Diplock, and the central issue before the House of Lords related to his 'executive discretion' whether to arrest her or not.[105] This in its turn requires, not a positive showing of reasonable cause by the executive officer (a policeman in this case), but a showing by the aggrieved person that there has been an abuse of discretion on the part of the executive officer according to the so-called *Wednesbury* principles 'that have become too familiar to call for repetitious citation.'[106] On the facts in *Holgate-Mohammed v Duke* the police officer decided to make an arrest because he thought that the person arrested 'would be more likely to confess to what he had reasonable cause to believe to be the truth if she were arrested and taken for questioning to the police station.'[107]

Should this consideration have been irrelevant to the exercise of his powers whether or not to arrest? The House of Lords thought not, and the appellant lost her claim for false imprisonment.

The implications of the decision have been well explored elsewhere,[108] but the application of the *Wednesbury* principles in the overlap between criminal and administrative law deserves fuller recognition. The *Wednesbury* guide should, of course, only be regarded as an initial statement of principle, because much depends on the context and the particular facts. In the exercise of preventive powers under *Duncan v Jones* and *Thomas v Sawkins*, for instance, there is scope for investigation of the type of preventive measures taken to avert a breach of the peace. In *Moss v McLachlan*, Skinner J spoke of 'reasonable preventive action including, if necessary, the measures taken in this case', namely, preventing the convoy of cars (conveying striking miners) from proceeding further to collieries nearby.[109] The inclination of the courts is, not surprisingly, to leave much to the discretion of the police on the spot — as in severely limiting the number of pickets in *Piddington v Bates*[110] or in asking for a street meeting to be moved 175 yards away as in *Duncan v Jones*[111] — and to make allowance for circumstances 'when the susceptibilities and passions of the public are in a state of tension and liable to be more easily aroused.'[112] A similar inclination is evident in the context of the scope of banning orders made with regard to public processions,[113] the adoption of a policy for the policing of Toxteth (in Liverpool) in the light of the Scarman Report on Brixton,[114] and the imposition of conditions upon the granting of bail.[115] On the other hand, a sharp awareness of the problem of police discretion is seen in the Australian case of *Forbutt v Blake*[116] where, in the context of a demonstration at the end of an Anzac Day parade, it was held that the police officer — who 'reasonably anticipated a real possibility of a breach of the peace if he did not intervene'[117] — was held not to have been acting in the execution of his duty in seeking to forbid the continuation of the demonstration. The judgment of Connor J in that case could be interpreted as an implicit injection of the *Beatty v Gillbanks* principle[118] into the application of the *Wednesbury* principles: in other words, the exercise of police discretion was wrong because insufficient weight was given to the need to protect those going about their lawful activities.[119] The *Wednesbury* principles, as has often been shown in administrative law, are very adaptable.[120]

3 Conclusions

The variability of the principles of judicial review, both in formulation and application, is a distinctive feature of administrative law. Examples of this variability can be seen in several areas of criminal law, criminal procedure and police powers. What is abundantly clear is that the special considerations of criminal law, criminal procedure and police powers need to be employed as important guides to the application of more general principles; and the examples given in this essay are intended to underline the interdependence of criminal law and administrative law.

Much else could have been considered. The omitted topics include the intricacies of procedure in the lower criminal courts; the various remedies available in judicial review; error of law on the face of the record; the law of search and seizure; and the topical and controversial subject of emergency powers. The latter area brings into focus the extent of judicial review of the use of exclusion orders, the special powers of arrest and search, and other refinements of the law; and the appropriate role of the courts in such cases is a matter of considerable interest and importance.[121] Special attention could also have been given, for instance, to the area of environmental safeguards where there are particular considerations as to the definition of offences, prosecution policies, and the various methods available to secure enforcement of the law.[122] In addition, the institutional aspects of administrative law — formal proceedings in tribunals and public local inquiries — could be regarded as relevant from time to time, whether, for instance, in the context of the problem of disruption of public inquiries[123] or in the wider context of the possible extension of the law of contempt of court to many types of administrative tribunals.[124]

The impact of administrative law was foreshadowed in the early case law on byelaws. Steadily the principles of administrative law have encroached upon various aspects of criminal law, criminal procedure, and police powers; and they are especially important in areas of procedure and discretion. The control of executive discretion, in particular, has become a major emphasis in judicial review of executive action, and the effect is seen both at the periphery of criminal law and in the content of some of the offences. The purpose of this essay has been to identify these and other examples of the interaction of criminal law and administrative law.

NOTES

1 *Council of Civil Service Unions v Minister for the Civil Service* [1985] AC 374 at 410, HL.

2 In 'The Task of Administrative Law' (1927) 75 Univ of Penn LR 614, 620 Professor Frankfurter argued that 'a subject like "judicial review", in any scientific development of administrative law, must be studied not only horizontally, but vertically, eg, "judicial review" of Federal Trade Commission orders, "judicial review" of postal fraud orders, "judicial review" of deportation warrants.'

3 On the distinction between 'review' and 'appeal', see HWR Wade *Administrative Law* (5th edn, 1982), pp 34–36.

4 For a useful short explanation, see PF Smith and SH Bailey *The Modern English Legal System* (1984), ch 19 ('Appeals and Judicial Review'). The authors point out (at p 745) that judicial review may be sought 'directly' (especially through an 'application for judicial review') or 'collaterally' ('where the argument that an act or decision, such as a byelaw, is ultra vires is raised as a defence to enforcement proceedings or prosecution').

5 See generally, JF Garner and BL Jones *Garner's Administrative Law* (6th edn, 1985), pp 68–74; CK Allen *Law and Orders* (3rd edn, 1965), pp 95–97 and 232–33; RM Jackson *The Machinery of Local Government* (1959), ch 7; Note 'Byelaws and the Criminal Law' (1947) 11 JCL 89–99.

6 See W Ivor Jennings *The Law Relating to Local Authorities* (1934), p 314. In any event, as Evatt J pointed out in *Swan Hill Corpn v Bradbury* (1937) 56 CLR 746 at 766, 'past decisions upon particular byelaws in exercise of one power are seldom of assistance in determining the validity of a byelaw made in exercise of another power.' See also, *Country Roads Board v Neale Ads Pty Ltd* (1930) 43 CLR 126, 135 (Aust HC).

7 'A power to make byelaws about horses cannot justify a byelaw about dogs': *Footscray Corpn v Maize Products Pty Ltd* (1943) 67 CLR 301 at 307, per Latham CJ.

8 On the three tests, especially as developed and applied in Australia and New Zealand, see DC Pearce *Delegated Legislation in Australia and New Zealand* (1977), chs 21, 23, 24.

9 *Cinnamond v British Airports Authority* [1980] 2 All ER 368 at 373, per Lord Denning MR, who added that the courts interpreted railway byelaws '. . . almost malevolently. Prepared to strike them down if on their literal interpretation they could be said to be too wide or too uncertain.'

10 [1898] 2 QB 91 at 99, DC (Lord Russell of Killowen CJ). See also *A-G v Hodgson* [1922] 2 Ch 429 at 438; *Townsends (Builders) Ltd v Cinema News and Property Management Ltd (David A Wilkie & Partners, Third Party)* [1959] 1 All ER 7 at 10, CA (Lord Evershed MR); *Aldred v Miller* 1925 JC 21 at 27, Ct of Justiciary; *Stiles v Galinski* [1904] 1 KB 615 at 621, DC; *Re the Invercargill Byelaw No 6, 1923* [1924] NZLR 1142 at 1143 (SC of New Zealand). In the latter case, Reed J said: 'A certain amount of latitude must be allowed to a Council, the members of which, after all, are the chosen representatives of the ratepayers and know a great deal more of its requirements than a Judge can.'

11 See eg, *United Bill Posting Co v Somerset County Council* (1926) 42 TLR 537 at 538, DC (Lord Hewart CJ).

12 *Cullis v Ahern* (1914) 18 CLR 540 at 542. The case concerned a byelaw requiring all vehicles to carry a lighted rear lamp between sunset and sunrise. A state statute (in Victoria) required a light, at the rear or the front, on vehicles; but this provided, said Griffith CJ (at 543), only 'the irreducible minimum of obligation.' (See also *Thomas v Sutters* [1900] 1 Ch 10 at 16, CA (Sir FH Jeune)).

13 On repugnancy, see *Powell v May* [1946] KB 330, DC, which concerned a Glamorgan County Council byelaw directed against betting on the streets and in public places. In the course of his judgment for the court, Lord Goddard CJ spoke of the difficulties of interpretation in this area. On uncertainty, see *Re Dartmouth and SS Kresge Co Ltd* (1966) 58 DLR (2d) 229 (SC of Nova Scotia).

14 [1898] 2 QB 91 at 99–100. Earlier cases on unreasonableness as to byelaws include *London and Brighton Rly Co v Watson* (1878) 3 CPD 429 (railway byelaw) and *Slattery v Naylor* (1888) 13 App Cas 446 (a case on a municipal byelaw, heard on appeal from the Supreme Court of New South Wales in the Judicial Committee of the Privy Council). In the latter, Lord Hobhouse (at 452) traced the development of unreasonableness as a ground of challenge to older cases involving manorial bodies, towns and corporations which had inherent powers or general powers conferred by charter of making such laws.

15 In *R v Powell* (1884) 51 LT 92, the defendant (a captain in the Salvation Army) was convicted at Truro because of his persistent playing of a concertina. Stephen J, in denying that the byelaw was unreasonable, declared that the 'liberty of the subject always consists in doing something a man is not forbidden to do, and why it is unreasonable and void that he should be forbidden to play a musical instrument in the public streets of Truro, I cannot see.' See also, *Munro v Watson* (1887) 57 LT 366 (byelaw in Ryde held unreasonable in a Salvation Army case) and *Johnson v Croydon Corpn* (1886) 16 QBD 708 (byelaw in Croydon — again on musical instruments — held unreasonable, with Hawkins J commenting (at 709) that it 'would include any sort of music played under any circumstances, and however harmless or free from offence such music might be'). Newspaper reports of byelaw cases involving the Salvation Army appear in the Times (1885) 25 August at 5 (byelaw in Ryde); the Times (1885) 15 December at 10 (Home Office considering proposals for byelaws in Colchester); and the Times (1886) 8 October, at 9 (convictions under a Torquay byelaw). In a much later case, *Slee v Meadows* (1911) 75 JP 246, a byelaw survived a Salvation Army challenge to the effect that it was ultra vires, uncertain, unreasonable, repugnant, partial and unequal.

16 On noise byelaws, see AH Davis *Noise* (1937) pp 134–35; *Noise in Public Places* (Report by a Working Group of the Noise Advisory Council, HMSO 1974), ch 3 and Appendix A (the Appendix sets out examples of model byelaws); Hylton Dawson *Noise & Society* (National Society for Clean Air, 1984), p 12.

17 See eg, *Hazledon v McAra* [1948] NZLR 1087; *Aldred v Miller* 1925 JC 21. In both cases, issues of free speech and public order were raised with regard to the regulation of meetings. See also *McGill v Garbutt* (1886) NZLR, 5 SC 73, an early Salvation Army case on the regulation of street processions; *Stanley v Scott* [1935] NZLR s 15.

18 See eg, *Strickland v Hayes* [1896] 1 QB 290 (where the important question, according to Lindley LJ, (at 291) was 'whether or not this byelaw is unreasonable because it goes too far').

19 *Scott v Pilliner* [1904] 2 KB 855.

20 *Westbrook v Innes-Jones* [1928] NZLR 46. *McCarthy v Madden* (1914) 33 NZLR 1251, which concerned a byelaw about cattle being driven along or across borough streets, saw an important analysis by Denniston and Edwards JJ of the concept of unreasonableness. It was stressed (at 1268) that the 'question whether a byelaw is reasonable or unreasonable being essentially one of fact, it is not possible to define in advance any test which will be conclusive

upon the validity or invalidity of any particular byelaw.'

21 *Stiles v Galinski* [1904] 1 KB 615; *Arlidge v Islington Corpn* [1909] 2 KB 127. The latter case, which involved the litigious Mr Arlidge (immortalised in *Local Government v Arlidge* [1915] AC 120, HL), saw Mr Avory KC arguing that a byelaw 'as to houses let in lodgings which may be reasonable in Islington may be unreasonable in Mayfair' — a statement of relativity echoing the dictum that what 'would be a nuisance in Belgrave Square would not necessarily be so in Bermondsey' (*Sturges v Bridgeman* (1879) 11 Ch D 852 at 865, CA) and later reformulated, in the context of a New Zealand byelaw, to suggest that that 'which may be perfectly reasonable as regards an abattoir at Blenheim may be quite unreasonable with regard to one situated in a large centre of population such as Wellington' (*Smith v Blenheim Borough Council* [1928] NZLR 536 at 550). It is perhaps a relief, however, to be told that a 'loudly played transistor radio is as much a nuisance in Torquay as it is in Scarborough' (*Noise in Public Places, op cit* (n 16), 3.10).

22 *Repton School Governors v Repton RDC* [1918] 2 KB 133, CA.

23 It was in 1877, for instance, that the Local Government Board issued its first model series of byelaws for the purpose of the Public Health Act 1875 (see Knight's annotated *Model Byelaws*, the first edition of which appeared in 1883). On byelaws directly related to the criminal law, see Sir Edward Troup *The Home Office* (1925), pp 223–25, where the author notes (p 224) that 'there is now a list of "model byelaws" dealing with such subjects as street music, street cries, street obstructions, indecent acts, etc which can be adopted in any locality where they are needed and which have so far stood the scrutiny of the courts'; and also, Sir Frank Newsam *The Home Office* (1954), pp 191–93; DCM Yardley *Source Book of English Administratve Law* (2nd edn, 1970), pp 13–16 (Specimen set of 'Good Rule and Government' Byelaws).

24 See (1962) *Times*, 2 January at 12 (Eastbourne Town Council decides to make a byelaw on lines suggested by the Home Secretary) and (1962) 8 March at 5 (Home Secretary approves the byelaw, and other towns interested include Bournemouth, Brighton, Christchurch, Hastings, Lytham St Anne's, Ryde and Torquay).

25 RM Jackson *The Machinery of Local Government* (1959), p 100.

26 'Local byelaws are not usually as local as they may seem . . . In this way a large measure of uniformity is presumed throughout the country, and this subordinate legislation is in reality far more the work of Whitehall than of local Solons' (CK Allen *Law and Orders* (3rd edn, 1965, p 96).

27 Public order measures which emerged from provisions in a number of (though not all) private statutes include s 5 of the Public Order Act 1936 and the provision for advance notice of processions in the Public Order Act 1986. On the latter, see *Review of Public Order Law*, White Paper, Cmnd 9510 of 1985, 4.3. The Home Affairs Committee of the House of Commons said, in its report on *The Law Relating to Public Order*, HC 756–1 (7 August 1980), para 37: 'As notice requirements already operate in many areas, through local Acts, there is a case for a uniform national policy.'

28 See the chapters on 'Administrative Law' in the issues of the *Annual Survey of Commonwealth Law* from 1965 to 1977, passim.

29 See the judgment of Diplock LJ in *Mixnam's Properties Ltd v Chertsey UDC* [1963] 2 All ER 787 at 799. This case was affirmed in the House of Lords, [1965] AC 735.

30 [1943] 1 KB 223 at 228 ff. See also, DC Pearce *op cit* (n 8), ch 23.

31 Lawrence Baxter *Administrative Law* (1984), p 479 (n 12); Christopher Forsyth *In Danger for their Talents. A Study of the Appellate Division of the Supreme Court of South Africa* (1985), pp 92–111. Dr Forsyth comments, in the latter work (p 94), that *Kruse v Johnson* 'has frequently been resorted to when litigants sought to have racial discrimination struck down by the courts.' See LC Green 'The Legality of Jim Crow Regulations' (1950) 3 ILQ 590. On the activities of South African courts in 1986, see eg (1986) Times, 30 July at 5 and (1985) 12 August at 1.

32 JM Evans *De Smith's Judicial Review of Administrative Action* (4th edn, 1980), p 353. The *Wednesbury* test, which is referred to later in this chapter, comes from the judgment of Lord Greene MR in *Associated Provincial Picture Houses Ltd v Wednesbury Corpn* [1948] 1 KB 223, CA. See *City of Edinburgh District Council v Secretary of State for Scotland* 1985 SLT 551.

33 Lawrence Baxter *op cit* (n 31), p 479.

34 It might be recalled, however, that Coke CJ, in his famous (but abandoned) dictum in *Dr Bonham's Case* (1610) 8 Co Rep 107a, spoke of the common law controlling an Act of Parliament which 'is against common right or reason, or repugnant, or impossible to be performed.'

35 See *McEldowney v Forde* [1971] AC 632, HL (a 3–2 decision of the House of Lords concerning regulation under the Special Powers Act in Northern Ireland). See *R v Immigration Appeal Tribunal, ex p Begum* (1986) Times, 24 July QBD.
36 'Crime and Crown Privilege' [1959] Crim LR 10–18. The judge (at Nottingham Assizes) was Stable J.
37 See respectively *Ellis v Home Office* [1953] 2 QB 135; *Auten v Rayner* [1958] 1 WLR 1300, CA; and *R v Governor of Brixton Prison, ex p Soblen* [1963] 2 QB 243, CA.
38 [1968] AC 910.
39 (1968) Times, 29 February at 11.
40 *R v IRC, ex p Rossminster Ltd* [1980] AC 952 at 999 *per* Lord Wilberforce. Lord Diplock spoke (at 1012) of 'a public interest immunity against premature disclosure of information relating to criminal investigations or pending prosecutions.'
41 *Malone v Metropolitan Police Comr* [1979] Ch 344.
42 *R v Lewes Justices, ex p Home Secretary* [1973] AC 388, HL. It is in this case that the term 'Crown privilege' was described as inaccurate and misleading, and the preferred term since then has been 'public interest immunity.'
43 *Williams v Home Office* [1981] 1 All ER 1151. The judge in this case (McNeill J) was following the lead of the House of Lords in *Burmah Oil Co Ltd v Bank of England* [1980] AC 1090. The plaintiff in *Williams* later failed in the trial of his action for false imprisonment (*Williams v Home Office (No 2)* [1981] 1 All ER 1211).
44 See *Neilson v Laugharne* [1981] QB 736, CA; *Hehir v Metropolitan Police Comr* [1982] 2 All ER 335, CA; *Conerney v Jacklin* [1985] Crim LR 234, CA; and *Peach v Metropolitan Police Comr* [1986] 2 All ER 129, CA. See also *Taylor v Anderton* (1986) *Times* 21 October.
45 (1978) 142 CLR 1. This arose from the 'Loans Affair' during the Labour Government under Mr Gough Whitlam: see SD Hotop *Principles of Australian Administrative Law* (6th edn, 1985), pp 497–500. It might be noted that, in response to the High Court's ruling, the New South Wales Parliament speedily amended the law (by legislation) in order to restrict disclosure: see Hotop, at 502, referring to the Evidence (Amendment) Act 1979. See also, HP Lee *Emergency Powers* (1984), pp 279–87.
46 (1984) 58 ALJR 97. See Hotop at 501–02. Reference might also be made, in the wider context of the criminal law, to *United States v Nixon* 418 US 683 (1974) (the Watergate tapes case) in the United States.
47 See *R v Metropolitan Police Comr, ex p Blackburn* [1968] 2 QB 118, CA (see DGT Williams 'The Police and Law Enforcement' [1968] Crim LR 351); *R v Metropolitan Police Comr, ex p Blackburn (No 3)* [1973] QB 241; *R v Metropolitan Police Comr, ex p Blackburn* (1980) Times, 6 March.
48 See *A-G v Harris* [1961] 1 QB 74; *Gouriet v Union of Post Office Workers* [1978] AC 435, HL; *Stoke-on-Trent City Council v B and Q (Retail) Ltd* [1984] AC 754. See generally, John LlJ Edwards *The Attorney General, Politics and the Public Interest* (1984), esp ch 5 and 6.
49 See *Hanratty v Lord Butler of Saffron Walden* (1971) 115 Sol Jo 386.
50 See *Re Findlay* [1985] AC 318, HL (relating to a policy statement on parole made by the Home Secretary).
51 In *Luttin v Benin* (1704) 11 Mod Rep 50 at 51, for instance, Holt CJ said a justice has no jurisdiction at all if he makes 'an order for a man to keep a bastard-child, which in reality was born two days after marriage.'
52 There is a considerable literature on standing. See generally, HWR Wade *Administrative Law* (5th edn, 1982), ch 18; *Standing in Public Litigation* (Report no 27 of the Law Reform Commission of Australia, 1985). The latter report (of 273 pages) covers a wide range of issues of standing including the role of private prosecutions in criminal proceedings. Recent cases where aspects of criminal law interpretation and enforcement have been examined include *Royal College of Nursing of the United Kingdom v Department of Health and Social Security* [1981] AC 800 (on abortion). See also, *Gillick v West Norfolk and Wisbech Area Health Authority* [1986] AC 112.
53 On the new approach to prerogative powers, see *Council of Civil Service Unions v Minister for the Civil Service* [1985] AC 374, HL. In the course of his speech Lord Roskill was not (at 418) disposed to include the prerogative of mercy among the prerogatives to be regarded as 'susceptible to judicial review.'
54 In the *Findlay* case (above n 50), the House of Lords ruled that a new policy on parole was not unacceptable in the manner of its operation. Reference was made to the leading case (on fettering discretion by policies) of *R v Skinner* [1968] 2 QB 700, where it was held that the Home Secretary's approval of a breath test device (under the Road Safety Act 1967) could be given by the appropriate departmental official.

55 In the first *Blackburn* case (above n 47), for instance, the Court of Appeal considered whether in principle mandamus should be refused on the ground that the applicant had available an equally effective alternative remedy, namely, the undertaking of a private prosecution. Edmund Davies LJ was content (at 149) with 'the simple observation that only the most sardonic could regard the launching of a private prosecution . . . as being equally convenient, beneficial and appropriate as the procedure in fact adopted by this appellant.'
56 [1969] 2 AC 147.
57 [1981] 1 NSWLR 644.
58 [1981] 1 NSWLR at 655, per Reynolds JA (from whose judgment most of the quotations are taken). On the wider problems of 'jurisdiction' since *Anisminic*, see Cooke J in *Bulk Gas Users Group v A-G* [1983] NZLR 129.
59 DC Pearce *Statutory Interpretation* (1974), para 199 (p 126).
60 See *London and Clydeside Estates Ltd v Aberdeen District Council* [1979] 3 All ER 876; *AJ Burr Ltd v Blenheim Borough Council* [1980] 2 NZLR 1.
61 *R v Bates* [1911] 1 KB 964, CCA.
62 *R v Salisbury and Amesbury Justices, ex p Greatbatch* [1954] 2 QB 142.
63 See *R v County of London Quarter Sessions Appeal Committee, ex p Rossi* [1956] 1 QB 682, CA (where the applicant was alleged to be the father of an illegitimate child), where Denning LJ said (at 691) 'that it is a fundamental principle of our law that no one is to be found guilty or made liable by an order of any tribunal unless he has been given fair notice of the proceedings so as to enable him to appear or defend them.'
64 [1964] AC 40. The decision of the House of Lords in this case, which arose from the dismissal of the Chief Constable of Brighton, was partly based on a breach of express procedural requirements and partly on a denial of natural justice. See also, with regard to natural justice, *Chief Constable of North Wales Police v Evans* [1982] 3 All ER 141, HL (respondent was denied an opportunity to refute allegations against him) and *Maynard v Osmond* [1977] QB 240, CA (on legal representation in disciplinary proceedings).
65 *R v Leyland Magistrates, ex p Hawthorn* [1979] 1 All ER 209. The problem, in the words of Lord Widgery CJ (at 210), 'is that breach of the rules of natural justice is primarily a remedy sought on account of an error of the tribunal, and here, of course, we are not concerned with an error of the tribunal: we are concerned with an error of the police prosecutors.' See Roderick Munday 'Natural Justice in the English Criminal Prosecution' (1981) 131 NLJ 6–9.
66 [1974] 2 All ER 1219. The applicant had been fined £5,000 for an offence under the Prevention of Oil Pollution Act 1971, s 2(1). In the words of Lord Widgery CJ (at 1223), the accused 'had no time to take samples, no time to see a report of the samples taken by the prosecution, no time to look for witnesses, no time to prepare any supporting evidence supportive to his own, and that too when he was a man with a very rudimentary knowledge of the English language in a country foreign to his own.'
67 'The temptation of many men of goodwill is to cut corners, take shortcuts, and reach the desired end regardless of the means' (*Hannah v Larche* 363 US 420 at 494 (1960) per Douglas J). In the *Polemis* case, (above n 66), what was apparently in the magistrates' minds 'was that the applicant's ship would be liable to sail with the tide that night.'
68 See Smith and Bailey *op cit* (n 4), at 679–80; DGT Williams 'Preventive Justice and the Courts' [1977] Crim LR 703, 707–09; *Veater v G* [1981] 2 All ER 304.
69 *Sheldon v Bromfield Justices* [1964] 2 All ER 131 at 133–34. The trial 'was one of those not unfamiliar domestic cases in which the son-in-law was blaming the mother-in-law and the father-in-law collectively for the disturbance which had occurred, and the mother-in-law and the father-in-law were blaming the son-in-law, and saying he was responsible' (*R v Woking Justices, ex p Gossage* [1973] QB 448 at 450, per Lord Widgery CJ). The son-in-law was the defendant.
70 [1984] QB 813.
71 *R v Woking Justices, ex p Gossage* [1973] QB 448. In *Ex p Boulding*, Watkins LJ said (at 820): 'It is one thing to impose a small or trivial sum of money as a recognisance without inquiring and so on; it is quite another to impose without inquiry into the means of the defendant, a relatively large sum.'
72 Watkins LJ said (at 819): 'The judge may have been wiser and spoken a little more temperately if he had avoided any reference to Hitler. But that apart, I can see nothing whatsoever objectionable in what he said. I cannot think that any right-minded person, sitting in court, listening to the judge, could sensibly have come to the conclusion that he was in any way biased against the applicant.' It might be recalled that McReynolds J, dissenting in a Supreme Court case concerned with the alleged anti-German bias of a judge in an espionage trial said that 'an amorphous dummy, unspotted by human emotions, [is not] a becoming

receptacle for judicial power.' (*Berger v US* 225 US 22, 43 (1921). See the case of *Ex p Church of Scientology of California* (1978) Times, 21 February, CA, where Lord Denning MR stepped down from a case involving the Church of Scientology, and *Public Utility Commission of the District of Columbia v Pollak* 343 US 451 (1952), where Frankfurter J withdrew from a case on the constitutionality of the transmission of radio programmes in streetcars because of his self-confessed strong emotions on the subject. See generally, Ross Cranston 'Disqualification of Judges for Interest, Association or Opinion' [1979] Pub Law 237, esp at 248.

73 *R v Liverpool City Justices, ex p Topping* [1983] 1 All ER 490 at 494. On the particular use of computers which gave rise to this case, Ackner LJ commented (at 496) that 'there is a real danger that administrative convenience is being given greater priority than the requirements of justice,' and the Divisional Court held the practice to be wrong in law.

74 This is a principle, according to Edmund Davies LJ in *Metropolitan Properties Co (FGC) v Lannon* [1969] 1 QB 577 at 604, which 'remains transcendent despite its enshrinement in the excessively quoted words of Lord Hewart' (in *R v Sussex Justices, ex p McCarthy* [1924] 1 KB 256 at 259).

75 *R (Donoghue) v County Cork Justices* [1910] 2 IR 271.

76 See eg *R v Sussex Justices, ex p McCarthy* [1924] 1 KB 256, *R v Camborne Justices, ex p Pearce* [1955] 1 QB 41.

77 See *Cooper v Wilson* [1937] 2 KB 309, CA in the context of police disciplinary proceedings.

78 See eg *Cooper v Wilson*, above, at 345–46.

79 *R v West Yorkshire Coroner, ex p Smith* (1982) Times, 13 October, where Webster J rejected allegations of bias made against the coroner in conducting the inquest into the death of Helen Linda Smith in Saudi Arabia.

80 *R v Abingdon Justices, ex p Cousins* (1964) Times, 14 October. The report on the defendant (a 16-year-old youth convicted of assault occasioning actual bodily harm) said inter alia that he was: 'Very aggressive. Very noisy. Unreliable. Anti-social, ill-tempered. Difficult to control. Continuously troublesome. A leader of a gang. Could not conform to discipline. Was given to wilful damage. His temper was almost uncontrollable . . . He was malicious, wanton and wilful; his dress was always that of a 'Teddy boy'; he would not conform to rules; he carried out wanton damage. Recorded punishments include punching girls, misbehaviour, wilful damage, disorderly conduct.'

81 See *Kruse v Johnson* (above, n 10).

82 See Francis Alexis 'Reasonableness in the Establishing of Bias' [1979] Pub Law 143.

83 See eg de Smith *op cit* (n 32), pp 346–354; HWR Wade *op cit*, n 52, pp 353–409.

84 [1942] AC 206, HL. See now the comments in *R v IRC, ex p Rossminster Ltd* [1980] AC 952 at 1011, and in *R v Home Secretary, ex p Khawaja* [1984] AC 74 at 110. For the position in South Africa, where the judiciary is accustomed to emergency situations, see Baxter *op cit* (n 31), pp 463–68; Forsyth *op cit* (n 31), ch 3 ('Judicial Attitudes towards Security Legislation'); Etienne Mureinik '*Liversidge* in Decay' (1985) 102 (1) SALJ 77. In *Hurley v Minister of Law and Order* 1985 (4) SA 709 (D) Leon ADJP spoke of Lord Atkin's dissent in *Liversidge v Anderson* as 'famous' and 'great' (715) and of the majority's decision as 'an aberration' (720).

85 [1942] AC at 228.

86 *Shaaban Bin Hussien v Chong Fook Kam* [1970] AC 942 at 948.

87 (1947) 176 LT 308 at 311 per Cassels J.

88 *Hayward v Metropolitan Police Comr* (1984) Times, 24 March per Caulfield J.

89 See de Smith *op cit* (n 32), at 348–50; LH Leigh *Police Powers in England and Wales* (2nd edn, 1985), pp 80–82; SH Bailey, DJ Harris and BL Jones *Civil Liberties. Cases and Materials* (2nd edn, 1985), pp 43–45; *Dumbell v Roberts* [1944] 1 All ER 326, CA; *McArdle v Egan* [1933] All ER Rep 611, CA.

90 *R v Howell* [1982] QB 416 at 426. See Glanville Williams 'Arrest for Breach of the Peace' [1954] Crim LR 578; Leigh *op cit* (n 89), ch 9.

91 [1961] NZLR 732. In the course of his judgment, Leicester J said (at 734) that 'bloody' could nowadays be regarded as an epithet which had become 'expansive rather than opprobrious.'

92 *Review of Public Order Law*, Cmnd 9510 of 1985, at 6.13. See generally, Michael Supperstone *Brownlie's Law of Public Order and National Security* (2nd edn, 1981).

93 *The Brixton Disorders, 10–12 April 1981*, Cmnd 8427 of 1981, at 7.35. The cases specifically referred to by Lord Scarman were: *Humphries v Connor* (1864) 17 ICLR 1; *Beatty v Gillbanks* (1882) 9 QBD 308; *Wise v Dunning* [1902] 1 KB 167; and *Duncan v Jones* [1936] 1 KB 218.

94 *Thomas v Sawkins* [1935] 2 KB 249. These powers are expressly preserved in the Police and Criminal Evidence Act 1984, s 17(6).

95 [1936] 1 KB at 223 per Humphreys J.
96 [1935] 2 KB at 256–57 per Avory J.
97 *Liversidge v Anderson* [1942] AC at 226.
98 De Smith *op cit* (n 32), p 349.
99 Cmnd 9510 of 1985, 4.25. Earlier in the same paragraph it is stated: 'When the Public Order Act [of 1936] was enacted Parliament insisted that the question of whether the police were justified in imposing conditions should be capable of challenge in the courts . . . Since then the availability of judicial review as an effective remedy has been greatly extended, by case law and by the procedural reforms of recent years . . . ' See DGT Williams *Keeping the Peace* (1967) p 58.
100 Report of the Royal Commission on the September Moratorium Demonstration, South Australia 1971, at 21. See *Wooster v Webb and Sussum* (1936) in The Solicitor 26 and 309 HC Official Report (5th series) cols 1619 ff.
101 *Piddington v Bates* [1960] 3 All ER 660 at 663. See also, *Innes v Weate* (1984) 12 A Crim R 45 at 52 (SC of Tasmania).
102 See generally, NCCL *Civil Liberties and the Miners' Dispute* (First Report of the Independent Inquiry), at 3.38–3.47; Times (leading article on 'Preventive Policing'), 24 March 1984, at 9.
103 [1985] IRLR 76, 78 (also in (1984) Times, 29 November).
104 [1984] AC 437. See especially, Christopher L Ryan and Katherine S Williams 'Police Discretion' [1986] Pub Law 285.
105 The Criminal Law Act 1967, s 2(6), provided: 'Where a constable, with reasonable cause, suspects that an arrestable offence has been committed, *he may arrest* anyone whom he, with reasonable cause, suspects to be guilty of the offence' (italics added). See now the Police and Criminal Evidence Act 1984, s 24(6).
106 [1984] AC at 443. The case referred to is *Associated Provincial Picture Houses Ltd v Wednesbury Corpn* [1948] 1 KB 223, CA where Lord Greene MR delivered an unreserved, widely-stated and infinitely malleable explanation of the grounds of irrationality or unreasonableness or improper purpose or irrelevancy (and lack of relevancy) under the doctrine of ultra vires.
107 [1984] AC at 444.
108 Ryan and Williams, above, n 104.
109 [1985] IRLR at 78.
110 [1960] 3 All ER at 663: 'The real criticism, I think, is this: "Well, to say that only two pickets should be allowed is purely arbitrary. Why two? Why not three? Where do you draw the line?" For my part, I think that a police officer charged with the duty of preserving the Queen's peace must be left to take such steps as, on the evidence before him, he thinks are proper.' (Lord Parker CJ).
111 [1936] 1 KB at 219. In the House of Commons (314 HC Official Report (5th series) col 1551) DN Pritt later said: 'You can always lend an air of plausibility to the enterprise of stopping the meeting by offering, as was offered in one case, an alternative site 175 yards away. It sounds so plausible, but if you cannot get an audience 175 yards away you might as well be 175 miles away.'
112 *Burton v Power* [1940] NZLR 305 at 307 per Myers CJ. See, more recently, *R v Howe* [1982] 1 NZLR 618 at 630, CA, with regard to anti-Springbok demonstrations in New Zealand. With regard to allegedly inflammatory placards in Ireland in 1878, the Attorney-General for Ireland saw no reason for questioning the legality of the police action in removing the placards, since the police 'must necessarily act in such matters promptly upon their own knowledge of the locality and the facts.' He added that the language used on the placards 'might cause no discomfort or alarm to the police in London, but it might be very different in Kilkenny' (318 HC Official Report (3rd series) col 195).
113 *Kent v Metropolitan Police Comr* (1981) Times, 14 May, CA. A ban imposed for 28 days within the entire Metropolitan Police district was unsuccessfully challenged as too broad, or covering such a wide number of organisations, and as extending over such a wide area. The Court of Appeal, in agreeing with a refusal of leave to apply for judicial review, was apparently referring both to the condition precedent to and the nature of a ban under the Public Order Act 1936, s 3(3).
114 *R v Oxford, ex p Levey* (1985) Times, 18 December. The applicant claimed inter alia that it was ultra vires for the chief constable to declare or adopt a policy whereby Toxteth was deemed on some or all occasions to be a 'no go' area for the police force. See CA at (1986) Times, 1 November.
115 *R v Mansfield Justices, ex p Sharkey* [1984] IRLR 496, where striking miners had been

charged with picketing offences. A condition was imposed in each instance to forbid further picketing or demonstrating 'in connection with the current trade dispute between the NUM and the NCB other than peacefully to picket or demonstrate at his usual place of employment.' The discretion as to conditions on bail is expressly referred to (at 500–01) as subject to the *Wednesbury* conditions.

116 (1980) 51 FLR 465 (SC of ACT). See Bailey, Harris, and Jones *op cit* (n 89), pp 179–80. The demonstration was by women protesting about women raped in war. See generally, Human Rights Commission (Occasional Paper no 8, prepared by Robin Handley, 1985), *The Right of Peaceful Assembly in the ACT*, paras 18 and 72–74.

117 (1980) 51 FLR at 470.

118 (1882) 9 QBD 308. See DGT Williams 'The Principle of Beatty v Gillbanks: A Reappraisal' in Anthony N Doob and Edward L Greenspan, QC (eds), *Perspectives in Criminal Law* (1985), pp 105–131; DL Keir and FH Lawson *Cases in Constitutional Law* (6th edn, 1979, by FH Lawson and DJ Bentley), pp 184–89.

119 See the comments of Fitzgerald J in *Humphries v Connor* (1864) 17 ICLR 1; Williams *op cit* (n 99), at 117.

120 See *R v Barnet and Camden Rent Tribunal, ex p Frey Instruments Ltd* [1972] 2 QB 342, CA.

121 See generally, HP Lee, *Emergency Powers* (1984), esp ch 7; David Bonner *Emergency Powers in Peacetime* (1985); Clive Walker *The Prevention of Terrorism in British Law* (1986); Review of the Operation of the Prevention of Terrorism (Temporary Provisions) Acts 1974 and 1976 (Lord Shackleton), Cmnd 7324 of 1978; Review of the Operation of the Prevention of Terrorism (Temporary Provisions) Act 1976, Cmnd 8803 of 1983; Prevention of Terrorism (Temporary Provisions) Act 1984.

122 See generally, Genevra Richardson, Anthony Ogus and Paul Burrows *Policing Pollution. A Study of Regulation and Enforcement* (1982); GM Bates *Environmental Law in Australia* (1983); David Hughes *Environmental Law* (1986); DGT Williams 'Developments in British Environmental Law' (1984) Natural Resources Journal (New Mexico) 511–34.

123 See *Review of Public Order Law*, Cmnd 9510 of 1985, 5.17.

124 See *A-G v British Broadcasting Corpn* [1981] AC 303, HL. See Annual Report of the Council on Tribunals for 1980–81, paras 3.8–3.14; Note (1980) 38 Camb LJ 229.

Child witnesses

Glanville Williams

The law of evidence and procedure relating to a child as a witness in a legal proceeding is overdue for radical reform. With luck, this contribution on the subject will be published in time for a forthcoming parliamentary debate.

Generally, though not necessarily, the case to be considered is one where the child is the victim of an offence. (Occasionally the child will be the witness of an offence against another person.) Generally, though not necessarily, the offence against the child will be sexual, and then the child is likely to be female, though young boys are also quite frequently interfered with. Where the case is one of ordinary cruelty, the prosecution will often have other evidence, and the child will not be a necessary witness; but when sexual interference takes place in private the evidence of the child is generally essential. So I shall principally be concerned with the girl victim testifying to a sexual offence; but when I speak of girls it must be understood that the female embraces the male (subject to context). The word 'child' will primarily bear its legal meaning (a juvenile up to 14), but I do not exclude its extension in some circumstances to young persons.

The problems are manifold.

Children's evidence produces a danger of wrongful convictions. The notion that the trial itself is a safeguard of innocence is often ill-founded, and it is so here. Defending counsel is not allowed to interview the child (and other prosecution witnesses) before the trial, in order to pursue a detective enquiry.[1] Very much depends, therefore, upon the enquiry made by or on behalf of the police; but when the police think they have got their man they frequently fail to probe further.

By the time the child comes to court, her evidence may be a well-rehearsed lesson. Counsel when cross-examining does not like to ask questions in the dark, because he is afraid of merely reinforcing the case for the prosecution. It is said, also, that counsel is inhibited from cross-examining the child complainant thoroughly, for fear of offending the jury. And some defence counsel are inexperienced in dealing with children.[2]

Some lawyers hold that, under controlled conditions, the evidence of children is reliable; others, to the contrary, emphasise the dangers of fabricated evidence.[3] Certainly it has been known for children to invent elaborate fantasies and tell rank falsehoods. Children can be extraordinarily precocious, well versed in sexual language and quite capable of making false accusations, especially when they believe this to be a form of self-defence. So it is dangerous for the jury or magistrates to suppose that just because a young girl can describe so clearly what she says happened, and knows (for example) what an erection is, her tale that she was interfered with by the defendant must be true. She may have seen her brother with an erection, or been told by an older sister or school friend. She may have heard her mother questioning an elder sister about similar conduct in which she was involved. The incident, after being mentioned by the alleged victim of the sexual interference, may have been discussed in the family and additional details may have been suggested by other members. The mother may have deliberately put ideas into the child's head in order to get rid of her husband and go off with a lover.

One actual example of false evidence is given by Gibbens and Prince.[4] A brother and sister aged 9 and 10 from a problem family said that a man of 62 interfered with both of them. In fact, as it afterwards transpired, the girl had been 'put up' to her story by another girl, and the only person who had interfered with her was her brother, with whom she slept. This one example is enough to contradict the remark of two experts in child abuse that the child's story of sexual molestation should be believed — 'children do not fabricate stories of detailed sexual activities unless they have witnessed them, and they have, indeed, been eyewitnesses to their own abuse.'[5] Among the reasons suggested for false evidence by children are: the fact that children are not born knowing the difference between right and wrong, or truth and untruth, and some are slow to learn; children fantasise, and having made up a tale may find that they cannot retreat from it; a child may falsely accuse a person of sexual abuse in order to protect another person who is the real offender, or in order to hide her voluntary involvement with the real offender; the child may make a false accusation against a disliked stepfather or her mother's lover, in the hope of getting rid of him; the child may be actuated by a desire to gain attention, and finds that accusations of being sexually abused are an excellent way of getting it.

Error may creep into a child's evidence even without her conscious intent. All experienced observers agree that children are highly suggestible, which makes it very important that false ideas are not put into the child's head by the person interviewing her. Circumstantial details suggested by questioning may easily become part of a stereotyped recital.

Counterbalancing the danger of unjust convictions is the much greater (though far less important) danger of unjust acquittals. Judges tend to view child evidence with great reserve, and certain rules as to corroboration and jury-warnings have been devised to reduce its impact. They obviously assist the defendant, whether he is innocent or guilty.

Quite apart from such safeguards, the child will often make an unsatisfactory witness in court. The atmosphere of the courtroom is intimidating to a child. Boys as old as 9 and girls as old as 11 have been known to be too tongue-tied to relate in the witness-box what the man did to them.[6] Where the sexual abuse occurred within the family, the girl may well be placed under pressure to retract or weaken her evidence when she comes to court. Perhaps the pressure comes from her mother, who fears that the offender will go to prison; all she may have to do to influence the child's evidence is to emphasise her fears to her child.

It is sometimes thought that children, in addition to being suggestible, have short memories; this may be true for the very young, but not, it seems, for older children. An experimental study of 10- and 11-year-olds required the children to report on an incident they had witnessed. It was found that delay in being required to report (for up to two months after the incident) did not increase inaccurate recall, though it did (as one would expect) reduce comprehensiveness of recall.[7] Putting this finding into a legal context, it would seem that delay in the court hearing operates in favour of the defendant, since, by causing the child to forget details, it makes her vulnerable on cross-examination.

So, for one reason or another, convictions of child-molesters who do not admit the offence are hard to secure. Knowing this, the police generally decline to charge such persons. Parents, who come to know from newspaper articles how harrowing the experience of giving evidence is for their daughter, may refuse to allow the charge to proceed even though the police are prepared to make it. Another source of weakness in the law follows from the fact that the outcome of a prosecution is often very harmful to the child. Incestuous fathers are frequently sent to prison for long terms, for purely punitive reasons; this disrupts and impoverishes the family, and may result in the children having to be taken into care. This again is likely to cause the child who has given evidence to experience serious self-reproach, or to be bitterly blamed by her mother and siblings. Knowing this, doctors who suspect incest often keep silent upon it, not being able to decide what is the best course to take.[8] (Another explanation of their silence is that they fail to realise how common intrafamilial child-abuse is, and so have an unduly high threshold of suspicion.[9])

There is a natural assumption that weakness in law-enforcement is an evil; but in this instance the picture is mixed. Most child molestation is by the child's relative (brother, father, stepfather, adoptive father, uncle, grandfather), mother's lover, or other family acquaintance,[10] and has been going on for a long time when it is discovered. The primary purpose of intervention should be to stop it, to prevent it occurring again with other young members of the family, and to give any needed therapy to the victim and the family (the last being a matter in which our arrangements leave much to be desired). When the child is supported by her parents, investigation and detection are often enough to put an end to the trouble, and it may be highly undesirable to bring the criminal courts into the matter.[11]

The law fails to draw (perhaps cannot draw) distinctions that any reasonable person would draw between particular cases. It does not distinguish finely between trivial and gross molestation (for instance between mere sexual touching and many types of gross abuse short of intercourse), nor between young and older offenders. Obviously, its general prescriptions need great care in administration, particularly where the misbehaviour takes place within the family. Nevertheless, some cases of family child-abuse call for a criminal sanction.

When the child abuse is committed by a stranger, considerations of penal deterrence bulk larger, because the intervention of the law is less likely to add to the victim's distress. The paedophiliac who makes a practice of sitting next to young girls in cinemas and fumbling with them is, at the least, a public nuisance, a cause of annoyance to the girls and their parents. Others do great harm. Many promiscuous child-molesters are naturally recidivist; and if the molester gets to know that he is unlikely to be charged, or if charged convicted, he is encouraged to continue his practices. We do not, of course, know the full extent of child sexual abuse, but competent observers agree that it is more serious than is generally realised.[12]

The great majority of sexual interferences with children are probably minor. The girl may not realise that anything improper has occurred, or may herself enjoy it, at least when the molester is himself young. So no harm may be done;[13] but on other occasions, of course, the sexual abuse of children can result in great evils, including drug abuse, sexual dysfunction, prostitution, and other behavioural and psychological symptoms.[14]

The strain on the child witness

At the best of times it is a severe strain for a young girl to have to give evidence in court, particularly on a sexual matter, and particularly if the evidence incriminates her father or other member of her family. Children as offenders are protected by confining nearly all charges against them to the juvenile court, which is relatively informal; but children as victims or other witnesses of an offence by an adult must appear in the adult court. When the child is perhaps already upset by the offence itself, or by her parents' reaction to her complaint or admissions, common sense suggests that the addition of this further distress may contribute significantly to the bad effects of the whole incident upon the emotional development of the child.[15]

Cross-examination makes things far worse. The defence advocate has no choice but to put his client's case to the child. The fact that the offence is relatively minor does not necessarily eliminate the upset caused to the child in having to give evidence in court. Take the case where a man is charged with indecently touching a girl of 11 in a cinema. Her parents and all connected with the case know from the whole background that she is telling the truth in saying that she did not invite or encourage the interference; but the man's defence is that the girl led him on and started to open his flies. The girl must submit to being cross-examined on this since the defence is relevant to mitigation. When the parents know of even the possibility of the defence, they are not going to allow their daughter to give evidence.[16]

The very great hardship for the child witness has often been pointed out, and by way of support I choose only three quotations, each from an experienced observer. The first is from an article by Dr Nesta Wells, who acted as woman police surgeon in Manchester (apparently the first such appointment in England):

> 'Carnal knowledge cases are those most likely to be sent on to the higher courts for trial, which nearly always means waiting weeks or even months. This is a long and anxious period and can be a big strain to even the calmest of girl victims. They are not allowed to forget; but almost certainly times, sequences, and other details may get a bit confused, and instead of being helped to get over the shock and feeling of shame and loss of self-respect the wound is deepened when the evidence has to be repeated in a more overwhelming court atmosphere. This repetition especially needs to be avoided somehow in these higher court cases.'[17]

Similarly Sir Basil Henriques:

> 'The child should have to repeat her story as few times as possible — constant repetition will only result in parrot-like recitation or else in an increasingly exaggerated and embroidered account of what took place. So far as possible the re-living and re-experiencing of what is often a most unpleasant and traumatic experience must be avoided.'[18]

Dr AP McEldowney wrote:

> 'In over 25 years as a Metropolitan Police Surgeon I saw a large number of cases of children who had had sexual interference by an adult and it was always my conviction that far more harm was done by the repeated questioning by parents, police and myself, and any subsequent examination, than by the act itself, which if left alone the child would have soon forgotten. Children are far more matter of fact than adults generally realise and such sexual experiences should be played down rather than up.'[19]

From the point of view of the child victim, much the happiest outcome of a sexual offence generally is that the offender should not be caught. When he is not found, the child often makes a good recovery, her chief source of distress frequently being the agitation and disapproval of her parents when they come to know the facts.[20] Long-term effects need not be serious even in cases of rape resulting in conception and the birth of an illegitimate offspring. But if the offender is discovered and in the hands of the police, the consequent proceedings are often very disturbing to the victim. She may have to undergo a physical examination, often in the frightening atmosphere of a police station; and then there is the interrogation and giving of evidence. We have no general provision enabling the court to dispense with the child's personal evidence at the trial, even a summary trial.[21] Substantially the court's only legal power to dispense with the evidence of the child at the trial, and to allow the child's deposition to be read instead, is where attendance in court would involve serious danger to her life or health.[22] The provision is unsatisfactory because it requires the taking of the deposition before a magistrate, which may be almost as disturbing for the child as telling her story at the trial. One of the worst features of the present position is the forced confrontation in court between the child and her attacker.[23]

Improving the examination of child witnesses

The basis of any reform of the present practice must be improvement of the interrogation of children. Some progress has been made. The first step will be a medical examination if it seems the girl may have been physically injured or if the examination may show evidence of sexual interference. The (woman) doctor who performs the examination will naturally talk to the girl about any injury and its cause; what the child says may indicate what special clues the doctor should look for. The doctor may be a police surgeon, who should be a woman where the child is female;[24] there are not nearly enough women police surgeons. (It has been suggested that women doctors might be recruited particularly for examining female complainants of all ages, given appropriate training and paid per session.)[25] The examination should be in premises designed for the purpose (which are also needed for adult women who complain of rape). Some forces have already set up Victim Examination Suites; but it is most undesirable that they should be located in a police station, as not infrequently happens.[26] Suitable rooms in hospitals and surgeries are sometimes used.[27]

An interview with the child (preferably in a room near the medical examination room) will often be necessary, and should obviously be conducted by a person with some degree of training. In some countries, like Sweden[28] and Israel,[29] provision is made for special child examiners; but in Britain we have no fixed qualifications for interviewers and no fixed procedure.

Certain desiderata can be formulated. The person conducting the interview should most certainly be of the same sex as the victim (at any rate if the victim is female); at present this is by no means always the case.[30] She should be suitably qualified and possess considerable interviewing skill (since a young girl is likely to be strongly averse to relating in detail a frightening or otherwise distressing experience, or an act regarding which she herself feels shame; she may be especially loath to incriminate a friend or a member of her family; and, quite apart from her natural reluctance, she may well have been warned or threatened by her mother or other person to prevent her making the required disclosure).[31]

The interviewer may be a psychiatrist, a paediatrician, a police surgeon[32] or other doctor, a child psychologist[33] or a social worker, but should in any case have the experience needed to understand the mental condition of the child. She should also receive some specialist instruction. She must, for example, know that answers must not be put into the child's mouth, or into her head, except to the extent that this cannot be avoided (of which more later). Avoiding what lawyers call leading questions is necessary not only to satisfy the lawyers but to give credibility to the child's evidence (which is, indeed, why the law frowns on leading questions). A body of experience has been gained in the interviewing of girls on complaints of sexual abuse,[34] and the results of this experience should somehow be communicated to interviewers.

As with the medical examination, the interview should not be in a police station. Dr Bentovim points out that while the presence at the interview of a trusted adult may give the child a sense of security, the child may need privacy to talk freely.[35] It must, therefore, be left to the interviewer to decide whether to suggest at some stage of the proceedings that she wishes to be left to continue the interview alone.

This brief account indicates that our arrangements are too improvised and casual; and the criticism applies to the investigation of sexual offences against adult women as well as against young girls. Also, the investigation of the offence may be inadequately linked to the provision of help for the victim. The child victim of incest, in particular, often needs referral to the psychiatric services, and family therapy may also be required. In Australia, Sexual Assault Centres have been developed, to which victims of rape and other sexual assaults can be referred for both physical and psychological help. Sydney, with a population of 3.28 million, now has five such centres, all fully used. We, too, should have special clinics in each major centre of population, where victims of sex offences can have both forensic examination and psychological help.[36]

Eliminating the child's appearance in court

The many disadvantages of requiring the child victim to give evidence in court prompted the adoption in Israel in 1955 of a bold reform. The child is examined by a 'child examiner', who is generally a social case worker; he gives evidence in court as to the result of the examination, the child not being called as a witness except with the examiner's consent.[37] It is found that these examiners are able to get more information from victims than the most experienced police interrogators.[38]

Nowadays the availability of videorecording naturally suggests the possibility of accepting as sufficient evidence a recording of the child's evidence given at the interview. This change of practice would be particularly beneficial when the child has been sexually abused by her father or other relative. As Dr Jane Wynne has said:

> 'It's quite intolerable to expect a child or teenager to go to court to give evidence against their father or grandfather. The court appearance is child abuse in itself.'[39]

A proposal to this effect was first seriously made in England by Gibbens and Prince in a study previously cited. In my opinion it should be adopted not only for the alleged victim of the indecency but in respect of other young witnesses of the act. As Sir Basil Henriques wrote, 'sometimes sexual assaults have a more traumatic effect on the child witnesses than on the victims of the offence.'[40] And it should be adopted not only for criminal but also for civil proceedings, such as care or wardship.

An incidental advantage of the procedure is that the addition of other defendants after the child's evidence has been recorded (eg when the child was a witness of gang-rape, and further persons are added as defendants from time to time) does not require the child to give her evidence over again. And, of course, the system of videorecording of a private interview with a sympathetic investigator is much more likely to procure the parents' consent to the child's evidence being used than the present procedure. Normally the recording, or the important parts of it, would be played for the court; the question of allowing a transcript in place of the recording would be the same as for other recorded evidence.

Gibbens and Prince acknowledged the objections that might be expressed to their reform:

> 'Many magistrates, although wishing to spare the child as much as possible, feel that it is distinctly helpful to see the child and be able to assess its personality, in a way which is hardly possible from the evidence alone. The clinical psychologist, naturally, sympathises with this desire to examine the child in person. In the case of adults one can understand that the stress of court appearance may help to reveal the truth. But whether a child's behaviour in court gives any reliable indication of its feelings or truthfulness is much more doubtful. In psychiatric reports to the juvenile court one frequently has to warn the court that the child is proposing to say something in court out of fear of its parents, when it has privately insisted on the opposite.'[41]

I passed on the proposal (with documentation and extensive argument, much of it in the present paper) to the Criminal Law Revision Committee in 1969, when it was considering the law of criminal evidence. I never had any great hope that a committee of lawyers would accept the proposal, and they did not. They rejected it after a very brief discussion, and, not being mentioned in the Committee's Report, it sank without trace. However, on another matter, the 'right of silence', the Report was thought to be too dangerously extreme for government endorsement. Had the committee accepted the proposal I put before it in respect of the evidence of children, its Report would have been even more decisively doomed.

At the time when I raised the question videorecording had not been invented. I spoke of sound recording, which is obviously far less satisfactory than a combination of sound and vision. A filmed record would have been regarded as even less of a practical proposition than the one I put forward.

Video, with reusable tapes and cameras that can work in poor light, has transformed the possibilities, and reformers may take heart from the fact that the question of videotaping evidence is now being publicly discussed.

The proposal, of course, cuts across cherished principles as to the criminal trial. The traditional attitude is that the best and indeed the only acceptable testimony is that given on oath in court. This assumption is open to question even for adult witnesses, but as applied to children it is ridiculous. To many small children the oath is a ceremony beyond their comprehension, but they may give true evidence all the same. For all witnesses, their most reliable account of an incident is generally the first unprompted account they give of it after the occurrence.

A recording of the interview is better because it vividly preserves the child's statement at an early stage in the proceedings, and shows precisely how it came to be made (the present system conceals this from the defendant and from the court). A jury or magistrates viewing the videorecording will be able to see for themselves the extent, if any, to which the child was prompted. Moreover, the child will speak more freely in private, to a sympathetic listener, than in a court, in response to questions from a (probably male) lawyer. (The number of persons present at the interview should be kept to the minimum, but other observers might view the proceedings through a one-way mirror, and might have the conversation relayed to them.)

An incidental advantage is that modern cameras showing the child in close-up can enable her facial expressions to be observed more closely, and her indistinct speech can, if necessary, be interpreted by an expert. Also, by seeing the videotape the defendant would be better placed to decide whether to plead guilty. And once the interview is on tape, there is no reason why it should not be made available to the defence. The recording may help the defendant, if innocent, to procure the evidence in his defence. With the evidence thus safely perpetuated, there is no reason why the defendant should not be allowed to interview prosecution witnesses (other than the child herself) in order to elicit supplementary facts. The usual objection to allowing the defence to interview prosecution witnesses before the trial is the fear that these witnesses will be bribed or intimidated, but this fear hardly applies in sexual cases.

The defendant could not be allowed to interview the child complainant independently, but if he has been arrested or charged before the interview arranged by the police, he and his lawyer could be enabled to sit behind the one-way mirror. The interviewer would be wearing a miniature earphone, so that the lawyer could suggest supplementary questions that he wishes to put to the child. These requests would be included in the record for the jury at the trial, who would be able to check that the interviewer dealt as well as she could with the requests she received. This procedure would supersede the defendant's normal right to cross-examine the witness.

If the defendant has not been arrested or charged at the time of the interview, the above procedure (substituting for cross-examination) could not be followed, and an awkward question arises. Doubtless, a formidable body of legal opinion would insist that the defendant's right to cross-examine his accuser before the jury or magistrates is sacrosanct. Yet to allow the defendant to insist upon the girl being brought to court as a witness would partly frustrate the object of the proposed procedure. He might be allowed to require a supplementary interview with the child, at which his questions are put to the child by the interviewer, the whole being recorded in the same way as the first interview. I do not much like this solution, because it would prolong the child's emotional stress; but it is the only acceptable way in which the defendant can be enabled to test the reaction of the child (particularly an older child) to his own version of the facts.

An ethical problem that has not been considered is whether it is proper to use as evidence the recording of an interview with the child, when the child did not know it would be used in court, perhaps in a prosecution of her own father. If the prosecution is of a stranger there is no real difficulty, because if any consent to the use of the recording is necessary the parents can, on ordinary principles, consent on behalf of the child. As to cases of child-abuse within the family, my own inclination would be to say that although great care and discretion should be exercised in deciding whether to prosecute, any evidence lawfully obtained from the child should be admissible without the child's consent or that of her parents.

My proposal is not mentioned in the Report of the CLRC, but the reasons for rejecting it given by some members are stated in the confidential minutes. On the question of confidentiality, I regard the proceedings of the committee as absolutely confidential in the sense that I would think it utterly improper to divulge the opinion of any particular member of the committee; but after this lapse of time there can be no harm in summarising the objections stated by members of the committee who contributed to the discussion. Unless answered, they are likely to be shared by many other lawyers.

(1) It would be difficult to decide what should be the age below which the procedure would operate. (This difficulty of fixing the age applies, of course, to all special provisions relating to juveniles. I would apply the procedure not only to the evidence of children but to that of persons under 16, since a girl of 14 or 15 may suffer extreme distress in being required to testify publicly against, say, her father. If this is not politically acceptable, the procedure could be confined to the evidence of children in the technical sense (under 14).) (2) It would be repellent for the jury to be able to convict the defendant without seeing the child and hearing his evidence in person. (The possibility of videorecording seems to answer this objection.) (3) In practice children are rarely called to give evidence in these cases. (But numberless cases never reach court simply because the police and the parents realise the stress that is involved for the child victim. The cases that come to court tend to be those in which the defendant is prepared to plead guilty.[42])

The committee did not seem to realise the great assistance that the proposal would give in the administration of the law. Unfortunately, the esteemed recipient of these essays was not a member of the committee for the reference.

Some other countries have put the idea into practice. In Sweden, the use of a recording of the child's evidence in sexual abuse cases has been regular for many years. Legislation to allow videorecordings to be used has been passed in some of the United States, notably Texas.[43] Interest is also stirring in Australia.[44]

Even in dear old stick-in-the-mud England, some movement has taken place. Interviews with the child victims of sexual offences have been videotaped for psychiatric training, or 'diagnostic purposes', or for confronting the male relative in order to induce him to cease his objectionable behaviour.[45] Although not made for legal purposes, these tapes have proved useful to the police, because when shown to the accused offenders they produced an unusually large number of guilty pleas.[46]

An English judge allowed the videotaping of depositions in a civil case under letters rogatory from a Californian court (where videotaping of witnesses is permitted).[47] Marvels will never cease: the government is even reported to be considering the converse, that British courts (even criminal courts) should be allowed to admit videotaped statements taken abroad.[48] The move is prompted by the difficulty of convicting international fraudsters, and the government does not seem to be contemplating any extension of the procedure for domestic witnesses. The principle of action in Britain is to change the law to the very minimum extent needed to correct flagrant anomalies, and then only long after the anomalies have been perceived.

In a few civil proceedings, such as wardship, video tapes of the interview with the child have been allowed in evidence.[49] The legal basis of admitting them is not reported; certainly they could not be used on a criminal charge without legislation.

The practice evidenced by the tapes seems to have received a chilly reception from lawyers. Anita Ryan QC criticised them, apparently to a Times reporter, in the following words:

> 'It seemed to us that a leading question would be put, and on the basis of an affirmative answer a second leading question would be put; so that a whole edifice would be constructed on the basis of assumptions.'[50]

A similar criticism was made by Ewbank J of a videotape used in a wardship proceeding before him.[51] Of course, the criticism related only to the particular tapes before the court, and better training of the interviewers should meet it. It seems that the particular tapes were originally produced for one of the non-legal purposes previously mentioned. But, whatever the purpose of the recording, it is important that information given by the child should be correct, not something put into the child's head.

The legal criticisms of videotapes just mentioned received considerable publicity, sometimes with lurid headlines ('Lawyers and doctors reeling over growing use of video tapes', a cheap joke for the Times), which was all the more unfortunate because these reports were so easily misinterpreted. Supposing that no videotape had been made in the cases in question, the child might have given evidence herself in the usual way, but her evidence might have been coloured by unsatisfactory questioning before the trial. Normally, this blemish in the evidence is not known, whereas the videotape makes it known. It is irrational to blame the medium for the message: to regard the device of videotaping as at fault because the interviewers have bungled their job.

Interviewers have discovered the utility of using dolls with correct anatomical features in order to help the child to explain herself.[52] Perhaps such dolls were used in the questioned interviews. But there is no objection to their use if the interviewers use them properly. The interviewers should be instructed that the child should so far as possible be left to tell her own story without assistance. Questions may be asked to direct her mind to the general subject of investigation, but should be as general as possible and should not suggest the answer. Some questions should be asked to which the answer 'no' is expected, because an interview in which the child answers only 'yes' may give the appearance that the child is not exercising her own judgment. Nude dolls should not be introduced unless the child has indicated nudity.

Here is a boiled-down example of the central part of what I conceive to be an unexceptionable interview.

> What did the man do? — No response. Did he touch you? — Affirmative response. Where did he touch you? — No response. Did he hurt you? — Negative response (as by shaking the head). Did he take something from you? — Affirmative response. What did he take? — No response. Was it your dolly that he took? — Negative response. Was it your handbag? — Negative response. Was it one of your clothes? — Affirmative response. Was it your frock? — Negative response. Was it your panties? — Affirmative response.

Nudity has now been acknowledged, so it would be proper for the interviewer to introduce the nude female doll, in order to help the child to acknowledge that the man touched her genitals. The doll both helps her to break taboo and offers a way of expressing herself without searching for words which may not be at her command. Similar remarks apply where a male doll has to be used.

In the last resort it should be permissible for an interviewer to lead the child. Leading questions can be asked even in court, with the leave of the judge, if the witness is not doing his/her best to answer properly. The judge cannot be consulted in a pre-trial interview, but the tape will show whether it was justifiable in the circumstances for the interviewer to lead the witness. And the trial judge could apply the voire dire procedure, scrutinising the tape (or a transcript) in the absence of the jury (at the instance of the defendant) to determine whether the interview was fairly conducted.

Certain arguments by analogy may be advanced to support the proposal for videotaped evidence. The common law rule admitting complaints in evidence in sexual cases is an acknowledgment of the importance of the fresh complaint. But the complaint is not regarded as probative in itself, and does not save the complainant from having to give evidence. Another analogy is the section in the Children and Young Persons Act 1933 already referred to,[53] allowing the child's deposition to substitute for his appearance before the court; but the provision is limited to cases where the child's life or health would be seriously endangered by a court appearance. Some doctors may be prepared to say that the endangerment occurs wherever the child is required to testify in court against a relative or friend; but the restrictive wording appears to have been effective to secure that the section is rarely invoked.

The proposal for video-linked evidence

I had completed this contribution up to the present point, and was about to post it to Peter Smith (on 9 October 1986), when the newspapers reported a statement by the Home Secretary, Douglas Hurd, to the Conservative Party Conference. He said that a forthcoming Criminal Justice Bill would allow live video links to be used to enable children to give evidence in child-abuse cases without the distress of testifying in the presence of the alleged attacker. One cheer for that. A commendable proposal, as far as it goes. We shall then at least have video screens installed in the principal criminal courts; and some day someone may venture to add recording equipment to the outfit. Why not go in for videorecording now?

Mr Hurd's cautious proposal would save the child from going into the courtroom, but it would lack the other advantages of a system of recorded evidence for child witnesses. So, to describe it as a half-measure would be unduly complimentary.

(1) The live-link interrogation would still mean another grilling for the child, in addition to those she has undergone before.
(2) And it would be the worst one of all. Presumably the child's evidence in chief would still be elicited by questioning by a (probably male) lawyer, the lawyer being in court and video-linked to the child who is in some other place. Presumably the child sees the prosecuting lawyer on a screen; she is answering questions coming from the screen, a procedure to which she is unaccustomed. If the lawyer is a barrister (as he will be if the prosecution is in a Crown Court) he will presumably be bewigged and begowned. This is a most unsuitable way of extracting evidence from a child, and anyway lawyers are unlikely to be the best people to do it. One has only to consider the type of questioning illustrated before, in connection with the use of sexually explicit dolls, to realise how preposterous it would be to subject a small girl to this type of examination in a public court.
(3) Perhaps the proposed legislation will permit the questioning in chief to be done by a non-lawyer, or a lawyer in mufti, the questioner being in the same room as the child. But presumably it is part of the plan that defending counsel can cross-examine the child from his place in court (otherwise there is little point in insisting upon a live video-link between the child and the courtroom). Perhaps counsel will shed his wig for the purpose, but other objections to formal cross-examination by this method will remain. The child should be questioned by one person seeking to arrive at the truth, not by two people, one trying to elicit the child's story and the other to dispute it. Moreover, a defendant is entitled to conduct his own defence: will he be entitled to cross-examine the child?
(4) The proposed procedure would operate only at the trial, which may be long after the incident, when the child has forgotten some of the details. Not only will the evidence lose some of its sharpness through the lapse of time, but it is universally agreed to be highly undesirable that the child should be required to keep the distressing incident in mind for any longer than is absolutely necessary.
(5) By the time of the trial the child will certainly have been questioned by various people, and this questioning may have been conducted in a highly unsatisfactory way, and have given the child false ideas. The rules forbidding leading questions in court may be nullified by assiduous leading questions asked of the child witness before the trial. And no one will know that they have been asked. A recorded interview will reveal any leading questions asked at the interview.
(6) The live-link procedure will not enable the defendant to see for himself, before the trial, the full force of the child's evidence, and so will not encourage him to admit his guilt and save the trial, as videorecordings have been found to do. On the admission being made, the prosecutor may be satisfied that alternative arrangements will justify the charge being dropped; even if it proceeds, the court hearing will be greatly shortened by a plea of guilty, and the necessity for much distressing evidence avoided.
(7) The videorecording, shown to the defendant before the trial, enables him to investigate and perhaps disprove the child's allegations, which he may not be able to do if he first knows of them at the trial itself.

(8) The proposed procedure would not save the child from having to repeat her evidence if a new defendant is subsequently added to the proceedings, whereas the videorecording retains its value in these circumstances.

In short, the proposal fails to offer most of the significant advantages of videorecording. Mr Hurd was perhaps moved to reject videorecording by reason of the unfavourable publicity given to the remarks of a judge and a barrister; but, as I have already said, these remarks may be read as having been directed rather against the way in which particular interviews were conducted than against the practice of videorecording itself.

Other necessary reforms

In order not to extend this essay unduly I do not deal with the somewhat naive, creaking and absurd rules relating to the taking of the oath by children and the corroboration of their evidence, but all these rules (or some of their details) need to be reconsidered with a fresh mind if common sense is to be infused into the use of child witnesses. It would certainly be absurd to try to administer an oath or affirmation to a child for the purpose of an interview by a child psychologist.

NOTES

1 For the dangers, see the fascinating Swedish case reported by Professor Trankell of Stockholm in (1958) 56 Jrnl of Abnormal and Social Psychology 385, and in his *Reliability of Evidence* (Stockholm 1972). The case did not go to court; had it done so, without Trankell's investigation, a conviction would have been very likely, since it would have been impossible for counsel at the trial to have conducted the kind of enquiry that was possible for Trankell. Some of the relevant witnesses (eg the mother) might not have been called by the prosecution, and therefore might not have been available for cross-examination. Also, essential evidence of what happened at the first full interview of the boy would have been missing. The great danger of a false conviction in that case would have been eliminated in England by our corroboration requirement, but the corroboration rule would not have prevented unmerited suspicion continuing to hang over the suspect.

2 The last point is mentioned, for example, in a memorandum approved by the Council of the Magistrates' Association in 1962. Gibbens and Prince remark: 'Counsel for the defence is apt to say: "We all wish to spare you as much as possible, but it is my duty to ask you certain questions. When you say he did this or that, what do you mean? Do you know what this word means?" etc. The procedure strikes anyone who works in the field of child care as a surprising anachronism.' (*Child Victims of Sex Offences*, Institute for the Study and Treatment of Delinquency, 1963).

3 For literature see Libai in 15 Wayne L Rev 977 n 81.

4 *Op cit* (n 2, above).

5 RS and CH Kempe *Child Abuse* (1978) 64.

6 For an instance where a prosecution collapsed because a boy of 9 'found difficulty' in answering questions, see 132 JPN 791.

7 Dent and Stephenson in (1979) 18 Br Jrnl of Social and Clinical Psychology 41.

8 May Duddle in 289 BMJ 1399.

9 Jane Wynne told a conference of paediatricians that 'our figures reinforce the belief that child sexual abuse is common and under-diagnosed' (Times, 17 April 1986).

10 See Duddle (n 8, above).

11 Some observers say that even father-daughter incest ceases as soon as it comes to light, the father being shamed by the public reaction. But the experience of others indicates cases where efforts to end incest without the authority of the law to back them up prove to be ineffectual: see the references in Duddle *op cit* (n 8, above).

12 Cp *Sexual Victimisation: Two Recent Researches into Sex Problems and Their Social Effects*, ed DJ West (1985). The number of cases reported to doctors, social workers or the police depends upon people's assessment of the advantages and disadvantages of doing so, and bears no relation to the number of incidents. Dr Bentovim reported that in the four years since the Hospital for Sick Children started its sexual abuse project, the number of referrals doubled each year, to 235 in 1985: 292 BMJ 1394. In 1985, 2,850 cases of sexual abuse of children were placed on child-abuse registers in local authorities, compared with 1,500 in 1984 — a 90 per cent rise (*Sexual Abuse Briefing*, NSPCC). This particular rise is probably due, in large part, to increased awareness of sexual abuse by the public, and increased readiness to report it. The term 'sexual abuse' as used by the NSPCC is not technical, but presumably indicates a serious abuse.

13 See below, text at n 19.

14 Sandra Buck in 284 BMJ 1875; May Duddle in 289 BMJ 1399, nn 11, 13, 14.

15 While the general bad effects are widely recognised, it is impossible to separate out the contribution of any particular factor. Some of the literature is referred to by David Labai in 15 Wayne L Rev 980–984.

To reduce the strain of appearing in court, various suggestions have been made for giving the girl witness the comfort of a woman companion. This is merely a palliative, but better than nothing. See the Report of the Departmental Committee on Sexual Offences Against Young Persons (1926); *The Criminal Law and Sexual Offenders* (1949) (Report of a joint committee of the BMA and the Magistrates' Association); Nesta Wells in [1958] 2 BMJ 1408; Sir Basil Henriques in [1961] 2 BMJ 1630. Some limited endorsement of the proposals was made in a Home Office Circular, no 208/1964; it would be interesting to know how far its instructions are still observed.

16 For this and similar instances see Claire Marks in the Sunday Times, 1 July 1973.

17 [1961] 2 BMJ 1633.

18 Ibid, 1630.

19 Times, 20 February 1978, endorsing a previous letter by Professor Ivor Mills.

20 See, for example, Lindy Burton *Vulnerable Children* (1968).

21 The Children and Young Persons Act 1933, s 41, enacts that a court can proceed with the case in the absence of a child or young person in respect of whom a scheduled offence is alleged to have been committed — but this does not dispense with evidence.

22 C & YPA 1933, ss 41–43. But a magistrate must take the child's deposition; the suspect must be given the opportunity of cross-examining the child; and the child must be the alleged victim of the offence — other children who witnessed it are not included. The most serious defect of the section is its old fashioned insistence on the formal sworn statement. What is wanted is a record of the actual interview at which the child gives his or her account, with the very words used in question and answer.

The Ingleby Committee (Cmnd 1191, para 262) proposed that the wording should be altered to cover cases where giving evidence 'would involve injury to his health'; and 'health' should be defined to include mental health. This recommendation was approved by the Council of the Magistrates' Association on 17 May 1962. But the CLRC, when considering the law of evidence, rejected it (by a majority), and no reference is made to it in the Report (Cmnd 4991 of 1972), though it was suggested on the committee that the inclusion of mental health would be effected by judicial decision. Would a psychiatrist testify that a serious danger of causing the child great distress involves a serious danger to his mental health?

The committee considered whether a medical certificate should be made admissible, to save the doctor having to testify in person, but in the event made no recommendation on this either.

The Criminal Justice Act 1967, s 9 (as amended by C & YPA 1969) allows evidence to be given by written statement, but only on certain conditions including non-objection by the defendant. See *Lister v Quaife* (1982) 75 Cr App Rep 313. Some provisions permit or require examining magistrates to allow in evidence a written statement taken from a child witness to a sexual offence, but they are limited in effect and occasion problems of interpretation: MCA 1980, s 103 (replacing C & YPA 1963, s 27 (1)), compared with CJA 1967, s 9, and MCA 1980, s 102, as amended by C & YPA 1969, s 72(3), and Sch 5, para 55. See 132 JPN 55, 127; 134 JPN 507.

23 See Gibbens and Prince *op cit* (n 2, above), for a graphic account of a case where two children who were brought to court to give evidence were said to be 'prostrate with terror when they saw the man again', and one who had to be brought from hospital insisted on all the doors and

windows being closed in case 'the man comes for me.' The man was acquitted because evidence on oath could not be taken from the children, and there were no other witnesses. The parents felt convinced that more damage had been done by the court appearance than by the assault.

24 This may seem to be too obvious to need saying, but it was slow in gaining acceptance. See Nesta Wells in [1961] 2 BMJ 1632.

25 See *Violence against Women*, the report by a Working Group of the Women's National Commission (Govt Offices, Great George St, London SW1P 3AQ, 1986), para 53. The necessary qualifications for a doctor who examines children in cases of suspected sexual interference are set out by Danya Glaser and Margaret Lynch in 290 BMJ 1145; cp Raine Roberts in 292 BMJ 1527.

26 Children associate police stations with wrongdoing, and readily assume that when they have to go to one it is because they themselves have erred. Glaser and Lynch, *op cit* (last note), say that 'the examination should not take place in a police station, since this is extremely likely to compound the guilt which many sexually abused children already experience' (290 BMJ 1145).

27 *Violence against Women* (n 25, above), paras 50–51.

28 Or, at least, Stockholm. See Libai in 15 Wayne L Rev 986–7. Also Copenhagen.

29 See below, text at n 37.

30 See May Duddle in 290 BMJ 771, who also catalogues other defects in our arrangements. A Departmental Committee of 1925 (Cmd 2561) recommended that suitable and properly trained women should be employed as child interviewers. Women police officers came to be used, and also women probation officers and social workers; but the use of male police officers continued where no woman was available.

31 There is much to be said for requiring the courts to honour a statement by an interviewer to a child witness that the molester will not be sent to prison if he does not do it again.

32 A police surgeon (who does not wear uniform) is a GP who has the advantage of being accustomed to giving evidence in court; also, he or she receives guidance from the Association of Police Surgeons. Although some are women, in many cases the victim still has no choice in the sex of the doctor examining her.

33 Owing to the greater prestige of the medical profession, judges often prefer the evidence of psychiatrists to that of psychologists; and doctors themselves frequently assume that the psychological examination of children should be by doctors. Of course, doctors are more widely available than psychologists. But a training in child psychology should be more relevant for this purpose than one in psychiatry. We do not make enough use of psychologists in our legal process.

34 See, eg, John Rich *Interviewing Children and Adolescents* (1967).

Dr Nesta Wells wrote: 'A rough assessment of the child's IQ is helpful, as it may explain why the child was slow to realise what the man was up to. Too often it happens that mention of "slowness" in court is wrongly interpreted, and the child's story is disbelieved. This is unfair to the subnormal child, as soon after the event she can give a good, obviously true account, simply because she has not got the intelligence to make it up; but her memory is poor, the details soon become blurred and patchy, with the result that after a time the story may vary and she gives the impression of an unreliable witness.': [1961] 2 BMJ 1632.

35 See below, n 52.

36 See May Duddle in 290 BMJ 771.

37 See the excellent article by David Reifen in 49 Jrnl of Criminal Law, Criminology and Police Science 30 (largely repeated in 12 Int Child Welfare Review 109), which should be studied by all who remain doubtful of the need for change in this part of the law. Also Judge Sten Rudholm in *Sexual Offences* (ed Radzinowicz 1957) 452, and the article by David Libai in 15 Wayne L Rev 977.

38 See the report of a meeting of the Federation of Committees for the Moral Welfare of Children in the Times, 29 October 1963. Gibbens and Prince *op cit*, n 2 above, comment: 'It seems probable that the general effect is to bring a higher proportion of offenders before the courts since there may be less reluctance on the part of the parents to bring a charge; but a rather higher proportion of offenders may be acquitted, as there is a natural tendency for the youth examiner to err on the side of caution in interpreting the child's statements.'

39 Address to the British Paediatric Association's Annual Conference, Times 17 April 1986.

40 [1961] 2 BMJ 1630.

41 Gibbens and Prince *op cit* (n 2, above). The authors made proposals about the persons who might interview the child, which are now somewhat outdated.

42 Gibbens and Prince found that in a sample of 87 cases coming before the courts, 11 defendants before a higher court pleaded not guilty, and the child presumably gave evidence in some at least of these cases; in the others she would probably have been present without being called.

43 This was the subject of a BBC documentary on 8 September 1986.
44 The possibility of legislation has been canvassed in official reports published in New South Wales and Victoria: [1986] Reform 73, 141. The Queensland report suggests that it should be a condition of the use of a recorded interview that evidence be given of the history of the interviews of the child leading up to the recorded interview, and the court must be satisfied that the interview was not edited in any way.
45 See as to the last, Bentovim in 290 BMJ 1431.
46 Statement by Detective Superintendent Peter Goodwin in the BBC programme referred to in n 43 above. He reported that in 235 cases, the tapes produced guilty pleas in 221.
47 *J Barber & Sons (a firm) v Lloyd's Underwriters* [1986] 2 All ER 845.
48 (1986) Times, 14 July. Cp the recommendation of the Fraud Trials Committee (Roskill) (1986), para 5.43. In New York, as early as 1982 a criminal court heard the evidence of witnesses on videotape even though they were within the jurisdiction, the purpose being to save the time of the court: (1982) Times, 23 March.
49 See Frances Gibb, Legal Affairs Correspondent, in the Times, 16, 17 June 1986.
50 Gibb *op cit* 17 June.
51 *Re E (a minor)* (1986) Times, 16 July.
52 See Bentovim (of the Child Sexual Abuse Project) in 290 BMJ 1431. But Dr Raine Roberts expressed the opinion that 'any use of these dolls should only be contemplated where the child is being videorecorded'; (292 BMJ 1527). It is not clear to me why the proper method of interviewing a child victim should depend on whether the interview is being recorded.
53 Above, n 21.

Disorder in public order law

Richard Card

Introduction

The purpose of this essay is to argue that for various reasons, 'public order law' is in an unsatisfactory state despite the enactment of the Public Order Act 1986, which was passed in the light of a number of official investigations in the last ten years.

This essay does not examine in technical detail the rules of public order law. Instead, it concentrates on whether or not public order law is in need of amendment or rationalisation, on whether or not it is based on clear, consistent and justifiable premises and is compatible with the international obligations of the United Kingdom, and on the process of law reform underlying the modern law of public order. It is hoped that, in the light of this, indications will be given for the future development of this area of our law.

1 The subject matter

A rough and ready definition of public order law is that it consists of those statutory and common law rules designed (or having an established application) either to prevent or control conduct which actually or potentially disturbs public order or to deal after the event with those involved in such conduct. In a practical sense, the rules relating to the prevention or control of public disorder are far more important than the others.

Potentially, this covers a wide area of law, and there is undoubtedly scope for argument as to whether or not a particular offence is a public order offence (for example, affray,[1] offences of entering and remaining on property, and being drunk and disorderly in a public place). With this in mind, it must be emphasised that this essay cannot attempt to describe or cover every candidate for inclusion under the heading of public order law. Instead, a selection has been made for discussion of a convenient number of offences and powers, most of which are clearly ones relating to public order and the rest arguably so. What is said about them is equally applicable to similar offences.

(a) RESTRICTIONS ON FUNDAMENTAL FREEDOMS

Some of the rules of public order law restrict the exercise of the rights of freedom of expression, of freedom of peaceful assembly and of freedom of association, prime examples of these being provided by Pt II (ss11–16) of the Public Order Act 1986. Section 11 introduces a requirement of advance notice to the police of certain kinds of public processions, while s 12 extends provisions formerly in s 3 of the Public Order Act 1936. It empowers a chief constable (or the senior officer present) to impose conditions on a public procession if he reasonably believes that it may result in serious public disorder, serious damage to property or serious disruption to the life of the community, or that its organisers' purpose is the intimidation of others with a view to compelling them not to do an act they have a right to do (or to do an act they have a right not to do). Section 14 introduces virtually identical provision for conditions to be placed on assemblies. Lastly, s13 substantially re-enacts other provisions in s3 of the 1936 Act. It provides for processions (but not assemblies) to be banned where the chief officer of police reasonably believes that his powers to impose conditions will be insufficient to prevent serious public disorder. There are various minor offences connected with a failure to notify a procession, or with non-compliance with a condition imposed on a procession or assembly or with a banning order.

Part III of the 1986 Act, which deals with incitement to racial hatred, imposes restrictions on freedom of expression. Particularly important are the provisions, formerly in the Public Order Act 1936, whereby it is an offence to publish or distribute written matter which is threatening, abusive or insulting and which is intended or likely to stir up racial hatred, or to use threatening, abusive or insulting words or gestures which are so intended or likely.

Other offences are designed to restrict manifestations of the freedom of association, examples being offences relating to the wearing in public of an item of dress signifying membership or support for a political organisation and offences relating to the training of quasi-military organisations.

Some applications of the above provisions not only restrict the freedoms of some but also protect the freedoms of others, as where a march is made subject to conditions or a ban in order to prevent others being intimidated in pursuing some freedom or right. Other provisions are designed specifically to protect the rights of others. An example is the offence of breaking up a meeting contrary to s 1 of the Public Meeting Act 1908.

(b) SERIOUS DISORDER

Other public order offences, while not specifically designed to restrict or protect the freedom of expression, peaceful assembly or association, nevertheless may often be invoked for this purpose.

Part I of the Public Order Act 1986 (ss1–10) provides a number of offences of this type, in descending order of seriousness. Section 1 of the Act provides the offence of riot, which is indictable only and punishable with a maximum of ten years' imprisonment. It requires that there must be at least 12 persons present who are using or threatening unlawful violence for a common purpose in such a way as would cause a person of reasonable firmness to fear for his personal safety, each of them who uses such violence being guilty of riot. Section 2 defines the offence of violent disorder in similar terms, save that no common purpose is required and that the minimum number of persons using or threatening violence is three. Each person so using or threatening violence is guilty of violent disorder, which is triable either way and punishable with a maximum of five years' imprisonment. Section 3 substantially reproduces the common law offence of affray, the new statutory offence of affray being triable either way and carrying a maximum of three years' imprisonment. The offences in ss 1–3 replace the common law offences of riot, rout, unlawful assembly and affray.

(c) THREATENING, ABUSIVE OR INSULTING WORDS OR BEHAVIOUR

The two other offences provided by Part I of the 1986 Act are both summary offences. Section 4, which replaces the frequently-used offence under s5 of the Public Order Act 1936, makes it an offence for anyone to use threatening, abusive or insulting words or behaviour towards another person (or to distribute or display any writing or other visible representation, which is threatening, abusive or insulting) with the intention of causing that person to believe that immediate unlawful violence will be used, or of provoking the immediate use of unlawful violence, or whereby that person is likely to believe that immediate unlawful violence will be used or it is likely that such violence will be used. Section 5 introduces a new offence of using threatening, abusive or insulting words or behaviour, or disorderly behaviour, or displaying any writing or other visible representation which is threatening, abusive or insulting, within the hearing or sight of a person who is likely to be caused harassment, alarm or distress thereby. Like s 4, s 5 is likely to prove to be useful to the police as a preventive measure enabling a constable to nip public disturbances in the bud by exercising against particular offenders (as 'group leaders') the special power of arrest attached to the offence, quite apart from being used after the event to impose criminal liability.

(d) FOOTBALL HOOLIGANISM

More specific offences are provided by the Sporting Events (Control of Alcohol etc.) Act 1985, as amended by the 1986 Act, which contains various provisions to deal with football hooliganism. These make it a summary offence to be in possession of intoxicating liquor, or to be drunk, on a train, coach or minibus being used for the principal purpose of going to or from a designated sporting event (basically any international football match or a match involving a Football League club), or to be in possession of intoxicating liquor or of a firework, smoke or visible gas bomb, or the like, at a designated football ground during the period of a designated football match, or to be drunk at such a place during such time.

The rest of the 1985 Act is mainly concerned with making provision for regulating sale or supply of intoxicating liquor and for the closure of bars at designated sports grounds. There are various minor offences dealing with the breach of these provisions.

Part IV of the 1986 Act makes further provision to prevent hooliganism at football matches, by empowering the courts to make orders excluding from entering grounds to watch a prescribed football match persons convicted of various offences committed during a prescribed football match or at a time immediately before or after it or while travelling to or from it. Breach of an exclusion order is a summary offence.

(e) AGGRAVATED TRESPASS

Provisions relating to trespass by groups of people were introduced by s 39 of the Public Order Act 1986. Under the section, the police are given power to direct people to leave land where it is reasonably believed that two or more persons have entered it as trespassers and are present there with the common purpose of residing there for any period; that reasonable steps have been taken to ask them to leave; and that any of them have damaged property there or used threatening, abusive or insulting words or behaviour to the occupier, his family or staff or that they have brought 12 or more vehicles on to the land.

Failure as soon as practicable to comply with such a direction is a summary offence, as is a return to the land within three months of a direction. A uniformed police officer may arrest without warrant anyone whom he reasonably suspects is committing one of these offences.

(f) POLICE POWERS

A particular facet of public order law is the powers of the police which are specifically designed to prevent or deal with conduct which actually disturbs, or is liable to lead to a disturbance of, public order. The statutory powers of the police in relation to public processions and assemblies and to aggravated trespass have already been referred to. In addition, there are various statutory police powers of arrest or search specifically provided in relation to some of the above offences.

More significant, there is a general common law power (for police and private citizens alike) to prevent or control a breach of the peace. According to the Court of Appeal in *R v Howell*, there is a breach of the peace whenever harm is actually done or is likely to be done to a person or in his presence to his property or a person is put in fear of being harmed through an assault, affray, riot or other disturbance.[2]

Anyone may arrest without warrant and detain a person who has committed a breach of the peace in his presence, or where a breach has been committed and it is reasonably believed that a renewal of it is threatened, or when he reasonably believes that a breach will otherwise be committed in the immediate future.[3]

Another aspect of the common law breach of the peace powers of the police is that if a constable reasonably apprehends an imminent breach of the peace he may take any necessary action to control or prevent it (and use reasonable force for this purpose),[4] including forbidding a meeting or limiting numbers in any particular place,[5] entering and remaining at meetings whether on public or on private premises,[6] dispersing an assembly,[7] or temporarily detaining a person.[8] It was under this power that the police stopped and turned back pickets during the miners' strike in 1984–85,[9] and that they stopped and turned back National Front members outside Wakefield in January 1984 after they had been banned from marching in the area.

Clearly, these common law powers of the police are a powerful 'back-up' to their various statutory powers.

(g) APPLICATIONS OF GENERAL OFFENCES

The offences described above may be called specific public order offences within the rough and ready definition of public order law on p 204. In addition, there fall within that definition certain well-established applications to actual or potential public disorder of more general offences which are not limited to actual or potential disturbances to public order and of which such a disturbance is not an essential element. Particularly noteworthy here are the summary offences of obstructing a constable in the execution of his duty (contrary to s 51(3) of the Police Act 1964); of obstructing the highway (contrary to s 137 of the Highways Act 1980), and of intimidation (contrary to s 7 of the Conspiracy and Protection of Property Act 1875) which, inter alia, punishes intimidating a person or watching or besetting his house or work-place, with a view to compelling him to do or abstain from doing an act he has a right to abstain from doing or to do. These offences have frequently been utilised in relation to public order situations. To give a well-known example deriving from *Duncan v Jones*,[10] an organiser of a meeting who persists in holding it after he has been forbidden to do so or told to hold it elsewhere by a constable may be convicted of wilfully obstructing the constable in the execution of his duty, provided the constable had reasonable grounds to apprehend a breach of the peace if the meeting took place as planned (and can therefore exercise the common law power referred to on p 207).

Another general offence which can have application in a public order situation is the common law offence of public nuisance. There is no precise definition of this offence, but in Stephen's *Digest of the Criminal Law*[11] it is defined as 'an act not warranted by law . . . which . . . obstructs or causes inconvenience or damage to the public in its exercise of rights common to all Her Majesty's subjects.' This offence, which is triable either way, has been used to deal with disturbances to public order by obstructions to the highway caused by sit-down demonstrations.[12]

2 Duplication of offences and powers

Consideration of public order law reveals a considerable duplication of offences and of police powers. In some cases the duplication is with other public order offences; in others it is with more general offences. In most, if not all, cases this duplication is unnecessary.

(a) DUPLICATION OF PUBLIC ORDER OFFENCES

Examples of such duplication are provided by s1 of the Public Order Act 1936 and s1 of the Prevention of Terrorism (Temporary Provisions) Act 1984, both of which contain summary offences relating to wearing items of dress signifying membership of, or support for, a political organisation (only the IRA or the INLA in the case of the latter offence). Admittedly, the latter offence is wider in that it also extends to articles (such as badges and banners) as well as dress, but there would be little difficulty in merging these two offences.

The same can be said for the more serious offences under s 1 of the Unlawful Drilling Act 1819 and s 2 of the Public Order Act 1936, both of which are concerned with the training of quasi-military organisations. Although the latter offence — unlike the former — only catches the organisers and trainers, and not mere participants, there would be a benefit, without any loss to the law, in tidying up this area as well (along the lines of s 2), removing in the process the antique language of the 1819 Act.

Duplication also exists between the statutory offence of wilful obstruction of the highway and the common law offence of public nuisance in so far as the latter applies to highway obstruction. The former offence is qualified by the provision that it must be without lawful authority or excuse, as well as wilful; the extent to which corresponding requirements exist for the latter offence remains to be determined by the courts. There is much to be said for a simple section providing that the offence of public nuisance shall cease to have effect in so far as it relates to obstruction of the highway.[13]

It is likewise questionable whether there is a need for the summary offence of breaking up a public meeting under s1 of the Public Meeting Act 1908, which provides that it is an offence for a person, at a lawful public meeting, to act in a disorderly manner for the purpose of preventing the transaction of the business for which the meeting was summoned. Given that the conduct required for this offence will constitute an offence under s 4 or under s 5 of the Public Order Act 1986, there seems to be no need to retain it, notwithstanding that the maximum penalty under s 5 is lower (a level 3 fine on the standard scale) than that for the offence under the Act of 1908 (6 months and/or a level 5 fine).

A particularly important instance of duplication relates, on the one hand, to the power of the police to deal with an anticipated breach of the peace, recognised in *Duncan v Jones*,[14] and its application via the offence of obstructing a constable, and, on the other, to the provisions in Pt II of the Public Order Act 1986 concerning the regulation of processions and assemblies. The reason is that, by the use of the former power to impose conditions on an assembly or procession (or even to ban it), it is possible to by-pass the various procedural safeguards laid down for the exercise by the police of their powers under Pt II.

(b) DUPLICATION WITH OTHER OFFENCES

Various offences under the Sporting Events (Control of Alcohol etc.) Act 1985 duplicate pre-existing offences under the general criminal law.

As a starting point, reference may be made to s2A of the Act, which makes it a summary offence to be in possession of a firework, or a smoke or visible gas bomb, or the like, at a designated sports ground during the period of a designated sporting event. It may be that some of the articles covered by the section contain 'a *noxious* liquid, *gas or other thing*', in which case there could be conviction for the serious offence of possessing a prohibited weapon, contrary to s 5 of the Firearms Act 1968. Of greater practical importance, a person who has in his possession at a designated sports ground any firework or bomb or the like can be convicted of another serious offence, possessing an offensive weapon in a public place, contrary to s 1 of the Prevention of Crime Act 1953, if the thing is made or adapted for causing personal injury or if he intends to use it for causing such injury. Alternatively, if the firework, bomb or the like is possessed with intent without lawful excuse to damage or destroy another's property, the serious offence under s 3 of the Criminal Damage Act 1971 will be committed by such a person.

The only likely situation where there is no duplication is where the thing is not so made, adapted or intended but carried for an innocent purpose (as where a firework was bought for bonfire night on the way to a football match). Does this require criminal liability and the associated police powers of search, when this is not necessary elsewhere? Why evade the normal requirement in the 1953 Act that, if not made or adapted, the thing must be proved to have been intended for use to cause injury, or in the case of the 1971 Act that an intent to damage or destroy another's property must be proved? Would it not be enough, if necessary, to leave it to the club to refuse admission or to reserve the right to have a person removed from the ground if such an article is seen?[15]

Another area where there is duplication relates to the offence of being drunk in a designated sports ground during a designated sporting event or while entering or leaving the ground during that period, contrary to s 2(2) of the 1985 Act. There would seem to be a complete overlap with the offence of being found drunk in the highway or other public place, contrary to s 12 of the Licensing Act 1872. True, the maximum sentence is a fine not exceeding level 1 on the standard scale, as opposed to level 2 for the offence under the 1985 Act. However, in cases deserving a higher penalty there would doubtless be an element of disorderliness, in which case a prosecution could be brought for the general summary offence of being drunk and disorderly in a public place, contrary to s 91 of the Criminal Justice Act 1967, or even a prosecution for the summary offence under s 5 of the 1986 Act, for either of which the maximum sentence is a fine not exceeding level 3.

The complaint of unnecessary duplication can also be made concerning the offences of being drunk in a vehicle to which s 1 or s 1A of the 1985 Act applies, contrary to s 1(4) or s 1A(4) of that Act. One reason is that both a railway carriage and a motor coach to which the public have or are permitted to have access on payment of money have been held to be public places in other contexts.[16] Second, it is arguable that a person in a minibus or other vehicle on the highway is thereby in the highway. Third, it is an offence under railway byelaws[17] to be in an intoxicated state on the railway. Consequently, in most, if not all, cases covered by s 1(4) or s 1A(4) one of the general offences or the offence under the railway byelaws is also committed.

(c) AFFRAY

By s 3 of the Public Order Act 1986, a person is guilty of affray if he uses or threatens unlawful violence towards another and his conduct is such as would cause a person of reasonable firmness present at the scene to fear for his safety.[18] As can be seen from this definition, an affray cannot be committed without committing some other offence. It is often charged with one or more other offences, including murder, manslaughter, wounding or causing grievous bodily harm with intent, unlawful wounding or infliction of grievous bodily harm, common assault, offences of threatening, abusive or insulting behaviour,[19] and possession of an offensive weapon. Alternatively, these offences may be charged instead of affray.

Despite this duplication, the Law Commission (in its investigation of the common law offence of affray) concluded that an offence of affray was necessary because it dealt:

> '. . . with a type of conduct in which, by contrast with offences against the person, both the identity of the victim and his injury are immaterial . . . The essence of affray lies rather in the fact that the defendant participates in fighting

> or other acts of violence inflicted on others of such a character as to cause alarm to the public: it is essentially an offence against public order.'[20]

Because the identity of the victim and his injury were immaterial, said the Commission, the evidential requirements were less than in the case of an offence against the person. The Commission clung to this view, relying on the reality of what occurs in street fighting:

> 'If a fight takes place, for example, late at night amongst a considerable number of people such as rival gangs of youths, precise identification of what is being done to whom in the course of a general mêlée at that time of day may well be impossible. It will, however, be clear that the participants concerned have engaged in acts of violence, or aiding and abetting others in such acts.'[21]

Nevertheless, the offence is open to the objection that it undermines the safeguards provided by the more serious offences against the person, with the result that there are substantial dangers of wrongful conviction if there is no detailed evidence of what the accused did; if there is, he can be charged with the relevant offence. As one commentator said: 'If there is insufficient evidence to convict a person of assault on another specific person, prima facie, there will also be insufficient to show that he was fighting at all'.[22]

As already indicated, there would be no gap in the criminal law if no offence of affray existed because, even if injury cannot be proved, there will still be a common assault, and, even if the identity of a particular victim cannot be proved, an offence under s 4 or s 5 of the Public Order Act 1986 will have been committed. However, it is arguable (as the Law Commission argued) that these offences are insufficient to deal with cases of a major character where there is not sufficient evidence to charge a serious offence against the person. In reply, one can say that a number of jurisdictions seem to manage without an offence of affray, for example New Zealand and Canada, and that English law survived for over 100 years without the offence (since there were no reported affray charges between 1845 and 1957, when the offence was re-discovered in *R v Sharpe, R v Johnson*).[23]

Like affray, the offences of riot and violent disorder cannot be committed without also committing one or more other offences. The arguments for and against them, in terms of duplication, are similar to those mentioned in relation to affray, but two other arguments can also be made in favour of them.

First, there is the argument that the conduct covered by them is marked by the numbers (a minimum of twelve for riot and of three for violent disorder) using or threatening violence. As the Court of Appeal said in *R v Caird*[24] in relation to the common law offence of riot: '. . . riot . . . is an offence which derives its gravity from the simple fact that the persons concerned were acting in numbers and using those numbers to achieve their purpose.' Undoubtedly, the use or threat of violence by groups of people can be extremely terrifying, more so than when perpetrated by a single individual.

Second, in relation to riot, there is the argument that the fact that public disorder is promoted pursuant to a common purpose increases the gravity of the conduct.

Both arguments have their attractions. They certainly justify a higher penalty for a relevant offence against the person or property than the conduct of each individual requires, but do they and the other arguments necessitate a separate offence?

3 Elasticity and uncertainty

Another complaint which can be made about public order law is the elasticity and uncertainty of parts of it. For example, ss 4 and 5 of the Public Order Act 1986 contain the words 'threatening, abusive or insulting', which words involve questions of fact for the magistrates[25] (with the consequent uncertainty of how the law will be applied by a particular bench in a given case), as well as other terminology which is notable for its width. The result is that, in any given case, it is the magistrates who determine the boundaries of the offence. It is they who decide what is legal and what is illegal behaviour (and, in some cases, the extent to which a fundamental freedom, such as that of expression, may be exercised).

Above all, the elasticity of the common law powers to prevent or control a breach of the peace means that they are easily expandable by the courts, as shown by *Moss v McLachlan*,[26] so as to justify after the event action by the police or, when used in combination with s 51 of the Police Act 1964, to impose criminal liability for obstructing a constable. In this way, in particular, there is a gradual 'creep' in police powers and in the scope of the criminal law, which comes near to, if not actually, infringing the principle of legality and hence infringing art 7 of the European Convention on Human Rights, referred to on p 216. Concern over this is increased by the performance of the courts which indicates that they will not be reluctant to discover new applications of the common law powers.[27]

By way of a last example, the wide definition of public nuisance means that it, too, is open to new applications in the area of public order — an opportunity which the courts may well accept, given that they have not been reluctant to discover new applications of this offence in other areas.[28]

It is unfortunate that the recent reviews of public order law have failed to grapple with the elasticity and uncertainty of parts of public order law. Unfortunate not only because it is essential that the law should be sufficiently precisely stated that it is clear in advance what is the minimum conduct covered by it, but also because public order law is inextricably bound up with restricting fundamental freedoms and there is a constant danger that these may be unjustifiably jeopardised by an extensive interpretation of the relevant law.

4 Complexity and fragmentation

Public order law is also open to the criticism that it is complex and fragmentary, being derived from a number of statutes (albeit fewer than used to be the case, following repeals effected by the Public Order Act 1986), as well as from judicial decisions and, even, byelaws. The duplication of public order rules referred to above adds to the complexity and fragmentation of public order law.

This complexity and fragmentation is going to be on the increase if recent additions to the law are indicative of Parliament's willingness to add to the law in this area. Examples of such additions are the offences introduced by the Sporting Events (Control of Alcohol etc.) Act 1985 and the Public Order Act 1986.

Other examples relate to the increase in police powers made by those Acts, in particular the 1986 Act. In the recent official investigations where the matter was raised,[29] the view was taken that new police powers in relation to public order were unnecessary, the existing powers being adequate. In the light of this, and of the partial codification of police powers by the Police and Criminal Evidence Act 1984, it was surprising to find powers of arrest being tacked on to pre-existing offences (viz offences relating to conditions on processions and the banning of them and the offences of inciting racial hatred by words or gestures and the offence of intimidation) by the 1986 Act, as well as to certain new offences (viz those under ss 5 and 14 of the Act and the back-up offences relating to aggravated trespass and to breach of an exclusion order). The addition of powers of arrest to the pre-existing offences is particularly surprising, given that Parliament had not thought them deserving of anything more than the limited power of arrest under s25 of the Police and Criminal Evidence Act 1984 when it enacted it two years previously. The question: 'What has changed to necessitate these powers now?' was not answered in Parliament and does not seem to be answerable. If Parliament continues in this trigger-happy way in other legislation the attempt made by the 1984 Act to simplify and pull together police powers will soon be set at nought.

5 Basis of public order law

We have seen that public order law not only protects the exercise of the rights and freedoms of individuals, but also places constraints on the exercise of the fundamental freedoms of expression, of peaceful assembly and of association, freedoms which are part of the foundation of a democratic society since they are essential to ensure the pluralism, tolerance and broad-mindedness which are characteristics of such a society. As Lord Denning MR said in his dissenting judgment in *Hubbard v Pitt*:[30]

> 'The right to demonstrate and protest are, like the right of free speech, rights which it is in the public interest that individuals should possess and exercise without impediment, so long as no wrongful act is done.'[31]

Although they are protected by the European Convention on Human Rights, none of these, or any other, human rights is constitutionally guaranteed by English law in a positive sense. Instead, such rights only exist in a negative sense, in that a person is free to do something unless it is specifically prohibited by law. It follows that it is important that public order law should be developed on the basis of clearly articulated premises, and be fully argued and justified in terms of those premises, lest (even if inadvertently) fundamental freedoms are unjustifiably reduced by the introduction of new offences and powers.

A point clearly recognised in the Wolfenden Report,[32] although rarely in other reports, is that so severe is the criminal law that its intervention must be justified up to the hilt. It need hardly be said that the mere fact that an activity is regarded as unacceptable or undesirable is not a sufficient ground for the intervention of the criminal law: there must be a pressing social necessity for it on a recognised ground of public interest. This is particularly true where fundamental freedoms may be constrained by the criminal law; regard must be had to the importance of the freedom in question as well as the evil which is intended to be repressed.

In his statement in *Hubbard v Pitt*, quoted above, Lord Denning MR spoke of the various freedoms as '. . . ones which it is in the public interest that individuals should possess and exercise without impediment, so long as no wrongful act is done.' This raises the question of what is a wrongful act, or, to adopt the terminology used above, when there is a pressing social necessity for the intervention of the criminal law.

(a) CRITERIA FOR INTERVENTION

The National Council for Civil Liberties[33] believes that the sole criterion for public order controls (both offences and the exercise of police powers) should be a minimum test of actual violence or of an immediate threat of violence to persons or property. In the case of a threat of violence, it would have to be immediate in the sense that it was proximate in time and place. Such a test would, for example, exclude from the intervention of the criminal law much of the activity covered by s 5 of the Public Order Act 1986, and also the grounds for imposing conditions on a procession or assembly relating to serious disruption to the life of the community or the case where the organisers' purpose is intimidation (or even the case of serious disorder or damage to property, where this is not immediately threatened). It would also exclude offences relating to obstruction of the highway or to picketing.

It is submitted that the NCCL view draws the line too high because there are other bases in a democratic society for the intervention of the criminal law in respect of public disorder. Nevertheless, it is doubtful whether the preservation of public order for its own sake can be regarded as a sufficient basis in a democratic society for the intervention of the criminal law since some protest and resulting disorder 'is a part of normal community life and serves a vital function in a democratic system of government.'[34] As Professor ATH Smith has said: 'Just as we tolerate risks to life and property inherent in our dangerous road traffic system, so we must sometimes be prepared to take risks with public order.'[35]

On the other hand, it is submitted that the intervention of the criminal law to preserve public order will be justifiable as necessary where there is a risk of otherwise unavoidable (although not immediate) violence to persons or property, or where there is a risk to national security, or where there is a risk of substantial alarm or distress being caused to a vulnerable sector of the public. On this basis, for example, the application of the criminal law to some cases covered by s 5 of the 1986 Act which would not be justified under the NCCL test is nevertheless justifiable.

Another type of case where the criminal sanction would seem justifiable is where it is necessary to protect the rights of others. More so than in most other areas of the criminal law, there may be a need to hold the balance between competing rights. The problem here is how to evaluate competing rights and social interests. Overall, the law appears to come down in favour of the majority against the minority (regardless of the value of their respective rights or interests).

Not the least of the difficulties in discussing the justifiability of the present law is that its basic criteria have not been articulated. Some of the controls seem to suggest that the social unacceptability of behaviour, such as some types of behaviour covered by s 5 of the 1986 Act, is itself the criterion for the intervention of the criminal law, and as already said this cannot suffice.

(b) OTHER COURSES

In answering the question of the necessity for the intervention of the criminal law in relation to particular behaviour, it should be borne in mind that there is not simply a stark choice between the imposition of criminal liability on the one hand and no legal intervention on the other. While an evil may justify some interference by the law, it may not be sufficiently serious or sufficiently likely to make interference by the way of the criminal sanction necessary; sufficient legal intervention (at least in the first instance) being achieved by preventive police powers or by reliance on rights or powers conferred by the civil law.

It is a notable feature of our statutory public order law that most of it is designed to deal with disorder after the event. In terms of preventive powers, it contains very little. The powers to impose conditions on processions or assemblies and to ban processions, the licensing restrictions at designated sports grounds, and the system of exclusion orders, are the only obvious examples, although the offences under ss 4 or 5 of the Public Order Act 1986 do have a preventive aspect in that each is accompanied by the power to arrest a person reasonably suspected of committing that offence, which is not required actually to have resulted in violence. Because of the relative dearth of statutory preventive powers, the preventive powers which exist at common law have a particularly important function, but they are open to objection by reason of their elasticity, as indicated on p 212.

(c) NEED FOR SPECIFIC PUBLIC ORDER OFFENCES

Another question which merits consideration is whether, if there is a need for intervention by the criminal law, there is a need for a specific public order offence or police power where there is some other offence or power available. Some cases of public disorder deserving punishment involve the commission of one or more offences against the person (ranging from common assault to murder) or against property (particularly criminal damage, but also theft, robbery or burglary). In talking about criminal liability for such offences, one must remember that it will be borne not only by those who perpetrate the violence against the person or property but also by others who are involved as aiders, abettors, counsellors or procurers. Liability for conspiracy, attempt and incitement to commit these offences must not be forgotten either. Nor must the various police powers relating to them be overlooked.

The provisions concerning aggravated trespass, for example, prompt the question of whether there is a need for specific provisions. The conduct in question is attended by the clear risk of a breach of the peace, since the landowner and others in the area may well be prompted to take action, with the result that the police can prevent the trespass taking place by exercising their common law power to prevent a breach of the peace by stopping them entering the immediate area or the land in question. If those concerned refuse to obey they will commit at the least the offence of obstructing a constable in the execution of his duty. If they then use or threaten force against the police or anyone else or against property in order to gain access to the land (or while they are there), they can be dealt with as appropriate by a prosecution for using or threatening violence to secure entry (contrary to s 6 of the Criminal Law Act 1977), or for an offence under Pt I of the Public Order Act 1986, or for an offence against the person, or for criminal damage, provided they can be identified. Where vehicles are used to enter land,[36] the offence is committed of driving without lawful authority on land which does not form part of a road (contrary to s 36 of the Road Traffic Act 1972).

With the exception of the last offence, all these offences are more serious than the aggravated trespass offence. In relation to police powers, most of these offences are arrestable, and where they are not, one or more of the conditions for an arrest under s25 of the Police and Criminal Evidence Act 1984, or one of the requirements for an arrest in relation to breach of the peace, is likely to be satisfied in the type of trespass situation covered by the aggravated trespass provisions.

Similar comments can be made about the offences of riot, violent disorder and affray, as shown on pp 210–11. Whether or not these offences are necessary in addition to the various offences against the person or against property depends on an evaluation of the arguments referred to on those pages.

6 Consideration of European Convention on Human Rights

Of the freedoms protected by the Convention, art 10 protects the right to freedom of expression, which right includes freedom to receive and impart information and ideas without interference by public authority, and art 11 the right to freedom of peaceful assembly and association with others.

The second paragraphs of arts 10 and 11 each provide that interference with the rights declared is permissible only if two conditions are satisfied. The first is that the interference must be 'prescribed by' law, which means that it must be 'pre-determined by substantive law',[37] whether statutory or common law. The validity of an interference cannot be derived from an ex post facto development of the law. In fact, in the case of criminal liability this would also involve a breach of art 7 which declares the principle of legality. The second condition is that the interference must be necessary in a democratic society to serve one or more stated grounds of policy, the prevention of disorder or crime and the protection of the rights of others being particularly relevant grounds in the area of public order.[38]

Space does not permit a detailed discussion here of whether or not all the various parts of public order law are compatible with the Convention. Suffice it to say that many obviously are. For example, the offences of riot, violent disorder and affray do not conflict with the Convention since, even if they could be said to interfere with the freedom of expression or the freedom of peaceful assembly or association, that interference is clearly necessary in a democratic society for the prevention of violent disorder or of crimes of violence against the person or property and, given the nature of these offences, is clearly justifiable under para (2) of arts 10 and 11.

On the other hand, the position is far less certain as far as particular applications of certain powers and offences relating to processions and assemblies are concerned.

(a) CONDITIONS AND BANS

It will be recalled that, inter alia, under Pt II of the Public Order Act 1986, the police have power to impose conditions on the conduct of a public procession or assembly if they reasonably believe that it may result in serious public disorder, serious damage to property or serious disruption to the life of the community or that the purpose of the organisers is the intimidation of others with a view to compelling them not to do an act they have a right to do (or to do an act they have a right not to do). The objective justifiability of these provisions under the Convention is questionable since, while the grounds themselves might be regarded as corresponding to the grounds of exemption under the Convention, it is not required that it be necessary (or even reasonably believed to be necessary) for a particular condition to be imposed. Instead, it is enough that the condition appears necessary to the police.

The power to ban all public processions or any class or public processions (eg 'processions of a politcal nature') in a particular area, the procedure for which can only be set in train if the chief constable reasonably believes that the power to impose conditions is insufficient, has already been mentioned. It is a defect with this power that, if a banning order is made, all processions or processions of a specified class are banned. In consequence, processions which pose no threat to public order may be prohibited. In such a case the interference with peaceful assembly does not seem justifiable as being necessary in a democratic society for any of the specified grounds. This defect would be avoided if it was possible for specific or selective banning orders to be made. Provided there was a pressing need for such an order there would be no contravention of the Convention. Unfortunately, in drafting the relevant provision in the 1986 Act the government decided against a selective banning power.[39]

(b) OBSTRUCTING THE POLICE

Clearly, the offence of obstruction of a constable in the execution of his duty can normally be justified under art 10(2) or 11(2) if it infringes one of the freedoms in art 10 or 11. However, in one case it is doubtful whether such an infringement can be so justified. As explained on p 208, if the organiser of a meeting persists in holding it after he has been forbidden to do so or has been told to hold it elsewhere by a constable, he may be convicted of obstructing the constable in the execution of his duty, provided the constable had reasonable grounds to apprehend a breach of the peace.

It could be argued that the imposition of criminal liability on the organiser of the meeting in such a case is necessary in a democratic society for the prevention of violent disorder or crime. This has a superficial attraction. However, given that he intended the meeting to be peaceful and that the risk of disorder comes from his opponents, can it be said that the prohibition etc of a meeting which is to be, or is being, conducted in a peaceful way by a person, and his subsequent conviction if he ignores the prohibition, is necessary in a democratic society to prevent disorder or crime when the police have not first tried to control the real offenders,[40] those who are likely to disturb the meeting and cause a breach of the peace? Bearing in mind the fairly strict meaning of 'necessary in a democratic society' under the jurisprudence of the European Commission of Human Rights and the European Court of Human Rights,[41] and the importance of freedom of expression and of peaceful assembly in a democratic society, it is submitted that the imposition of criminal liability in these circumstances, except as a last resort, cannot be objectively justified. In the type of situation at issue here, the imposition of conditions on a procession or assembly (or the banning of a procession) under the Public Order Act 1986 is equally open to objection.

(c) UNRULY MEETINGS

While convictions under s 4 of the 1986 Act are normally justifiable under the Convention as being necessary in a democratic society for the prevention of disorder or crime, the conviction of a speaker in the sort of circumstances just outlined would not seem to be so justifiable. This is because a person, who uses threatening, abusive or insulting words or behaviour in addressing an audience made up of hooligans who are there to prevent him continuing, can be convicted of an offence under s 4 if unlawful violence is likely to be provoked by his words or behaviour, even though he did not intend to provoke it and even though his words or behaviour would not have provoked reasonable people to violence, since a speaker in such a case must take his audience as he finds it.[42]

The present law makes it hazardous for a person to present unpopular or controversial views at a public meeting. However much one may disapprove of certain views, the freedom to express them in a public meeting must be protected rather than suppressed — unless all other attempts at preventing disorder fail. At present, the law gives what amounts to a veto on freedom of expression and assembly in the present type of circumstances to rowdies, who can prevent a meeting taking place by threatening violence. It can hardly be claimed that the present state of the law is objectively justifiable as necessary in a democratic society for any of the purposes specified by the Convention.

7 Law reform process

Various criticisms have been made in this essay about the existing state of public order law. The chances of rectifying the defects in that law would have been greater if the official investigations which preceded the Public Order Act 1986 had not proceeded as they did.

(a) THE INVESTIGATIONS

In 1980 the Home Office published a Green Paper, Review of the Public Order Act 1936 and Related Legislation,[43] hereafter referred to as 'the Green Paper', which was largely concerned with the law on processions and assemblies and incitement to racial hatred. Later in the same year, the House of Commons Select Committee on Home Affairs published its Report on the Law relating to Public Order,[44] which investigated the operation of the 1936 Act and made a number of recommendations (most of which were enacted in the 1986 Act). Then, in 1981, Lord Scarman's Report on the Brixton Disorders 10–12 April 1981[45] was published; it favoured a restatement of public order law, although it made no specific recommendations in relation to that law since Lord Scarman did not regard it as inadequate. Subsequently, in 1983, the Law Commission published, as part of its remit to codify the criminal law, its Report on Criminal Law: Offences Relating to Public Order,[46] which it had produced in the light of responses to its Working Paper on Offences against Public Order.[47] The Report concerned itself only with the four common law offences of affray, riot, rout and unlawful assembly and with certain ancient and obsolete statutory offences. It was followed, in 1985, by the Government White Paper, Review of Public Order Law,[48] referred to in this essay as 'the White Paper'. Although it dealt with a wider range of public order law than the previous reports, the White Paper was far from being a comprehensive review of all aspects of that law. Instead, it did not go much further than indicating the Government's response to the proposals made in the other reports, most of which were accepted on a pragmatic basis. The proposals endorsed or made by the White Paper were generally enacted in the Public Order Act 1986. Finally, there have been two Reports of the (Popplewell) Inquiry into Crowd Safety and Control at Sports Grounds, the Interim Report[49] being published in 1985 and the Final Report[50] in 1986.

(b) PIECEMEAL NATURE

Public order law itself has already been criticised as complex and fragmentary. Any chance of changing this in the recent Public Order Act was really lost at the outset of the law reform process because, as can be seen, none of the official investigations into it dealt with public order as a whole. True, the White Paper drew on the previous reports, but even it did not deal with everything found in the Public Order Bill when it appeared (because it did not deal with exclusion orders), let alone as it was amended. Moreover, the White Paper did not deal with matters not covered by the other reports, such as public nuisance and the obstruction offences, and it only dealt fleetingly with the common law powers.

It was particularly disappointing that the Law Commission decided to limit itself to the four common law offences and certain ancient statutory offences. In relation to the provisions in the Public Order Act 1936 (uniforms, quasi-military training, processions and so on), it justified this approach on the ground that they were already being investigated by the Home Office, which was a more suitable body for that purpose. Among the provisions in the 1936 Act was the offence under s 5 of threatening, abusive or insulting words or behaviour intended or likely to occasion a breach of the peace. The failure of the Law Commission to review this offence was a major factor in rendering its report, which was after all entitled Offences Relating to Public Order, an incomplete review of offences relating to public disorder, and so were its failures to consider the offences of obstructing a constable, obstructing the highway and public nuisance (in terms of their application to public disorder).[51] The reasons for these latter omissions were that these offences had implications in areas other than public disorder and considerations of the 'proper boundaries of our review and convenience' led to their exclusion.[52] Although it received some support,[53] the first of these reasons is unconvincing, since it would have been possible to consider in isolation the public order aspects covered by these offences and, if reform was found necessary, to draft a new offence and simply provide that the old offence should no longer be charged in a public order context. The second reason also gained some support on the ground that it would have been vain to hope for such a wide review.[54]

As a result of all these omissions, the interrelation of these and other public order offences and the common law powers with the four major offences reviewed by the Commission was not investigated by it. Nor was it investigated by any of the other investigations. Likewise, the question of duplication of offences was not considered, except (by the Law Commission) in the case of riot, violent disorder and affray.

Clearly, a comprehensive review of public order law would have imposed a major burden on the Law Commission, given the other demands on it. Nevertheless, the absence of such a review is most unfortunate, since the offences of threatening, abusive or insulting words or behaviour, of obstructing a constable and of obstructing the highway, along with the common law powers to prevent or control a breach of the peace, are among the key public order provisions, being invoked far more frequently than virtually any other public order provision.

The piecemeal review of an area of law, as has occurred in relation to public order law, undoubtedly militates against a thorough discussion of the law. It also prevents the development of rules which are consistent with each other. For these reasons, it is to be deprecated.

(c) PANIC REACTION

At one point in the Green Paper[55] it was said that the law on public order had 'on the whole succeeded in adapting flexibly to new situations'. This is a charitable way of putting things, since it might be more appropriate to describe changes in public order law as a panic reaction on the part of different Governments and Parliaments, and even judges, to particular events, in an effort to placate the law and order lobby or to allay public anxiety.

As a result our law has been loaded with statutory offences (often unduly specific ones), some of which are either doubtful in terms of need or duplicate other pre-existing provisions. Examples of such legislation are the Public Order Act 1936, passed in response to the Mosleyite disturbances in the 1930s, the Sporting Events (Control of Alcohol etc.) Act 1985, passed hurriedly in response to violent events at football matches at home and abroad and almost immediately requiring amendment by the Public Order Act 1986, and the Public Order Act 1986 itself, passed principally in response to urban unrest in the 1980s. If enacted, the proposals for increased powers of search and arrest in relation to football hooliganism made by the Popplewell reports would be open to the same objection.

Panic reaction legislation is to be deprecated. Not only does it reduce the freedoms of the general public simply to deal with special (often short-term) situations, but it also militates against the development of rational and consistent law. Both complaints are aggravated by the fact that, once enacted, such legislation tends to survive any short-term need.

(d) PRAGMATISM

The complaint of panic reaction is in fact merely part of a larger complaint, that the law reform process has essentially been a pragmatic exercise, a complaint which can also be made in other areas of our criminal law. Given the defects in public order law, there was a crying need for a more fundamental approach than simply starting with the existing law and ascertaining what its technical defects were and how they could be cured, which was the approach essentially adopted by the Law Commission and by the Green Paper and the White Paper. What was required was a true re-appraisal of all aspects of public order, starting afresh and examining the extent to which there is a pressing social necessity for the intervention of the criminal law (and, if there is, whether a specific public order offence is necessary where conduct is already covered by a more general offence). The reform process should have included a determination of the causes of public disorder, and it should have given attention to the prevention of public disorder as well as how it should be dealt with after the event. In addition, proper consideration should have been given to protecting freedom of expression, of assembly and of association (especially in relation to minority groups), and to balancing competing freedoms and rights, and proper consideration should also have been given to the compatibility with the European Human Rights Convention of the law as it was or as it was proposed to be; only lip-service was given to these matters (or, at least, some of them) by the various investigations (and some did not even do this).[56] Consideration should also have been given to the role of the police, and to the relationship of public order law with the system of criminal justice (including binding over). Lastly, in making proposals for the reform of the law in the light of such considerations, the process should have examined and articulated the basis of the intervention of the criminal law in this area. The failure to do so was no doubt partly due to the piecemeal nature of the law reform process in relation to public order law.

The reports of the various investigations make depressing reading. For the reasons just indicated, they do not provide a comprehensive programme for the future, nor do they even provide the groundwork upon which such a programme could be based.

(e) LAW REFORM MACHINERY

Criminal law reform does not benefit from being split between various agencies. The work must be undertaken comprehensively by one body. Clearly, this would be too big a job for the Law Commission (as presently constituted), given that criminal law reform and codification are only part of its functions. It is also too big for the part-time Criminal Law Revision Committee or any other such committee. What is needed is a full-time Criminal Law Reform Commission. It would be important to involve laypersons (as well as lawyers) in the work of this body, some of them as members, because they are less likely than lawyers to limit themselves solely to a technical systemisation and rationalisation of existing law and more likely to bring to bear a true re-appraisal of society's needs and how to fulfil them. As Lord Wilberforce said in Parliament when the Law Commission was proposed, law reform is '. . . much too serious a matter to be entrusted to lawyers.'[57] Policy advisory groups, like the one used by the Criminal Law Revision Committee in relation to the age of consent, should be used and evidence sought on a wide basis at an early stage. Something particularly to be avoided is consultation only after a working paper has been prepared; once matters have got as far as a working paper the approach and attitudes are likely to have hardened and become specific, with the result that major changes of appraisal and approach are unlikely.

Conclusion

There is far too much public order law,[58] just as there is far too much criminal law in general.[59] Public order law is unduly fragmentary and complex, and it is badly affected by unnecessary duplication, by elasticity and by uncertainty. Particular mention may be made in this context of the unduly elastic common law rules, whose escape from codification was openly based by the government on their flexibility in the hands of the courts.[60] Having developed pragmatically, often in response to essentially short-term needs, public order law lacks a rational and consistent basis.

Because of the piecemeal, pragmatic, superficial and over-simplistic nature of the recent investigations of public order law, it is clear that the modern law is not the result of a thorough review of all its aspects.

It would be pleasant to think that the Public Order Act of 1986 simply clears the way for a subsequent and far more comprehensive revision of public order law, but, unless the defects of the law reform process pointed out above are rectified, this is most unlikely to happen.

Lastly, mention must be made of codification, whose aims are identified in Codification of the Criminal Law: A Report to the Law Commission[61] as accessibility, comprehensibility, consistency and certainty. All these aims deserve fulfilment in the area of public order law. However, if reform and codification are, in fact, different exercises with different objectives, as the Report and the Law Commission claim,[62] then public order law requires both for the reasons set out in this essay.[63]

NOTES

1 Affray has typically been charged in cases of pitched street battles between rival gangs, spontaneous fights in pubs and clubs and revenge attacks on individuals. It is arguable that it is merely an offence against the person, and not part of the public order law. Compare the views of ATH Smith [1982] Crim LR 485 at 488 with Law Commission Working Paper No 82: Offences against Public Order, para 4.6

2 [1982] QB 416, [1981] 3 All ER 383, CA.

3 Ibid, applied in *Parkin v Norman* [1983] QB 92, [1982] 2 All ER 583, DC. This power was not abolished by the Police and Criminal Evidence Act 1984. Although it has been argued that, where conduct amounts to a specific offence, powers of arrest are confined to those in ss 24 (arrestable offences) and 25 (limited power of arrest for other offences, dependent on general arrest conditions) of the 1984 Act (see Leigh *Police Powers in England and Wales* (2nd edn), p 87), there is no warrant for this in the Act.

4 See, for example, *Albert v Lavin* [1982] AC 546 at 565, HL, per Lord Diplock.

5 *Duncan v Jones* [1936] 1 KB 218, DC.

6 *Thomas v Sawkins* [1935] 2 KB 249.

7 *O'Kelly v Harvey* (1883) 15 Cox CC 435.

8 *Albert v Lavin*, n 4 above.

9 *Moss v McLachlan* [1985] IRLR 76, DC.

10 [1936] 1 KB 218, DC.

11 (8th edn, 1900), p 184.

12 *R v Moule* [1964] Crim LR 303, CCA; *R v Adler* [1964] Crim LR 304, CCA; *R v Clark (No 2)* [1964] 2 QB 315, [1965] 3 All ER 884, CCA; Law Commission Report: Offences Relating to Public Order (Law Com no 123), para 1.8.

13 See ATH Smith 'Law Commission Working Paper No 82: Offences against Public Order' [1982] Crim LR 485 at 486.

14 [1936] 1 KB 218, DC.

15 'We Protest: The Public Order Debate' (1985) NCCL, p 73.
16 *R v Holmes* (1853) 22 LJMC 122; *Langrish v Archer* (1882) 10 QBD 44, DC.
17 British Railways Board, byelaw 16.
18 Law Commission Report: Offences Relating to Public Order (Law Com no 123), para 3.2.
19 *R v Oakwell* [1978] 1 All ER 1223, CA.
20 Law Commission Working Paper No 82: Offences against Public Order, para 4.6. Also see Law Commission Report: Offences relating to Public Order (Law Com no 123), para 3.3–3.6.
21 Law Commission Report: Offences Relating or Public Order (Law Com no 123), para 3.5.
22 Ibid, para 3.4.
23 [1957] 1 QB 552, [1957] 1 All ER 577, CCA.
24 (1970) 54 Cr App Rep 499 at 505. Also see Law Commission Report: Offences Relating to Public Order (Law Com no 123), para 6.9.
25 *Brutus v Cozens* [1973] AC 854, [1972] 2 All ER 1297, HL.
26 [1985] IRLR 76, DC.
27 Eg *Duncan v Jones* [1936] 1 KB 218, DC; *Piddington v Bates* [1960] 3 All ER 660, DC; *Hubbard v Pitt* [1976] QB 142, DC; *Moss v McLachlan* [1985] IRLR 76, DC.
28 For recent examples, see *R v Madden* [1975] 3 All ER 155, CA; *R v Soul* (1980) 70 Cr App Rep 295, CA.
29 Lord Scarman's Report on the Brixton Disorders 10–12 April 1981 (1981), Cmnd 8427; Review of Public Order Law (Cmnd 9510), para 6.13.
30 [1976] QB 142 at 177.
31 The UN International Covenant on Civil and Political Rights (to which the UK is also a party) contains similar guarantees of freedom of expression and of the right of peaceful assembly.
32 Report of the Committee on Homosexual Offences and Prostitution (1957), Cmnd 247.
33 'We Protest: The Public Order Debate' (1958) NCCL, pp 36 and 37.
34 Hewitt *Abuse of Power*, p 108.
35 ATH Smith 'Law Commission Working Paper No 82' [1982] Crim LR 485 at 487.
36 Merely trampling down grass in a farmer's field has been held to be damage for the purpose of the Malicious Damage Act 1861: *Grayford v Chouler* [1898] 1 QB 316, DC. Doubtless the same would be held in relation to the Criminal Damage Act 1971.
37 *Evans v UK* Report of the European Commission on Human Rights, vol 24, para 144 (1979).
38 The UN International Covenant on Civil and Political Rights likewise states that the exercise of the freedoms contained in it may be subject to restrictions of these types.
39 Reversing its decision in the White Paper, Review of Public Order Law (1985), Cmnd 9510.
40 It should be remembered that the police have the power to arrest those members of the audience who commit a breach of the peace or who use insulting or abusive language.
41 See, for example, *Handyside*, Publications of the Court, Ser A, no 24, paras 48 and 49; *Evans v UK* Report of the Commission, vol 24, para 207.
42 *Jordan v Burgoyne* [1963] 2 All ER 225, DC.
43 Cmnd 7891.
44 5th Report HC 756 -I & II.
45 Cmnd 8427.
46 Law Com no 123.
47 Law Com Working Paper no 82 (1982).
48 Cmnd 9510.
49 Cmnd 9585.
50 Cmnd 9710.
51 Although the Law Commission had initially decided to include in its review the offence of public nuisance in so far as it it used in the area of highway obstruction, it soon declined to do so. Its reasoning was that even in so far as the offence is used in this area, a review 'would be impracticable and would unduly protract our work: it would include many situations remote from the law relating to disturbances to public order.'
52 Law Commission Report (Law Com no 123), para 1.6.
53 DGT Williams [1985] Public Law 12 at 12.
54 Ibid at 16.
55 Cmnd 7891, para 21.
56 Passing reference was made in the Law Commission Report (Law Com no 123) para 2.15, and in the White Paper (Cmnd 9560), paras 1.8.2.11 and 2.15.
57 264 HL Official Report (6th series) col 177.
58 A comparison with other common law jurisdictions shows not only that they make do with far fewer public order offences but also that those offences carry much lower maximum sentences. For example, offences corresponding to the English offence of riot do not generally carry a

maximum of more than two or three years' imprisonment.

59 For example, since the present administration came into power in 1979, over 300 new offences have been created: 478 HL Official Report (6th series) Col 982.

60 Review of Public Order Law (Cmnd 9510), para 6.13.

61 (1985) Law Com no 143, Ch 1.

62 Ibid, paras 16 and 1.10.

63 The Law Commission's statement in its Eighteenth Annual Report (for 1982–83) (Law Com no 131, para 2.26), that the task of codification was seen by it primarily as the restating of the present law in a coherent and consistent manner coupled with the suggestion of limited reforms where the law was seen to be defective, is far too limiting.

Works by Professor JC Smith

Books

(Sole author)

The Law of Theft	1st edn 1968 2nd edn 1972 3rd edn 1977 4th edn 1979 5th edn 1984

(Joint author)

A Casebook on Contract (with JAC Thomas)	1st edn 1957 2nd edn 1961 3rd edn 1965 4th edn 1969 5th edn 1973 6th edn 1977 7th edn 1982
Criminal Law (with B Hogan)	1st edn 1965 2nd edn 1969 3rd edn 1973 4th edn 1978 5th edn 1983
Criminal Law: Cases and Materials (with B Hogan)	1st edn 1975 2nd edn 1980 3rd edn 1986

Lectures

Sexual Offences (Frank Dawtry Seminar, University of Leeds, 1980)
The Guilty Mind in the Criminal Law (Inaugural Lecture, University of Nottingham, 1959)

Cheque and Credit Card Frauds in the Criminal Law (Mary Share Jones Lecture, University of Liverpool, 1981)

Intoxication and the mental element in crime (1st Lawson Lecture, University of Lancaster, 1981)

Subjective or Objective? Ups and Downs of the Test of Criminal Liability in England (Donald A Gianella Memorial Lecture, Villanova University, 1982)

Attempts, Impossibility and the Test of Rational Motivation (Auckland Law School Centenary Lecture, 1983)

Towards a Rational Criminal Law (Presidential Address, Holdsworth Club, 1983)

The Penalty for Murder (Mary F Robertson Lecture, University of Nottingham, 1986)

Codification of the Criminal Law (Child and Co Lecture, London, 1986)

Articles

1 CRIMINAL LAW REVIEW

The Fraudulent Sub-Postmistress	1955:18
Stealing a Hut	1955:404
Fit for Human Consumption	1956:101
The Fraudulent Intent in Larceny: Another View	1956:238
Larceny by Finding Out	1956:516
The *Davenport* Case	1957:640, 722
Larceny and False Pretences	1958:92
Questioning by the Police: Some Further Points	1960:347
Success and Failure in Criminal Attempts	1961:436
The Scope of Fraudulent Conversion	1961:741, 797
Two Problems in Criminal Attempt Re-examined	1962:135,212
The Literature of the Criminal Law — 1954–63	1964:96
The New Judges' Rules — A Lawyer's View	1964:176
Developments in the Law of Evidence — 1954–63	1964:434
Burglary under the Theft Bill	1968:295, 367
The Element of Chance in Criminal Liability	1971:63
Obtaining Credit by Fraud and the Theft Act	1971:448
Restatement of a Judicial Nightmare—Section 16 of the Theft Act	1972:4
A Note on *Stowers v Darnell*	1973:699
A Note on Duress	1974:349

The Heilbron Report	1976:97
Conspiracy under the Criminal Law Act 1977	1977:598, 638
Intent: A Reply	1978:14
Mens Rea in Statutory Conspiracy: Some Answers	1978:210
Theft, Conspiracy and Jurisdiction: *Tarling's* Case	1978:220
The Admissibility of Statements by Computer	1981:387
Theft and Voidable Title: A Reply	1981:677
Arthur's Case and the Right to Life of a Down's Syndrome Child (with MJ Gunn)	1985:705
Arthur's Case: Comments on Comments (with MJ Gunn)	1986:390

2 LAW QUARTERLY REVIEW AND MODERN LAW REVIEW

The Right to Rescind for Breach of Condition in a Sale of Specific Goods under the Sale of Goods Act 1893	(1951) 14 MLR 173
Unilateral Contracts and Consideration	(1953) 69 LQR 99
Waiver of Contractual Rights	(1955) 18 MLR 609
Embezzlement and the Disobedient Servant	(1956) 19 MLR 39
Pothier and the Three Dots (with JAC Thomas)	(1957) 20 MLR 38
The Guilty Mind in the Criminal Law	(1960) 76 LQR 78

3 OTHERS

Note on *Canon v Hartley* (1950) 10 CLJ 466

The Personnel of the Criminal Law in England and the United States (1955) 13 CLJ 80

Void Promises as Consideration (1956) 20 Conveyancer 7

Two problems in Criminal Attempts (1957) 70 Harv LR 422

The Theft Bill — a rejoinder (1968) 118 NLJ 401

Civil Law Concepts in the Criminal Law [1972B] CLJ 197

Intention in Criminal Law [1974] CLP 93

The Reform of the Law against Violence (1975) 5 Forensic Sci

Some Problems of the Reform of the Law of Offences Against the Person [1978] CLP 15

The Law of Contract — Alive or Dead? (1979) 13 Law Teacher 73

Majewski Down Under (1981) 1 OJLS 127

The Reform of the Law of Sexual Offences (1981) 1 The Staffordshire Jurist 1

An Academic Lawyer and Law Reform (1981) 1 Legal Studies 119

Subjective or Objective? Ups and Downs of the Test of Criminal Liability in England (1982) 27 Villanova LR 1179

Liability for Omission in the Criminal Law (1984) 4 Legal Studies 88

Codifying the Criminal Law [1984] Stat LR 17

R v Ralph Roffel (1985) 9 Crim LJ 320

Codification of the Criminal Law, A Report to the Law Commission, 1985 (with E Griew and I H Dennis)

Contributions to collections

Aid, Abet, Counsel or Procure in *Reshaping the Criminal Law* (ed P Glazebrook, 1978)

Secondary Participation and Inchoate Offences in *Crime, Proof and Punishment* (ed CFH Tapper, 1981)

The Trend to Subjectivism in English Criminal Law in *The Cambridge Lectures* (ed D Mendes da Costa, 1980)

Responsibility in Criminal Law in *Barbara Wootton, Essays in her honour* (ed P Bean and D Whynes, 1985)

Intoxication and the Mental Element in Crime in *Essays in Memory of Professor FH Lawson* (ed P Wallington and R Merkin, 1986)

The Evidence Provisions of the Police and Criminal Evidence Act 1984 in *The Police* (ed J Benyon and C Bourn, 1986)

Criminal Law Review Commentaries

The name of JC Smith first appeared as the author of the commentaries in the Case and Comment section of the Criminal Law Review in November 1956. In the course of the succeeding thirty years he has written well in excess of 3000 commentaries ranging in length from the briefest observation, note or reference expressed in a single sentence to a complete analysis of the failings, merits and implications of a decision. For the majority of the time he has shouldered the burden of commentary alone, although since 1981 he has shared the task with DJ Birch.

Index